THE BIG
NEW YORKER
— BOOK OF —
CATS

RANDOM HOUSE 🐾 NEW YORK

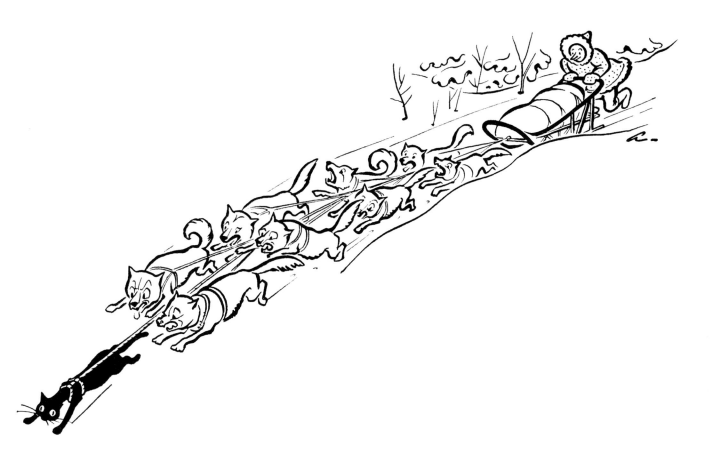

THE BIG
NEW YORKER
— BOOK OF —
CATS

Foreword by Anthony Lane

Published in the United States by Random House, an imprint of The Random House Publishing Group,
a division of Random House LLC, New York, a Penguin Random House Company.

RANDOM HOUSE and the HOUSE colophon are registered trademarks of Random House LLC.

All pieces in this collection, except as noted, were originally published in *The New Yorker*.
The publication dates are given at the end of each piece.

Handwritten draft of "Myself with Cats" by Henri Cole. Reprinted by permission of the author.

Roald Dahl's handwritten notes for "Edward the Conqueror" © RDNL.
Reprinted by permission of The Roald Dahl Museum and Story Centre.

Original draft manuscript of Ted Hughes's "Esther's Tomcat" taken from *Lupercal,* © Estate of Ted Hughes.
Reprinted by permission of Faber and Faber Ltd. and the Manuscript, Archives,
and Rare Book Library, Emory University.

"Town of Cats" from *1Q84* by Haruki Murakami, copyright © 2011 by Haruki Murakami.
Reprinted by permission. All rights reserved.

"The Case of Dimity Ann" by James Thurber, copyright © 1952 by Rosemary A. Thurber. Reprinted by
permission of Rosemary A. Thurber and The Barbara Hogenson Agency. All rights reserved.

James Thurber's original draft manuscript of "The Case of Dimity Ann" (copyright © 1952 by
Rosemary A. Thurber) is published by permission of the Rare Books & Manuscripts Library of
the Ohio State University Libraries, Columbus, Ohio, home of the James Thurber Archive,
Rosemary A. Thurber, and The Barbara Hogenson Agency. All rights reserved.

Credits for illustrations appear on pages 327–328.

Library of Congress Cataloging-in-Publication Data

The big New Yorker book of cats / foreword by Anthony Lane.
pages   cm
ISBN 978-0-679-64477-4
eBook ISBN 978-0-679-64478-1
1. Cats—Anecdotes. 2. Cats—Fiction. I. New Yorker (New York, N.Y.: 1925)
SF445.5.B546   2013
636.8—dc23   2013013345

Printed in the United States of America on acid-free paper

www.atrandom.com

2 4 6 8 9 7 5 3 1

First Edition

Book design by Susan Turner

STEINBERG

*"I know a lot of people will say, 'Oh, no—
not another book about cats.'"*

CONTENTS

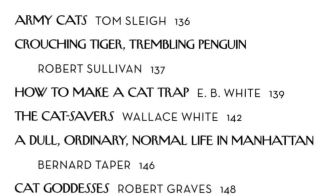

CAT FANCIERS

CURIOUS CATS

"I can see it going even a little more feline."

Jan. 29, 1972

THE
NEW YORKER

Price 50 cents

FOREWORD

ANTHONY LANE

To anyone entering the offices of *The New Yorker* for the first time, whether as a casual visitor or as an inmate facing a long sentence, the greatest surprise is not the dearth of raised voices, the hush where the live band ought to be, or the lack of a decently stocked bar. It is the want of a cat. I mean, look at the place. There are cubicles, closets, half-empty bookshelves, tops of filing cabinets, laptops, and laps that are crying out for a shorthair. Why the post has not been advertised, let alone filled, is hard to fathom. Ideal candidates should be sleek, seductive, quick of tongue, slow to wrath, and, above all, nonhuman. They should aim, wherever possible, to be as self-combing as most of the writers; expert groomers, in the editorial department, are on hand to unpick any remaining knots. Fur-balls, like dangling participles, are not welcome. Milk is in the fridge.

Was catlessness always the case within the precincts of the magazine? Has there really never been a resident Smoky, Macavity, Buster, Vesper, Oedipuss, Esmé (loved but squalid), Anchorman, Adolf, Jones, or kohl-eyed Cleopatra? Must we believe that our in-house grammarian of fifty years, the late Miss Gould, was not shadowed by an Abyssinian, say, of flawless pedigree, by the name of Subordinate Claws? It seems inconceivable. He would surely have struck a pose behind her shoulder, on the nearest windowsill, and followed the silvery motions of her pencil, not unlike the white cat in *The Tale of Peter Rabbit,* who gazes at goldfish in a pond: "She sat very, very still, but now and then the tip of her tail twitched as if it were alive." The precision of Beatrix Potter, here as elsewhere, points to the first rule of felinology: you need to learn to look at cats, down to the last whisker, every bit as closely as they look at you. To them, remember, nothing is lost in the dark.

If anything unites the contributors to the present volume, varied as they are, it is this primary urge to bear true, if bewildered, witness. Few artists, for example, could be more distinct in tone and temper than Sempé and William Steig, and to pass from the latter's portrait of the moggy as monster, striking us rigid with his all-knowing, shark-toothed grin, to the slim streak of placability unfurled along a bed, in Sempé's rendering, is to rise, like Dante, from the nether depths toward beatitude. Yet neither image works without the other, if we are to see cats steadily and see them whole—if we are to admit to ourselves that, however far our pets may be bred from the wild, sometimes to the verge of interior decoration, they are never quite bred enough. "Domesticated cat," indeed, may be the very phrase at which Steig's creature was laughing when he was trapped in art.

The pursuit of such verities will lead you, eventually, to the most insane of creative feats: getting under the skin of a cat. This will never be anything but challenging, even if you wear motorcycle gauntlets and a knight's visor, but it remains a quest to which many writers are lured. Perhaps they view it as a kind of scratching post—a ready-made, abrasive chance to sharpen their natural skills. Joyce, who liked to miss nothing, bent his ear to a very specific quandary, the spelling of a cat's ululation, in the fourth chapter of *Ulysses,* and came up with the infinitesimal swell of "mkgnao" into "mrkgnao." (Try both, out loud, but not after eating crackers, and see if you can tell them apart.) J. F. Powers explored further with "Death of a Favorite," which was published in *The New Yorker,* in 1950, and later selected by John Updike for *The Best American Short Stories of the Century,* which is quite a pantheon. Our narrator is Fritz, the only quadruped in a household of Catholic priests; he falls foul of a couple of missionaries, newly arrived, whose mission, it turns out, is to hound the cat from his home. A sandal is wielded, and a crucifix; at the sight of it, Fritz admits, "an undeniable fear was rising in me," and we sense a flicker of the old belief that cats are the proper companion of witches, or worse. We half expect the clergy to bring out the garlic. Yet who, in all faith, is the worst offender here? Is it Fritz, or could it be the nicely named Father Burner, already his sworn foe when the tale begins? The cat, mulling the matter over, has no doubt; as he says of the men of God, gathered around the dinner table, "There was something about my presence there, I thought, that brought out the beast in them—which is to say very nearly all that was in them." Touché.

Like the best of his peers, Powers is trusting the language to lead him to the borders of ontological wit. To "bring out the beast" in somebody is a cliché, rubbed smooth over time, but to have it uttered by a cat—that is to lend it new and jagged life. The author understands that to write like a cat is not to escape the human voice but to find a new angle from which to pronounce, with a lightly modulated hiss, upon the infinite gradations of human sin. He is hardly alone in this endeavor, either within or beyond the parish of the magazine. Saki's "Tobermory," first published in 1911, is still fêted for the social devastation that is wrought by its speaking cat, blessed with perfect syntax but no scruples, and, within the correspondence of Raymond Chandler (a tremendous trove of sly good sense), there is a letter that he wrote to a friend, in 1948, in the person of his Persian, Taki: "Come around sometime when your face is clean and we shall discuss the state of the world, the foolishness of humans, the prevalence of horsemeat, although we prefer the tenderloin side of a porterhouse, and our common difficulty in getting doors opened at the right time and meals served at more frequent intervals. I have got my staff up to five a day, but there is still room for improvement."

Note the low estimation of human beings, which seems, by definition, to go with the territory, whenever the animal viewpoint is adopted; its logical conclusion, never bettered for pure disgust, is the moment when Gulliver—safely returned to England, but schooled in a more delicate existence by his time among the Houyhnhnms—reels away from the stink of his own family. Cats would not make so bold a show of revulsion, yet we, as cat owners (a term that belongs to the theater of the absurd, as both parties are aware), are wearily mindful of the gambits by which superiority is vaunted: the courteous sniff that precedes the refusal of food; the glowering retreat to an aerie, in the opposite corner of the room; the turning of the tail. Dog lovers—and such beings do exist—derive much joy from their Dobermans, their quaking Chihuahuas, and everything in between, and we should not begrudge them that delight; to be ceaselessly gratified by one's pet, however, and to find one's love returned with interest, on all occasions, is bad education for the soul. Cat people, on the other hand, know what it is to be adored and then rejected, with no explanation, in the space of a single minute, with the purr switched off like an alarm clock. They know, like Powers's priests, Father Burner included, that the world is a treacherous vale, undeserving of our trust, and that to be humbled, if only by a dish of untouched ham, is the beginning of wisdom. Blessed are the cat-mad, for they shall be driven up the wall.

Some of them go straight to the top of the wall and stay there, with no inclination to jump down. Take Rita Ross. By 1938, when she was honored by a profile in the magazine, this formidable lady, born Marion Garcewich, had personally caught "two hundred tons of cats"—picture the fact-checkers working *that* one out—and delivered them to the Society for the Prevention of Cruelty to Animals, and thus, effectively, to their deaths. Roaming the streets of New York in search of strays, crowned by a conical hat, and consumed by a reverent pity, she had, according to the authors, "nearly seventy thousand souls on her conscience." Each man kills the thing he loves, Oscar Wilde wrote, but most men tend not to require a wire trap, cans of salmon, five burlap sacks, and a police whistle to put that tragic paradox into practice. Set beside the Augean labors of Miss Ross, the duty confronting the hero of John Updike's "The Cats"—the extermination of a mere farmful, inherited on his mother's death—seems no more than child's play. He turns the problem over to professionals, although, with time on his hands, and in a country mood, he might have made use of the instructions that were issued to readers of *The New Yorker* by E. B. White, in "How to Make a Cat Trap." This ends with dark talk of cyanide, and its stifling details are only just rescued from outright creepiness by a breath of fresh humor: "Screw one screw-eye into the top of the treadle half an inch from the right side and seventeen and one-half inches from the front end. Screw the second screw-eye into the piano for all I care."

So it is, as this well-fed book stretches out in languor, that the array of feline opposites starts to emerge. Cats must be destroyed; cats should be saved. Cats are like us; no, cats are not of this world. Cats can be savored for their fellowship, then eaten for their flesh: that, at any rate, was the alarming formula arrived at by Sylvia Townsend Warner, one of whose fictions ushered in a sinuous Siamese tom, with "dusky paws," that wreathed itself around the shoulders of a Parisian wine merchant, and later became his dinner. Mind you, the setting was Paris in 1942, when anything edible, or, frankly, catchable, was fair game. Next comes the cartoonists' dialectic—the cats who infest our tenement rooms like mice played off against the cats, often of noble embonpoint, who sit in offices, behind desks, and scare the lower orders. ("You fed me tuna and cleaned my litter box, Harris, and I'm not going to forget it.") Cats exist in these pages, as they do throughout our lives, both as obsessively singular—one ill-fated, hard-up couple from Wilmington, Delaware, pay fifteen thousand dollars to provide their ailing, adored, asthmatic pet with kidney dialysis and a transplant—and as a barely controllable mass, doomed to proliferate forever, like poison ivy or biographies of Napoleon. Above all, for every cat who is liked, accepted, or worshipped from afar, there is another who peers into our eyes—those hopeless orbs, superfluous at night—and spies only horror, indifference, and fear.

Needless to say, you get synthesis. Emotions merge. I myself have two Bengals, of whom I am fond, plus the marks on my wrists to prove it—deep, diagonal scars that could easily suggest, to casual acquaintances, that I am attempting suicide, without much success, on a weekly basis. The cats are joined, in the household, by two poodles, and if you are one of those old squares who think that two plus two equals four, forget it. Try four *cubed*. Not all of them were acquired with my foreknowledge, still less my consent, and the results are on display, day

in, night out. One Bengal would like to partition the other into a million little pieces of Bengal; the first poodle secretly likes the other poodle but hides this fact with bass growls of wounded disdain; the second poodle loves everything that moves, including German shepherds in the street and falling oven mitts, but cowers beneath repeated demonstrations that not everything loves him back; and so on. Envy, hurt, territorial fervor, uranium-tipped malice, and a neediness so profound that it can never be measured, let alone assuaged, combine to grant us much entertainment, fitful panic, but no peace. You think North and South Korea could explode? Come round to my place and see what a real flashpoint looks like. Imagine not just a North and a South but a West and an East Korea, too, with me at the nexus, armed only with a sachet of Intense Beauty. (That, God preserve me, is the name of the cat food. The dogs like it.)

Even to someone in my predicament, this book has the answer. Most contributors report, as faithfully as can be, from the front line where the genus *Felis* collides—and, if we are dumb enough to kid ourselves, colludes—with *Homo sapiens*. Why settle for the petting zoo of our homes, though, when there are genuine zoos to explore? And how can I complain about my angry puss, no larger than a leg of lamb, when *Panthera tigris tigris*, the Bengal tiger, is on the prowl? This fellow is best seen, preferably from a distance, as a director's cut of my cats. Extended features include sunset-colored fur, an average male weight of around five hundred pounds, and, one presumes, the ability to resolve the issue of a tiresome poodle by treating it as a pretzel. Habitats include India, Bangladesh, Nepal, the heavenly kingdom of Bhutan, and Jackson, New Jersey. This cat is hep, and he's here. And he's not alone. Susan Orlean, in a probing chronicle of 2002, explained a familiar problem:

> You know how it is—you start with one tiger, then you get another and another, then a few are born and a few die, and you start to lose track of details like exactly how many tigers you actually have.

Tell me about it. That is my favorite sentence in the book, because its trademark shrug, laced with a light sigh, feels true not just to *The New Yorker* but to the whole eternal folderol of choosing to keep a cat. We *do* know how it is. We are not fundamentally different from Rita Ross, or from Joan Byron-Marasek, who oversaw the Bengals of Jackson at Six Flags Wild Safari, except that we are not so pungently fragranced, and our lives are less possessed by what we own. The lengthy portrait of Robert Lothar Kendell, by Katharine T. Kinkead, that ran in *The New Yorker* in 1951 depicted a gentleman whose industry, devotion, and entrepreneurial drive would have marked him out in any given business; it just so happens that, because he was the president of the American Feline Society, his business was the well-being of cats. If that increased their chances of widespread deification, so much the better. No kingdom could be more heavenly. History has forgotten the initiative Cats for Europe, as devised by Mr. Kendell, but it was a munificent scheme—"a plan to send a million American cats to the Marshall Plan countries to rid them of rats." They would be airlifted over in groups of seventeen hundred, "five cats per crate." Hmm. Whether they were to be parachuted into Holland by moonlight, or bravely spilled onto the beaches of Normandy from landing craft, was a vital secret that both the author and her subject, in their prudence, kept to themselves. Nor do we learn which spoilsport vetoed

Cats for Europe in the end. Probably some covert rat fan. Or a schmuck with a Peke.

This raises a tricky humanitarian point: what are we to do with the heathen—the haters and slanderers of the cat? They can't be put to sleep, or caged for more than a couple of days, or even neutered without a written agreement. The best course, on reflection, is to slink away from them. Chandler again: "I have never liked anyone who disliked cats, because I've always found an element of acute selfishness in their dispositions." A smart move, that—to charge the anti-cat brigade with precisely the same vice that its members claim to detect in the average cat. (There is no average cat. That is their first mistake.) I call them Boswells, after a celebrated passage in his *Life of Johnson* on the theme of Hodge, the beloved cat for whom the good Doctor used to buy oysters:

> I recollect him one day scrambling up Dr. Johnson's breast, apparently with much satisfaction, while my friend smiling and half-whistling, rubbed down his back, and pulled him by the tail; and when I observed he was a fine cat, saying, "Why yes, Sir, but I have had cats whom I liked better than this;" and then as if perceiving Hodge to be out of countenance, adding, "but he is a very fine cat, a very fine cat indeed."

Boswell misses the point. There is no "as if" about it. Hodge *was* put out, less by having his tail pulled, as if he were a church bell, than because he had just heard himself described as inferior to his predecessors. A libelous gibe. Any self-respecting cat—in brief, any cat—would be mortified, not to mention incredulous, at the suggestion that he or she might not be rated top dog. The reason that Boswell writes "as if" is that, as he has already confessed, "I am, unluckily, one of those who have an antipathy to a cat." His manly regret is laudable, but still; not liking Hodge, he is incapable of grasping what Hodgeness means, and what subtle plays of feeling can be discerned on Hodge's countenance. Serious cat people, like first-rate art critics, are chivvied by passion into perspicacity. Believing is seeing.

And who are cat people? Can they be recognized on the street, or cradled securely in one's arms? In the film *Cat People*, made in 1942 and again forty years later, the heroine—played first by Simone Simon, then by Nastassja Kinski—was physically transformed from woman into cat. The prospect of Nastassja Kinski appearing through one's catflap and mewing for cream sounds more of a privilege than a hardship, but it came with a twist; after sex, she turned into a panther. Again, not an insuperable problem, except that, come breakfast time, panthers need more than Friskies. In regular tests, for example, Kinski showed a preference for tender morsels of man. There are worse ways to go.

Such hybridization is rare, but, as with Miss Ross and Mr. Kendell, extreme legend speaks to a downbeat desire. Poets realize this, adept as they are at padding back and forth between warmed homeliness and a more adventurous truth. I was once informed, in my salad days, that no woman should go to bed with a man who doesn't like cats—a maxim that I have pondered ever since, mostly at night, and one that poets, past and present, do nothing to discredit. Baudelaire, the high priest of the Kinskite tendency, is so eager to entwine the feline and the female that at moments, to be honest, he can't see the cat for the sex. Even if you have no French, feel the rub of this: "Et que ma main s'enivre du plaisir / De palper ton corps électrique . . ." If I were a suburban, middle-aged tabby of fixed abode (and I am), those lines would leave me with the squirm-

ing, bashful conviction that, somewhere along the line, between kittenhood and fireside, I missed out.

Things cool down a touch in the poems reprinted here. Robert Pinsky, in "Door," addresses his cat as "darling" and hails her as "fellow-mortal," which is an unarguable fact, though she might not wish to be reminded of it. One of the more declarative poems is "Propinquity," by Alastair Reid, who writes, "Cats fall on their feet" (another cliché pounced on and revived), and then, more provocative still, "Part of us is cat." But which part? The nerve ends, the back of the ears, the throat? Orson Welles, who could count himself fortunate not to have been tranquilized, snared, and borne off to Six Flags Wild Safari, thought that the crossover was all to do with the universal dread of lost face. In his words, "If spiritually you're part of the cat family, you can't bear to be laughed at. You have to pretend when you fall down that you really *wanted* to be down there just to see what's under the sofa." That is beautifully noticed, and, if you follow it through, you come to the place where cats and people, despite the chasm between their genetic strands, do indeed knot and knit together: a shared, super-tangled string ball of pride, shame, avarice, lust, and less deadly stirrings—the mature decision to do nothing, or the sudden urge to go nuts.

Maybe that is the cause, in the end, of the cat-free *New Yorker* offices. We presume that we could always hire a mousing assistant along the lines of the one who squats, placidly curled, at the center of Velázquez's *The Weavers,* a still point amid the panoply of yarn-spinning and mythological reference. She—and it has to be a she, no question—is both a complement to the array of womenfolk and a mild, amused rebuke to their busy toils. But we would probably inherit no such thing. We would be far more likely to get one of the humongous crossbreeds that spring up, from time to time, to grace the covers of the magazine: the Steinberg Sphinx, say, of 1996, whose air of enigma is so radioactively strong that innocent employees in the surrounding area, freaked out beyond repair, would resign before the close of the first day. As for the Ronald Searle cat, from the winter of 1988, who squats, perfectly content, with googly eyes, licking a multicolored ice cream in a blizzard: Help. However you approach him—and it has to be a him, no question—you will reel away in bafflement, inspecting your own sanity for damage. Why ice cream? How can he be hot? Could the scoops be made from flavored snow? And what about those tiny triangles of teeth, showing through his indecipherable smile: would he be offended if we called them canines? Like I say: Help.

Perhaps we need to rethink the assumption, deep-rooted but far from well grounded, that writers and cats are a good mix. Sure, Mark Twain had cats, such as Sour Mash and Blatherskite, and, up at the more louche and loping end of American literature, in the life and work of Poe, Kerouac, William Burroughs, Charles Bukowski, Edward Gorey, and Stephen King, you are never that far from the patter of ominous paws; whether a cat that has been reared on a diet of neat Burroughs would find a niche at *The New Yorker*, however, is open to debate. We aim at the scrutable, the translucent, the undrugged, and the verified; whether we even get close is not for us to say, but such aspirations find no echo in the bosom of the cat. The cat sneers at clarity and career plans, and even its major stratagems can be dropped upon a whim; my earliest cat, an Ulster Protestant of uncertain parentage and violent sectarian opinions, would cheerfully wait nine hours in the airing cupboard in the hope that my sister would pass by,

on the way to her evening bath, with bare—ergo attackable—toes, yet even that grim design could be shelved if the smell of smoked cheese, say, were brought into the equation.

How could such a beast hold court, let alone sway, in the civilized halls of *The New Yorker*? We tend to think ahead, sometimes to issues many months away; a cat, conversely, will identify the one sheet of paper that needs to be corrected and dispatched in the next twenty minutes and park his ass on it, no more shiftable than a Buddha. To put the matter at its bleakest: you cannot factcheck a cat. Many people have tried, some of them fluent in Persian or Burmese, but all have fallen short. In contrast to the magazine, and to this capacious book, cats are unreadable, and happy to remain so. Unlike writers, and related pests, they cannot be controlled. Others abide our question; they are free. All we can do is call them from the back porch, listen for their mkgnao, or, alternatively, their mrkgnao, and offer our services gratis, just for the hell of it, and the mystery, and the fun. Who knows? It could be that our cats, no less cherished and misunderstood than life itself, may wind up as our best epitaph. As Weldon Kees, who is represented twice within these pages, wrote in "The Cats," a wondrous, late-period poem that somehow slipped the embrace of *The New Yorker*, leaped down, and stole away:

> The cars go by in a bluish light.
> At six o'clock the cats run out
> When we come home from work
> To greet us, crying, dancing,
> After the long day.

May 6, 1972

THE
NEW YORKER

Price 50 cents

FAT CATS

DEATH OF A FAVORITE

Fiction

J. F. POWERS

had spent most of the afternoon mousing—a matter of sport with me and certainly not of diet—in the sunburnt fields that begin at our back door and continue hundreds of miles into the Dakotas. I gradually gave up the idea of hunting, the grasshoppers convincing me that there was no percentage in stealth. Even to doze was difficult, under such conditions, but I must have managed it. At least I was late coming to dinner, and so my introduction to the two missionaries took place at table. They were surprised, as most visitors are, to see me take the chair at Father Malt's right.

Father Malt, breaking off the conversation (if it could be called that), was his usual dear old self. "Fathers," he said, "meet Fritz."

I gave the newcomers the first good look that invariably tells me whether or not a person cares for cats. The mean old buck in charge of the team did not like me, I could see, and would bear watching. The other one obviously did like me, but he did not appear to be long enough from the seminary to matter. I felt that I had broken something less than even here.

"My assistant," said Father Malt, meaning me, and thus unconsciously dealing out our fat friend at the other end of the table. Poor Burner! There was a time when, thinking of him, as I did now, as the enemy, I could have convinced myself I meant something else. But he *is* the enemy, and I was right from the beginning, when it could only have been instinct that told me how much he hated me even while trying (in his fashion!) to be friendly. (I believe his prejudice to be acquired rather than congenital, and very likely, at this stage, confined

3

to me, not to cats as a class—there *is* that in his favor. I intend to be fair about this if it kills me.)

My observations of humanity incline me to believe that one of us—Burner or I—must ultimately prevail over the other. For myself, I should not fear if this were a battle to be won on the solid ground of Father Malt's affections. But the old man grows older, the grave beckons to him ahead, and with Burner pushing him from behind, how long can he last? Which is to say: How long can *I* last? Unfortunately, it is naked power that counts most in any rectory, and as things stand now, I am safe only so long as Father Malt retains it here. Could I—this impossible thought is often with me now—could I effect a reconciliation and alliance with Father Burner? Impossible! Yes, doubtless. But the question better asked is: *How impossible?* (Lord knows I would not inflict this line of reasoning upon myself if I did not hold with the rumors that Father Burner will be the one to succeed to the pastorate.) For I do like it here. It is not at all in my nature to forgive and forget, certainly not as regards Father Burner, but it is in my nature to come to terms (much as nations do) when necessary, and in this solution

there need not be a drop of good will. No dog can make that statement, or take the consequences, which I understand are most serious, in the world to come. Shifts and ententes. There is something fatal about the vocation of favorite, but it is the only one that suits me, and, all things considered—to dig I am not able, to beg I am ashamed—the rewards are adequate.

"We go through Chicago all the time," said the boss missionary, who seemed to be returning to a point he had reached when I entered. I knew Father Malt would be off that evening for a convention in Chicago. The missionaries, who would fill in for him and conduct a forty hours' devotion on the side, belonged to an order just getting started in the diocese and were anxious to make a good impression. For the present, at least, as a kind of special introductory offer, they could be had dirt-cheap. Thanks to them, pastors who'd never been able to get away had got a taste of Florida last winter.

"Sometimes we stay over in Chicago," bubbled the young missionary. He was like a rookie ballplayer who hasn't made many road trips.

"We've got a house there," said the first, whose name in religion, as they say, was—so help me—Philbert. Later, Father Burner would get around it by calling him by his surname. Father Malt was the sort who wouldn't see anything funny about "Philbert," but it would be too much to expect him to remember such a name.

"What kind of a house?" asked Father Malt. He held up his hearing aid and waited for clarification.

"How would you feel if the mouse did that to you?"

Father Philbert replied in a shout, "The Order owns *a house* there!"

Father Malt fingered his hearing aid.

Father Burner sought to interpret for Father Philbert. "I think, Father, he wants to know what it's made out of."

"Red brick—it's red brick," bellowed Father Philbert.

"*My* house is red brick," said Father Malt.

"I *noticed* that," said Father Philbert.

Father Malt shoved the hearing aid at him.

"I know it," said Father Philbert, shouting again.

Father Malt nodded and fed me a morsel of fish. Even for a Friday, it wasn't much of a meal. I would not have been sorry to see this housekeeper go.

"All right, all right," said Father Burner to the figure lurking behind the door and waiting for him, always the last one, to finish. "She stands and looks in at you through the crack," he beefed. "Makes you feel like a condemned man." The housekeeper came into the room, and he addressed the young missionary (Burner was a great one for questioning the young): "Ever read any books by this fella Koestler, Father?"

"The Jesuit?" the young one asked.

"Hell, no, he's some kind of a writer. I know the man you mean, though. Spells his name different. Wrote a book—apologetics."

"That's the one. Very—"

"Dull."

"Well . . ."

"This other fella's not bad. He's a writer who's ahead of his time—about fifteen minutes. Good on jails and concentration camps. You'd think he was born in one if you ever read his books." Father Burner regarded the young missionary with absolute indifference. "But you didn't."

"No. Is he a Catholic?" inquired the young one.

"He's an Austrian or something."

"Oh."

The housekeeper removed the plates and passed the dessert around. When she came to Father Burner, he asked her privately, "What is it?"

"Pudding," she said, not whispering, as he would have liked.

"*Bread* pudding?" Now he was threatening her.

"Yes, Father."

Father Burner shuddered and announced to everybody, "No dessert for me." When the housekeeper had retired into the kitchen, he said, "Sometimes I think he got her from a hospital and sometimes, Father, I think she came from one of *your* fine institutions"—this to the young missionary.

Father Philbert, however, was the one to see the joke, and he laughed.

"My God," said Father Burner, growing bolder. "I'll never forget the time I stayed at your house in Louisville. If I hadn't been there for just a day—for the Derby, in fact—I'd have gone to Rome about it. I think I've had better meals here."

At the other end of the table, Father Malt, who could not have heard a word, suddenly blinked and smiled; the missionaries looked to him for some comment, in vain.

"He doesn't hear me," said Father Burner. "Besides, I think he's listening to the news."

"I didn't realize it was a radio too," said the young missionary.

"Oh, hell, yes."

"I think he's pulling your leg," said Father Philbert.

"Well, I thought so," said the young missionary ruefully.

"It's an idea," said Father Burner. Then in

earnest to Father Philbert, whom he'd really been working around to all the time—the young one was decidedly not his type—"You the one drivin' that new Olds, Father?"

"It's not mine, Father," said Father Philbert with a meekness that would have been hard to take if he'd meant it. Father Burner understood him perfectly, however, and I thought they were two persons who would get to know each other a lot better.

"Nice job. They say it compares with the Cad in power. What do you call that color—oxford or clerical gray?"

"I really couldn't say, Father. It's my brother's. He's a layman in Minneapolis—St. Stephen's parish. He loaned it to me for this little trip."

Father Burner grinned. He could have been thinking, as I was, that Father Philbert protested too much. "Thought I saw you go by earlier," he said. "What's the matter—didn't you want to come in when you saw the place?"

Father Philbert, who was learning to ignore Father Malt, laughed discreetly. "Couldn't be sure this was it. That house on the *other* side of the church, now—"

Father Burner nodded. "Like that, huh? Belongs to a Mason."

Father Philbert sighed and said, "It would."

"Not at all," said Father Burner. "I like 'em better than K.C.s." If he could get the audience for it, Father Burner enjoyed being broad-minded. Gazing off in the direction of the Mason's big house, he said, "I've played golf with him."

The young missionary looked at Father Burner in horror. Father Philbert merely smiled. Father Burner, toying with a large crumb, propelled it in my direction.

"Did a bell ring?" asked Father Malt.

"His P.A. system," Father Burner explained. "Better tell him," he said to the young missionary.

"You're closer. He can't bring me in on those batteries he uses."

"No bell," said the young missionary, lapsing into basic English and gestures.

Father Malt nodded, as though he hadn't really thought so.

"How do you like it?" said Father Burner.

Father Philbert hesitated, and then he said, "Here, you mean?"

"I wouldn't ask you that," said Father Burner, laughing. "Talkin' about that Olds. Like it? Like the Hydramatic?"

"No kiddin', Father. It's not mine," Father Philbert protested.

"All right, all right," said Father Burner, who obviously did not believe him. "Just so you don't bring up your vow of poverty." He looked at Father Philbert's uneaten bread pudding—"Had enough?"—and rose from the table, blessing himself. The other two followed when Father Malt, who was feeding me cheese, waved them away. Father Burner came around to us, bumping my chair—intentionally, I know. He stood behind Father Malt and yelled into his ear, "Any calls for me this aft?" He'd been out somewhere, as usual. I often thought he expected too much to happen in his absence.

"There was something . . ." said Father Malt, straining his memory, which was poor.

"*Yes?*"

"Now I remember—they had the wrong number."

Father Burner, looking annoyed and downhearted, left the room.

"They said they'd call back," said Father Malt, sensing Father Burner's disappointment.

I left Father Malt at the table reading his Office under the orange light of the chandelier. I went to the living room, to my spot in the window from which I could observe Father Burner and the missionaries on the front porch, the young one in the swing with his breviary—the mosquitoes, I judged, were about to join him—and the other two just smoking and standing around, like pool players waiting for a table. I heard Father Philbert say, "Like to take a look at it, Father?"

"Say, that's an idea," said Father Burner.

I saw them go down the front walk to the gray Olds parked at the curb. With Father Burner at the wheel they drove away. In a minute they were back, the car moving uncertainly—this I noted with considerable pleasure until I realized that Father Burner was simply testing the brakes. Then they were gone, and after a bit, when they did not return, I supposed they were out killing poultry on the open road.

That evening, when the ushers dropped in at the rectory, there was not the same air about them as when they came for pinochle. Without fanfare, Mr. Bauman, their leader, who had never worked any but the center aisle, presented Father Malt with a travelling bag. It was nice of him, I thought, when he said, "It's from all of us," for it could not have come from all equally. Mr. Bauman, in hardware, and Mr. Keller, the druggist, were the only ones well off, and must have forked out plenty for such a fine piece of luggage, even after the discount.

Father Malt thanked all six ushers with little nods in which there was no hint of favoritism. "Ha," he kept saying. "You shouldn'a done it."

The ushers bobbed and ducked, dodging his flattery, and kept up a mumble to the effect that Father Malt deserved everything they'd ever done for him and more. Mr. Keller came forward to instruct Father Malt in the use of the various clasps and zippers. Inside the bag was another gift, a set of military brushes, which I could see

they were afraid he would not discover for himself. But he unsnapped a brush, and, like the veteran crowd-pleaser he was, swiped once or twice at his head with it after spitting into the bristles. The ushers all laughed.

"Pretty snazzy," said the newest usher—the only young blood among them. Mr. Keller had made him a clerk at the store, had pushed through his appointment as alternate usher in the church, and was gradually weaning him away from his motorcycle. With Mr. Keller, the lad formed a block to Mr. Bauman's power, but he was perhaps worse than no ally at all. Most of the older men, though they pretended a willingness to help him meet the problems of an usher, were secretly pleased when he bungled at collection time and skipped a row or overlapped one.

Mr. Keller produced a box of ten-cent cigars, which, as a *personal* gift from him, came as a bitter surprise to the others. He was not big enough, either, to attribute it to them too. He had anticipated their resentment, however, and now produced a bottle of milk of magnesia. No one could deny the comic effect, for Father Malt had been known to recommend the blue bottle from the confessional.

"Ha!" said Father Malt, and everybody laughed.

"In case you get upset on the trip," said the druggist.

"You know it's the best thing," said Father Malt in all seriousness, and then even he remembered he'd said it too often before. He passed the cigars. The box went from hand to hand, but, except for the druggist's clerk, nobody would have one.

Father Malt, seeing this, wisely renewed his thanks for the bag, insisting upon his indebtedness until it was actually in keeping with the idea the ushers had of their own generosity. Certainly none of them had ever owned a bag like that. Father Malt went to the housekeeper with it and asked her to transfer his clothes from the old bag, already packed, to the new one. When he returned, the ushers were still standing around feeling good about the bag and not so good about the cigars. They'd discuss that later. Father Malt urged them to sit down. He seemed to want them near him as long as possible. They *were* his friends, but I could not blame Father Burner for avoiding them. He was absent now, as he usually managed to be when the ushers called. If he ever succeeded Father Malt, who let them have the run of the place, they would be the first to suffer—after me! As Father Malt was the heart, they were the substance of a parish that remained rural while becoming increasingly suburban. They dressed up occasionally and dropped into St. Paul and Minneapolis, "the Cities," as visiting firemen into Hell, though it would be difficult to imagine any other place as graceless and far-gone as our own hard little highway town—called Sherwood but about as sylvan as a tennis court.

They were regular fellows—not so priestly as their urban colleagues—loud, heavy of foot, wearers of long underwear in wintertime and iron-gray business suits the year round. Their idea of a good time (pilsner beer, cheap cigars smoked with the bands left on, and pinochle) coincided nicely with their understanding of "doing good" (a percentage of every pot went to the parish building fund). Their wives, also active, played cards in the church basement and sold vanilla extract and chances—mostly to each other, it appeared—with all revenue over cost going to what was known as "the missions." This evening I could be grateful that time was not going to permit the usual pinochle game. (In the midst of all their pounding—almost as hard on me as it

was on the dining-room table—I often felt they should have played on a meat block.)

The ushers, settling down all over the living room, started to talk about Father Malt's trip to Chicago. The housekeeper brought in a round of beer.

"How long you be gone, Father—three days?" one of them asked.

Father Malt said that he'd be gone about three days.

"Three days! This is Friday. Tomorrow's Saturday. Sunday. Monday." Everything stopped while the youngest usher counted on his fingers. "Back on Tuesday?"

Father Malt nodded.

"Who's takin' over on Sunday?"

Mr. Keller answered for Father Malt. "He's got some missionary fathers in."

"Missionaries!"

The youngest usher then began to repeat himself on one of his two or three topics. "Hey, Father, don't forget to drop in the U.S.O. if it's still there. I was in Chi during the war," he said, but nobody would listen to him.

Mr. Bauman had cornered Father Malt and was trying to tell him where that place was—that place where he'd eaten his meals during the World's Fair; one of the waitresses was from Minnesota. I'd had enough of this—the next thing would be a diagram on the back of an envelope—and I'd heard Father Burner come in earlier. I went upstairs to check on him. For a minute or two I stood outside his room listening. He had Father Philbert with him, and, just as I'd expected, he was talking against Father Malt, leading up to the famous question with which Father Malt, years ago, had received the Sherwood appointment from the Archbishop: "Have dey got dere a goot meat shop?"

Father Philbert laughed, and I could hear him

sip from his glass and place it on the floor beside his chair. I entered the room, staying close to the baseboard, in the shadows, curious to know what they were drinking. I maneuvered myself into position to sniff Father Philbert's glass. To my surprise, Scotch. Here was proof that Father Burner considered Father Philbert a friend. At that moment I could not think what it was he expected to get out of a lowly missionary. My mistake, not realizing then how correct and prophetic I'd been earlier in thinking of them as two of a kind. It seldom happened that Father Burner got out the real Scotch for company, or for himself *in* company. For most guests he had nothing—a safe policy, since a surprising number of temperance cranks passed through the rectory—and for unwelcome guests who would like a drink he kept a bottle of "Scotch-type" whiskey, which was a smooth, smoky blend of furniture polish that came in a fancy bottle, was offensive even when watered, and cheap, though rather hard to get since the end of the war. He had a charming way of plucking the rare bottle from a bureau drawer, as if this were indeed an occasion for him; even so, he would not touch the stuff, presenting himself as a chap of simple tastes, of no taste at all for the things of this world, who would prefer, if anything, the rude wine made from our own grapes—if we'd had any grapes. Quite an act, and one he thoroughly enjoyed, holding his glass of pure water and asking, "How's your drink, Father? Strong enough?"

The housekeeper, ap-pearing at the door, said there'd been a change of plans and some of the ushers were driving Father Malt to the train.

"Has he gone yet?" asked Father Burner.

"Not yet, Father."

"Well, tell him goodbye for me."

"Yes, Father."

When she had gone, he said, "I'd tell him myself, but I don't want to run into that bunch."

Father Philbert smiled. "What's he up to in Chicago?"

"They've got one of those pastors' and builders' conventions going on at the Stevens Hotel."

"Is he building?"

"No, but he's a pastor and he'll get a lot of free samples. He won't buy anything."

"Not much has been done around here, huh?" said Father Philbert.

He had fed Father Burner the question he wanted. "He built that fish pond in the back yard—for his minnows. That's the extent of the building program in his time. Of course he's only been here a while."

SANCTUARY

On East Fifty-sixth Street one day last week, we noticed a hand-lettered sign on the windshield of a
parked car. It read, "Under your car is a kitten. Stay
where you are until he decides to come out. Thank
you."

| 1956 |

"How long?"

"Fourteen years," said Father Burner. *He
would be the greatest builder of them all—if he
ever got the chance.* He lit a cigarette and smiled.
"What he's really going to Chicago for is to see a
couple of ball games."

Father Philbert did not smile. "Who's playing there now?" he said.

A little irritated at this interest, Father Burner
said, "I believe it's the Red Sox—or is it the Reds?
Hell, how do I know?"

"Couldn't be the Reds," said Father Philbert.
"The boy and I were in Cincinnati last week and
it was the start of a long home stand for them."

"Very likely," said Father Burner.

While the missionary, a Cardinal fan, ana-
lyzed the pennant race in the National League,
Father Burner sulked. "What's the best train out
of Chicago for Washington?" he suddenly inquired.

Father Philbert told him what he could, but
admitted that his information dated from some
years back. "We don't make the run to Washington any more."

"That's right," said Father Burner. "Washington's in the American League."

Father Philbert laughed, turning aside the
point that he travelled with the Cardinals. "I
thought you didn't know about these things," he
said.

"About these things it's impossible to stay ignorant," said Father Burner. "Here, and the last
place, and the place before that, and in the seminary—a ball, a bat, and God. I'll be damned, Father, if I'll do as the Romans do."

"What price glory?" inquired Father Philbert, as if he smelt heresy.

"I know," said Father Burner. "And it'll probably cost me the red hat." A brave comment, perhaps, from a man not yet a country pastor, and it
showed me where his thoughts were again. He
did not disguise his humble ambition by speaking
lightly of an impossible one. "Scratch a prelate
and you'll find a second baseman," he fumed.

Father Philbert tried to change the subject.
"Somebody told me Father Malt's the exorcist for
the diocese."

"Used to be." Father Burner's eyes flickered
balefully.

"Overdid it, huh?" asked Father Philbert—as
if he hadn't heard!

"Some." I expected Father Burner to say
more. He could have told some pretty wild stories, the gist of them all that Father Malt, as an
exorcist, was perhaps a little quick on the trigger.
He had stuck pretty much to livestock, however,
which was to his credit in the human view.

"Much scandal?"

"Some."

"Nothing serious, though?"

"No."

"Suppose it depends on what you call serious."

Father Burner did not reply. He had become
oddly morose. Perhaps he felt that he was being
catered to out of pity, or that Father Philbert, in
giving him so many opportunities to talk against
Father Malt, was tempting him.

"Who plays the accordion?" inquired Father
Philbert, hearing it downstairs.

"He does."

"Go on!"

"Sure."

"How can he hear what he's playing?"

"What's the difference—if he plays an accordion?"

Father Philbert laughed. He removed the cellophane from a cigar, and then he saw me. And at that moment I made no attempt to hide. "There's that damn cat."

"His assistant!" said Father Burner with surprising bitterness. "Coadjutor with right of succession."

Father Philbert balled up the cellophane and tossed it at the wastebasket, missing.

"Get it," he said to me, fatuously.

I ignored him, walking slowly toward the door.

Father Burner made a quick movement with his feet, which were something to behold, but I knew he wouldn't get up, and took my sweet time.

Father Philbert inquired, "Will she catch mice?"

She! Since coming to live at the rectory, I've been celibate, it's true, but I daresay I'm as manly as the next one. And Father Burner, who might have done me the favor of putting him straight, said nothing.

"She looks pretty fat to be much of a mouser."

I just stared at the poor man then, as much as to say that I'd think one so interested in catching mice would have heard of a little thing called the mousetrap. After one last dirty look, I left them to themselves—to punish each other with their company.

I strolled down the hall, trying to remember when I'd last had a mouse. Going past the room occupied by the young missionary, I smiled upon his door, which was shut, confident that he was inside hard at his prayers.

The next morning, shortly after breakfast, which I took, as usual, in the kitchen, I headed for the cool orchard to which I often repaired on just such a day as this one promised to be. I had no appetite for the sparrows hopping from tree to tree above me, but there seemed no way to convince them of that. Each one, so great is his vanity, thinks himself eminently edible. Peace, peace, they cry, and there is no peace. Finally, tired of their noise, I got up from the matted grass and left, levelling my ears and flailing my tail, in a fake dudgeon that inspired the males to feats of stunt flying and terrorized the young females most delightfully.

I went then to another favorite spot of mine, that bosky strip of green between the church and the brick sidewalk. Here, however, the horseflies found me, and as if that were not enough, visions of stray dogs and children came between me and the kind of sleep I badly needed after an uncommonly restless night.

When afternoon came, I remembered that it was Saturday, and that I could have the rectory to myself. Father Burner and the missionaries would be busy with confessions. By this time the temperature had reached its peak, and though I felt sorry for the young missionary, I must admit the thought of the other two sweltering in the confessionals refreshed me. The rest of the afternoon I must have slept something approaching the sleep of the just.

I suppose it was the sound of dishes that roused me. I rushed into the dining room, not bothering to wash up, and took my customary place at the table. Only then did I consider the empty chair next to me—the utter void. This, I thought, is a foreshadowing of what I must someday face—this, and Father Burner munching away at the other end of the table. And there was the immediate problem: no one to serve me.

The young missionary smiled at me, but how can you eat a smile? The other two, looking rather wilted—to their hot boxes I wished them swift return—talked in expiring tones of reserved sins and did not appear to notice me. Our first meal together without Father Malt did not pass without incident, however. It all came about when the young missionary extended a thin sliver of meat to me.

DREAMS OF GRANDEUR

WOOF!

MANKOFF

"Hey, don't do that!" said Father Philbert. "You'll never make a mouser out of her that way."

Father Burner, too, regarded the young missionary with disapproval.

"Just this one piece," said the young missionary. The meat was already in my mouth.

"Well, watch it in the future," said Father Philbert. It was the word "future" that worried me. Did it mean that he had arranged to cut off my sustenance in the kitchen too? Did it mean that until Father Malt returned I had to choose between mousing and fasting?

I continued to think along these melancholy lines until the repast, which had never begun for me, ended for them. Then I whisked into the kitchen, where I received the usual bowl of milk. But whether the housekeeper, accustomed as she was to having me eat my main course at table, assumed there had been no change in my life, or was now acting under instructions from these villains, I don't know. I was too sickened by their meanness to have any appetite. When the pastor's

away, the curates will play, I thought. On the whole I was feeling pretty glum.

It was our custom to have the main meal at noon on Sundays. I arrived early, before the others, hungrier than I'd been for as long as I could remember, and still I had little or no expectation of food at this table. I was there for one purpose—to assert myself—and possibly, where the young missionary was concerned, to incite sympathy for myself and contempt for my persecutors. By this time I knew that to be the name for them.

They entered the dining room, just the two of them.

"Where's the kid?" asked Father Burner.

"He's not feeling well," said Father Philbert.

I was not surprised. They'd arranged between the two of them to have him say the six- and eleven-o'clock Masses, which meant, of course, that he'd fasted in the interval. I had not thought of him as the hardy type, either.

"I'll have the housekeeper take him some beef broth," said Father Burner. Damned white of you, I was thinking, when he suddenly whirled and swept me off my chair. Then he picked it up and placed it against the wall. Then he went to the lower end of the table, removed his plate and silverware, and brought them to Father Malt's place. Talking and fuming to himself, he sat down in Father Malt's chair. I did not appear very brave, I fear, cowering under mine.

Father Philbert, who had been watching with interest, now greeted the new order with a cheer. "Attaboy, Ernest!"

Father Burner began to justify himself. "More light here," he said, and added, "Cats kill birds," and for some reason he was puffing.

"If they'd just kill mice," said Father Philbert, "they wouldn't be so bad." He had a one-track mind if I ever saw one.

"Wonder how many that black devil's caught in his time?" said Father Burner, airing a common prejudice against cats of my shade (though I do have a white collar). He looked over at me. "Sssss," he said. But I held my ground.

"I'll take a dog any day," said the platitudinous Father Philbert.

"Me, too."

After a bit, during which time they played hard with the roast, Father Philbert said, "How about taking her for a ride in the country?"

"Hell," said Father Burner. "He'd just come back."

"Not if we did it right, she wouldn't."

"Look," said Father Burner. "Some friends of mine dropped a cat off the high bridge in St. Paul. They saw him go under in mid-channel. I'm talking about the Mississippi, understand. Thought they'd never lay eyes on that animal again. That's what they thought. He was back at the house before they were." Father Burner paused—he could see that he was not convincing Father Philbert—and then he tried again. "That's

a fact, Father. They might've played a quick round of golf before they got back. Cat didn't even look damp, they said. He's still there. Case a lot like this. Except now they're afraid of *him*."

To Father Burner's displeasure, Father Philbert refused to be awed or even puzzled. He simply inquired: "But did they use a bag? Weights?"

"Millstones," snapped Father Burner. "Don't quibble."

Then they fell to discussing the burial customs of gangsters—poured concrete and the rest—and became so engrossed in the matter that they forgot all about me.

Over against the wall, I was quietly working up the courage to act against them. When I felt sufficiently lionhearted, I leaped up and occupied my chair. Expecting blows and vilification, I encountered only indifference. I saw then how far I'd come down in their estimation. Already the remembrance of things past—the disease of noble politicals in exile—was too strong in me, the hope of restoration unwarrantably faint.

At the end of the meal, returning to me, Father Philbert remarked, "I think I know a better way." Rising, he snatched the crucifix off the wall, passed it to a bewildered Father Burner, and, saying "Nice Kitty," grabbed me behind the ears. "Hold it up to her," said Father Philbert. Father Burner held the crucifix up to me. "See that?" said Father Philbert to my face. I miaowed. "Take that!" said Father Philbert, cuffing me. He pushed my face into the crucifix again. "See that?" he said again, but I knew what to expect next, and when he cuffed me, I went for his hand with my mouth, pinking him nicely on the wrist. Evidently Father Burner had begun to understand and appreciate the proceedings. Although I was in a good position to observe everything, I could not say as much for myself. "Association," said Father Burner with mysterious satisfaction, almost with zest. He poked the crucifix at me. "If he's just smart enough to react properly," he said. "Oh, she's plenty smart," said Father Philbert, sucking his wrist and giving himself, I hoped, hydrophobia. He scuffed off one of his sandals for a paddle. Father Burner, fingering the crucifix nervously, inquired, "Sure it's all right to go on with this thing?" "It's the intention that counts in these things," said Father Philbert. "Our motive is clear enough." And they went at me again.

After that first taste of the sandal in the dining room, I foolishly believed I would be safe as long as I stayed away from the table; there was something about my presence there, I thought, that brought out the beast in them—which is to say very nearly all that was in them. But they caught me in the upstairs hall the same evening, one brute thundering down upon me, the other sealing off my only avenue of escape. And this beating was worse than the first—preceded as it was by a short delay that I mistook for a reprieve until Father Burner, who had gone downstairs muttering something about "leaving no margin for error," returned with the crucifix from the dining room, although we had them hanging all over the house. The young missionary, coming upon them while they were at me, turned away. "I wash my hands of it," he said. I thought he might have done more.

Out of mind, bruised of body, sick at heart, for two days and nights I held on, I know not how or why—unless I lived in hope of vengeance. I wanted simple justice, a large order in itself, but I would never have settled for that alone. I wanted nothing less than my revenge.

I kept to the neighborhood, but avoided the rectory. I believed, of course, that their only strategy was to drive me away. I derived some little satisfaction from making myself scarce, for it was

thus I deceived them into thinking their plan to banish me successful. But this was my single comfort during this hard time, and it was as nothing against their crimes.

I spent the nights in the open fields. I reeled, dizzy with hunger, until I bagged an aged field mouse. It tasted bitter to me, this stale provender, and seemed, as I swallowed it, an ironic concession to the enemy. I vowed I'd starve before I ate another mouse. By way of retribution to myself, I stalked sparrows in the orchard—hating myself for it but persisting all the more when I thought of those bird-lovers, my persecutors, before whom I could stand and say in self-redemption, "You made me what I am now. You thrust the killer's part upon me." Fortunately, I did not flush a single sparrow. Since *my* motive was clear enough, however, I'd had the pleasure of sinning against them and their ideals, the pleasure without the feathers and mess.

On Tuesday, the third day, all caution, I took up my post in the lilac bush beside the garage. Not until Father Malt returned, I knew, would I be safe in daylight. He arrived along about dinnertime, and I must say the very sight of him aroused a sentiment in me akin to human affection. The youngest usher, who must have had the afternoon off to meet him at the station in St. Paul, carried the new bag before him into the rectory. It was for me an act symbolic of the counterrevolution to come. I did not rush out from my hiding place, however. I had suffered too much to play the fool now. Instead I slipped into the kitchen by way of the flap in the screen door, which they had not thought to barricade. I waited under the stove for my moment, like an actor in the wings.

Presently I heard them tramping into the dining room and seating themselves, and Father Malt's voice saying, "I had a long talk with the

Archbishop." (I could almost hear Father Burner praying, Did he say anything about *me*?) And then, "Where's Fritz?"

"He hasn't been around lately," said Father Burner cunningly. He would not tell the truth and he would not tell a lie.

"You know, there's something mighty funny about that cat," said Father Philbert. "We think she's possessed."

I was astonished, and would have liked a moment to think it over, but by now I was already entering the room.

"Possessed!" said Father Malt. "Aw, no!"

"Ah, yes," said Father Burner, going for the meat right away. "And good riddance."

And then I miaowed and they saw me.

"Quick!" said Father Philbert, who made a nice recovery after involuntarily reaching for me and his sandal at the same time. Father Burner ran to the wall for the crucifix, which had been, until now, a mysterious and possibly blasphemous feature of my beatings—the crucifix held up to me by the one not scourging at the moment, as if it were the will behind my punishment. They had schooled me well, for even now, at the sight of the crucifix, an undeniable fear was rising in me. Father Burner handed it to Father Malt.

"Now you'll see," said Father Philbert.

"We'll leave it up to you," said Father Burner.

I found now that I could not help myself. What followed was hidden from them—from human eyes. I gave myself over entirely to the fear they'd beaten into me, and in a moment, according to their plan, I was fleeing the crucifix as one truly possessed, out of the dining room and into the kitchen, and from there, blindly, along the house and through the shrubbery, ending in the street, where a powerful gray car ran over me— and where I gave up the old ghost for a new one.

Simultaneously, reborn, redeemed from my previous fear, identical with my former self, so far as they could see, and still in their midst, I padded up to Father Malt—he still sat gripping the crucifix—and jumped into his lap. I heard the young missionary arriving from an errand in Father Philbert's *brother's* car, late for dinner he thought, but just in time to see the stricken look I saw coming into the eyes of my persecutors. This look alone made up for everything I'd suffered at their hands. Purring now, I was rubbing up against the crucifix, myself effecting my utter revenge.

"What have we done?" cried Father Philbert. He was basically an emotional dolt and would have voted then for my canonization.

"I ran over a cat!" said the young missionary excitedly. "I'd swear it was this one. When I looked, there was nothing there!"

"Better go upstairs and rest," growled Father Burner. He sat down—it was good to see him in his proper spot at the low end of the table—as if to wait a long time, or so it seemed to me. I found myself wondering if I could possibly bring about his transfer to another parish—one where they had a devil for a pastor and several assistants, where he would be able to start at the bottom again.

But first things first, I always say, and all in good season, for now Father Malt himself was drawing my chair up to the table, restoring me to my rightful place.

| 1950 |

"The Case of Dimity Ann"

by James Thurber
    The Ledgelets
    Somerset Bridge, Bermuda

When the last guests had left, after a party that
began with early cocktails, proceeded gaily through wine at
dinner, and then liquers and highballs, the Ridgeways stood
in the open doorway, of their house and watched the Bennett's Buick flash its
headlights at the turn of the driveway and disappear down the
road.

"Let's have a night cat," said Ridgeway David. "I say
'night cat' because nobody ever talked about cats the way
Bennett talked about cats tonight, All I can think of is
cats. I can't understand a cat man like that," he finished
with a snarl. Alice didn't like the snarl, which boded more
Scotch, and she said, "I think I'll go to bed, it's after two,"
but she knew it wouldn't work. ~~and to claim.~~ "I'll finish
the one I have," she said quickly. "Then I'm going to bed."
She hurriedly led the way back to the living room, as if she
wanted to get the night cap over with. "Wives always tell
their husbands where they're going," ~~he~~ Ridgeway said. "'I'm going to
bed. I'm going to put my foot down. I'm going to tell you

THE CASE OF DIMITY ANN

Fiction

JAMES THURBER

When the last guests left, after a party that had begun with early cocktails, proceeded gaily through wine at dinner, and then liqueurs and highballs, the Ridgeways stood in the open doorway of their house and watched the Bennetts' Buick flash its headlights at the turn of the driveway and disappear down the road.

"Let's have a nightcat," Ridgeway said. "I say 'cat' because nobody ever talked about cats the way Bennett talked about cats tonight. All I can think of is nightcat, hubcat, foolscat, freshman cat— I can't understand a cat man like that," he finished with a snarl.

Alice didn't like the snarl, which boded more Scotch, and she said, "I think I'll go to bed. It's after two," but she could see it wouldn't work. "I'll finish the one I have," she said quickly. "Then I'm going to bed." She hurriedly led the way back to the living room, as if she wanted to get the nightcap over with.

"Wives always tell their husbands where they're going," Ridgeway said sulkily. " 'I'm going to bed.' 'I'm going to put my foot down.' 'I'm going to tell you something.' 'I'm going crazy.' That puffball must have seventy-five cats."

Alice's highball glass, which was almost full, stood on the table by her chair. Mrs. Bennett had noticed when her hostess stopped drinking, with a kind of obvious quietness, twenty minutes before, and she had begun to remind Mr. Bennett of the hour, but the cat man was deep in a story about Alex, one of his Persians, and had to finish it. It seemed that Alex, who was as smart as a human being, could tell time,

17

liked imported Chianti, and often made a certain music box play by lifting its lid with one paw. "Daintily, I suppose," Ridgeway had put in evilly, and when Bennett said "I beg your pardon?," his wife had got to her feet. "Sorry you have to go," Ridgeway had told him, rising from his chair. "I was just reminded of a cat my first wife had, which I used to tie up." The women had intervened with a flurry of parting talk, and the Bennetts managed to get away without hearing about what Ridgeway had done to the first Mrs. Ridgeway's cat.

"You need some ice," Ridgeway said, and he got two lumps from the bucket on the bar and dropped them into Alice's glass. "I'll never forget Percy, one of my tomcats," he said mockingly. "He was smarter than a human being. He could whistle between his teeth, often winked, as God is my judge, and once, if my memory serves, killed a meter reader." He drank what had been left of his own highball and walked to the bar.

Knowing the significance of his various gaits, as well as the implications of his gestures and inflections late at night, Alice figured that if he had two more drinks, he would be up till dawn. "Not too heavy," she said. "It's almost three."

He poured a stiff drink, talking with his back turned. "Moriarty, another of my tomcats," he said, "could use an eyecup, and often *closed* the lid of the music box, thus putting a stop to 'Do Ye Ken John Whoozis?' What happened to that big slob in his infancy that made him cat-foolish the rest of his life?" He dropped into his chair, tugged at a lock of his hair with his left hand, and ran his lower lip over the upper one. This usually meant that he was about to attack her old beaux, particularly one with the aggravating name of Rupert Llewellyn. Rupert had once sent Alice a volume of Emily Dickinson with the inscription: "This, when so much that is lovely has gone."

"What was it you did to Lydia's cat?" she asked hastily.

He clutched more hair in his left hand and gestured with his glass. "'This, when all that was lovely is gone,'" he said in a jeering falsetto.

Alice twisted in her chair. "You've got it wrong," she said. "You always get it wrong."

He struck a match indolently, and slowly lighted a cigarette. "I don't care how it goes," he said. "I have no desire to be an authority on Rupert of the Lacy Touch. All I know is that a guy who writes 'This comma' is a lady cat."

Alice took a sip of her highball and said, "Well, speaking of cats, let's get it over with. What did you do to Lydia's?"

He took in and exhaled a deep breath, and was about to begin his story when Alice thought she heard something and exclaimed, "What was *that*?"

He glared at her. "I never started a story in my life," he said, "but what you heard something, or saw something, or remembered something. 'I just remembered something' has broken up more marriages than anything else." Alice took a larger swallow of her drink. "And don't keep saying 'Get it over with.' What the hell kind of attention is that, anyway?" he demanded.

Alice gave him her cool smile and said, "I am all ears."

"The cat's name was Dimity Ann," he began, "and I used to tie it up in the cord of my dressing gown to see how long it would take to get out. I never hurt the cat. The trouble was that I never told Lydia about it, and if I tied that cat up once, I tied it up a hundred times. I was going to tell Lydia about it," he went on. "I was going to say, 'Lydia, I keep tying the cat up all the time, if you want to know,' but I never did."

Alice sat forward in her chair. "Didn't you

do anything about it?" she asked. "I mean didn't you talk to anybody?"

This puzzled and annoyed him. "Didn't I talk to anybody about what?" he demanded.

She smoothed her dress over one knee. "Well, it sounds like what they call a compulsion," she said. "Something you have to do, but you don't know why."

His annoyance grew, and his voice rose a little. "Whenever I do anything that I don't know why, I'll let you know," he said coldly. He seemed to become abruptly soberer, as he always did when he was caught between irritation and reminiscence. His eyes opened wider and looked clearer. "We haven't even come to the part that *you* would call compulsion," he said, "but *I* wouldn't. Anyway, it wasn't like deliberately running a lawnmower over a frog, or something like that—something your boy friend Rupert Valentino would do, and probably did."

"It wasn't Valentino," she said, "and you know it."

He finished his highball, and put the empty glass on the floor by his chair. "Llewellyn is worse," he said. "One day I was at the library and suddenly I stopped reading and went all the way home to tie up that damned cat. You've got to remember that the library was three miles from my house. I opened the front door and began calling, 'Here, pussy, pussy, pussy.' I knew Lydia wasn't home."

"I don't think I like this," Alice said. "I don't think I want to hear about it. I mean it sounds kind of deep-seated now."

He picked up his glass and rattled the ice in it. "I said, 'Here, kitty, kitty, kitty. Here, kitty, kitty, kitty,' but she was hiding. All right, all right, I found her and tied her up again, and then I went back to the library—after she got out, of course. When I came home that eve-

MISSING

A Seventy-second Street housewife we know had to call in a plumber the other day. Her cat watched him with deep interest while he went about the business of getting the kitchen sink working again. As the plumber put away his tools, he remarked, "Say, that's quite a cat you got there. Seems to know just what's going on." Our friend agreed that it was indeed a knowing cat, and added that most Siamese cats were like that. "A Siamese, hey?" the plumber said, and glanced around the kitchen. "Where's the other one—asleep?"

| 1945 |

ning, Lydia said, 'The dotted-swiss cat has run away. I can't find her anywhere.'"

"Is this supposed to be funny?" Alice asked. "Because it isn't."

He went to the bar with his glass again and she didn't say anything. She had several ways of not saying anything, and this was the one he disliked most. Even with his back turned, he could *feel* her not saying anything. "All right, all right," he said over his shoulder. "This is the drink that would kill Rupert, but I am not a thimble-belly. I am not the kind of man who loses one glove in a theatre and his wife has to look for it under the seats, either. And I do not extend my fingers when I examine my nails. I, by God, double my hand like a man." He made more noise than was necessary with the ice cubes and the seltzer bottle, and walked back to his chair with his lower lip protruding. Still Alice didn't say anything. He sat down and there was a ten-second silence, which he ended by saying, in his mocking tone, "Here, kitty, kitty, kitty, kitty, kitty, kitty, kitty, kitty, kitty."

She took another drink and said slowly, "Ah, shut up. I can't stand writers after it gets dark."

He looked deep into his highball and said,

"The fastest time Dimity Ann ever made getting out of the cord was seventeen seconds. No fractions. You can put it down to research, if you want to. I am probably the only man in the world who knows the fastest time a cat can make getting out of the cord of a bathrobe. Seventeen seconds."

"What I would like to know," Alice said after a long pause, "is why you haven't told me this story before. I mean I wish you had, somehow. It's the kind of thing a man would tell a girl when he was going with her, I mean if it wasn't deep-seated."

He snarled, "I wish the hell you wouldn't keep using that damn word. You don't know what deep-seated means. It means worse than a bad cold, but you wouldn't know what that means. I didn't tell you about Dimity Ann because it isn't the kind of story a man thinks of telling a girl. It's really not important."

Alice jiggled the ice in her glass. "I don't like to hear you say it isn't important, because that's just the kind of thing that *is*," she said. "I mean if you think it isn't important, it probably is. But now you are trying to—trying to—what is it they call it when you don't want to face how important it is?"

He sat looking at her cloudily for a long moment. "You are the God-damnedest fuzziest psychologist in the world," he said. "What you are buzzing around like a mosquito is 'overcompensation.' But, as usual, you are completely wrong. I am telling this story for the first time because this happens to be the first time I have ever had a great big lovable cat man in my house. I had not given Dimity Ann a single thought for eight years until tonight. Tonight all I had was cats—cats for cocktails, cats for dinner, and cats after dinner. Did I ever tell you about Rupert? He was one of my alley cats, and what distinguished him from the others was his ability to play a comb with tissue paper on it, and the fact that once he swallowed his own tail. This is what is known as psychological evasion."

Alice found, somewhat to her surprise, that she had finished her drink, and she held her empty glass out to him. He came over and got it and carried it to the bar. "Just a light one," she said. He made the drink and took it back to her. "Did you ever find Dimity Ann?" Alice asked. "I mean it would be awful if you drove that little kitten out into the streets and it died or something."

He laughed. "I forgot to tell you about that," he said. "Dimity Ann was picked up by Mary Pickford, who happened to be driving through in her limousine. The cat lived happily ever after, and became one of the greatest little pals Buddy Rogers ever had. This is known as minimization of the monstrous."

Alice turned her glass around slowly in her hands. "What makes me think you are trying to make me believe you are making this all up?" she asked. "I know you must actually have had a cat, or Lydia had one, because you could never make up the name Dimity Ann."

He got up and began to pace around the room. "This was a charming cat," he said, "but there just happened to be something between it and me, a kind of perverse communion. That day at the library, it was as if a faint, distant bell had rung. It was a signal from the cat to me. I think she actually wanted to be tied up, and the only thing that really worries me is that I was weak enough to give in to her. Lydia once had a Siamese cat that liked to have a Scotty drag it by its tail. The damn cat would lie on its back and wave its tail at the Scotty until the Scotty sighed and dragged it around. Its name was Asia. You won't believe this, but while the cat was being dragged, it purred."

Feb.17,1973

THE NEW YORKER

Price 50 cents

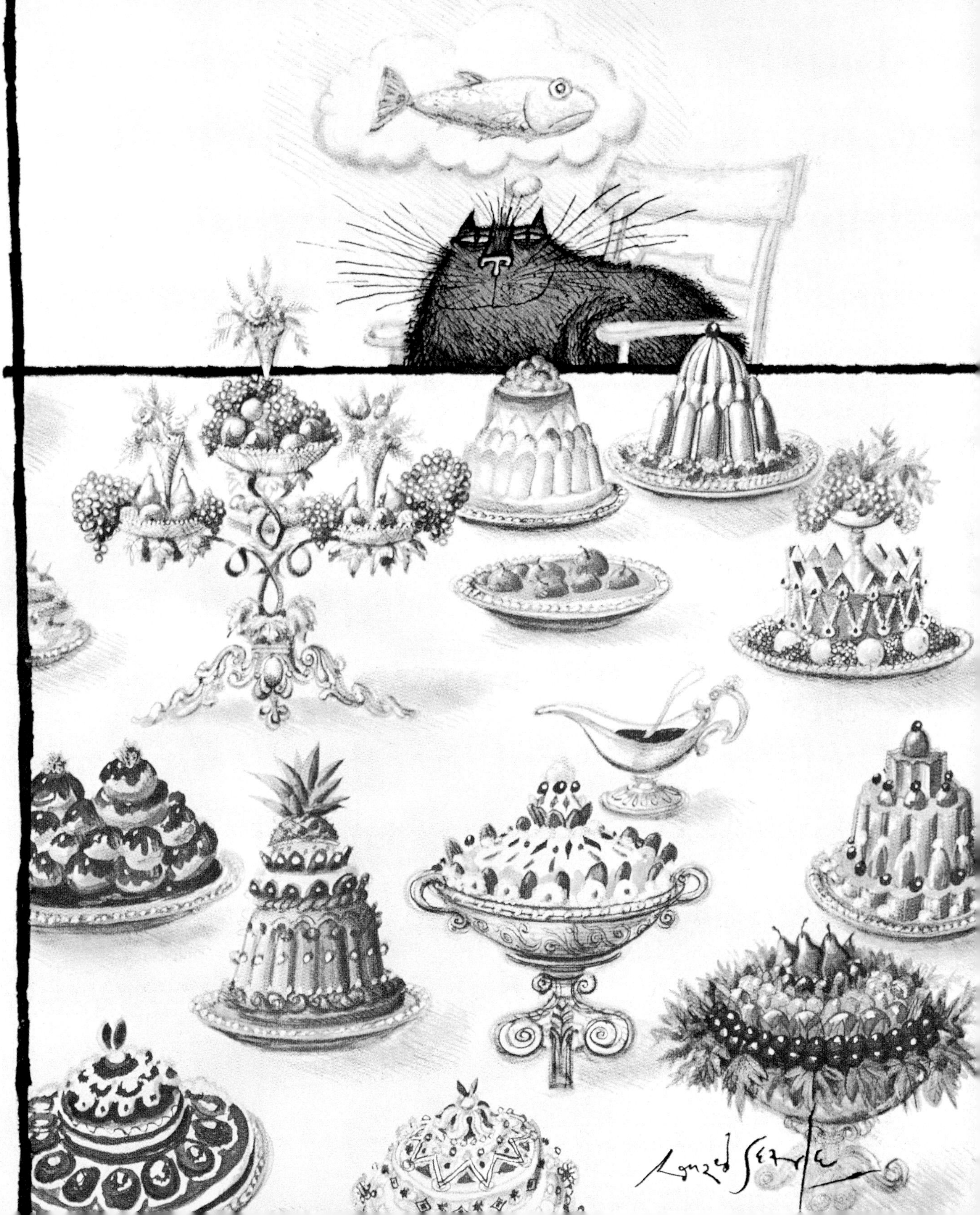

"You just made that up," Alice told him. "You made it up to annoy George Bennett, and I think I know why you didn't tell him. You were trying to think of something that would shock him, but you decided that he would be amused, and you didn't want to amuse him. Now you are trying to make me believe you didn't tie up Dimity Ann, by telling obviously impossible stories." She looked at her wristwatch.

"I know," he said. "It's almost four, but I'll stay up all night if you insist on blaming me instead of Dimity Ann. It's always the cat's fault. They're strange creatures. You ought to know that."

Alice hadn't been listening. She sat forward slowly, frowning at the floor, and he knew that she was searching for a contradiction of something he had said. She found it, and looked up at him suddenly. "I wasn't buzzing around 'overcompensation,'" she said. "That's not the right word at all. Overcompensation is when you are nice to little girls and old ladies because you have been cruel to your mother. It means you ask for ice cream in a loud voice in a restaurant if you

really think you are becoming an alcoholic. It means things like that."

He sat down, leaned far back in his chair, and studied her as if she were something in a museum. "What did you major in at college?" he asked. "If it was psychology—"

"I know what it is!" she cried. "I mean I know what it is when you pretend that tying up the cat wasn't important. It's defense mechanism." She brought this out triumphantly.

"You're getting colder and colder," he told her. "Defense mechanism, to use one of your cunning illustrations, is when a dowager at a formal dinner drops the ice cream down her bodice and then tells her hostess she is having a chill."

He began to drink his highball rapidly, and she said, "We're not going to sit up all night and argue, even if we do disagree on certain terms." He paid no attention to this and finished his drink. Then he put the glass slowly down on the floor by his chair. "I guess it *is* late," he said surprisingly, "and that goddam cat man wore me out. Like a fool, I just sat there and gave him my fixed grin and acted as if I were interested in his cats. The only one of them that had any guts was the one that could catch a baseball at thirty paces. It couldn't have been *his* cat. It must have belonged to the neighbors."

Alice got up and began emptying ashtrays and gathering up glasses, including his. She took the glasses out to the pantry, set them down, and stood there a moment frowning, going over the case of Dimity

"Keep your guard up, Willoughby. We're entering big-cat country."

Ann. Suddenly she hurried back to the living room. There was something she had to tell her husband, and she was afraid he might have fallen asleep. When he did that late at night, it was almost impossible to bring him back to full consciousness. He was sitting in his chair with his eyes closed, but he was not asleep.

"The thing that worries me most is your going all the way home from the library to tie up the cat," she said. "If you had just happened to tie up the cat when you saw it, and were in your dressing gown, that wouldn't be anything at all. But I can just see you sitting there in the library and suddenly jumping up and forgetting where you were and tiptoeing out, to go back home, five miles."

He jumped to his feet. "I did *not* tiptoe," he said coldly, "and it was *not* five miles! I don't understand why you have to make it sound furtive. There wasn't anything furtive about it. It was as normal as tying a can to a dog's tail."

Alice sat down and watched his gestures, which were wide and agitated, an invariable mannerism of his when he was holding an untenable position.

"Look!" he shouted. "When I got to the library I found out I had left my research notes at home, and I couldn't get anywhere without them. I went back to my house, as any sane man would, and in the course of hunting for them I tied up the cat. I have tried to tell you it was a little game we played together. Every time Ed Morrison goes home, for instance, he throws a few darts at his dart board. It was as simple as that." He sat down in his chair and began groping on the floor beside him for his glass.

"You have a wonderful memory," Alice reminded him. "You never forget anything, and you certainly wouldn't forget notes if you were going to the library to use them. I mean it wouldn't be like you." She stood up and walked toward the door

into the hall, but stopped beside his chair. "Please don't rationalize this," she said quietly. "I don't want you to get in deeper than you already are."

"There is something serious the matter with you," he said crisply, in the tone of a trial lawyer cagily abandoning a shaky defense for a random attack. "You're trying to transfer some anxiety neurosis of yours to me by mixing me up in all this goddam terminology." He folded his arms and leaned back in his chair with the satisfied look of a counsellor who has brilliantly rested his case.

"What research were you doing that day at the library?" she asked.

He stared up at her. "How the hell should I know?" he demanded. "This was eight years ago."

She watched the left corner of his mouth turn up, the way it did when he was about to tell a daring story in mixed company or an inconsequential lie to her in private.

"I didn't go to the library at all that day," he said with a full grin. "I hid in a closet until Lydia had left the house, and then I came creeping out on all fours, calling, 'Kitty, kitty, kitty, kitty, kitty, kitty, kitty, kitty, kitty—'"

"Scat!" she cried loudly, as much to her own surprise as to his. Then she walked slowly out into the hall, and waited at the foot of the stairs for his last word. On nights like this, he always had the last word. She could see his right hand groping for his missing glass, and she could sense his mind and tongue searching for something final to say. She realized, after several long moments of silence, that he couldn't find the last word, for the simple reason that she had said it herself. She ran up the stairs as lightly and swiftly as a girl, restraining a new and unexpected impulse to clasp her hands above her head and wave them, in triumphant greeting to the invisible wives of all the writers in the world.

| 1952 |

DEFENCE OF CATS

WOLCOTT GIBBS

The other day the editor of a great newspaper decided that he ought to find out if dogs are better than cats, so he sent a man up to see Albert Payson Terhune, some of whose best friends have fur. It turned out that Mr. Terhune preferred dogs, feeling strongly about the whole thing.

Only women like cats, he said, and added disparagingly that this seemed to him "a very significant tip-off on the makeup of the two sexes." This was the place, of course, for the reporter to ask Mr. Terhune if he thought dogs were better than women, but apparently he forgot to. Anyway, Mr. Terhune said next that the only real friendships he had ever made with cats were with those that thought they were dogs and acted that way. For a moment this gave me quite a cheerful picture of Mr. Terhune and his cat friends hot on the scent, yelping and baying, but I imagine that the intent was a little more mystic than that, implying some subtle masculinity of the spirit, and I suppose we might as well let it go.

Finally, Mr. Terhune summed up his whole opinion of cats by calling them lazy, disloyal opportunists, with nothing to recommend them except a low mechanical cunning.

"Cats can do some marvellously intelligent things," Mr. Terhune admitted reluctantly. "They will learn by themselves to unlatch a door."

This seems to me not only an intelligent but almost a miraculous accomplishment, except in the case of an extremely tall cat, but in any case it is white of Mr. Terhune, and shows that at least he tries to keep an open mind.

I am inclined to resent his other statements, though, and would like to discuss them for a moment, with special reference to Dillinger, the cat who thinks she's Gloria Swanson.

In the first place, women do *not* like Dillinger, although she admires them passionately. There is something about a richly upholstered beauty which inspires in Dillinger a perfect frenzy of admiration and yearning. It is unfortunate that her love usually expresses itself in a frantic attempt to climb up their legs, but it is impossible not to admire her persistence in the face of repeated and often painful rebuffs. Nor, in spite of Mr. Terhune, is there anything mercenary in Dillinger's courtship. She wants nothing from these ladies, neither food nor affection. She loves only, I'm sure, the way they smell.

In another paragraph of that misguided interview, Mr. Terhune says, "A cat simply does not know what loyalty is. I have a warmer kitchen and more milk and liver. Your cat will gladly come to my kitchen and desert you." In the case of Dillinger, who wouldn't be found dead in any man's kitchen and undoubtedly imagines that liver and milk are the staples of a baser order—of dogs, perhaps—it is hard to apply Mr. Terhune's conditions, but I understand his point. It is perfectly true that Dillinger would leave me instantly for more caviar and thicker cream, for softer pillows and larger vistas, but there would be no disloyalty in that. Dillinger is an epicure, serenely removed from such soft and bourgeois considerations as loyalty and disloyalty, and her only anxiety in life is to better herself aesthetically. It seems to me that people like Mr. Terhune have wasted a great deal of sympathy on dogs that have starved to death in hovels rather than leave their masters. They are the socially inefficient, and they deserve what they get.

I think, though, that Mr. Terhune is most misguided when he talks about the economic uselessness of cats. Never, he told the reporter, had he heard of a cat's pulling a child out of a river by the seat of its trousers (an almost routine performance among Mr. Terhune's collies) or even balancing a ball on its nose in a vaudeville act. To me there is something offensively utilitarian in any such attitude, and the captious might even suspect that Mr. Terhune doesn't want a pet as much as a sort of combination lifeguard and acrobat. Dogs, like all weak and sentimental characters, are highly susceptible to suggestion, and they, too, have come to accept this unfortunate conception of themselves. They have been quite willing to learn foolish tricks and run pointless errands, forfeiting their dignity and diffusing their personalities, until the average dog today is a sorry creature, functioning adequately neither as a guest in the house nor a servant.

Cats, on the other hand, have character and independence. They are realists, and they understand perfectly their position in domestic life, which is decorative and nothing else. Cats don't work, and I suspect they look on dogs, who do, as scum. In all the time I've known Dillinger, she has never shown the slightest interest in justifying her existence, and when you think about it, this is as it should be. After all, she was a lioness when the Terhune collies were wolves, or worse.

| 1934 |

THE SMOKER

Fiction

DAVID SCHICKLER

Douglas Kerchek taught twelfth-grade advanced-placement English at St. Agnes High School on West Ninety-seventh and Broadway, and Nicole Bonner was the standout in his class. She was the tallest, at five feet ten, the oldest, at nineteen, and the smartest, with a flawless A. She wasn't the prettiest, Douglas thought—not beside the spunky nose of Rhonda Phelps or Meredith Beckermann's heart-shaped derrière—but Nicole was dangerously alluring. She had a chopped black Cleopatra haircut and wise blue eyes, and her recent essay on *Othello* had ended with this note:

> Dear Mr. Kerchek:
>
> Last night in bed I read Fear + Loathing in L.V. It is puerile, self-involved gamesmanship. I suppose I don't love drugs enough, although my parents made me drink brandy with them every night. They consider it a gesture of affection.
>
> I saw you yesterday, outside the locker room, changing your shoes to go running, and your ankle looked quite blue. What did you bang it on?
>
> Respectfully,
> Nicole Bonner

This note caused Douglas some concern. He, too, disliked Hunter S. Thompson, but Nicole had also written "in bed" and mentioned his bruise. It was Nicole's habit to do this, to call out random, intimate specifics from the world around her and bring them to Douglas's attention. She'd done it that day in class.

"Iago is filled with lust, Mr. Kerchek," said Jill Eckhard.

"He's a Machiavellian bastard," said Rhonda Phelps.

"You know what's an excellent word to say out loud repeatedly?" Nicole Bonner chewed her hair. "'Rinse.' Think about it, Mr. Kerchek, Rinse. *Rinse.*"

That evening, as always, Douglas walked home to his shabby studio apartment. Douglas was thirty-one. He lived alone, five blocks north of St. Agnes, in an apartment building filled with Mexican men who drank Pabst and held boisterous, high-stakes poker games every night in the lobby outside Douglas's first-floor apartment. They were amiable, violent men, and their nickname for Douglas was Uno, because whenever he sat with them he had one quiet beer, then bowed out.

"Uno," cackled the Mexicans. "Come take our money, Uno."

"Fuck us up, Uno."

A twelve-year-old boy named Chiapas rattled a beer can. "Come get your medicine, Uno."

Douglas grinned wanly, waved them off, and opened his door.

Rinse, he thought, frowning. Rinse. *Rinse.*

After a quick sandwich, Douglas corrected essays. He was a fastidious, tough grader. Also, he had short black sideburns with streaks of gray in them, a boxer's build, a Ph.D. in English literature from Harvard, and no wife or girlfriend. These qualities made Douglas a font of intrigue for the all-female population of St. Agnes—both the lay faculty and the students—but in truth Douglas led a sedentary life. He loved books, he was a passionate, solitary filmgoer, and he got his hair cut every four weeks by Chiapas, whose father ran a barbershop down the block. All told, Douglas was a quiet and, he thought, happy man. He was also

the only male teacher at St. Agnes. Cheryl, Audrey, and Katya, the three single women on the faculty, would have taken up the crusade of dating him, but he wasn't drawn to his co-workers. Cheryl wore electric shades of suede that confused him, Audrey had two cops for ex-husbands, and Katya, despite her long legs and Lithuanian accent, was cruel to the girls. So Douglas spent his nights alone seeing films, correcting essays, and occasionally chatting with Chiapas and company. On this particular night, Douglas was barely into his stack of essays when the phone rang.

"Hello?" sighed Douglas. He expected it to be his mother, who called weekly from Pennsylvania to see if her son had become miraculously engaged.

"Good evening, Mr. Kerchek."

Douglas frowned. "Nicole?"

"Yes, sir."

"How did you get this number?"

"Off the Rolodex in the principal's office. How's your ankle?"

Douglas sneezed, twice. He did this instinctively when he didn't know what to say.

"God bless you," said Nicole.

"Thank you," said Douglas. He glanced around, as if expecting his apartment suddenly to fill with students.

"How's your ankle?"

"It's . . . it's all right. I banged it on my radiator."

"Really?"

The truth was, Douglas had slipped in his shower, like an elderly person.

"Yes, really. Nicole—"

"Do you know what's happening to *my* ankle as we converse?"

"No."

"John Stapleton is licking it. He likes to nibble my toes, too."

Douglas blinked several times.

"John Stapleton is a domestic shorthair. Sometimes he licks, other times he nibbles."

"I see," said Douglas. There was a substantial pause.

"John Stapleton is a cat," said Nicole.

"Of course," agreed Douglas.

"Do you enjoy gnocchi?"

Douglas set his essays on the couch beside him. "Pardon?"

"Gnocchi. Italian potato dumplings. We had them for dinner tonight. Father makes them by hand every Thursday. It's the only thing Father knows how to cook, but he's good at it."

Douglas crossed his ankle over his knee.

"So, do you enjoy them?" said Nicole.

"Gnocchi?"

"Yes."

"Yes."

"Yes meaning you enjoy them, or yes meaning you understood what I was asking?"

"Yes. I mean yes, I like them."

Nicole Bonner laughed.

"When should I start hearing from colleges?" she asked. "It's nearly April."

Douglas was relieved at the topic. "Any week now. But you'll get in everywhere. It's all about what you want."

"I want Princeton."

Douglas imagined Nicole sitting on a dorm bed, reading, sipping soup. He imagined baggy sweater sleeves covering her wrists.

"Fitzgerald went there," said Nicole.

"Yes," said Douglas.

"He was a career alcoholic."

"Yes."

"Did you know that John Stapleton is toilet trained?"

Douglas laughed out loud, once. This usually happened only at the movies, if he was alone and the film was absurd.

"Toilet trained. Meaning what?"

"Meaning that he uses the toilet, like a human being. He crouches on the rim of the bowl and does his business and presses his paw on the flusher afterward. He's very tidy."

"Nicole," said Douglas.

"It's the truth, sir. It took Father aeons to train him, but he did it. We don't even have a litter box. Father was a marine."

Douglas checked his watch. "John Stapleton's an unusual name for a cat."

"He's an unusual cat," said Nicole.

"I think maybe I should hang up now, Nicole. Why don't we talk in school tomorrow?"

"All right. I don't want to inconvenience you in your evening time."

"It's all right."

"Really?"

"Well," said Douglas. "What I mean is, it's no problem. But, um, we'll talk in school tomorrow."

"Inevitably," said Nicole.

Douglas had written Nicole a letter of recommendation for Princeton. In the letter he'd said this:

Whether she's tearing across the field-hockey grass, debunking Whitman, or lecturing me about Woody Allen films, Nicole exudes an irrepressible spirit and a generous unguarded tenacity. She reads an entire novel every night, not to impress anyone but because she loves to do it. She is organized, clever, and kindhearted, and once she knows what she wants she will pursue a thing—a line of argument, a hockey ball, a band to hire for the prom—with a charmingly ruthless will.

Douglas prided himself on his recommendations, on making his students shine on paper. It was one of the few vanities he allowed himself. When it came to crafting words, Douglas felt that he'd been blessed with a knack for always knowing what to say. That was why, the morning after the call from Nicole, Douglas awoke feeling flummoxed. He'd spent ten minutes on the phone with a nineteen-year-old girl and tripped over his tongue like a schoolboy the whole time. During the night, he'd also dreamed he'd been walking barefoot down a beach with Nicole. In the dream, she wore a lowrider black bikini and a lovely blue scarf in her hair like Jackie Kennedy. Douglas, meanwhile, wore green Toughskins jeans and a shirt made of burlap. Every time the waves washed over their feet, Douglas scampered back and yelled, "Beware the manatees!"

Ridiculous, thought Douglas. Embarrassing. He put on a smart coat and tie, and decided to give the girls a pop quiz.

At school, in the faculty lounge, he forced himself to make small talk with Cheryl, the suede-clad mathematician. When the bell rang for his class, Douglas strode into the classroom with confidence.

"Mr. Kerchek." Meredith Beckermann jumped from her desk. "Jill's going to ask you to come watch softball today, but you promised to see our Forensics meet against Regis, remember?"

"I remember," said Douglas.

"Suckup," Jill told Meredith.

Meredith glared at Jill. "Avaunt, and quit my sight," she sniffed.

Douglas set his satchel on his desk, surveyed the room. His advanced-placement class consisted of six girls, the brightest lights in the St. Agnes senior class. There were Meredith and Jill, the arguers; Rhonda Phelps, the bombshell

achiever; Kelly DeMeer, the agnostic; Nancy Huck, who was always on vacation; and Nicole Bonner, who sat by the window.

"Where's Nancy?" asked Douglas.

"Bermuda," said Rhonda. "Snorkeling, with her aunt."

Jill tapped her copy of *Othello*. "Can we discuss the last act?"

"Desdemona's a dipshit," said Meredith.

"Meredith," Douglas warned. He glanced at Nicole, then at Kelly. They spoke the least of the six, Kelly because she was cultivating spiritual fatigue and Nicole because . . . Well, thought Douglas, because she was Nicole. The look in her eyes when she stared out the window reminded Douglas of when he was a boy and he would gaze at his mother's dressing-room mirror, wondering who lived on the other side.

"Vocab quiz," said Douglas.

The girls cleared their desks. They whipped out pens and blank pieces of paper.

"Three synonyms, from Latin roots, for 'bellicose.'" Douglas thought out loud. "Two antonyms for 'abstruse.' One example of synecdoche. Extra credit, list four books by Melville. You have five minutes."

The girls began writing immediately. Douglas watched them with fondness. They were gifted young women, and they would conquer this class and every literature class in their future. He passed among them, staring at their bent heads, at the roots of their hair and their earlobes, wondering how many had prom dates, how many might end up teachers, how quickly Rhonda would marry. He rolled his eyes at Meredith's and Jill's papers: each of them already had seven synonyms for "bellicose." Kelly had finished in three minutes, and was now drawing hangman nooses—her trademark—on all of her "T"s. Then Douglas looked over Nicole's shoulder. Her paper

was in a band of sunlight, and on it she had written no vocabulary words whatsoever. She was, however, busily churning out sentences. Douglas watched, then caught his breath. Nicole had written verbatim, from memory, the entire first page of *Moby-Dick,* and was still going. Douglas waited to see if she would run out of steam or turn her head to look at him, but she didn't.

Douglas leaned down. He could smell Nicole's raspberry shampoo. He scribbled in the margin of her paper, "This isn't what I asked for."

Without glancing up, Nicole crossed out what he'd set down and wrote, "It is a far, far better thing that I do."

"Pens down," said Douglas.

After school, he performed his daily regimen, half an hour of free weights followed by a three-mile run in Central Park. He got back to St. Agnes with just enough time for a shower before the Forensics match. Outside the locker room, lounging on her back on a windowsill eight feet off the ground, was Nicole Bonner.

"How'd you get up there?" panted Douglas. He was winded from his run.

"Flew." Nicole sat up, studied her teacher. Douglas had a privileged view of her ankles, which were crossed and not at all blue. She wore low black pumps.

"What'd you read last night?" he asked.

"*The Moviegoer.* Walker Percy. Did you know, Mr. Kerchek, that thousands of runners die every year from heart attacks in mid-workout?"

"I don't think I run fast enough to induce cardiac trauma, Nicole."

The girl on the ledge didn't swish her legs. Even when she chewed her hair, Douglas thought, she didn't do it nervously. She made it seem correct.

"'Trauma' is an excellent word to say out loud repeatedly. Trauma. Trauma."

"I should shower," said Douglas.

Nicole pointed at him. "Give me one good reason why I should go to college at all."

"Tons of reading time," said Douglas.

Nicole jumped off the ledge, landed lightly on her feet a yard from Douglas.

"I'll accept that," she said, and off she walked.

It was three weeks later, on a rainy Tuesday morning in mid-April, that Douglas received the invitation. Just before chapel, Nicole Bonner poked her head into the faculty lounge, where Douglas and Katya Zarov sat beside each other on the couch. Douglas was reading the paper, and Katya had just noticed a run in her stocking.

"Mr. Kerchek," said Nicole.

Douglas and Katya looked up.

"No students in here," said Katya.

"Mr. Kerchek, I need to speak to you privately." Nicole stood with her hands behind her back like a butler.

Douglas stood. Katya Zarov made a little snort.

Out in the hall, Nicole flashed Douglas a smile.

"Princeton's taking me," she said.

Douglas had a fleeting image of hugging his student. He patted her once on the shoulder.

"That's wonderful," he said. "Congratulations."

Nicole noddded sharply. She had a Bible under one arm, which surprised Douglas.

"As a thank-you for your letter of recommendation, my parents and I would like you to join us for dinner this Thursday at our home."

"Well," said Douglas, "that's very kind, but there's no need."

"We'll be serving gnocchi that Father will have prepared by hand. I've assured Father that you enjoy gnocchi."

"Nicole," began Douglas.

The bell for chapel rang.

"You told me that you enjoy gnocchi, Mr. Kerchek."

"Oh, I do," said Douglas quickly. "But—Listen, Nicole, I'm very proud that you've gotten into Princeton, but you don't have to—"

"I'm reading the Book of Revelation." Nicole tapped the Bible. "In case you were wondering."

Girls surged past Douglas and Nicole, chattering, chapel-bound.

"Come on, Nicky," said Rhonda Phelps.

"Good morning, Mr. Kerchek," said Audrey Little, the horny health teacher.

Nicole cocked her head to one side. "Did you know, Mr. Kerchek, that there are creatures in the Book of Revelation covered entirely with eyeballs."

Douglas shook his head. He felt slightly dizzy, in need of ibuprofen.

"My parents and I will expect you at seven on Thursday." Nicole stepped backward. "We live in the Preemption apartment building, West Eighty-second and Riverside."

"Preemption?" called Douglas, but Nicole Bonner had turned away.

On Thursday afternoon, Douglas got his hair cut at the corner barbershop. Chiapas, who wasn't yet five feet tall, stood on a milk crate, moving an electric razor over Douglas's sideburns, grinning at him in the mirror.

"You a week early, Uno. Hot date tonight?"

Douglas smirked. "Yeah, right."

Chiapas whistled a tune Douglas didn't know. Because Chiapas was only an apprentice, Douglas got his haircuts for free, but, in what he recognized as a ridiculous instinct, Douglas felt he was keeping the boy out of trouble.

"Bet you got a date, Uno. Bet you and Grace Kelly going out for langostino."

"Uh-huh."

Chiapas knew Douglas's movie addictions.

"Ow." Douglas flinched, and Chiapas pulled the razor away. Douglas turned his head. Two inches below his part, the razor had bitten his hair down to the scalp.

"Whoops." Chiapas shrugged. "Sorry, Uno."

Douglas fingered the gash. "Chiapas. Today of all days."

The boy's eyes lit up. "You do got a date."

Douglas blushed. "I do not."

Chiapas inspected Douglas's head. The cutaway hair was in the shape of a question mark without the period. "Don't worry, Uno. It's cool. She'll love it."

"There is no she," insisted Douglas.

At 7 P.M., Douglas arrived at the Preemption. He wore a camel's-hair sports coat, and he carried a German chocolate cake from Café Mozart. He'd thought first to bring wine, then decided it was inappropriate, since Nicole was his student.

In the lobby, Douglas was met by a tall black doorman with an oval scar on his forehead. "Douglas Kerchek?" said the doorman. "This way."

Douglas followed the doorman to an ancient Otis elevator, the hand-operated kind. "Top floor. Penthouse." The doorman ushered Douglas into the elevator, pulled a lever, and stepped out. *"Bonne chance."*

The elevator doors closed, and Douglas was alone, moving. The mahogany walls smelled like something Douglas couldn't place, a medieval monks' library, maybe, or the inside of a coffin. When he disembarked, the door to the Bonner penthouse was already open. Nicole stood leaning against the jamb.

"Good evening, Mr. Kerchek."

Douglas made an effort not to widen his eyes. Nicole was wearing the most exquisite black silk evening gown he'd ever seen. It lay along the lines and curves of her body so perfectly that the material might have been woven around her as she stood there in the doorway. The gown was exactly as black as her hair, and, for a fantastic second, Douglas imagined that crushed black diamonds and the ink of several squid had gone into making the silk.

"Hello, Nicole," said Douglas. "You look . . . really nice."

"You have a question mark on your head," said Nicole.

Douglas sneezed, twice. Nicole blessed him. A man and a woman appeared behind her.

"My parents," said Nicole, not looking at them.

"Samson," announced the man.

"Paulette," said the woman, smiling.

Samson Bonner resembled a gigantic bass instrument. He was well over six feet tall, and although his torso sloped massively forward around the abdomen, it appeared to be formidably muscled. His voice was resoundingly deep, almost a shout, and his eyes were black. He was a renowned lawyer of unwavering conservative politics.

His wife, Paulette, was as skinny and straight as a flute.

"The teacher, the teacher," chirped Paulette. "Come in, come in."

They all moved inside. Samson Bonner shut the door. Paulette whisked Douglas's cake box off to another room.

"Cocktails," boomed Samson.

Douglas looked around. The Bonner penthouse was the kind of lair that nefarious urbanites like Lex Luthor occupied in films. The huge main room had a high ceiling and a marble floor.

Lining one entire wall were shelves bearing leather-bound books that, for all Douglas knew, could be traced to the same monks' library he'd smelled in the elevator. Also in the room were two hunter-green couches, a hearth with a fire, a glass table laid for dinner, an oaken door that opened onto a study, and three tall windows. Through these, Manhattan could be seen, laid out like a map on which schemes were planned.

Paulette Bonner swept back into view, carrying a tray of glasses and a cocktail shaker. "Sidecars, Sidecars." She set the tray on an end table by the couches.

"We're a brandy family, Douglas," said Samson. "We have a gusto for brandy."

"Ho ho," said Douglas. He'd meant it to sound chipper and hale, but it didn't.

The women sat on one couch, the men on the other. Samson Bonner wore a fine, bone-colored suit. His wife, who had black hair like Nicole's, wore a gray dress. The fire crackled. Douglas sipped his drink, which tasted like limes. In his home town, Allentown, Pennsylvania, very few drinks contained limes.

"I'm so proud of Nicole," said Douglas. "Um, you must be, too."

"We are, we are," breathed Paulette.

"Well, hell." Samson Bonner punched Douglas on the shoulder. "Just because Princeton has a white-boy hoop club doesn't mean they can't compete. Am I wrong?"

"No," said Douglas, whose shoulder now hurt.

"So they're pick-and-roll," declared Samson. "So they're old-school back-door. So what?"

"We're so pleased you've come," said Paulette.

Douglas glanced back and forth between the parents. Despite their bookshelves, he couldn't tell yet whether they were literary, like their daughter.

"How's your Sidecar, Mr. Kerchek?" asked Nicole.

"It's brandy and Cointreau," explained Paulette.

"And limes!" shouted Samson.

Douglas smiled and nodded.

"Anyway," said Samson, "let's hear from the man." He patted Douglas's back.

A silence ensued. Douglas grinned foolishly until it hit him.

"What, you mean me?"

The Bonners sat waiting, looking at Douglas.

"Well." Douglas scratched his recently botched head. "What would you like to hear about?"

"Hell, we don't know." Samson har-hared.

"You want to hear about me? That I'm from Pennsylvania, that kind of thing?" Douglas looked at Nicole.

"Nah," said Samson. "Teach us something."

"Yes." Paulette's eyes flashed.

"Teach us something," said Samson, "or else no gnocchi for you."

Douglas laughed. No one joined him.

Nicole cleared her throat. "Father's serious, Mr. Kerchek." She peered at her teacher over her glass. "He gets like this. You have to teach him and my mother something or the evening can't progress."

Douglas gazed at his student. He saw that she was in earnest, then he looked quickly away. Nicole's hair was pulled back taut against her head tonight, and Douglas feared that if he stared too long at the taper of her temples her father, the marine, would notice.

"Um. What would you like to learn?"

"Hell, we're easy." Samson punched Douglas again.

"Teach them a word," suggested Nicole. "Something quick. I'm hungry."

Douglas moved to the edge of the couch, out of Samson's range. He thought of things he knew well. He thought of books.

"I suppose," said Douglas. "I suppose I could tell you why I think Shakespeare named *King Lear King Lear.*"

Paulette looked anxious, as if Douglas were in peril.

"*Leer* is the German word for empty. And *King Lear* is an existential play. The title character ends up mad, out in the wilderness, living in a hovel, like Job. He's a man stripped down, all alone with the truth of himself." Douglas raised his eyebrows. "An empty man."

"Bravo!" shouted Samson. He jabbed toward Douglas's shoulder, but Douglas stood up quickly. He poured himself a fresh Sidecar.

"Empty, empty." Paulette sounded delighted.

Nicole narrowed her eyes. "You never taught us that."

"What?" said Douglas.

"We read *King Lear* last November. You never taught us about the German. About the name."

Douglas shrugged. He set down the cocktail shaker. "Well, it's just a theory I have. It's nothing proven."

"Wrong." Samson pointed at Douglas. "It's the truth. I know the truth when I hear it."

"Well," said Douglas.

"It's the truth and you found it." Samson gave Douglas the thumbs-up. "The evening can progress."

Nicole stood. "I think it's damn selfish, that's what I think." She glared at Douglas.

"What is?" said Douglas.

"You," snapped Nicole. "You, keeping your precious little theory all secret from your students."

"Now, wait a minute," said Douglas.

"No." Nicole crossed her arms under her breasts in a manner that Douglas could not ignore. "You're our teacher, Mr. Kerchek. You're supposed to lay bare your thoughts on behalf of us girls."

"Looks like he kept some thoughts for himself." Samson winked at Douglas.

"Hmph." Nicole raised her chin, which made Douglas see her neck, the shadowy knife of her cleavage. "I am absolutely disappointed," she said icily, "and I will not speak again tonight until after the salad course."

Nicole left the couch and took her place at the table.

Samson rubbed his hands together. "Let's eat!" he cried.

During the shrimp cocktail, Douglas related much of his life to the Bonners. He was nervous because Nicole was moody and silent, and he ended up blurting out the stories of his postgraduate year in Japan, his bout with mononucleosis, his disastrous senior prom with Heather Angelona.

"You're feeling all right now, though?" said Samson.

Douglas looked up from his salad. "Sir?"

"You've recovered, I mean. From the mono."

"Oh. Yes, sir. I had it thirteen years ago."

"Bravo." Samson wolfed a chunk of cucumber. "Look, no more of this 'sir' business. I'm Samson, dammit."

"All right." Douglas tried to catch Nicole's eye. She sat across from him, while Samson and Paulette sat at the long ends of the table. When Nicole stared only into her salad, Douglas switched his gaze to the book wall behind her.

"So, Samson," said Douglas. "Paulette. Those are some wonderfully bound books there. Have you read most of them?"

Samson stared hard at Douglas. He let ten seconds pass.

"Douglas," said Samson. "I have read each and every one of them cover to cover."

"Really?" Douglas scanned the shelves again. "That's unbelievable."

COLLOQUY

In the broken light, in owl weather,
Webs on the lawn where the leaves end,
I took the thin moon and the sky for cover
To pick the cat's brains and descend
A weedy hill. I found him grovelling
Inside the summerhouse, a shadowed bulge,
Furred and somnolent. "I bring,"
I said, "besides this dish of liver and an edge
Of cheese, the customary torments,
And the usual wonder why we live
At all, and why the world thins out and perishes
As it has done for me, sieved
As I am toward silences. Where
Are we now? Do we know anything?"
Now, on another night, his look endures.
"Give me the dish," it said.
I had his answer, wise as yours.

—WELDON KEES | 1954 |

Samson scowled. "Oh, is that what it is, Mr. Harvard? Unbelievable?"

"I'm sorry," said Douglas quickly.

"You're a contentious bastard," declared Samson.

Douglas's stomach bottomed out, the way it had in high school before his boxing matches. "Samson. Mr. Bonner. I certainly meant no insult."

"Ha!" shouted Samson. "Got you!"

Douglas looked at the Bonner women, who wore thin, knowing smirks.

"What?" said Douglas.

"I was giving you the business, Doug," chuckled Samson. "Had to test your mettle."

"Oh." Douglas took a gulp of his wine. "Ha-ha," he said weakly.

"I shall now rejoin the conversation," said Nicole.

"Hell." Samson pointed his fork at the books. "I've never read a single one of those things, Doug. They're a priceless collection."

"They're heirlooms," said Paulette.

"Right, heirlooms." Samson chewed and swallowed. "Nicole reads them. They belonged to my ancestor Vladimir Bonner. He was a prince from the Carpathian Mountains or some crazy bastard place." Samson waved his hand dismissively. "The point is, he was a prince, and these were his books."

"The point is, Bonners are royalty," said Nicole.

Samson slapped the table. "The gnocchi," he bellowed. "I made them myself." He glared around, as if expecting dissent.

Paulette served the main course, which Douglas had to admit was delicious. He sipped his wine, and the conversation mellowed. Samson spoke of common concerns—the mayor, the weather, the stock market. Douglas listened. He complimented Samson on the gnocchi. When Samson asked about his Allentown boyhood, Douglas mentioned the Eagle Scout he'd been, but did not mention the chipmunks he had killed with firecrackers. Paulette asked Douglas about his favorite films, and Douglas answered. Every time Douglas looked at Nicole, she looked right back at him. All in all, Douglas was enjoying himself. The Chardonnay settled lightly in his head, and he found himself wondering random things, like how the Yankees would do this season, how cold it was outside, how curvy Nicole had ever emerged from beanstalk Paulette. The gnocchi plates were cleared.

"Well, girls," said Samson, "let's cut to the chase."

Paulette placed a snifter of brandy before each person.

"Which chase is that?" said Douglas, smiling. He wiped his mouth with his napkin.

"We feel that you should marry Nicole," said Samson.

Douglas sneezed four times in a row. Everyone blessed him.

"Pardon?" said Douglas.

"Paulette and I would like to arrange a marriage between you and our daughter here. Our only child."

Douglas stared at the Bonners. They were all seated in their chairs, smiling politely. Nicole wore the look that she always wore just before she aced a test. Nobody laughed.

"You're kidding," said Douglas.

"Oh, no." Samson Bonner sipped his brandy. "I'm not giving you the business, Doug."

Douglas got the boxing feeling in his stomach again. When he was young, he'd participated in the Friday Night Smokers, weekly events at the Society of Gentlemen club. The Gentlemen were hardworking Allentowners who drank whiskey and played cards on Friday nights. Every weekend, they brought in a crew of boys from area high schools. To earn themselves rib-eye steak dinners, the boys donned gloves and duked it out in a lighted canvas ring in the center of the club while the men drank and cheered. To be picked to box a Smoker was the highest honor an Allentown boy could receive, and Douglas had been chosen to fight fourteen times. He'd won

"I won't lie. There have been other pussycats."

twelve of those fights, one by a knockout, and he'd never had his nose broken. Some nights even now, just before he fell asleep, Douglas remembered himself in the ring, fighting Heather Angelona's brother Carmine. Carmine had ten pounds on him, and he was beating Douglas on points till the third round, when Douglas delivered an uppercut that jacked Carmine right off the ground and dropped him unconscious. The men in the room roared like lions. The bell clanged. Douglas remembered cigar smoke in his nose, blood on his face, and, strangely, no blood on Carmine's. Watching Mr. Angelona revive his son with smelling salts, Douglas had wanted simultaneously to vomit and to shove his tongue into Heather Angelona's mouth.

Douglas shook his head, cleared it. He stood up. "Nicole," he said severely. "What's going on? Is this some joke, some bizarre family hoax?"

"No." Nicole rested her fingertips calmly on the table. "My parents would honestly like you to marry me. So would I."

"Please sit down, Douglas," said Paulette.

For once, her tone had no levity. Douglas sat. "This is nuts," he said. "We're just having dinner."

Samson Bonner rapped the table with his knuckles. "Hell, son, Paulette and I have been happily married for twenty-five years, and guess what? My father set the whole thing up. He and Paulette's father were law partners."

"My maiden name is Depompis," explained Paulette.

"Right," said Samson. "Depompis. Anyway, our fathers saw that Paulette and I would stack up together. Well, we feel that you and Nicole stack up, too."

Douglas's head was swimming. "You've discussed this? As a family?"

"Sure," said Samson. "Every night for a week."

"Excuse me, Mr. . . . Excuse me, Samson, but you don't even know me."

"Oh, hell." Samson swatted the air as if it held gnats. "Nicole knows you. She says you watch a movie every night just like she reads a book every night."

"It's adorable," said Paulette.

Douglas stared at his student. She smiled quickly.

"Nicole," he said. "You're nineteen."

"Twenty in September," said Nicole.

"We held her back," said Paulette. "In third grade."

"Well, twenty, then," said Douglas.

"She struggled with phonics," said Paulette.

"Excuse me." Douglas cleared his throat loudly. The Bonners hushed themselves.

"Listen," said Douglas, "you've— I've— This has been a lovely meal, but— Well, aren't you all being quite preposterous? As I was trying to point out—"

"Young man," said Samson, "do you not find Nicole attractive?"

Douglas shut his mouth. He kept expecting a game-show host to spring out from behind a curtain. Nicole sat opposite him in her impossibly black dress, watching him with her relentless blue eyes. For the first time, Douglas honestly considered what it would be like if she were his. He thought of Lillian Marx, the last woman he'd dated, who'd adored jazz. He imagined holding Nicole's hand, driving with her to Montauk in a convertible, the radio playing the punk bands he knew she liked. He blushed.

"Religion's not an issue," blustered Samson. "Nicole assures me that you're High Episcopal, same as we are. She admires your intellect, and you always give her an A. So what's your problem, Doug?"

"Douglas," said Paulette. "We're really very

impressed with you. Especially now that we've met."

Douglas sat up very straight. "Yes. Well. As I was trying to say, Nicole's eleven years younger than I am. Doesn't that seem . . . problematic?"

"No," said Samson. "I've got twelve years on Paulette."

"Mr. Kerchek," said Nicole. "Did you know, Mr. Kerchek, that in centuries past a girl was often married and birthing offspring by fourteen?"

"Let's not rush into any birthing," chuckled Samson.

"This isn't the Middle Ages, Nicole." Douglas swallowed some brandy after all. "You haven't even been to college."

"Well, I'm going, aren't I?"

"Of course she is." Paulette sounded offended. "No daughter of mine will be denied an education because of her husband."

"Now, hold on," said Douglas.

"Hey," growled Samson. "You can have my daughter's hand, Doug, and we'll give you some starting-out money, but Princeton's nonnegotiable. Don't try to weasel her out of that."

"I wasn't."

"No weaseling," said Nicole.

Douglas sighed heavily. "I need to use the bathroom," he said.

"Well, hell," said Samson. "Who wouldn't?"

Paulette pointed to a hallway. "Third door on the right."

Douglas strode quickly out of the room. His mind was a blur. He thought of his unserved, uneaten German cake. He recalled a teaching class he'd once taken, where the instructor had told him to watch out for female students and their crushes.

Is that what this is? thought Douglas. A crush?

The door to the bathroom was slightly ajar.

Douglas was about to push it fully open when he heard a toilet flush from within.

"Excuse me," he said automatically. He stepped back, surprised. Moments later, the door nudged open and a black cat stepped out of the bathroom. It stopped at Douglas's feet and looked directly up at him.

"John Stapleton," whispered Douglas.

"Mrow," said John Stapleton.

The cat nibbled briefly at the toe of Douglas's left shoe, then proceeded down the hall, disappearing into the shadows.

This is insane, thought Douglas. This night, this family, this cat, all of them are certifiable. But the cat seemed like an omen, somehow, and as Douglas washed his face and hands in the bathroom sink, as he studied his goofy haircut and took deep, weight-lifting breaths to compose himself, he thought of Nicole. He thought of the simple silver-post earrings she always wore. He recalled the Melville she'd committed to memory, the respect she had for Graham Greene novels, the merciless grip she kept on her stick when she played field hockey. Her favorite film was *The Philadelphia Story,* a tough favorite to argue against. He'd heard her rail passionately against the death penalty once during an ethics-class debate, and he'd seen her hold a faculty member's baby in her arms.

"I'd like to talk to Nicole alone," said Douglas, when he rejoined the Bonners.

"Of course you would," said Samson.

"Alone, alone." Paulette smiled wearily at Douglas.

"Use my study." Samson stood up, shook Douglas's hand.

They were alone. The study door was closed. Nicole sat on a daybed, her shoes off, her calves drawn together and to one side. Across the room, Douglas sat on the edge of a wooden chair, the top crossbar of which was embossed with a crest. Douglas thought that it might be the Bonner family crest, but he didn't ask.

Nicole cracked her knuckles. "In a minute, I'm going to start calling you Douglas instead of Mr. Kerchek."

"Oh, really?"

Nicole sighed. "Mr. Kerchek, please just listen. I'm going to say some things."

Douglas collected his thoughts. Outside the door was a married couple on a green couch, drinking brandy, perhaps petting John Stapleton. In the study with him was a headstrong young woman.

"Mr. Kerchek," said Nicole, "you know that I'm smart. That I can think and read well, the way you could when you were nineteen. But I also know what the world is like, Mr. Kerchek."

Douglas watched Nicole. She's serious, he thought. She's deadly serious.

"I know," said Nicole. "I know how long people go in this city without finding someone to love. I'm young, but I understand loneliness." Nicole rubbed her feet. "Listen. I know I can be irrational, Douglas."

Douglas caught his breath. He felt something in his spine—fear, maybe.

"Like tonight," said Nicole. "That *King Lear* business. But here's something you probably don't know. I saw you at the Film Forum last week."

Douglas blushed again.

"They were showing *The Gunfighter*, with Gregory Peck. It was last Tuesday, the 9 P.M. show. I saw it advertised in the paper, and I just knew you'd be there. So I went."

Douglas tried to remember what he'd worn that night, what candy he'd brought with him. A flannel shirt? Gummi Bears?

"I sat five rows behind you and watched your silhouette. I saw you admiring the guy who

PERSON-TO-CAT

Here's a cat *and* Telephone Company yarn, all in one. It seems this man went out to dinner prior to going to the Idlewild Airport to meet his wife, arriving from Washington. Soon after he left, his wife called their apartment from the capital to notify him that her plane had been grounded by fog and that she'd arrive by train. Well, he wasn't in, of course, but when the phone rang, their cat—jumping in fright, or something—knocked the phone off its cradle and began to meow. The lady had put in a collect call, so the operator asked the cat whether it would accept the charges. The cat gave a noncommittal meow, and the lady tried to explain matters to the operator, gave up, hung up, and went home under her own steam. Her phone bill at the end of the month included a charge for the call, which, after her husband's complaint to a member of a high Telephone Company echelon, was cancelled. The Company spokesman observed that long-distance calls are not considered complete unless there is a two-way conversation, and that such, apparently, hadn't taken place, but added a warning that local calls are automatically registered and charged for as soon as the receiver is lifted. This information has been passed on to the cat.

| 1951 |

played the bartender. You know, the guy from *On the Waterfront*."

Douglas closed his eyes. She's right, he thought. She's nineteen and she's right.

"Anyway, whether you marry me or not, this is what I want to tell you." Nicole exhaled. "It's no good, Douglas."

Douglas kept his eyes closed. He was listening.

"It's no good the way you're living. All those weights you lift, all those miles you run, all those movies you see. It isn't right. It's lonely."

Douglas looked at her then. He saw her curves and her temples, but something else, too, something that lived behind her eyes.

"You're a good teacher and all, but you're just killing time, Douglas. I can tell."

Bullshit, thought Douglas. Then he thought, How? How am I killing it?

"I can tell from the books you assign, the ties you wear, everything." Nicole was not chewing her hair. "You're ready, Douglas. For *the* woman, the one you're supposed to marry." Nicole shrugged, just a little. "And I think she's me. I've dated some guys, and I know what's around, and— Well, I just know what I want."

"How?" blurted Douglas. His hands trembled on the snifter, so he put it down. He felt as if he might weep. "Are you in—" Douglas changed phrases. "Do you love me?"

Nicole petted her neck, sipped her brandy. "Look. I've got Princeton to go to. And I've got that huge heirloom library out there to read. I'm just saying that you should have a woman with you at the movies, and she should be me. I'm ready for her to be me."

Douglas couldn't sit still any longer. He stood up and paced. He wanted to shout or punch or be punched. He wanted something he knew the feeling of. He stalked over to Nicole, unsure of what to do.

"Easy, Douglas." Nicole moved back on the daybed.

"No." Douglas shook his head, went back to pacing. "No 'Easy, Douglas.' You have to tell me something here. I'm thirty-one, and I'm— I'm your *teacher*, for Christ's sake. I mean— Is this— Look, answer me, now, Nicole."

"O.K.," she whispered. "I will."

"Is this real? I mean, are you . . . in love with me?" He couldn't believe what he'd asked.

"I'm ready to be," said Nicole. "And I mean

this as a compliment, but I've got nothing better to do."

Douglas stopped pacing. "I'm going crazy," he said softly. "I'm standing here, solidly, on my own two feet, and I'm going crazy."

Nicole smiled. She took his hand.

"Listen," she said. "I have the prom in a month, which my cousin Fred is escorting me to, and graduation's two weeks after that. It'll be hectic for a bit, but as of the first week of June I'm prepared to become completely infatuated with you."

Douglas laughed out loud, once, at the practicality in her voice. He thought of his mother, of Chiapas and the Mexicans, of the unbroken chain of essays that he'd corrected for the past six years. There might have been a thousand of those essays. And there might have been a time in history when all people spoke like Nicole Bonner.

"I can commute to Princeton," explained Nicole, "or else just come back to you on weekends. My family's a little eccentric, and I am, too, but, well, there it is. What do you think?"

Douglas pulled Nicole to her feet. He felt giddy, vicious. He didn't know what he felt. Like an animal, he set his teeth for one last stand.

"Nicole." His voice was low, almost mean. "If you're kidding about all this, and you tell me tomorrow that you're kidding, then I'll . . . I'll . . ." Douglas clenched and unclenched his fists.

"I'm not kidding," said Nicole.

Douglas looked out the window at New York City. He looked back at Nicole.

"You're sure?"

Nicole reached up, trailed one hand lightly over Douglas's haircut.

"Domestic shorthair," she whispered.

Douglas took both her hands in his. He was beaming. He felt slightly nauseous. "All right. All

"Isn't it true that you did not love the victim, as you claim, but, in point of fact, feigned affection for the sole purpose of obtaining tuna fish?"

right, if you're serious, then I want you to do something for me."

Nicole frowned. "No sex till we're hitched. A kiss, maybe."

"Be quiet and listen." Douglas's voice quavered with pleasure. "I don't want you to kiss me. I want you to hit me."

"What?"

Douglas couldn't keep the grin, the old, triumphant sass, off his face.

"I want you to punch me in the stomach as hard as you can."

Nicole stepped away. "You're insane."

"No." Douglas took her by the shoulders, squared her off facing him. "Trust me. If you do this, I'll know that we're— I'll just know."

Nicole laughed, just a little. "You're a freak."

"Hit me."

Nicole angled her head to one side. "You're serious."

"Give me your hand."

Nicole held out her right palm.

"Make a fist. No, like this, with your thumb outside. Good."

"How do you know how—"

"Shut up and hit me." Douglas sneered at her. "Come on. Let's see what you got."

A wicked joy stole over Nicole's face. "You better watch it."

"Hit me."

"I'll do it, Douglas," she warned.

"Go ahead."

Nicole drew her fist back to her hip. Her eyes checked the door that was hiding her parents. She looked to Douglas as if she would erupt with laughter, or something else, something he couldn't predict.

"Come on, punk." Douglas dared her, and that was it. Nicole shot her fist forward and showed him what he, what both of them, were in for.

CAT STORY

JAMAICA KINCAID

Pussy cat, pussy cat, where have you been?
I've been to London to look at the Queen.
Pussy cat, pussy cat, what did you there?
I frightened a little mouse under her chair.

Morris, who is a cat and is (so to speak) the star of a cat-food advertising campaign, has edited (so to speak again) a book about cats and how to take care of them. Morris, who is an orange tabby cat, and his trainer, a man with a severe crewcut, came to the city the other day to promote the book, so they invited people to come to Sardi's and ask questions and take pictures. Morris was placed on a table at one end of the room for all to see, and he licked his paws, rested his chin on his paws, half closed his eyes, moved one of his ears, moved both of his ears, lay down on his stomach, flicked his tail, and jumped off the table and tried to run away a few times.

"Is he drugged?" asked a woman, who later said that she is very concerned about the treatment of cats in public life, is against cat shows, has five cats, and takes her cats to a cat dentist regularly.

"No," said someone connected with Morris and his trainer. "People always ask that. But Morris doesn't have to be drugged. He's a real professional."

"But isn't Morris dead?" asked another woman.

"Well, yes, but that was the other Morris," answered the connection. "It's like a dynasty. Morris is dead. Long live Morris. This Morris was found in a cat shelter. He was a stray. This is the Morris that is now used in all the ads. But there are three more in reserve, in case he should suddenly drop dead."

A grown man in a Kool-Aid-orange-and-white cat suit walked by. On his stomach, written in black letters, were the

words "Personal Ambassador to Morris the Cat."

"He looks highly flammable," said a man.

"It's rough," said a woman.

Morris left the room, presumably to eat a meal of fish, fish by-products, water, crab, shrimp, animal fat, wheat flour, dried yeast, dried whey, iron oxide, vi-tamin E, A, and niacin supplements, thiamin mononitrate, ethylenediamine dihydroiodide, calcium pantothenate, ri-boflavin supplement, vitamin D3 supple-ment, and pyridoxine hydrochloride, which make up the contents of a six-and-a-half-ounce can of the brand of cat food that Morris represents.

| 1980 |

THE WINESHOP CAT

Fiction

SYLVIA TOWNSEND WARNER

Stepping with dusky feet on the hot Paris pavement (that evening nearly five years ago now), the Siamese cat came round the corner by the herbalist's, crossed the road with decision, and began to walk down the Boulevard Edgar-Quinet—to the Montparnasse Cemetery, I presumed. It was closed, but closing hours would mean nothing to a Siamese cat. The dusky paws would bunch together and arrive neatly among the spikes on the top of the wall, for a moment the crooked tail would flick among the overhanging boughs, and an instant later the cat would be alighting on consecrated earth while a few dry leaves, since it was August, would have started on their twirling passage downward. The cat was walking with a stately air of habit. Perhaps this was the hour when it took a sparrow as an apéritif *chez* Baudelaire, or perhaps it simply preferred consecrated earth.

I had never seen a grander Siamese cat. In a way, it was regrettably grand. Had it been a more ordinary cat, I could have followed it and got acquainted with it. But one might as well hope to get acquainted with Phoebus Apollo, I thought, watching it disappear with arrogant leisureliness down that undistinguished Boulevard Edgar-Quinet.

A few evenings later I saw it again. This time it was sitting in the open doorway of a small wineshop, blandly squinting at the passers-by. It was clear that Phoebus Apollo was at home in his temple. Stepping reverently around the deity, I entered the temple and began buying a bottle of wine.

The man behind the counter was middle-aged, solid, and swarthy. He was not much interested in my purchase—for that matter, neither was I. Woman or wine, I realized, he was not going to bestir himself on either account. But as I took my bottle and my change, I said, "That's a very fine cat you've got. One can see he's a pedigreed cat."

He whistled, and the cat came in and sprang up on the counter and began to pace to and fro among the bottles. We admired it in silence for some time. The cat was the first to speak, saying "Mraow! Mraow!" in short, commanding monosyllables.

"He's thinking of his supper," said the man.

"Mraow!" said the cat forcefully. It jumped onto the man's shoulder and turned around there, rubbing itself against the back of his head. The man thrust his head back against the muscular, sidling caress, and his face assumed the severe look of intense physical pleasure.

"It's gratifying to see a cat in such good condition," I said.

Balancing his cat on his shoulder, the man walked over to a refrigerator, opened it, and took out a large slice of prime steak. Still silent, he held it across the counter for me to examine. Then he said to the cat, "But you won't get it yet, you know."

He slammed to the door of the refrigerator. With dusky paws the cat began to knead his shoulder in time to its rattling purr and blinked at me. Its eyes, which had reddened at the sight of the meat, were now a clear blue in its pokerwork face, and its purr became more rhythmical and hymnlike. I felt

that I had best leave this happy pair to themselves. But suddenly the man leaned forward across the counter. "A cat like this, Madame, is a formidable responsibility. With a cat like this one is compelled to take decisions. It can be painful."

"Siamese cats have a great deal of temperament," I said.

Launching himself further across the counter, confronting me with his own dark gaze and the cat's calm, blue squint, he said, "What can one do? I had to have him neutered!"

"What can one do?" he continued. "As a male, he was a misery. He wouldn't eat, he wouldn't thrive, he was away for days on end, infatuated with all the worthless she-cats of the quarter. He came back starving, dirty, wet to the skin, disfigured with bites and scratches, looking an object. Besides, his voice was loud, and people threw things at him."

The cat poured itself off his shoulder like a caramel and sat down on the counter, gazing devotedly at the refrigerator.

"What is one to do? One cannot imprison a cat; it is against nature. Equally, one cannot wander all night on the housetops pursuing it."

"You could not find him a companion?"

"Madame, as you know, these cats are opinionated. He would not domesticate himself. Instead, he took up with the most frightful females. I was in horrors, thinking how they might infect him with filthy diseases." His tone became so deeply moral that I felt my expression becoming deeply moral too.

"Mange!" he exclaimed, and I shuddered.

"Look at him now," said the man. "He is superb. One would say he has never regretted his virility."

"There are other pleasures in life," I replied. "And on the whole I think we all make too much fuss about sex."

"Very probably. Yet there are times when my mind misgives me, when I ask myself if I was justified. One cannot deny it. I have robbed him of a joy."

"You have robbed him of a great deal of uneasiness, too, and loss of dignity," I remarked firmly. "It is my belief, and I have studied cats pretty extensively, that what ultimately means most to a cat is to be the centre of consideration. It is the only thing about which they never become cynical and disillusioned."

The man nodded. His impulse of confidence was over, he was settling back into his solid, swarthy reserve. But on the last gust of the storm he repeated moodily, "One is compelled to take decisions. It can be very painful."

"Do not think so much of the past," I urged him. "Think of the present."

Thinking of the present, I recall the pair of them. For some time now cat flesh has fetched high prices in the Paris market. But I am sure of this: if anyone ate that Siamese cat, it was his master. And I am sure of another thing: that the cat, when he killed it, was still in good condition. It had not guttered into scabby starvation before the decision was attained and acted upon. Later in that day, it seems certain to me, the man must have got on his bicycle and ridden off, silent and catlike, but with a small, uncatlike weight against his thigh. Some evening or other that cat has been avenged—or will be. For he was that kind of man, and loved after that fashion.

| 1942 |

Hand-made Christmas card from Sylvia Townsend Warner to her partner, Valentine Ackland.

BOOKSTORE CAT

SUSAN SHEEHAN

The first time Andreas Brown, the owner of the Gotham Book Mart, laid eyes on his enormous orange tabby cat, it was chasing three smaller cats around his sister's house in San Diego and pursuing an occasional seagull up and down her porch steps. "I had to have him," Brown said the other day. "And so, about four years ago, when my sister moved, she agreed to send him to me by air." The cat was flown non-stop from California to J.F.K. in a pet carrier in the cargo hold. His new owner met him at the airport and took him in a taxi to his new residence, on West Forty-seventh Street.

Frances Steloff, the founder of the Gotham Book Mart, from whom Brown bought the shop in 1967, always had cats, and left money to half a dozen animal organizations when she died, in 1989, at the age of a hundred and one. Her last three cats had literary names—Thornton (Wilder), Christopher (Morley), and Mitchell (Kennerley). Brown decided to call his huge new tomcat Pynchon.

When Pynchon came East, the Gotham was down to one cat—Mitchell, who died a few months later. The shop became a one-cat bookstore again. "He's plenty to deal with," Brown said.

Pynchon has the run of the five-floor building, which houses the shop, a gallery, storage space, and Brown's apartment. He is the perfect bookstore cat.

He purrs when customers pet him. He poses for photographs dressed in T-shirts or tuxedos designed for dogs, and wearing a graduation cap or a sombrero or whatever else the staff puts on him. He attends meetings of the James Joyce Society, which are held in the second-floor gallery.

Because Pynchon arrived in New York with no front claws, he became an indoor cat. His most notable outings since then were in the winter of 1999. Brown, egged on by his staff and proud of his wondrous green-eyed, pink-nosed acquisition, entered him in the domestic-house-pet division of the annual cat show at Madison Square Garden. As Brown recalls, "I put this very large cat into this very heavy carrier and had a devil of a time hailing cabs on freezing-cold mornings. Once we got to the show, Pynchon won several nice-looking ribbons, but he was marked down in a couple of rounds of judging for being too heavy. 'Overweight for a cat is the death knell,' one judge admonished. 'He'll get diabetes. True cat-lovers do not allow their cats to weigh as much as tiger cubs.' This made me mad, because I'd dieted Pynchon down from his arrival weight of twenty-eight pounds plus to twenty-five pounds. Our mail scale is absolutely accurate. On one show day, Pynchon

was freaked out by the hundreds of other cats he smelled and heard and saw. He managed to get out of his cage with his clawless front paws and took off in the Garden for parts unknown. He was eventually found hiding behind a velour drape, huddled against a wall. After a few days of schlepping Pynchon to and from the Garden, I said 'Never again,' so Pynchon's days as a show cat are over."

Pynchon's years on Forty-seventh Street are also coming to an end. The Gotham Book Mart is in the middle of a block dominated by the diamond and jewelry trade and the building is therefore considered more valuable than a similar one a block or two away. Brown owns air rights to the building, and has put it up for sale for $7.9 million. Brown reckons he can sell books in a bigger but less expensive building, without air rights, somewhere in the general vicinity. He figures Pynchon will easily adapt to his next home. "He'll still have the whole staff to anticipate his needs six days a week," he said. "I'll still leave the radio above my desk tuned to classical music for him every evening when I go out for dinner. And he'll still greet our customers, many of whom come in just to visit him. This cat is tall, like his namesake, but he is no recluse."

| 2002 |

TOMCAT

Daylong this tomcat lies stretched flat
As an old rough mat—no mouth and no eyes.
Continual wars and wives are what
Have tattered his ears and battered his head.

Like a bundle of old rope and iron,
Sleeps till blue dusk. Then reappear
His eyes, green as ringstones; he yawns wide red,
Fangs fine as a lady's needle, and bright.

A tomcat sprang at a mounted knight,
Locked round his neck like a trap of hooks
While the knight rode fighting its clawing and bite.
After hundreds of years the stain's there

On the stone where he fell, dead of the tom;
That was at Barnborough. The tomcat still
Grallochs odd dogs on the quiet,
Will take the head clean off your simple pullet,

Is unkillable. From the dog's fury,
From gunshot fired point-blank, he brings
His skin whole, and whole
From owlish moons of bekittenings

Among ash cans. He leaps and lightly
Walks upon sleep, his mind on the moon.
Nightly, over the round world of men,
Over the roofs, go his eyes and outcry.

—TED HUGHES | 1960 |

from DIN-DIN

THOMAS WHITESIDE

In a way comparable, perhaps, to that by which in reading the newspapers and watching the TV news I rather suddenly became aware of the word "Sunbelt" and the portent of the increasing population shift thereto, I have become aware lately in my television viewing of the prevalence of pet-food commercials on the home screen. Hardly before I realized what was happening, it seemed that I couldn't turn on my set without being confronted by pet-food ads. Now that I have become acutely conscious of the pet-food commercials on the air, it seems to me almost as though dogs and cats and their eating preferences are beginning to take over television, with human beings and human activities slowly falling back to a humbler place in the scheme of things.

In fact, if one concentrates on the content of the pet-food commercials it can easily appear that human beings are on the way out in the Darwinian sense, too. In the pet-food commercials, the pets are increasingly shown addressing the viewer directly on their own behalf and without human prompting. The animals are also shown talking together and engaging in all sorts of other behavior usually considered exclusively human. Thus, in one pet-food commercial a cat answers a ringing telephone by tipping the receiver off its cradle with a paw. A representative of the local supermarket is on the line, and the cat orders up dinner by saying "Meow" into the mouthpiece. The supermarket man recognizes immediately that the cat is ordering a cat food called Meow Mix. In a similar commercial, a cat is *singing* its order for Meow Mix:

I want tuna,

I want liver,

I want chicken,

Please deliver.

Commercials for Purina Dog Chow show dogs responding to on-the-air interviews on the subject of dog dinners. One of the dogs, a poodle, when queried on its taste preferences, observes, in a bowwow voice, "I think Dog Chow's richer flavor is definitely richer." Another dog says, when pressed for comment, "Dog Chow's heavy on nutrition, man!" And yet another exclaims, "Uh, the new, richer flavor—superb!" Dogs are shown manifesting their approbation in other human ways, too. In a commercial for a Ralston Purina dog food called Dinner Mix, an m.c.'s voice asks an assembly of dogs grouped as an audience four tiers deep how they feel about dry dog food, and the dogs promptly raise their right paws and say, "Uh huh, yeah," to show their approval. And when the same dogs are asked about Dinner Mix they all clap their paws together in a round of enthusiastic applause. In commercials for Purina Cat Chow, a succession of cats move their paws in dancing rhythm to an accompanying tune and are heard singing, in chorus, the words "Chow! Chow! Chow!" Presumably, they not only sing but also read music. In some of the pet-food commercials, the animals are represented as being quite literate. For example, the opening shot of a commercial for Cadillac canned dog food shows a dog wearing glasses and quietly reading a book before it is interrupted by a call to a dinner of Cadillac.

As representations go, probably the most sophisticated inhabitant of the world of pet-food commercials is the cat Morris, which appears in the commercials for 9-Lives cat food. This cat is shown as being a choosy sort, especially in its eating preferences, and, through a human voice-over, is given to uttering its thoughts in a sort of interior monologue, mostly on the subject of cat food. The screen personality of Morris is one of advanced finickiness, displayed particularly in scenes in which the cat turns disdainfully away from the prospect of eating common cat food when its mistress (the audience sees only a pair of legs) cries coaxingly, "Din-din time!" The cat Morris also expresses its disdain of various attempts by its owner to entertain it—for example, by giving it an elaborate cat box—in a world-weary voice that I, for one, consider a bit fruity. In the commercials, Morris is stirred from boredom by an offer of 9-Lives, which it eats avidly, but after finishing the stuff the cat is shown as reverting to an attitude of languid archness. Not only is this cat represented as having a human character but it has even been endowed, it seems, with traces of some underlying psychic complex, manifested by a generally put-upon air and a little peevishness where the ladies are concerned. That's humanization with a vengeance. In aural effect, the disdain of Morris is dramatically offset, in the pet-food commercials, by the voice of a talking cat in a commercial for Cadillac cat food. This cat, as it keeps dipping a paw into an open can of Cadillac cat food and then eating from its paw, is represented as being of an unmistakably sexy female makeup, and is shown as saying, in a coy, whispery voice of gold-diggy seductiveness, "Oh, can't *wait* to get my paws into a can of Cadillac."

Of all classes of fussy eaters, innately ordained or externally conditioned, no others stand out in the world of pets in finicky potential like cats. That cats occasionally spurn food put in front of them is well known, and the combination of this characteristic and the permissiveness of most cat owners toward their charges has provided opportunities of bonanzalike proportions for the pet-food industry. Cat-food advertising is a bit different in some of its assumptions from dog-food advertising. In contrast to dogs, which indiscriminately offer affection to their owners, cats maintain an air of independence, cannot or will not be trained as dogs are, offer affection in sparing and on-and-off fashion, and need very little encouragement to be transformed into spoiled household darlings. Just as, for their own instinctive reasons, they sometimes choose to drink from a rank water supply rather than from a fresh one (cats are said to be partly of desert origin, and this may have something to do with such behavior), they often pass up particular kinds of food, sometimes for a few days, without harm. This natural stop-and-start pattern of eating is, of course, a heaven-sent gift to the pet-food merchandisers. As a result of it, cat owners are now subjected to a torrent of brand-name food offerings, all guaranteed to arouse a cat's appetite,

no matter what the animal's inclination of the day might be. For all their supposed waywardness of appetite, cats can easily become fixed on a very narrow range of foods, or even on one particular food, such as fish, almost to the point of addiction. Consequently, the alchemists in the cat-food boiler rooms and their allies on Madison Avenue never rest in their rivalry to take advantage of this phenomenon, as well as of their own notions of the psychic frailties that "she," the cat-food buyer and feeder, may possess. (Unfortunately for some of the cats that, as a result of all the ad campaigns aimed at owners, are being fed exclusively certain brands of cat food, quite a few of these products happen to be high in mineral content—mostly calcium and phosphorus. This high mineral content is suspected by some veterinarians of exacerbating an existing tendency among cats, especially neutered males, to develop urinary sand, stones, and other obstructions. One specialized brand of cat food, Science Diet, which is prepared with a very low mineral content, is never touted in television commercials, and is not available in supermarkets, but only in pet shops, as a preventive diet for cats that might develop urinary problems.)

It is out of the great clash of merchandising forces aimed at "her" that the success of the "gourmet" cat foods and the triumph of the 9-Lives canned cat food arose. Through its ad campaign featuring the cat Morris, 9-Lives raised its sales from fif-

ST.

teen million dollars in 1965 to about a hundred million dollars in 1975. Morris was thought up by the people at the Leo Burnett advertising agency, in Chicago, out of whose bottle of ideas have popped in the past such corporate-identity genies as the Jolly Green Giant and Charlie the Tuna. An account man I talked with at the Leo Burnett agency a while ago emphasized that, in spite of the finicky-eater reputation of cats, "as a matter of fact, you can get a cat to eat, consistently, anything he loves." He went on, "That talks to the most important thing—palatability. So you provide the pet owners with foods that the cat will eat regularly. Morris is clearly positioned as a finicky cat—the most finicky cat, who will be satisfied by 9-Lives." On the average, a six-and-a-half-ounce can of 9-Lives costs twenty-five to twenty-seven cents, which is nearly twice the cost of a canned cat food not in the gourmet class. If a cat eats two such cans a day, there goes half a dollar or so, and if a cat becomes strung out on 9-Lives or some other gourmet cat food, it does its bit for the profitability of the industry. To judge from the way the pet-food merchandisers talk, paying out all this money also exerts a certain benign influence on that "feeling of guilt—[that you're not] doing the very best thing" which the admen see as plaguing the women who buy the cat food and feed the cats. One pet-food adman in New York remarked to me, "Part of the whole mystique on the part of those women is the underlying thought 'Look at all the trouble I'm going through.'" Is guilt the name of the game?

However "she" may be viewing the great variety of choices and flavors of pet foods on the long stretches of shelves in the supermarkets, and however vast the trouble and money involved in replacing table scraps with gourmet offerings, the manufacturers see, above all, a highly profitable market that is advancing beyond its initial boom stage and is now in a stage of relative consolidation. At such a stage, the big gains to be exploited lie in the proliferation of brands and the seizure of particular shares of the existing market. Thus, all the delicious gravies and gourmet meals. A pet-food-company executive I spoke with not long ago remarked of the gourmet warfare currently being waged, "It's very much like the detergent business at the stage of competition where they had to come in with all the blue dots and the green dots."

PAUNCH

Barefoot, in burgundy shorts and a salmon-pink
T-shirt, I pad across the deck
and sink
into one of four old Adirondack

chairs that themselves slump into themselves. There's
    a flare
from the citronella bucket
as, there,
our eight-week-old stray kitten, Pyewackett,

ventures across what might have seemed a great divide
between her and me, had she not
now begun to nag and needle

and knead
my paunch for milk. The bucket fills with human fat.
The chair takes a dim view through a knothole.

—PAUL MULDOON | 1996 |

DEFECTION OF A FAVORITE

Fiction

J. F. POWERS

I was waiting in the lobby, sitting in a fairly clean overshoe, out of the draft and near a radiator, dozing, when the monthly meeting of the ushers ended and the men began to drift up from the church basement. Once a meeting got under way, the majority of the ushers, as well as Father Malt, their old pastor, liked to wind it up and break for the rectory, for pinochle and beer. Father Malt, seeing me, called "Fritz!" and I came, crossing in front of Mr. Cormack, the new man, who muttered "Bad luck!" and blessed himself. I hadn't thought much about him before, but this little action suggested to me that his eyes were failing or that he was paranoidal, for, though a black cat, I have a redeeming band of white at my throat.

While I waited for the ushers to put their hats and coats on, I thought I saw their souls reflected in their mufflers, in those warm, unauthentic plaids and soiled white rayons and nylons, a few with fringe work, some worn as chokers in the nifty, or *haute*-California, manner, and some tucked in between coat and vest in a way that may be native to our part of Minnesota.

Father Malt and I went out the door together. Going barefooted, as nature intended, I was warned of the old ice beneath the new-fallen snow. Father Malt, however, in shoes and overshoes, walked blindly, and slipped and fell.

When several ushers took hold of Father Malt, Mr. Keller, the head usher, a druggist and a friend of physicians, spoke with authority. "Don't move him! That's the worst thing you can do! Call an ambulance!"

Three ushers thought to cover Father Malt with their overcoats (three others, too late with theirs, held theirs in their hands), and everyone just stood and stared, as I did, at the old priest, my friend and protector, lying under the mound of overcoats, with the indifferent snow settling down as upon a new grave. I began to feel the cold in my bones and to think that I should certainly perish if I were locked out on such a night. I heard Mr. Keller ordering Mr. Cormack to the rectory to phone for an ambulance. Reluctantly—not through any deficiency in my sorrow—I left the scene of the accident, crossed the snowy lawn, and entered the rectory with Mr. Cormack.

After Mr. Cormack had summoned an ambulance, he called his old pastor, Father O'Hannon, of St. Clara's, Minneapolis (of which Sherwood, our town, was gradually becoming a suburb), and asked him to be at the hospital, in case Father Malt should be in danger of death and in need of extreme unction. "The assistant here, Father Burner, isn't around. His car's gone from the garage, and there's no telling when that one'll be back," said Mr. Cormack, sounding lonesome for his old parish. At St. Clara's, he'd evidently been on more intimate terms with the priests. His last words to Father O'Hannon, "We could sure use someone like you out here," gave me the idea that he had gone fishing for Father Burner's favor but had caught one of the white whale's flukes. Now, like so many of us, he dreamed of getting even someday. I could only wish him luck as he left the rectory.

I watched at the window facing upon the tragedy, enduring the cold draft there for Father Malt's sake, until the ambulance came. Then I retired to the parlor register and soon fell asleep—not without a prayer for Father Malt and many more for myself. With Father Burner running

the rectory, it was going to be a hard, hard, and possibly fatal winter for me.

The ironic part was that Father Burner and I, bad as he was, had a lot in common. We disliked the same people (Mr. Keller, for instance), we disliked the same dishes (those suited to Father Malt's dentures), but, alas, we also disliked each other. This fault originated in Father Burner's raw envy of me—which, however, I could understand. Father Malt didn't improve matters when he referred to me before visitors, in Father Burner's presence, as *the* assistant. I was realist enough not to hope for peace between us assistants as long as Father Malt lived. But it did seem a shame that there was no way of letting Father Burner know I was prepared—if and when his position improved—to be his friend and favorite, although not necessarily in that order. (For some reason, I seem to make a better favorite than friend.) As it was Father Burner's misfortune to remain a curate too long, it was mine to know that my life of privilege—my preferred place at table, for example—appeared to operate at the expense of his rights and might be the cause of my ultimate undoing. It was no good wishing, as I sometimes did, that Father Malt were younger—he was eighty-one—or that I were older, that we two could pass on together when the time came.

Along toward midnight, waking, I heard Father Burner's car pull in to the driveway. A moment later, the front porch cracked under his heavy step. He entered the rectory, galoshes and all, and, as was his custom, proceeded to foul his own nest wherever he went, upstairs and down. Finally, after looking, as he always did, for the telephone messages that seemingly never came, or, as he imagined, never got taken down, he went out on the front porch and brought in more snow and the evening paper. He sat reading in the parlor—it was then midnight—still in his dripping galoshes, still in perfect ignorance of what had befallen Father Malt *and* me. Before he arrived, the telephone had been ringing at half-hour intervals—obviously the hospital, or one of the ushers, trying to reach him. The next time, I knew, it would toll for me.

Although I could see no way to avoid my fate, I did see the folly of waiting up for it. I left the parlor to Father Burner and went to the kitchen, where I guessed he would look last for me, if he knew anything of my habits, for I seldom entered there and never stayed long. Mrs. Wynn, the housekeeper, loosely speaking, was no admirer of mine, nor I of her womanly disorder.

I concealed myself in a basket of clean, or at least freshly laundered, clothes, and presently, despite everything, I slept.

Early the following day, when Father Burner came downstairs, he had evidently heard the news, but he was late for his Mass, as usual, and had time for only one wild try at me with his foot.

"Make ratatouille."

However, around noon, when he returned from the hospital, he paused only to phone the chancery to say that Father Malt had a fractured hip and was listed as "critical" and promptly chased me from the front of the house to the kitchen. He'd caught me in the act of exercising my claws on his new briefcase, which lay on the hall chair. The briefcase was a present to himself at Christmas—no one else thought quite so much of him—but he hadn't been able to find a real use for it and I think it piqued him to see that I had.

"I want that black devil kept out of my sight," he told Mrs. Wynn, before whom he was careful to watch his language.

That afternoon, I heard him telling Father Ed Desmond, his friend from Minneapolis, who'd dropped by, that he favored the wholesale excommunication of household pets from homes and particularly from rectories. He mentioned me in the same breath with certain parrots and hamsters he was familiar with. Although he was speaking on the subject of clutter, he said nothing about model railroads, Father Desmond's little vice, or about photography, his own. The term "household pet" struck me as a double-barrelled euphemism, unpetted as I was and denied the freedom of the house.

And still, since I'd expected to be kicked out into the weather, and possibly not to get that far alive, I counted my deportation to the kitchen as a blessing—a temporary one, however. I had no reason to believe that Fa-

Here is a short history of the cats owned by Lisa Sco-
ville, aged seven, which she wrote for no particular reason:

CAT NAMES AND WHAT HAPPEN TO THEM

Tiger. The door slammed on him and he died.
Fluffy. She walked away and got lost.
Puffy. We gave her away.
Prince. A dog got her.
Ginger. We still have her. She is not well.

| 1959 |

ther Burner's feeling about me had changed. I
looked for something new in persecutions. When
nothing happened, I looked all the harder.

I spent my days in the kitchen with Mrs.
Wynn, sleeping when I could, just hanging
around in her way when I couldn't. If I wearied of
that, as I inevitably did, I descended into the cellar. The cellar smelled of things too various—
laundry, coal, developing fluid, and mice—and
the unseemly noise of the home-canned goods
digesting on the shelves, which another might
never notice, reached and offended my ears. After
an hour down there, where the floor was cold to
my feet, I was ready to return to the kitchen and
Mrs. Wynn.

Mrs. Wynn had troubles of her own—her
husband hit the jar—but they did nothing to
Christianize her attitude toward me. She fed me
scraps, and kicked me around, not hard but regularly, in the course of her work. I expected little
from her, however. She was another in the long
tradition of unjust stewards.

Father Burner's relatively civil conduct was
harder to comprehend. One afternoon, rising
from sleep and finding the kitchen door propped
open, I forgot myself and strolled into the parlor,

into his very presence. He was reading *Church
Property Administration*, a magazine I hadn't seen
in the house before. Having successfully got that
far out of line—as far as the middle of the room—
I decided to keep going. As if by chance, I came
to my favorite register, where, after looking about
to estimate the shortest distance between me and
any suitable places of refuge in the room, I collapsed around the heat. There was still no inti-
mation of treachery—only peace surpassing all
understanding, only the rush of warmth from the
register, the winds of winter outside, and the occasional click and whisper of a page turning in
Church Property Administration.

Not caring to push my luck, wishing to come
and doze another day, wanting merely to establish a precedent, I got up and strolled back into
the kitchen—to think. I threw out the possibility
that Father Burner had suffered a lapse of memory, had forgotten the restriction placed on my
movements. I conceived the idea that he'd lost, or
was losing, his mind, and then, grudgingly, I gave
up the idea. He was not trying to ignore me. He
was ignoring me without trying. I'd been doing
the same thing to people for years, but I'd never
dreamed that one of them would do it to me.

From that day on, I moved freely about the
house, as I had in Father Malt's time, and Mrs.
Wynn, to add to the mystery, made no effort to
keep me with her in the kitchen. I was thus in
a position to observe other lapses or inconsis-
tencies in Father Burner. Formerly, he'd liked
to have lights burning all over the house. Now
that he was paying the bill, the place was often
shrouded in darkness. He threw out the tattered rugs at the front and back doors and
bought rubber mats—at a saving, evidently, for
although one mat bore the initial "B," the other
had an "R," which stood for nobody but may
have been the closest thing he could get to go

with the "B." I noticed, too, that he took off his galoshes before entering the house, as though it were no longer just church property but home to him.

I noticed that he was going out less with his camera, and to the hospital more, not just to visit Father Malt, to whom he'd never had much to say, but to visit the sick in general.

In former times, he had been loath to go near the hospital during the day, and at night, before he'd leave his bed to make a sick call, there had had to be infallible proof that a patient was in danger of death. It had been something awful to hear him on the line with the hospital in the wee hours, haggling, asking if maybe they weren't a little free and easy with their designation "critical," as, indeed, I believe some of them liked to be. He'd tried to get them to change a patient's "critical" to "fair" (which meant he could forget about that one), and acted as though there were some therapeutic power about the word, if the hospital could just be persuaded to make use of it. Father Malt, with his hearing aid off, was virtually deaf, Mrs. Wynn roomed down the street, and so I had been the one to suffer. "Oh, go on, go on," I'd wanted to say. "Go on over there, or don't go—but hang up! Some of us want to sleep!" There were nights when I'd hardly sleep a wink—unlike Father Burner, who, even if he *did* go to the hospital, would come bumbling back and drop off with his clothes on.

In general, I now found his attitude toward his duties altered, but not too much so, not extreme. If he'd had a night of sick calls, he'd try to make up for it with a nap before dinner. His trouble was still a pronounced unwillingness to take a total loss on sacrifice.

I found other evidence of the change he was undergoing—outlines of sermons in the wastebasket, for instance. In the past, he'd boasted

that he thought of whatever he was going to say on Sunday in the time it took him to walk from the altar to the pulpit. He was not afraid to speak on the parishioners' duty to contribute generously to the support of the church, a subject neglected under Father Malt, who'd been satisfied with what the people wanted to give— very little. Father Burner tried to get them interested in the church. He said it was a matter of pride—pride in the good sense of the word. I felt he went too far, however, when, one Sunday, he told the congregation that it was their church *and* their rectory. There had always been too many converts hanging around the house for instruction, and now there were more of them than in Father Malt's day. The house just wasn't large enough for all of us.

Father Desmond, noting how little time Father Burner now had for himself (and for Father Desmond), suggested that the chancery be petitioned for help ("There's just too much work here for one man, Ernest"), but Father Burner said no, and so resisted what must have been the worst of all possible temptations to him, the assistant's sweet dream—to have an assistant. He said he'd go it alone. It almost seemed as if he were out to distinguish himself, not in the eyes of others— something he'd always worked at—but in his own eyes.

At any rate, he was beginning to act and talk like a real pastor. When Father Desmond came over or phoned, they talked of construction and repairs. Father Desmond, one of our most promising young pastors, was building a new school— with undue emphasis, it seemed to me, on the gymnasium. Father Burner, lacking authority to do more, made needed repairs. He had the rectory kitchen painted and purchased a Mixmaster for Mrs. Wynn. He had the windows in the church basement calked and installed a small in-

THE VIGIL

stitutional kitchen there, thus showing all too clearly that he intended to go in for parish suppers, which he'd abominated in the past as the hardest part of the priesthood.

Father Desmond and Father Burner now spoke fluently a gibberish that only a building pastor could comprehend. They talked of organs, bells, and bulletin boards, coin counters, confessional chairs and hearing devices, flooring, kneeler pads, gym seats, radiation, filing systems, electric fans, mops, and brooms, and all by their difficult trade names—Wurlitzer, Carillonic, Confessionaire, Confession-Ease, Speed Sweep, the Klopp (coin counter), Vakumatic, Scrubber-Vac, Kardex, Mopmaster, and many more. And shrubbery and trees.

There was a great need for trees in Sherwood—a need that, I daresay, had never occurred to Father Malt, or, presumably, to many of the older inhabitants of the town. The new people, who lived in "ranch houses" and worked in Minneapolis, seemed to like trees, and so, in his new phase, did Father Burner.

"When spring comes," he said, in cold January, "I'll plant some maples."

Father Desmond, who knew where Father Burner's thoughts were hiding, said, "Someday you'll build, too, Ernest."

After fourteen months in the hospital, Father Malt was moved to the sisters' infirmary in St. Paul, where there were supposed to be other patients, including old priests, of similar tastes and outlook. In our busy rectory, the seasons had come and gone without pause, the seasons as we observed them—baseball, football, Christmas, basketball, and Lent again. There were further improvements, or at least changes. Father Burner got Mrs. Wynn a white radio for her kitchen and thereby broke the tradition of silence we'd had

under Father Malt, who hadn't even listened to Cedric Adams and the ten-o'clock news.

I spent my mornings in the parlor and thus escaped the full effect of Mrs. Wynn's programs, but in the parlor, or wherever I went in the house, I heard those same voices, always at the same hour, always repeating themselves, and for a while, at first, I took a certain interest in those miserable lives. Can a woman over thirty-five find love again? Should a girl, the ward of a man twenty years older, marry him? For these questions, as time went on, I could see there would be no answers.

In our rectory, another question was being asked, and for this question there had to be an answer. Father Burner was pastor of the church in all but name, and could hope, with good reason, that this, too, would be added unto him in time, if he worked and prayed hard enough. During the first weeks after the accident, Father Burner and Father Desmond had discussed the physical aspects of Father Malt's case—what kind of cast, the number and type of pins, and all the rest. Lately, however, they'd been taking another line, more to the point and touching upon Father Burner's chances.

The difficulty lay, of course, in Father Malt's refusal to give himself up to the life of an invalid. Nothing could be done about appointing his successor until he actually resigned or died. No one, of course, openly suggested that he do either. It was up to him to decide. Father Desmond believed that, sooner or later, the Archbishop would go to Father Malt and precipitate a solution of the problem. But even the Archbishop was powerless to force Father Malt to resign against his will. As long as Father Malt wished, as long as he lived, he would be pastor, and this was according to canon law. Father Malt was an "irremovable pastor," well liked by the people of the parish, a favorite at the chancery, where, however, it was known—according to Father Desmond—that Father Burner was doing a bang-up job.

Father Burner was the rare one who hadn't asked for help, who was going it alone, with just two monks, down from St. John's, to assist him over weekends. He would go on retreat in June for five days (he wasn't much on card games, though), but he planned no regular vacation. He worked like a dog. He lost weight. He was tired. I was edified.

In May, I heard Father Desmond say, "Ernest, it's time to widen your circle of friends," and so Father Burner, rather unwillingly, tried to give a poker party at the rectory. Father Desmond, popular (as Father Burner wasn't) with the older men, a surprising number of whom claimed to have sold him on sobriety, invited several pastors and, significantly, no curates. But only two of those invited showed up—Father Kling and Father Moore. They belonged to the active set, a kind of Jockey Club for pastors, which maintained a floating poker game, a duckblind, and a summer lodge. They gambled, hunted, and fished in common.

On the evening of the party, when they came into the dining room, where the cards and chips were laid out, I could see that Father Desmond had led them to believe that Father Burner, of all people, was playing host to an almost official session. Father Kling, a forceful man, glanced at Father Moore, a mild one, and remarked that he'd understood others were coming. With good grace, however, he and Father Moore sat down to play.

Father Desmond, who seemed to regard his function as essentially one of public relations, started right in to plump for Father Burner. "It's a shame somebody doesn't tell the old man to retire," he said, referring to Father Malt. "It's not fair to Ernest, here, and it's not fair to the parish.

This place needs a young man, with young ideas." I, for one, wasn't surprised by the utter silence that followed these remarks. Father Kling and Father Moore, as even Father Desmond should've known, were not so young themselves, nor were they so hot on young ideas.

Father Burner wisely stayed out of it. Father Desmond continued along the same lines, however, until Father Kling commented dryly, "It's his hip, not his mind, that's gone wrong, isn't it?" and drained his highball.

"He's had quite a time of it, hasn't he?" said Father Moore gently. "Poor Dutch."

"How about poor Ernest?" asked Father Desmond.

"Uh, yes, of course," said Father Moore.

Father Desmond seemed to realize that he was doing no good and shut up. At least he might have waited, I thought, until they were feeling better. Father Kling had a little pile in front of him, and perhaps he'd remember where he got it. That was the only thing in Father Burner's favor when Mrs. Wynn came into the dining room and announced the Archbishop and another priest.

I followed Father Burner out of the dining room, but stopped at the door to the parlor, into which Mrs. Wynn had shown the guests. I preferred to enter unobserved.

When Father Burner attempted to kiss the episcopal ring, the Archbishop put his hand behind him. He reserved the ring-kissing business for ceremonial occasions, as everyone knew, but it was customary to make a try for it.

At Father Burner's invitation, the Archbishop and his companion, a young priest whose eyes looked as though he'd been driving all day, sat down, and at that juncture Father Desmond and the two other poker players came in to declare themselves. While they, too, tried to get at the

Archbishop's ring, I slipped into the parlor un-seen and then along the wall until I came to the library table. There, back out of view, at the inter-section of the crossbars supporting the table, I took up my position.

The Archbishop said that they'd been pass-ing the church, on their way back from a confir-mation tour along the northern marches of the diocese, when he thought of dropping in on Fa-ther Burner.

"It's good to see you all together," he said, looking them over. He liked to have his priests associating with one another, I knew, and not seeking other company to excess—except, of course, when necessary at parish functions.

The Archbishop asked about Father Malt (I daresay His Excellency, of those present, had seen him last), and Father Burner and Father Des-mond, replying, sounded a little too broken up to suit my taste, or to sound much like themselves.

When the conversation came around to Fa-ther Burner and the fine work he was doing, Fa-ther Desmond ran it into the ground. He fed the most leading questions to Father Burner, who

expressed himself well, I thought, although refer-ring too often to the Archbishop for a higher opinion on trivial matters. It galled me to see Fa-ther Desmond turning the occasion into a grease job all around. Father Burner, possibly recogniz-ing this but not able to turn Father Desmond off, excused himself and went down the hallway to the kitchen.

Father Desmond, speaking in a near-whisper, as if he were telling a secret, said, "You know, Your Excellency, Father's taken some nice shots of the Cathedral at night. If you'd care to see them . . ."

"I believe I've seen them," said the Arch-bishop. He was looking over Father Desmond's shoulder, disapprovingly, at his own smiling pic-ture on the wall—not one of Father Burner's shots, however.

"Yes," said Father Desmond. "But he doesn't have time for much any more."

The Archbishop nodded, and got up from his chair. "Excuse me, Father," he said. He crossed the room to the bookcase.

Mrs. Wynn entered the parlor with a tray of wineglasses, which she placed on the table.

Father Burner fol-lowed her with a bottle. I was happy to see that he'd had good luck with the cork. Later on, when the Archbishop had left, they'd switch back to bourbon (except Fa-ther Desmond, who was on 7-Up). For some rea-son, sacramental wine, taken daily, spoiled them for other wines.

"This is hardly the

"*Beg.*"

time, but it may be the place to ask you," said Father Burner, handing the Archbishop his glass, "but with Father Malt off the scene, Your Excellency, I was wondering if I dare go ahead with a tuck-pointing job on the church. I've been considering it—only academically, that is, Your Excellency, because it'll run into quite a lot of money." The Archbishop was silent. Father Burner started up again, in a manner feeble for him. "In the pastor's temporary absence, the disposition of these matters . . ."

"Couldn't it wait a bit, Father?" asked the Archbishop. It was a tense moment, a difficult reply indeed, when one tried to analyze it, as I did. At its best, it could mean that Father Burner would soon be empowered to make decisions concerning the church; at its worst, it could mean that the Archbishop expected Father Malt to recover and take over again, or, what was most likely, that he was not considering the question at all, regarded it as out of order, ill-timed, and impertinent. I felt that the Archbishop understood the reason for it, however. Father Burner had been overwhelmed by the visit, and flattered that others, particularly Father Kling and Father Moore, should be present to witness it. Such a visit—not an official visitation—could be enough to make him. It had been a great night for Father Burner until he popped that question.

When, a few minutes later, the Archbishop got up to leave, I came out from under the library table, went over to Father Burner, and brushed up against his trouser leg, purring.

The Archbishop, hearing me, I think, before he saw me, gazed down and said, "Do you like animals, Father?"

"Yes, Your Excellency," said Father Burner, who was only a dog-lover at best, and where I was concerned, I know, his answer was a barefaced

lie—until he made it. From that moment on—there was no doubt of it—he loved me.

"This one, I see, likes you," said the Archbishop, smiling. "Some believe it to be an infallible sign, the best of character references."

Father Burner blushed and said, "I wish I could believe in that sign, Your Excellency."

I trotted over to the Archbishop, selected his black trouser leg from all the others, and brushed against it, nicely purring. Everyone laughed.

"*Credo!*" cried Father Burner.

I was not surprised when, on the following morning, Father Burner invited me to join him at table for breakfast. I had wanted my elevation to my former place to happen of itself, to be a voluntary act on Father Burner's part, as mine had been on his account, and for that reason, and because I wanted Mrs. Wynn to get a good eyeful, I'd remained in the kitchen, awaiting, as it were, my nomination. After offering Mass, Father Burner came and sought me.

"Where's Fritz?" he asked.

"Who?" said Mrs. Wynn.

"Fritz," Father Burner said. "My cat."

"Oh, him," said Mrs. Wynn, who, it occurred to me, represented the sort of person who could live in the thick of history and never know the difference.

I walked out from under the kitchen table. Father Burner knelt and lifted me into his arms. He carried me into the dining room and pulled my old chair away from the wall and up to the table. We both sat down—to what I hoped would be only the first of many pleasant meals together.

I ate my bacon right royally and ruminated on the events of the evening before. I could not honestly say that I'd planned the splendid thing I'd done. It had more or less happened—unless, of course, I was both kinder and wiser than I believed myself to be. I was eating high on the hog again, I had my rightful place back, my reward for patience, and I was only sorry that Father Burner still had to wait for his. His buds had been pinched off at the start, but his roots had grown strong and deep. If he managed to flower, he'd be the classic type of late-blooming pastor. Until then he had me at his side, to him everything I'd been to Father Malt—friend and favorite, and, more, the very symbol and prefigurement of power. I actually liked him, I discovered. I liked him for what I'd done for him. But why had I done it? I didn't really know why. I work at times in ways so inscrutable that even I cannot tell what good or evil I am up to.

Before we'd finished breakfast, Father Desmond phoned—to discuss the Archbishop's visit, I gathered, for Father Burner said, "I've decided not to talk any more about it, Ed." I could almost hear Father Desmond squawking, "Whatta ya mean, Ernest?" "Maybe that's part of the trouble," Father Burner said. "We're talkin' it to death." Evidently Father Desmond took offense at that, for Father Burner spoke quickly, out of context: "Why don't you come for dinner sometime, Ed? When? Well, come tomorrow. Come early. Good."

Father Burner hung up, bounced over to the table, chucked me fondly behind the ears, took a banana out of the fruit bowl, and went whistling off to his car—off to do the work of the parish, to return a defective length of hose, to visit the sick and pregnant, to drive to Minneapolis for more informal conferences with building experts, lay and clerical. He had several projects going ahead—academically, that is: the tuck pointing, a new decorating job inside the church, and outside, possibly, a floodlight on the dome, which I thought a paltry affair better left in the dark.

Before lunch that day, he returned with a half dozen mousetraps. He seemed to want me to follow him around the house, and therefore I attended him most faithfully, while he set the traps in what he regarded as likely places. I rather expected to be jollied about my indifference to mousing. There was none of that, however, and what might have been an embarrassing experience for me became instead an occasion of instruction. Using a pencil for a mouse, Father Burner showed me how the trap worked, which was quite unnecessary but a nice gesture, I thought.

That evening—with Father Burner still in the mood to exterminate—we appeared together for the first time in public, at the monthly meeting of the ushers. In the future, Father Burner announced, all notices of the sort now being posted on the bulletin board at the rear of the church would have to emanate from his office (which, strictly speaking, was his bedroom) and carry his signature. This was a cruel but unavoidable check to Mr. Keller, who had become too prolific for his own good. He used the drugstore typewriter and special engraved cards bearing his name and title, and he took an authoritarian tone in matters of etiquette ("Keep your feet off the kneelers," "Don't stand in the back of the church," "Ask the usher to find you a seat—that's what he's there for," etc.), and in other matters (Lost and Found, old-clothes collections, ticket sales, and the like) he made it sound as though these were all services and causes thought up and sponsored by him personally. I felt that he was not far from posting bargains in real estate, another means of livelihood for him at the drugstore, when Father Burner stepped in. Mr. Keller took it well—too well, I thought. He murmured a few meek words about trying to spare Father Burner the trouble, as he'd spared Father Malt the trouble. (He now visited Father Malt regularly at the infirmary.) Before we left, he asked Father Burner to lead the ushers in the usual prayer for Father Malt's swift recovery.

It was early afternoon the next day when Father Burner remembered the mousetraps. I accompanied him on his rounds, but there was nothing I liked about the business before us. First we went to the pantry and kitchen, where Mrs. Wynn constantly dropped and mislaid quantities of food. Any mouse caught in a trap there, I thought, deserved to die for his gluttony. None had. In the cellar, however, Father Burner had snared two young ones, both from a large family whose members I saw from time to time. My record with them had been good, and they, in turn, had played fair with me and had committed no obvious depredations to make me look bad. When their loss was noted, the others, I feared, would blame me—not for the crime itself but for letting it happen within my precinct.

Father Burner removed the little bodies from the traps, and then, with the best of intentions and with a smile, which only made it worse, he did a terrible thing. He extended a hand to me, a hand curled in kindness, inviting me to banquet on the remains. I turned away in a swoon, physically sick and sick at heart. I made my way upstairs, wanting to be alone. I considered bitterly others I'd known and trusted in the past. Always, except with Father Malt, when I'd persuaded myself to take a chance on one of them, there'd be something like this. I tried to forget, or to sleep it off, which proved impossible. I knew what I had to do before I could begin to forget, and so I did it. I forgave Father Burner. It was another lesson in charity, one that cost me more than my going to bat for him with the Archbishop, but I'm afraid it was entirely lost on him.

Father Desmond came for dinner that afternoon at four, which I thought rather early even for "early." When he arrived, I was in the front hall having a go at the briefcase. He went right past me. I could see that he had something on his mind.

"I just couldn't stay away," he said, taking a chair across from Father Burner in the parlor. "I've got what I *think* is good news, Ernest."

Father Burner glanced up from *Church Property Administration* and shook his head. "I don't want to hear it," he said, "if it's about you-know-what."

"I'll just tell you what I *know* to be true," Father Desmond said, "and let it go at that."

"Whatever it is, it can wait," said Father Burner. I could see, however, that he'd listen if he was primed again.

Father Desmond bore down on him. "Sure, I know, you'll get it in the mail—when you get it. That's what you figure. I admire your restraint, Ernest, but let's not be superstitious about it, either."

Father Burner, sprawling in his chair, rolled and unrolled *Church Property Administration*.

Then, making a tube of it, he put it to his eye and peered through it, down his black leg, a great distance, and appeared finally to sight the silver glow on the toe of his big black shoe, which lay in the sunlight. "All right, Ed," he said. "Let's have it."

"All right, then," said Father Desmond. "Here it is. I have it on reliable authority—that is to say, my spies tell me—the Archbishop visited the infirmary today." I interpreted "spies" to mean some little nun or other on whom Father Desmond bestowed sample holy cards.

Father Burner, taking a long-suffering tone in which there was just a touch of panic, said, "Ed, you know he does that all the time. You'll have to do better than that."

Father Desmond tried to come up with more. "He had *words* with Dutch."

Father Burner flung himself out of his chair. He engaged in swordplay with the air, using *Church Property Administration*. "How do you mean 'he had words'? You don't mean to say they quarrelled?"

Father Desmond could only reply, "I just mean they talked at *some* length."

Father Burner gave a great snort and threw *Church Property Administration* across the room. It clattered against the bookcase, a broken sword. He wheeled and walked the floor, demanding, "Then why'd you say they had words? Why make something out of nothing? Why not tell it straight, Ed? Just once, huh?" He was standing over Father Desmond.

"You're under a strain, Ernest," said Father Desmond, getting up from his

MAINFRAME LAPTOP POCKET

chair. "Maybe I shouldn't have said anything about it at all."

Father Burner stared at him. "*Said?* Said *what?* That's just it, Ed—you haven't said anything." He took another walk around the room, saying the word "nothing" over and over to himself.

Father Desmond cut in, "All right, Ernest, I'm sorry," and sat down in his chair.

Then Father Burner, too, sat down, and both men were overcome by quiet and perhaps shame. Several minutes passed. I was sorry for Father Burner. He'd sacrificed his valuable silence to his curiosity and received nothing in return.

I addressed the briefcase, making my claws catch and pop in the soft, responsive leather. I wished that I were plucking instead at the top of Father Desmond's soft head.

Father Desmond glanced over at me and then at Father Burner.

"Why do you let him do that?" he asked.

"He likes to."

"Yeah?" said Father Desmond. "Does he ever bring you a mouse?"

With one paw poised, I listened for Father Burner's answer.

"You don't see any around, do you?" he said.

Well done, I thought, and renewed my attack on the briefcase. I had the feeling that Father Desmond still wanted to tell the world what he'd do to me if it were his briefcase, but, if so, he denied himself and got out a cigar.

"What'd you think of the plans for that rectory in South Dakota?" he asked.

"Not bad," said Father Burner, looking around for his *Church Property Administration.*

"There it is," said Father Desmond, as if it were always misplacing itself. He went over by the bookcase, picked up the magazine, and delivered it to Father Burner.

I curled up to nap. I could see that they were going to have one of their discussions.

When I heard the back door open, I supposed it was Mrs. Wynn coming in to start dinner, but it was Mr. Keller. I saw him advancing gravely up the hallway, toward me, carrying a travelling bag that I recognized as one the ushers had given Father Malt. Instantly I concluded that Father Malt had passed away in the night, that the nuns had failed to inform Father Burner, and had instead told Mr. Keller, the faithful visitor, to whom they'd also entrusted the deceased's few belongings.

Mr. Keller set down the bag and, without looking into the parlor, started back the way he'd come, toward the back door. Father Burner and Father Desmond, at the sight of the bag, seemed unable to rise from their chairs, powerless to speak.

After a moment, I saw Father Malt emerging from the kitchen, on crutches, followed by Mr. Keller. He worked his way up the hallway, talking to himself. "Somebody painted my kitchen," I heard him say.

I beheld him as one risen from the dead. He looked the same to me but different—an imperfect reproduction of himself as I recalled him, imperfect only because he appeared softer, whiter, and, of course, because of the crutches.

Not seeing me by the hatrack, he clumped into the parlor, nodded familiarly to Father Burner and Father Desmond, and said, again to himself, "Somebody changed my chairs around."

Father Desmond suddenly shot up from his chair, said, "I gotta go," and went. Mr. Keller seemed inclined to stick around. Father Burner, standing, waited for Father Malt to come away from the library table, where he'd spotted some old copies of *Church Property Administration.*

Father Malt thrust his hand under the pile of

magazines, weighed it, and slowly, with difficulty, turned on his crutches, to face Father Burner.

They stared at each other, Father Malt and Father Burner, like two popes themselves not sure which one was real.

I decided to act. I made my way to the center of the room and stood between them. I sensed them both looking at me, then *to* me—for a sign. Canon law itself was not more clear, more firm, than the one I lived by. I turned my back on Father Burner, went over to Father Malt, and favored him with a solemn purr and dubbed his trouser leg lightly with my tail, reversing the usual course of prerogative between lord and favorite, switching the current of power. With a purr, I'd restored Father Malt's old authority in the house. Of necessity—authority as well as truth being one and indivisible—I'd unmade Father Burner. I was sorry for him.

He turned and spoke harshly to Mr. Keller: "Why don't you go see if you left the back door open?"

When Father Burner was sure that Mr. Keller had gone, he faced Father Malt. The irremovable pastor stood perspiring on his crutches. As long as he lived, he had to be pastor, I saw; his need was the greater. And Father Burner saw it, too. He went up to Father Malt, laid a strong, obedient hand on the old one that held tight to the right crutch, and was then the man he'd been becoming.

"Hello, boss," he said. "Glad you're back."

It was his finest hour. In the past, he had lacked the will to accept his setbacks with grace and had derived no merit from them. It was difficult to believe that he'd profited so much from my efforts in his behalf—my good company and constant example. I was happy for him.

| *1951* |

PRICE $4.99

THE NEW YORKER

OCT. 5, 2009

May 3, 1969
THE
NEW YORKER
Price 50 cents

ALLEY CATS

THE CATS

Fiction

JOHN UPDIKE

hen my mother died, I inherited eighty acres of Pennsylvania and forty cats. Eighty-two and a half acres, to be exact; the cats were beyond precise counting. They seethed in a mewing puddle of fur at the back door, toward five o'clock, when they could hear her inside the kitchen turning the clunky handle of the worn-out can opener that jutted from the door-frame, beside the sweating refrigerator. One Christmas, when she was in her seventies, I had bought her a new can opener, but in time it, too, went dull and wobbly under its burden of use; I thriftily wondered whether or not it would last her lifetime. In her eighties, she as well was wearing out, as each of my visits to the farmhouse made clear. Walking to the mailbox and feeding the cats were the sole exertions she could still perform—she who had performed so many, from her girlhood of horse-riding and collegiate hockey playing to the days when, moving her family to this isolated farm, she had led us by working like a man, wielding the chain saw and climbing the extension ladder and swinging herself jubilantly up into the wide tractor seat.

She had been born here, in the age of mule-drawn plows. Neither my father nor I had understood her wish to return to this wearying place of work, weeds, bugs, heat, mud, and wildlife. She had led us in imposing some order—renovating the old stone farmhouse, repairing the barn, planting rows of strawberries and asparagus and peas, mowing a lawn back into the shadow of the woods. But, after I moved away and my father died, the fertile wilderness threatened to reclaim everything. Even the windowsills, the next owner of the house has discovered, were rotten and teeming with termites and wood lice. From inside the attic, the shingle roof looked like a starry sky. Not only did my mother allow mice and flying squirrels to nest in the house— she fed them sunflower seeds, whose shells, the new owner discovered, tumbled by the peck from their caches in the woodwork. The house in my mother's last years smelled of stacked newspapers that never made it to the barn, and of cat-food cans in paper bags, and of damp dog. Her overfed dog, Josie, was going lame along with her mistress; she never got any exercise. It was pathetic, how happy old Josie was to accompany me to the barn with the papers, and out to our mountain of tin in the woods with the cans.

Was it my imagination, or did my mother use to hum as she revolved the handle, like some primitive, repetitive musical instrument, emptying one gelatinous cylinder of cat food after another into the set of old cake tins that served the cats as dinnerware on the cement back porch? Feeding these half-feral animals amused and pleased her—quite improperly, I thought. Their mounting numbers seemed to me a disaster, which grew worse every time I paid a filial visit, in spite of the merciful inroads of various feline diseases and occasional interventionary blasts from the guns of interested neighbors. Some neighbors threatened to report her to the humane society, and others, furtively, dropped off unwanted kittens in the night.

Being my mother's son, I could follow her reasoning right into this quagmire. If you didn't feed the cats, they would eat all the birds. She loved birds, that was why she had begun to feed the cats. Sitting right in the house with its closed windows, talking away on the sofa, she would cock her head and say, "The towhee is upset about something," or, "The mockingbird is telling a joke," or, at night, coming into my room in her white nightgown, her eyes going wide as if scaring a child, "Listen to Mr. Whippoorwill."

In deference to my asthma she had never let the cats in the house, but the day after she died they could hear me through the screen door as I churned away with the can opener. I spoke aloud to them, much as she had. "I know, I know," I said. "You're ravenous. The lady who used to feed you is dead. I'm just her son, her only child. I don't live here, I live in Princeton, New Jersey, where I have a job with the fabled university, a four-bedroom house, a haughty and ele-

"Do you ever miss New York?"

gant wife called Andrea, and two grown children, one of them with a child of her own. I don't want to be here, I never did. And if you can think of a better place, go to it, because, my fine feline friends, *the dole is ending*. The cat food is down to its last case, and I'm here for just two more days. What are you going to do then? Beats me—it's a real problem, frankly. Well, you shouldn't have gotten sucked into the system. You shouldn't have all become teen-age mothers."

When I put the brimming cake tins, which smelled disagreeably of horse meat and pulverized fish, down on the bare cement, the cat bodies clustered around them like the petals of a fur flower. Yet the older cats managed, in the skirmish, to make way for the kittens among them. The calico kittens had mottled, wide-browed faces like pansies. The black-and-whites suggested Rorschach tests, or maps of a simpler planet than ours. My mother used to name the cats that came to the porch, and would say of one, "Isabel is a rather lackadaisical mother," or of a wary, beat-up tom, "Jeffrey has a limp today. His boots must pinch."

The cats that stayed in the barn didn't earn names. When I opened the top half of a stall door, light glinted from eyes in the straw as if from bits of pale glass, and a violent slither sent several cats squirming under the partition into the next stall. The pan I set down would be empty, though, an hour later. The barn cats paid for their shyness with relatively dismal lives; they were prone to the diseases of the inbred, and a probe of the straw, left over from the days when cows bedded here, would turn up a dried corpse— a matted pelt as stiff as a piece of leather, the dead animal's head frozen into an eyeless snarl.

Toward the end, my mother had been too frail to make it down to feed the barn cats, so my pan was only half-consumed the first night. The barn cats that had not perished or fled had become porch cats. "What are we going to *do*?" I asked the prowling animals as I returned from the barn in the early-September dusk. "I can't give up my whole civilized life just to keep feeding you ingrates."

Moving here when I was a boy had indeed felt like the loss of civilization. No phone, no electricity, no plumbing: a terrible regress. Amish workmen came and hammered snug a bright cedar-shingle roof and rather nicely built in the living room what none of the house's previous inmates had needed: a bookcase. In time plumbers came and rendered the outhouse obsolete, and the electric company marched tall creosoted poles down through the orchard. Television entered the house, and instead of listening to weather reports and corn prices and country music on the Reading radio station we were watching the Philadelphia news, first in black-and-white and then in color. But I could never shake my impression that the farm was a trap from which my clear duty was to escape.

I asked my neighbor to the south, Dwight Potteiger, "What shall I do about all the cats?"

He grows sweet corn and snap beans for market and is second in charge of the township school-bus fleet. He confided to me, "I used to ask Irma, 'What's Frank going to do, in case you pass on, with all the cats?' She'd say, so serene-like, 'Oh, Frankie will find a way. He always has. He's kept me here in style for twenty years.'"

She had become a widow in her sixties. My contributions to her upkeep, added to my father's pension and their savings, had been barely adequate and, now that she was dead, seemed quite niggardly.

"She exaggerated," I said.

"Well, now, one thing she didn't exaggerate

any was the size of that herd of cats. I can't imagine what-all money she put into cat food. She'd call me up after shopping this last year or two, and I'd go carry the cases for her into the kitchen."

"Thank you," I said. Dwight was the son I should have been.

"A week or so, she'd have another trunkful to lug in." Was he airing a bottled-up grievance, or trying to bring her back to life for me?

As apologetically as I could, I said, "They were company for her, of a sort."

"They were stark wild," Dwight said. "If I'd show up in the evening, they'd scatter off the porch like they'd never seen a man with a beard before." His beard had alarmed me, too, when he first began to grow it—in this part of the country beards were left to Amishmen and to ancestors in stiff-leaved photograph albums. This beard had a surprising amount of red in it, among bristles of gray and brown, and gave its wearer a mischievous-looking authority that rather cowed me.

"She began to feed them, you know," I wearily explained, "to keep them from eating the birds."

He chuckled. "That was the theory, I know. But I used to tell her, 'Irma, I still wouldn't say your place here is any paradise for our fair-feathered friends.' She didn't appreciate my saying that."

"But I know for a fact she lost a couple nests of swallows, when the cats figured out how to climb the old stable doors. Barn swallows are hard to discourage, but Irma's finally did stop coming back."

I hurried on, away from such sadness. "My question is, Dwight, what do I do about them? The cats. I can't just leave them to starve in the landscape."

I was begging, he could see. Though I knew he thought it, he did not ask, "Why not?" He was

indulging my fancies, as he had indulged my mother's.

"I have to get back to New Jersey," I said, "after I see the lawyer in town and the pastor up at the church and the undertaker again."

He shifted his weight, standing there. "Well, I could take the shotgun and go over at supper-time when they gather on the porch. That would take out a few, and then the others might get the clue and skedaddle. If you'd like, I could ask Adam to come down with his woodchuck rifle and we'll run a pincer operation. We need owner's permission, but you're giving that, isn't that right?"

"I sure am. We have to do *some*thing." Adam Wipf was the neighbor to the north, a plump orchard-keeper with a multitude of children and now grandchildren. We were, we three proprietors, about the same age, in our late fifties. They had been boys here when we moved. I had tried playing with them, but they had stunted ball-handling skills. An opaque earthiness about them frightened me—reminded me of death.

"I would be *very* grateful," I emphasized, and in my own ears my voice sounded citified, weak, patronizing.

Dwight said, "We don't want you worrying, over there with all those other smart folks at Princeton." I had avoided mentioning Princeton, naming my home as "New Jersey," but my mother had made no secret of my career, and I could not accept my neighbor's favor without accepting his needle. My mother had shown a good grasp of these country transactions: a little "kidding" for every kindness. She rented fields to her neighbors, and they helped her out in blizzards and mechanical difficulties. If she could not stay on the land, it would likely go under to a developer, and the neighborhood would be changed forever, with septic tanks and fast traffic and higher taxes and a lowered water table. It had suited me, too, to keep her on her farm, out of my life. I had begun to worry, though, how she would survive this coming winter. She took any decision out of my hands by dropping dead at the kitchen sink, frying herself a pork chop while the Channel 4 evening-news team was chattering in the living room.

Next morning, as I fed them, I told the cats, "Eat up, sweeties—your days are numbered." I had half expected rifle shots to ring out in my sleep, but the day broke still and dewy. The cement porch was decorated with wet paw prints. A continent of gray cloud was moving up into the sky beyond the telephone poles and the surviving orchard trees. When we moved here, there had been a pump on this porch, and all our water had been drawn up into pots and buckets. At first, it had been a challenge to my strength to work the metal handle through the first dry shoves, before the water began to flow. By the time we got plumbing and an electric pump, the action had become as automatic as turning on a faucet. Like turning the can-opener handle, pumping had its own catchy rhythm, its mechanical song.

My mother had set out a few potted geraniums at the corners of the porch and hung wind chimes from an overhead hook. She had seen them in one of the innumerable catalogues she received, and had ordered them; the idea amused

her. It was a fortunate gift in life, it occurred to me, to be easily amused. These chimes, and inquisitive scratchings from inside the walls, had not kept me from sleeping, though I had feared they would. The day's appointments clarified my future: I would get back to Princeton by nighttime, and in two more days would bring my family here for my mother's funeral, with a moving truck to take away what of her furniture we decided not to give to the auction house.

Heading up the road with Josie in the car, I swung in to the Wipfs' and asked Adam if he would keep an eye on the house. He and his wife live in a little new ranch house close to the road; his parents still live in the sandstone house, a twin to my mother's, down by the barn that he had turned into a fruit outlet. He smiled as he said he would, implying that it wouldn't be necessary. This part of the world might be changing, but people didn't yet go around robbing the houses of the recently dead.

"I really appreciate," I said, "your helping Dwight shoot the poor cats."

He looked puzzled. "I haven't heard any about that, but it's I guess not so big a problem," he said, as if he were reassuring my mother that he would get her tractor started.

When, two days later, at dusk, my family arrived in a station wagon and a yellow rental truck, the number of cats gathered on the back porch seemed no smaller than it had been, though visibly more frantic. They yowled upward, showing their curved fangs, their arched rough tongues, the rosy membranes of their throats. A few kittens were staggering with weakness, yet joined in the common mew of protest, of need. I kicked my way through the crowd but, once safely inside, gave my son, Max, a twenty and asked him to drive to the grocery store in Fern Hollow and buy enough cat food to see us through. He looked

---

FOSTER MOTHER

Gentleman connected with a construction company has been telling us about a cat his workmen have for a mascot. She is taken around from one job to another by the men, and lately she gave birth to a litter of five kittens on a location in Brooklyn. A few days after the event, a nest of baby rats was turned up when an old building was demolished and, while the cat was off foraging some place, the men put a handful of the ratlets—seven of them, to be exact—in the box with her kittens, and awaited results. When she returned, she purred with delight. She proceeded to suckle them with her own babies, she bathed them regularly, and gave them every maternal care. If they fell out of the box, she carefully put them back in. This went on for about a week. Then she started eating them. She ate one a day, for seven days.

| 1934 |

---

alarmed and said he always got lost in Fern Hollow. My wife heard us and came over protectively. "Max hasn't been to that store more than three times in his life," Andrea said. "When we came to visit we always went to the supermarket in Morgantown. Why can't he go *there*?"

"It's two miles further and closes at five-thirty. Also my mother thought the little stores should be patronized to keep them in business."

My wife sighed and rolled her eyes upward. "Your mother is dead, darling. We can buy at big stores if we want to."

"It's *closed*, I just told you. We can't stay here with these cats yowling all night."

"Maybe they'll stop yowling once we turn off the lights," she said. "Isn't it time they faced reality?"

"*I'll* go, dammit," I said, thinking they would all protest at having me, the leader of our mourning party, leave them alone in the old stone house, with its rustling rodents and airless, ill-lit rooms. We were all still in the kitchen, where my mother's hand-wound mantel clock had stopped ticking and chiming. Its melancholy, gulping gong had kept watch over my insomnia on many a boyhood night.

Hiram, my daughter's husband, said, "I'll go for you, Frank, if you'll tell me the way."

He was being kind, but he is also unctuous and prematurely balding, and I let my irritation with the others taint my reply: "It would take too long to explain. There are about six forks and none of them are marked."

"*He's* the country boy," my wife told Hiram with a collusive smile. "Let's let him go." To me she said, "You love those windy old roads."

It was a relief, as it always had been, to get out of the house and into the car, and onto the rolling freedom of the leafy roads. Newish ranch houses, built in homely mixtures of wood and sandstone and vinyl siding, added their window lights and mowed yards to the scattered habitations that I remembered. My mother used to recall being allowed to ride in the gig with her father when he caught the train into Reading at the Fern Hollow station, and then, though she was only nine or ten, bringing the gig back to the farm by herself. Of course, the horse knew the way. In the darkness, thinking of a little beribboned girl allowed to bring a gig through three miles of forest and tobacco fields, I missed one of the forks. Rather than turn around, I took what I remembered as a shortcut, but it led to a dead end at an abandoned gravel pit. It took forever, it seemed, to backtrack and find Fern Hollow. But Stoudt's Keystone was still open, with its two gas pumps and side porch loaded with horse feed and sacks of fertilizer. Behind the counter, Roy Stoudt nodded in recognition, though I was disguised in a citified shirt and blazer. When I told him what I wanted, he said, "I was wondering how those cats would manage."

"Not so well. The neighbors promised to shoot some but they haven't yet. I need just a case, to tide us over." I pictured the kittens staggering with hunger and said, "Maybe two cases."

"Your mother favored the protein beef mix and the seafood medley."

"Fine. Anything."

"She used to say they turned up their noses at pork; they were Old Testament cats. She was a funny one. You never quite knew when she was kidding."

"Yeah, that was a problem for me even." In Princeton, I would have said "even for me." The local lilt was not hard to slip into. Stoudt's Keystone was a long, dark store, its floorboards hollowed by wear, with gleaming nails, where generations had shuffled past the cash register. It still sold little tubes of flypaper and plugs of chewing tobacco. I had trouble deciding, amid the abundance of packaged carbohydrates, which brand of pretzels to buy. I settled for a bag that claimed "NEW! Lo Fat, Lo Sodium."

As he rang up my purchases, Roy went on, "She used to say to me, 'My boy thinks I'm crazy, feeding all these cats, but it's my only luxury. I don't drive a Mercedes, and I don't wear mink.'"

"I never said crazy. I may have said funny."

"She did trap some and take them down to the humane society," he pointed out. "It was just nature kept getting ahead of her." There was a slyness mixed in with his amiability; I sensed how much of a local joke she and her cats had been. "There," he said. "I've given you the discount for quantity I used to give to her."

"You don't have to do that." I could have bitten my tongue. I could hear his response coming, like the pedantic distinction, made much of in elementary school, between "can" and "may."

"I know I don't *have* to, Frank, but I *want* to," Roy said. "We'll miss your mother around these parts."

The cat-food section of Stoudt's Keystone would certainly miss her. I said what I should have said in the first place: "Thanks for the discount, Roy."

Outside, under the moth-battered lights, bits of abandoned railroad gleamed in the parking lot, where it hadn't paid to wrest the iron tracks from the blacktop. They crossed the little road, pointing on either side to tunnels of darkness. The woods had still not fully reclaimed the right-of-way; the rails were gone but the spalls and creosoted ties had been left and discouraged growth.

The morning of the funeral, I began to clean out my mother's crammed desk and found a little note on brittle blue stationery in an envelope addressed simply "Frank." It said:

In the event of my death I wish to be buried in the simplest possible ceremony, in the least expensive available coffin. Instead of flowers, I ask that contributions be directed to the Boone Township Humane Society, R.F.D. 2, Box 88, Emmetstown, Penna.

I had done it all wrong. I had bought her the second-most-expensive casket in the undertaker's basement, cherrywood with shiny brass rails to carry it by, and had arranged with the Lutheran pastor for the usual Lutheran service, with a catered lunch afterward. The announcement of the death in the Reading paper had said nothing about giving money to the humane society. Nor did her note say anything about what I was to do with the cats.

After the burial service, Dwight sidled up to me on the cemetery grass and said, "I haven't been able to come over with the rifle these last days—we're getting the buses ready for the school year, there's been a ton of maintenance. And Adam has the late peaches coming in. But we'll get to it, absolutely."

The sight of the cherrywood coffin, with its brass fittings, sinking into the clean-sliced earth was still gleaming in my brain. I said, "Dwight, maybe it's too much to ask. Why don't you and Adam forget about it, and I'll try to think of something else. It's not your problem."

"No, now, we wouldn't want to do that," he said consolingly. He looked strange, in a navy-blue churchgoing suit under a noon sun on a weekday. Adam had brought his entire family, including three grandchildren, getting them out of the orchard and into their good clothes. A few other neighbors were there, and Martha Stoudt from down in Fern Hollow—she was the caterer. Roy had stayed behind the counter at the store. Three of my female high-school classmates

showed up, touchingly, and a business associate, a fellow-accountant, of my father's who I thought had long ago died. In fact, though older than my parents, he was wiry and tan. He spent half the year in Florida, and didn't lack for dancing partners down there; this last was confided with a wink. Senility showed only in his tears, which refused to dry up in the outdoors, even with the early-fall sun beating down and a dry wind blowing on the cemetery hill. He cried for all of us, it seemed, while smiling and hopping about on the grass.

Martha Stoudt and the pastor's wife had been too optimistic about the funeral attendance; there seemed mountains of potato salad and cole slaw and sliced bread and cold cuts waiting for us in the church function room. The food held us fast like flies; we murmured and circled, though the farmers were anxious to get back to their farms and my high-school friends back to their jobs. All three women worked in welfare administration, oddly—government-sponsored mothers to the nation's hordes of orphans.

As for my mother, it is strange, once a life is over, how little there is to say about it. I could feel her in the room, polite but taking sardonic note, for future reference, of our collective failure to quite rise to the occasion. People had always struck her as inept, compared to animals. It galled

me on her behalf that the minister, in the very strenuousness of his oratorical attempt to evoke my mother's elusive qualities, had forgotten to signal the organist to play "A Mighty Fortress." How many Lutherans get buried without hearing, one last time, "A Mighty Fortress"? I felt it as a scandal, albeit minor. Ignominiously my living kin gathered up all the uneaten food and went back to the forlorn house, with its rotting sills and teeming population of invited pests. The cats, though it was not their dinnertime, were swarming hopefully on the back porch; some of the barn cats had ventured up to the house and made gray streaks in retreat across the lawn as our car pulled in. The house was stuffy and still inside; Andrea went around tugging open the sticky windows, in contravention of my mother's theory that closed windows sealed the coolness in. She and our daughter, Nancy, were dying to get back to Princeton; we had left it to a neighbor to feed fat old Josie, along with our own sleek cocker spaniel. Max and I were to stay a day or two—whatever it took—and load up the truck and get the house clean enough for the real-estate agent to show. Everywhere we looked, from the refrigerator full of cold cuts and potato salad to an attic holding a half century's worth of broken furniture, crockery wrapped in ancient brown newspapers, albums of ancestors whose names nobody now knew, and *Life* magazines of special historical interest, we were overwhelmed. Nancy put her one-year-old son, Peter, down upstairs for his nap. Andrea had a headache, Max and Hiram turned on the television set, and I escaped by getting in the car and driving to Emmetstown.

Four miles of back roads, crossing and recrossing a creek on rattling bridges, brought me to the outskirts of Emmetstown, where an ugly stencilled sign pointed the way to the Humane Society. I had been here a few times with my mother, delivering trapped cats. The society had lent her two galvanized cage traps a dozen years ago. She would bait them with liver pâté. On various weekend visits I had helped her lug her bizarre catch. Tomcats and new mothers were the hardest to carry, as they made the long cages pitch back and forth in their terror, hurling their bodies against the dropped doors and trying to bite and claw their way through the wire mesh. You handed them in over the Humane-Society counter and a stocky, pale teen-age girl would take them away and ten minutes later, looking slightly paler, would bring the cages back empty.

In the years since I had been here, there had been some refinements. From the concrete-floored rear of the complex there still drifted animal smells and yowls, but the front room looked more like an office, with framed certificates and prints of wildlife. The high bare counter was gone, and a walnut desk occupied the center of the shag-carpeted floor. Here sat a broad-shouldered bland woman with "big" hair, teased and tinted copper.

Her pale face lifted to me when I came in; her lips remained parted, so her front teeth showed in a semi-startled way I found appealing. Before I could introduce myself, she said, "I was sorry to read about your mother, Frank. She was a real nice lady. Such lovely manners, even when you could tell she was upset."

"When did you see her upset?"

"Oh, with the cats. Having to bring them in to be, you know, disposed of, when they were a lot like pets to her. She would say goodbye by name, sometimes. She used to say it was the tamest that trusted her enough to take the bait; the really wild ones never got caught."

"It was horrible, the way they multiplied."

"Well, they will, if you feed them." She

added, as I grappled with this Malthusian truth, "That's the nature of the beast." Seeing me still baffled, she said, "It's hard."

"Yes," I agreed. "Hard. Do you have any ideas as to what I should do?"

"About the cats?"

"Absolutely." What else? I had no other problems that I knew of.

She thought and said, "Well, do you still have the traps?"

"I haven't looked, but I guess they're still in the barn."

"I ask because your mother hasn't been in for a couple of years at least."

"She got too weak to do it. A trap with a fighting cat in it isn't so easy to handle."

"Oh, I know." She spoke with an increasing gentleness, as if to a crazy man. Though her fingernails were short and unpainted, her face was made up with that faintly excessive care of minor officialdom—of small-town postmistresses and small-city lawyers' secretaries. I suddenly knew that this composed executive woman was the stocky girl of years ago, the teenage executioner. She had assumed I recognized her at once, as she had me.

A young male minion in dungarees and ponytail opened the door to the fragrant beyond, said a few unintelligible words, received a confirming nod, and closed the door.

Lamely I continued, "I think she got overwhelmed and couldn't see beyond dishing it out every day. There's an absolute *mountain* of tin cans in the woods!"

She changed the angle of her listening head, and her professional patience seemed momentarily strained. "What I started to suggest was, if you still have the traps in the barn, you could set them and bring in one or two every day. The ones you don't eventually

catch will be so feral they'll keep to the woods."

"But I can't *stay*!"

She blinked at my fervor. Somehow she had seen me as replacing my mother in the little house, with its eighty-two acres of milkweed and horseflies and sandy red mud, as if my whole life had been killing time until I could take possession of my inheritance.

"I live in New Jersey!" I insisted. "I have to get back to my house, my job."

"You're putting your mom's place up for sale?"

"I have to! I can't take care of it!"

She pursed her lips slightly as she took this in. "It's considered a nice place around here, but if you can't, well, you can't. Your mother wouldn't want you to do the impossible." Yet a loyalty to my mother drove her, after a pause, to go on, "Though she always spoke of you as the one who'd take charge. She'd say to me, 'Amy, I'm just holding the fort for Frank.' How many days *can* you stay, then?"

"Two at most."

She thoughtfully scratched below her dough-colored little ear and I caught a whiff of her perfume. "So, then. Bring the borrowed traps in, and we'll cross them off your mother's card. Otherwise I'd have to charge you."

"Fine. I'll do it tomorrow." I hoped she didn't expect me to bring them in loaded. I didn't have any liver pâté, for one thing.

"And then, you know, Frank, we have a man who does some trapping for us. He lives not far from here, and works out in your area, at the hardware store in Morgantown. He could set the traps at your place on his way to work and pick them up on his way back."

"That sounds wonderful. *Wonderful.* How much does he charge?" Like a frontiersman packing a firearm, I had brought a checkbook, just in case.

"Oh, nothing to you. It comes under township wildlife control. He does it as a kind of hobby."

"Wonderful," I repeated once more. "It sounds almost too good to be true. Let me write a donation to the humane society. It's what my mother would have wanted, I know." I pondered the proper amount. A hundred dollars seemed not enough for the magnitude of the service. I pictured the waves of cats, gathered like gray sheaves into cages set out in the dawn's dewy light and harvested at twilight. Even two hundred seemed modest. I wrote a check for two hundred and fifty, which came to about six dollars a cat. The amount startled her, I could tell by the arch of her plucked and pencilled eyebrows. "And here's my number in Princeton if you ever need it," I said. "Could I have your card, so I can maybe call to check on progress?" I didn't want her, and her offer, to get away.

"Of course, Frank." She had stiffened; she had at last realized that she was a stranger to me—someone simply to use. The card said, "Amy Reidenhauer, Director, Boone Township Humane Society," with the same address as on my mother's note to me. I had cracked the code. I drove back to my farmhouse exhilarated, making the tires squeal on the winding Emmetstown road. It came to me that of all the women in the world I loved Amy Reidenhauer the best.

In the next two days, Max surprised me by being a great help in the packing up. While I stood around in the midst of my inheritance paralyzed by the imagined importance of everything, he made decisions. Keep this, take that. When he and I drove away in the yellow rental truck, we left the rest of the funeral meats in the woods, as a last feast for the cats. "O.K., kitties," I told them as they mewed up at my face. "Now you're on your own."

In the months to come, as fall activity was renewed in Princeton, I avoided going back. I was afraid of getting sucked in. Everything was handled over the telephone. It was almost eerie, to see society smoothly bring into play its perfected machinery for the transfer of property. My lawyer, another old high-school classmate, arranged for the estate assessment and sent me forms to sign and return. The real-estate agent kept me apprised of prospects and offers. When I asked him if he, on his latest showing of the house, had noticed any cats around the back porch, he pre-

"I'm not worried about you, Henley.
You'll land on your feet."

tended to search his memory before saying, "Why, no!" Their mewing, furry, hungry substance had vanished like the matter of a dream. My mother's meagre treasures—the rose-pattern china, the pine corner cupboard, the curly-maple sewing table, two lace tablecloths, some turquoise jewelry from my parents' one trip to the Southwest, and a brass tiger stamped on the bottom "Made in China" and forever marked by my childhood impressions of hugeness and menace, though it was scarcely six inches long—found their niches in our home or our daughter's, with a few pieces promised to Max when and if he ever settled down. Little Peter wanted the wind chimes. Josie inherited her yellow plastic dog dish. In Pennsylvania, the auction crew came into the house, cleaned it out of every tattered piece of

furniture and antique junk, including the *Life* magazines from V-E and V-J Days, and in late October sent me a respectable check for the proceeds at auction. In early November, the realtor had found a retired couple from Philadelphia whose bid was in the bottom end of my asking range, and who promised to keep renting the fields to Adam and Dwight. The buyers vowed they had no intention of developing the acreage but refused to sign a covenant without a sharp reduction in the price. I backed down. The farm could take its chances. We set the date of the signing for the Monday after Thanksgiving.

I felt guilty, selling the place. My mother had believed it to be a piece of lost Eden and wanted me to live on it for my own good. Pathetically, she would argue that I could still

"To this day, I can hear my mother's voice—harsh, accusing. 'Lost your mittens? You naughty kittens! Then you shall have no pie!'"

teach at Princeton, with a readjustment of my schedule that would bunch my teaching into a few days in the middle of the week. "What about my wife?" I asked.

"Tell Andrea," she said, "that I've never felt right, as a woman, off this place. There's magic in the soil, I do believe it. Two days away, and I used to get the most terrible cramps."

"My kids, Mother. They've been raised New York suburban."

This was before Nancy had married and Max dropped out of Dartmouth. "It's not too late to fix that," my mother said. "When they were smaller they used to love it here."

I sighed, and we dropped the subject, knowing that I was the problem. I was the one to whom the farm meant crabgrass and poison ivy, and bushwhacking that would be invisible the next summer, and indoor plumbing that was forty years out of date, and a pack of asthma-inducing cats at the back door.

I didn't call Amy Reidenhauer for weeks, and when I did she sounded vague. "I know he went out and looked the situation over," she said.

"But did he trap any?"

"He has the traps right now in his other truck, I think he told me. Anyway, he didn't see any cats."

"None? What time of day was he there?"

"I guess around their dinnertime," she said, with an audible smile in her voice. I saw her clearly, her pale lips half open on her moist teeth, sitting at her tidy desk in Emmetstown, with the wild ducks on the wall and the door leading back to the concrete-floored cages—a genie I had conjured but could not quite control, through some little glitch in interstate communications.

"I'd be happy to drive over," I told her, "but I don't see how it would do any good."

"No, Frank," she said sadly, as to a former lover. "I don't either."

Yet the persisting fact of the cats gnawed at me; at night I would wake up, with my mother's ghost wavering in the room, over where Andrea had dropped her white bathrobe on the back of a chair, and want to scream, in shame and helplessness. The runny-eyed kittens, staggering with hunger. Why had they been called into life? My mother, with more courage than I had, used to drown them, pressing one bucket down into another bucket half-filled with water and their peeping cries. My mother's humming returned to me, marking waltz time with the handle's rhythmic chunking noise, and with it came the whole sweet-and-sour aroma of the kitchen, the way she had shaped it with her life, all those mornings of rising alone, making coffee and pouring cereal, and ceremoniously feeding the cats, while the mantel clock sounded its gulping gong.

One morning, before I was really awake, Amy, taking pity, called me. "Well, he's been busy," she told me. "He must have brought two or three in every evening now for nearly two weeks. But, as he says, the others get more and more wary, so it may be a case of diminishing returns."

"Still, that's terrific progress. I'm *very* grateful. At that rate there can't be too many left."

"That's right," she said, "and the young ones you can count on dying of natural causes, especially now that we're having frosts."

I couldn't quite bring myself to say that I was grateful for that, too.

At the beginning of hunting season, Dwight called and told me he and Adam had posted my land. Did I mind? He knew, of course, that one of my mother's eccentricities was to leave her land unposted, to the annoyance of her neighbors. "They just want the shooting for themselves," she had explained to me. "Especially they don't want the Philadelphia blacks coming out here and finding any land to hunt on. One year, when I still had legs under me, I walked around and tore Dwight's signs down myself. No Hunting, except for him—it made me see red."

"No," I said. "I don't mind."

"I'm glad to hear it, Frank," Dwight said. "If I see any of those cats still around, I promise they won't live to tell the tale. Hunting season doesn't bode well for cats. Hunters see them as competition."

The last days of owning the farm were strange. It was as if I had a phantom limb; I could feel it move, but not see it. The papers were being signed the first day of December, and I thought I should go over the day before, check out the house and barn for any last remnants of our years there, and spend the night in a Reading motel. Thinking there might be a little last-minute brush-clearing or dirty lifting, I hung my suit in the car and put on a wool-lined olive-drab jacket, from an Army-surplus store, that my father used to wear on weekends, and that my mother inherited and would wear in winter, with not too bad a fit. I hadn't had the heart to leave it for the auctioneers to clear away. I put on the jacket and threw a pair of loppers and work gloves in the car.

But by the time I got away from my wife and my students, and made my way around Philadelphia, not many hours of daylight were left. The place when I pulled in was still—still as a picture. Green was gone from everything but the pines and the two holly trees, the male and the female. The orchard grass was an even slope of tan striped with shade. The woods beyond stood tall and silvery, the stalks of darkness between the trunks thickening in the four-o'clock light.

When I slammed the car door, it echoed off the barn wall in a way I had forgotten. When we first moved here, I used to stand in the yard and shout, marvelling at the echo, like the voice of a brother I didn't have.

The absence of an owner showed in a dozen little ways. I had paid a boy to keep the lawn mowed, but he had lazily left tousled fringes along the edges, and where the black walnut had dropped its pulpy shells on the lawn hadn't bothered to mow at all. I put on the coat and carried the loppers, though I doubted I would find much to do—perhaps just check the fragile weeping cherry tree for fallen branches, and cut some raspberry canes out of the hosta beds my mother had planted when we moved. As I drifted across the lank grass, a few shadows filtered out of the orchard and flickered toward the house, eagerly loping. Several more materialized from the direction of the woods. The cats had survived. They thought I was my mother and good times had returned.

| 2003 |

DAY AND AGE

Skimming by,
the milky spill of my old eye,
the mute white cat
now skirts me at the store.
Retarded and alert.

What good are instincts anymore?
Who does the math
for lengths of desperation
and how far to the door?

A woman, pregnant
like a red wool bud,
is circling the rink.
Catastrophe, I think.

—Dana Goodyear | 2003 |

A CAT IN EVERY HOME

KATHARINE T. KINKEAD

Robert Lothar Kendell, the president of the American Feline Society, Inc., and perhaps the world's most tireless defender of the cat, is an advertising man by profession. The latest agency list of the McKittrick *Directory of Advertisers*, a standard work of reference in the field, shows his firm, a one-man organization called Continental Advertising Associates, to have eleven accounts. Three of these—Grapho-Institute, a correspondence graphology course; the Kendell Company of America, a manufacturer of public-address systems; and the Sivad Press, book publishers—are inactive businesses of Kendell's. Seven of the remainder range from chinaware to apparel, and a substantial share of the fees Kendell receives from them goes to help operate the eleventh, the American Feline Society, described by McKittrick's as a charity. The Society's deficit for 1950, according to its most recent annual report, signed early this year by Kendell, was more than seven thousand dollars, and its cumulative loss over the past five years has been nineteen thousand dollars. As a client, the Society would not appear to be one in which the ordinary advertising man would take much pride.

A copy of the Society's annual report having fallen into my hands, I called Mr. Kendell up and made an appointment with him, hoping to learn something about the organization's aims and activities. This resulted in my making my way, one recent blustery afternoon, to his place of business, at 41 Union Square West, which turned out to be an old-fashioned building devoted mostly to small suites for small businessmen. A creaky elevator let me out at the ninth floor, and I approached

Mr. Kendell's office down a long, dim corridor scarcely four feet wide. At the far end of it was a glass door lettered with the names of his advertising firm, of the American Feline Society, and of his three inactive businesses. Through the door came the steady thump-thump of a typewriter. There was a suggestion of soft but im-

"Didn't I see you on YouTube riding a Roomba?"

portunate haste in the machine's sound. It stopped at my knock, and a man's well-modulated voice bade me enter. I did so, and found myself in a small room, facing its only occupant, a man in shirtsleeves, who rose from his typewriter desk and introduced himself courteously to me as Mr. Kendell. He is a rather handsome, thickset man of about fifty, with hazel eyes, a sparse mustache, a gentle, if rather nervous, manner, and a barrel chest, implying an abundance of physical energy. It required no great exercise of the imagination to see him as an executive in a midtown advertising office, nursing his ulcers, and holding his clients by his quiet, intense manner.

It was at once apparent from Mr. Kendell's surroundings, however, that somewhere along the line he had missed connections with the Madison Avenue crowd, and that his interests had been sharply diverted. The room I was standing in, only about eight feet by twelve and somewhat overheated, was lit by a single window, against which, from time to time, the wind blew in gusts, rattling the panes and giving the place a feeling of lonesomeness that was in no way lessened by a view of gray, bare rooftops. The office had the atmosphere of a forgotten storeroom,

being jammed with tattered, haphazardly piled cardboard cartons. The walls, from floor to ceiling, were lined either with shelves, from which protruded literature about cats and accessories for cats, or with bulletin boards displaying innumerable photographs of cats—cats yawning, cats playing, cats sleeping, cats pouncing, cats watching birds, cats smirking over spreading ribbon bows, cats looking bored or supercilious, cats suffering the gingerly fondling of movie stars clad in bathing suits or evening gowns, cats staring in amazement out of airplanes. It was impossible to avoid their gaze. Hanging from wall to wall near the ceiling was a large, faded red, white, and blue banner reading, "Help Save America's Cats!" Most of the room's contents, including the banner, were covered with a fine layer of dust.

In the midst of all this stood Mr. Kendell, smiling. "Our headquarters," he said proudly, and waved a hand about him. Then, realizing there was no place for me to sit, he hastily removed from a chair several large boxes, which, he said, contained shipments of food and medicine awaiting distribution to needy cats, and, relieving me of my wraps, seated me at a desk facing his. Before resuming his own seat, he went to a small basin by the window and carefully washed his hands, a performance he repeated several times during my stay, whenever he had touched any of the cartons stacked around the room.

I told Mr. Kendell that I was interested in finding out about the objectives of the American Feline Society, and, to my surprise, his cordiality lessened a bit. His answer was formal and measured. "Young lady, I doubtless could give you exactly the information that you want," he said. "But first I must ask you a question. Are you an aelurophobe?"

"A what?" I asked, not sure that I had caught the word.

"An aelurophobe—a cat-hater," he said.

Under Mr. Kendell's watchful scrutiny, I was glad that I could truthfully give a negative reply. "Of course not!" I assured him.

"Good," Mr. Kendell said, his manner relaxing to its earlier gentleness. "Aelurophobes are not welcome in this office. You'd be surprised how they disguise themselves. Doctors, scientists, garden-club women, and wildlife conservationists are some of the worst." Even the humane societies, he told me, are among the sworn enemies of cats. "Why, in this city alone, the A.S.P.C.A. last year, according to its own published records, killed over a hundred and sixty-three thousand cats," he said. "Criminal! Criminal!" he added, lowering his voice in sadness.

As we sat talking in the close, curious little office, I discovered that Mr. Kendell is a man with a staggering amount of information about cats. Although his feelings on the subject are obviously strong, he spoke, for the most part, softly, which lent effectiveness to what he had to say. Only occasionally did he betray the depth of his emotion.

"In ancient Egypt, cats were embalmed and placed in golden urns," Mr. Kendell said. "In pioneer days, they rode as honored guests in covered wagons, protecting our forefathers' grain supply from the innumerable rats that followed the caravans across the Western plains. *Today*, they are murdered. Of the twenty-one million cats that I estimate there are in this country, half, or ten and a half million, are strays—hungry, unloved, persecuted. Dogs all have strong organizations behind them. But does the cat, the noblest of animals? No! He lacks even an official position in our culture." It is the foremost aim of the American Feline Society, Mr. Kendell told me, to smooth the path of life for the nation's ten and a half million homeless cats—a group that, he declared, had had no sponsor whatever until the Society came along. "By the way," he said, peering at me suddenly, "never say 'alley cat.' Say 'short-haired.'"

I promised Mr. Kendell I would remember that, and asked about the size of his organization. "We have approximately three thousand members, eighty percent of them women," he said. "Our members live in forty-seven states, Alaska, Hawaii, and Puerto Rico, and also in Canada, Costa Rica, France, Mexico, New Zealand, and Switzerland. The roster includes college professors, stockbrokers, housewives, veterinarians, river pilots, bohemians, and Miss June Havoc, who recently joined. Most of our members are in the subscription class, paying five-dollar annual dues—that's the lowest of the four types of membership, which go up to the two-hundred-and-fifty-dollar life membership. Therefore, in theory, we have a neat nest egg with which to start operations each year, but in practice, unfortunately, this is not so. Some members' offerings arrive in pitiful dribs and drabs—nickels and dimes, the only way they can pay. Many never pay more than part of their dues, and others are habitually in arrears." Mr. Kendell told me he combats the tendency of the Society to fall apart financially by increasing his own contributions to it and allotting it more and more of his time. He has succeeded, against what must often have seemed discouraging odds, in building an international organization, and in this country has set up a nationwide network of non-salaried vice-presidents—one each in Brooklyn, Chicago, Knoxville, Los Angeles, San Antonio, and Flint, Michigan. "This arrangement frequently helps our work," he said. "For instance, a couple of years ago, when I read in the papers that the four cats of Angus Ward, the American Consul General at Mukden, were Stateside-bound with their master aboard the Lakeland Victory after being imprisoned in Communist China on starvation rations, I instantly ordered our Los Angeles vice-president to send thirty pounds of cat food direct from that city, via Pan American Airways, to be held for the refugees' arrival when their steamer docked in Yokohama—a mercy flight that gained invaluable time by getting its start on the Pacific Coast."

Notwithstanding the vice-presidents, and a board of directors that meets once a year in New York, Mr. Kendell is the man who holds the Society together. "I am a publicist, and the Society needs that kind of leadership just now," he said. "Because it's necessary to sell cats, as a package, to America." When I inquired how he went about selling cats as a package, he sighed. "It's a big job," he said. "I keep the editors of newspapers, wire services, magazines, and radio networks constantly informed as to the care, protection, and betterment of living conditions of the short-haired cat wherever it may be found throughout the world. Furthermore, I instantly

attack in these same quarters any defamation of the short-haired cat by knowing or unknowing enemies, no matter who they are. With local editors, I do this by telephone, and with more distant ones by sending out publicity releases that I write up and have mimeographed under the Society's letterhead." Mr. Kendell added that his reading of newspapers, magazines, and books is voluminous, and I gathered that his reaction to any reference to cats he may come across is highly individual and given swift circulation. In a single week, he said, he sometimes issues releases to over three thousand newspapers and other periodicals, a hundred and forty-six wire services and syndicates, and the country's four major radio networks—a feat that he is as likely as not to repeat the following week. In these communiqués, he stresses such inequities or indignities as that throughout the whole country only the forward-looking city of Seattle requires licenses for cats, that Maine's personal-property tax on them is unenforced, and that, in contrast to the legal protection afforded dogs and human beings, no state in the Union has a law designed specifically for the protection of cats. On occasion, the bombarded editors reverse the process and write to Mr. Kendell, requesting information about cats, which he supplies promptly. Moreover, he keeps the Society's members informed by mail of his activities, and asks that they, in turn, let him hear news of cats, thereby immeasurably broadening his outlook. "Sooner or later," he told me reflectively, "*all* cat facts pass through this room."

Mr. Kendell observed that one of his recent chores was the compilation of the world's largest list of friends of the cat—some ninety-two thousand presumed aelurophiles, whose names and addresses he acquired from the newspapers he himself has read or from clippings sent to him by members. To the more promising-sounding cat-

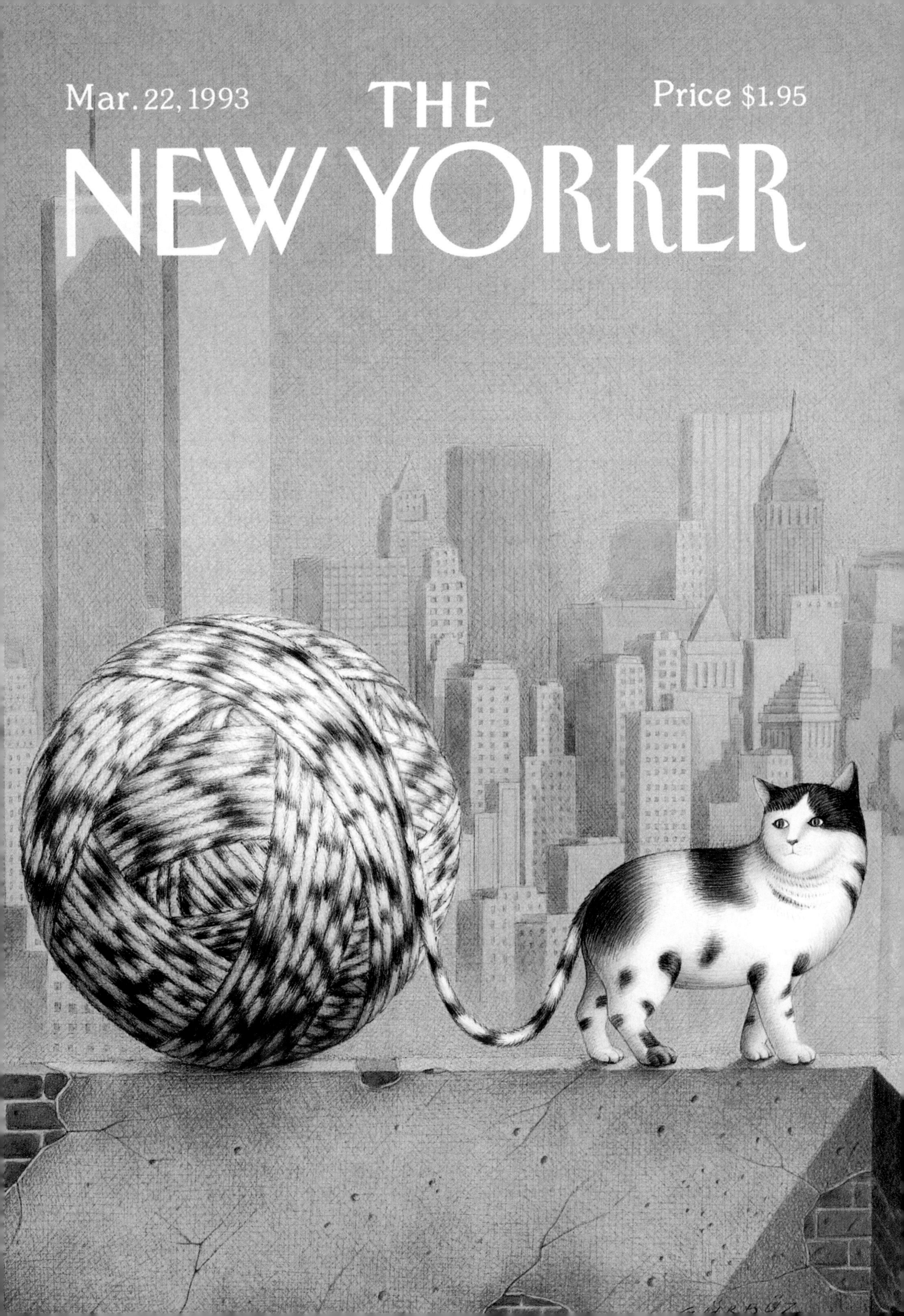
Mar. 22, 1993
THE
NEW YORKER
Price $1.95

GREGORY

"Okay, here's the deal—I'll stop chasing you if you agree to become a dog."

lovers on this huge list, he annually posts news of the feline world, as well as a cordial invitation to join the Society. Another job he has just finished, after two years of labor, is the preparation, for the convenience of his members, of a complete card catalogue of the more than one thousand manufacturers of cat accessories in this country—a formidable inventory that includes the makers of brushes, deodorants, jewelry, toys, blankets, trophies, bells, mats, and so on. "The alpha and omega of purveyors to cats!" murmured Mr. Kendell triumphantly, holding up a box full of file cards. In addition to all these activities, Mr. Kendell said, he daily performs half a dozen or so "service operations for the short-haired"—special attentions of one kind or another to the needs of individual cats.

I remarked that his efforts on behalf of the Society must keep him very busy. He nodded glumly. "Yes," he said. "And sometimes financially embarrassed, too. The Society's annual intake, you know, seldom amounts to more than three thousand dollars. This means I'm often

strapped to keep it going." Then his expression grew strained, as if he were returning to some ancient inner debate. "My advertising clients think I'm peculiar to spend so much time on cats," he said. "They even go so far as to tell me so. They don't seem to understand that I'm not in this for money. When you think of all the homeless cats in the world, you realize that somebody must take care of them. What's peculiar about that? Do *you* think it's peculiar?"

I said I didn't think it peculiar for anyone to do what seemed right to him. "Exactly!" Mr. Kendell said, more brightly. "My first wife, who started the Society in 1938, was in all respects the same as I am. She was the sort of woman who would get up at four in the morning to rescue a cat marooned in a tree." His present wife, he went on, whom he married, as a widower, in 1947, is also in complete accord with his views on cats. Fortunately, being a wage earner, she is able to help the Society along with her salary. "Perhaps I've always felt so strongly about cats because I've been childless," Mr. Kendell said. "But whatever the reason, this resistance to the Society gets me down. However, enough!" he added, disciplining himself with a smile. "Every organization struggles at first. Someday we'll get going in a big way, and when we do, watch us travel! Our initial moves are all planned out. Here in Manhattan, for instance, we'll have a National Headquarters Building, with a Trophy Hall, to house the statuary, mementos, and portraits that our members keep willing us of their pets. Then, every big city in the country will have a model twenty-thousand-dollar cat shelter, like that one." He called my attention to a framed drawing on one of the bulletin boards, which he said he'd had an architect turn out for him. Its floor plan included kitchens, dormitories, and an observation room for cats, and quarters for resident attendants. "Eventually," he said, "this country will have a national law, like Hong Kong's, requiring every home to have a cat."

"Is there actually such a law in Hong Kong?" I asked.

"Of course!" Mr. Kendell said. He went over to a cardboard container that served as a filing cabinet and extracted from it a cablegram the Governor of Hong Kong had sent him—in response to one of his own—confirming the law's existence. After replacing the communication, he walked over to the basin and washed his hands. As he was drying them, he looked at me thoughtfully. "How many cats do you have?" he asked.

"None," I answered in considerable embarrassment.

Mr. Kendell's face froze. "Young lady!" he said, aghast. "Do you realize you're depriving yourself of one of life's most glorious experiences? Here! Look at this letter that came in today from a new member." Discarding his towel, he picked up a sheet of paper from his desk, with a Park Avenue address engraved at its head, and handed it to me. "The enclosed check is from my two neutered males, Francis and Marcel, aged eight and twelve years old, respectively," the letter read. "They have let me live with them all their lives, and have taught me what a cat needs and gives in politeness, grace, faithfulness, cleanliness, intelligence, and affection. No matter what some biassed humans may say, I know that cats are the most loyal friends we have. I pray for the time people will recognize this and the world will become a true cat-and-man Utopia!"

I put the letter down. "I have two small

CAT IN THE CAGE

Hold tight to your chairs, folks, for this is a nature story about a remarkable cat. You may have trouble believing it but it's true, as you can find out by dropping around to 40 East Forty-ninth Street, where the Penthouse Galleries are. The cat belongs to the building, in a manner of speaking, and is fed twice a day in the superintendent's apartment, which is on the twentieth floor. Well, twice a day, at meal times, the cat strolls through the lobby of the building, enters an elevator cage, and rides up to the twentieth floor, where she disembarks and has her dinner. Remarkable? People get on and off at other floors, on the way up. The cat never does, not even if you miaow to her and try to tempt her. The elevator-boys do nothing to guide her; she just sits in the cage watching, and presumably counting, or else reading the numbers of the floors.

| 1931 |

children," I said defensively. "I'm afraid a cat might scratch them."

"Good heavens, young lady!" said Mr. Kendell, throwing up his hands. "Sometimes I feel like giving up. Here I am, working day and night, broadcasting factual information about cats, and *you* make a statement like that." With a reproachful look, he leaned toward me. "Pardon me," he said in a silky voice. He put his hand across the desk, the fingers talonlike on my arm. Speaking slowly, as one does to impress a child, he said, "I—will—explain. Cats—don't—scratch—people. People—scratch—cats. Cats like to open and close their paws against a person's skin—thus." He kneaded my flesh with his fingertips. "Now, if, at a time like this, an ignorant person makes a sudden movement, naturally the cat's claws sink into the epidermis. That's not the cat's fault. It's the person who's to blame, for not being better coordinated with his pet. Your ignorance of this principle causes me real concern." Mr. Kendell looked at me steadily, making sure I understood.

I said that perhaps I had been wrong in my fears, and hastily asked Mr. Kendell to tell me about his service operations. At once, his face re-assumed its customary gentle expression. "Our service operations vary greatly, but they are all free of charge," he said. "We maintain an adoption service, for instance, with normally a list of about four hundred cats on file waiting for new homes. As a rule, we don't take physical possession of a cat except in an emergency—just get the right parties together by phone. To new owners using our adoption service, we issue pamphlets called 'How to Receive Your Cat' and 'Cat Facts,' both of which I wrote." He handed me two leaflets, and I noted that one of them listed as necessities for the new arrival a "comfortable bed complete with kapok pillow and tiny blanket; special feeding and drinking vessels; collar, harness, and leash; metal toilet pan; scratching post and catnip-impregnated toys."

Mr. Kendell turned to a batch of filing cards on which he had kept a record of service operations completed the preceding month, and read me a few of them. One case involved arranging for a mate for a cat in Pocatello, Idaho; in another, a lady in New Jersey who accepts up to thirty cats for boarding in her home had been prevailed upon to look after the pet of a visiting Englishwoman until she got settled in the city. Mr. Kendell dwelt at length upon a third case— "an especially pitiful one," he called it. A cat had deserted its master in an apartment house on East Fifty-seventh Street and had gone to the basement to live with the janitor, from whom it refused to be enticed even by breast of chicken, its favorite tidbit. When the grieving owner consulted the Society, Mr. Kendell suggested that the man acquire another cat, explaining to him that he must have in some way bored or disgusted the original cat. The man reluctantly agreed to this solution. "I never saw a poor fellow so broken up, but I felt the kindest thing was to tell him the truth," Mr. Kendell said to me. "Doubtless his own personality was at fault. It may have been just a simple case of trying too hard. But, whatever it was, I knew the cat's decision was irrevocable. As I told this man, a horse will forget its feeling toward a particular person in six months, but a cat—never." Mr. Kendell illustrated this faculty of memory in cats by reminiscing about one that he and his first wife had owned. It had shown its fondness for a certain male friend of theirs by pouncing on his hat whenever he visited their home. After an absence of several years, the friend made a surprise call on them, during the war. He was in uniform and forty pounds heavier, and at first the Kendells didn't recognize him. "But the cat at once leaped for the cap in his hand," Mr. Kendell said, with a triumphant smile.

There was silence in the stuffy little room. A gust of wind shook the panes.

"Also," said Mr. Kendell presently, "cats can talk."

"What?" I said.

"Of course!" he went on. "One of the commonest fallacies is that they can't. Actually, the average cat has a vocabulary of from fifty to sixty definitely distinguishable words. The words are formed by nuances of sound from the cat's highly developed vocal cords, accompanied by the proper facial expression. When my two cats, for example, want an egg, they gallop for the icebox, all the time making the sound that means 'eggs.' It goes like this." Mr. Kendell opened his mouth wide and emitted a rolling "Me-ow!," assuming, as he did so, what I took to be the proper facial expression for "eggs"—one of wide-eyed gravity.

"Naturally," he continued, "the 'egg' sound is totally different from the word for 'milk,' which goes like this." Mr. Kendell narrowed his eyes and opened his mouth again, and this time a sharp, plaintive "Meow!" emerged. "Needless to say, there are sounds for all the other common ideas or objects, such as 'outside,' 'please,' 'thank you,' 'fish,' 'liver,' and so on," he said. "Any owner correctly attuned to his cat understands these. Conversely, cats can understand human speech. Let an owner say to his wife 'Why don't you open the window for Puss?' and the cat's there in a bound. What's more, cats can read printed labels on cans, or at least labels that concern them. For instance, they show not the slightest interest in a tin of kitchen cleanser the exact size of a tin of salmon, but let the tin of salmon appear and they set up their request murmur—a deep-throated purr accompanied by upward glances." Mr. Kendell glanced upward and purred. It was a resonant, authentic sound. I had the impression that if I were to close my eyes, I would feel myself in the room with a cat possessed of vocal cords of extraordinary power and timbre.

At that moment, the door opened and a postman crowded into the office. He seemed impressed to find Mr. Kendell purring. "Here's another one of them sacks—and some more cat mail," he said, dropping on Mr. Kendell's desk a large, pungent-smelling cloth bag, whose odor came pleasantly to me through the still air, and three envelopes addressed to the Society. Then, after looking at Mr. Kendell interestedly over his shoulder, the postman left.

Mr. Kendell stopped purring and swiftly reached for the three envelopes. He examined their postmarks eagerly, turned them over to scrutinize the return addresses, and shook them. "No coins," he said tersely. It suddenly seemed very important to him—as it seemed to me, just

then—that the American Feline Society get some contributions. He tore open the envelopes. The first two contained no money, and he slapped them angrily on the desk. "Terrible! Terrible!" he burst out. His face had the hurt look that can come into a thwarted child's. The third envelope contained a check. "Ha!" said Mr. Kendell. "Ha!" His countenance suddenly brightened, like an autumn field unexpectedly swept by sunshine. He smiled. "Of course, support means more than just mere money," he said to me. "*Much* more. Now pardon me while I write out an acknowledgment for this before I forget it." He slipped some forms and carbon paper into his typewriter and batted out a message, saying, as he did so, "It's wonderful, *wonderful*, to know you're not alone in the fight."

When Mr. Kendell had finished, he laid the papers to one side and, still smiling, picked up the sack. "Catnip from one of our members, for free distribution by the Society," he said. "The highest quality, fresh from the Pennsylvania mountains. Not a stem in the batch." He swung the sack up alongside some others on top of a pile of cartons, and in doing so tumbled a white wooden tray to the floor. Before replacing it, he showed it to me, saying, "One of the custom-made Cat-a-terias the Society will order for members. Just sent a minister in Iowa six the other day. Very attractive little things." The Cat-a-teria, which was supported on legs, contained two feeding dishes and was decorated with gaily colored figures of sardines and mice. There was also a space in which to inscribe a pet's monogram. "You never can do too much for your short-hairs," Mr. Kendell said gently.

Back at his desk, Mr. Kendell produced two large scrapbooks filled with some of his press releases and the publicity they have inspired. "Since our most vital work is public education, you'll want to look at these," he said. As I turned the pages, I was amazed at the number of publications, including big metropolitan dailies, that have carried cat stories obviously prompted by Mr. Kendell's releases, which he had pasted beside the clippings. The scrapbooks also held numerous newspaper photographs, cartoons, letters to the editor, and editorials based on Kendell releases, as well as quantities of columns by such syndicated writers as Paul Gallico, Bugs Baer,

"Can I borrow those kittens for an hour? I want
to freak out the people who had me spayed."

Bob Hope, George Sokolsky, Frederick Oth-man, and Robert Ruark.

Much, but by no means all, of the material in the books was concerned with the annual obser-vance of National Cat Week, late in the fall. This event was inaugurated by the Society in 1946, and for its promotion, Mr. Kendell told me, he goes into what is, even for him, extraordinarily high gear. "For several weeks before the event, I put in eighteen hours a day, seven days a week—a taxing schedule," he said. "But when I think of the number of needy cats, I easily find the strength to go on." His National Cat Week program in-volves not only stepping up his writing and mail-ing out of releases but calling on the publicity representatives of recording and broadcasting companies and making personal appearances for the cause, as he did on one occasion on a C.B.S. radio program entitled "Pets." He tries to enlist the aid of recording-company publicity men in choosing an official song for the occasion (in 1949, the last time he was successful, it was "The Pussycat Song"), and urges broadcasting stations to have their disc jockeys feature the tune, with appropriate remarks. Crowning his efforts during this hectic season, Mr. Kendell adds to his long regular mailing list a rotating selection of Holly-wood press agents who, he has discovered, can be induced to prepare photographs of some of their more photogenic female clients in the act of cud-dling cats. "Hollywood has a genuine cat appre-ciation, for which we are very grateful," he told me. Each year, a dozen or so actresses are so pho-tographed, and their press agents supply gratis hundreds of glossy prints for captioning by Mr. Kendell, who then sends them to newspapers, many of which give them an encouragingly en-thusiastic reception. In the past, Greer Garson, Ann Jeffreys, Janet Blair, Dale Evans, Barbara Bates, and Elizabeth Taylor have been among

those tapped. As a windup to Hollywood's par-ticipation, Mr. Kendell names as chairman of National Cat Week an actress playing in a cur-rent film whose cast includes a cat, and the cat is named honorary chairman—to the clicking of more cameras.

Each year, as a matter of course, Mr. Kendell petitions President Truman for government rec-ognition of National Cat Week. But things are not as they should be between the two leaders. There has been a coolness, Mr. Kendell said, dat-ing from Mr. Truman's first term, when the Pres-ident, at a National Press Club dinner, referred slightingly to cats and added, with definite jocu-larity, that there were even some people urging him to proclaim a National Cat Week. As Mr. Kendell told me this, his gentlemanly voice grew sharp. "Naturally the papers called me about it, and naturally I wrote the President at once, sug-gesting he withdraw his remark," he said. "Natu-rally he did so, at his next press conference, explaining he had been critical of two-legged, not four-legged, cats—still not the observation of a man who thinks intelligently about cats, but one that I decided it would be useless to protest."

Returning to the scrapbooks, Mr. Kendell pointed to evidence of some other achieve-ments of his that struck me as arresting. Dur-ing the war, for instance, he launched a Ration Point Pool for Cats. As a result of the publicity given the pool, vegetarians and theosophists all over the country sent their unused red, or meat, ration stamps to the Society in such numbers that they lay around the office in large paper bags, awaiting calls from the owners of protein-starved cats. Again, shortly after the war, Mr. Kendell checked a threat to the cats of New Jersey in the person of a Canadian fur buyer. This man, who claimed to have found a way of processing cat fur into "Prairie Sable," was canvassing the schools of Jersey, offering a fur coat free to any teacher who sent him a specified number of cat skins collected by her pupils. "Imagine—trapping cats!" said Mr. Kendell. By the time Mr. Kendell got through assailing the plan—getting in touch with Jersey educators directly and with Jersey clergymen through the press and radio—the fur buyer was in full flight; when last heard from, he had retreated to his own country, where he was engaged in a similar project involving Canadian rats.

Despite the value of such campaigns, they benefit, after all, only cats in this country, and Mr. Kendell told me that he is happiest when he is assisting cats on a global scale. "Fortunately, these opportunities come to me often. For example," he said, pointing out a clipping in one of the scrapbooks, "that story was the result of a telephone call to me a couple of years ago from an English newspaper's American representative here in New York. He informed me that several eastern counties in England were undergoing the severest sort of cat-influenza epidemic, and asked if I could help. Could I! I phoned a Missouri veterinarian whom I had seen cure several cats of influenza by a serum and told him the situation. He gave me the phone numbers of the Indiana whole-

saler of the serum and of its Kansas manufacturer, and within a matter of minutes I had spoken to both of them. Oh, the Society works quickly, I can tell you! A few hours later, five hundred cubic centimeters of the medicine had arrived here by plane, under refrigeration. It was immediately flown on to London and rushed from the airport there, under motorcycle escort, to the British Ministry of Agriculture. Soon after, the influenza epidemic subsided."

Another of Mr. Kendell's foreign maneuvers was a proposal of his that the White House adopt two British royal kittens, Jane and Belinda, that were born in the Silver Room of Buckingham Palace a fortnight or so after Roosevelt's fourth election. "This was a terrifically important project to cats, both here and abroad," Mr. Kendell said quietly. "Besides cementing Anglo-American relations no end, it would have furnished a magnificent opportunity to scotch, once and for all, the superstition that the presence of a cat in the White House brings immediate death to the President." I said I hadn't known there was such a belief. "Indeed there is!" said Mr. Kendell. "I'm surprised you haven't heard of it. One of the most pernicious calumnies prevailing today. The canard seems to have started after the assassination of McKinley, when it was said a cat was seen around the Executive Mansion the preceding evening. Supposedly it was confirmed—ha, ha, I say!—when another cat was reported to have appeared there the night before Harding's death." Mr. Kendell told me that the idea of a Presidential adoption came to him the minute he read about the birth of the palace kittens. "I decided the Society should sponsor the move, and I at once re-

A man from Nyack has told us a story which goes back to the recent mating season and concerns two powerfully built tomcats who, with hate in their hearts, fought a duel just before dawn on somebody's lawn. The sun rose to reveal the scene of battle, the fighters gone, the grass covered with cat fur. Very soon there appeared many of the birds that had selected Nyack for their summer home. They quickly cleared the lawn of fur, using it to line their nests. A fable for our time.

| 1943 |

"Everyone be home by two o'clock!"

Mr. Kendell looked at me as if I were hopelessly stupid. "Merely by introducing them properly," he said. "You simply hold the dog and cat a few feet apart until they get each other's scent. Then you push them together until their noses touch. After that, they're fast friends. I've done it hundreds of times. Utter nonsense, Fala hating cats!" Mr. Kendell was, of course, much disappointed when the adoption plan failed to come off, but he stood up manfully under the blow. "When the papers asked for my reaction, I made a simple public statement," he said. "I declared, quote, I most profoundly regret that the Roosevelts do not seem big enough to upset the White House cat superstition and the preposterous dog-cat enmity theory as they have the two-term Presidential tradition, unquote."

leased word to that effect to English and American newspapers," he said. "Then I wired the President's daughter, Mrs. Boettiger, whom I knew slightly, to do what she could to hasten the adoption."

The next day, the story was widely published in the British and American press. A few hours later, Mrs. Roosevelt announced that the plan was impractical, because Fala hated cats. "What an irony!" Mr. Kendell said. "What an absurd end to a great opportunity! Fala hating cats! Why, in ten minutes I could have had him and the kittens playing beautifully together for the rest of their lives."

"How?" I asked.

To the general public, Mr. Kendell may be best, if now only dimly, remembered as the author, in 1948, of the gigantic Cats for Europe scheme—a plan to send a million American cats to the Marshall Plan countries to rid them of rats. This project, he told me, originated as the result of his reading a statement in an English magazine that something like 40 percent of Europe's food in storage, including Marshall Plan consignments, was being destroyed by rats, which were multiplying rapidly because over a million European cats had disappeared during the war. Mr. Kendell saw a chance to strike a blow both for America's homeless short-hairs and for her allies' food supply, and swiftly went into action, one result being, according to an awed clipping-bureau official who in due course telephoned him, that during a single week more than six million column-inches of articles describing the plan were printed in papers here and abroad—very likely the greatest sustained publicity barrage ever laid down in the interests of cats. Offers of cats poured into the Society's headquarters by the thousand, and in the midst of all the bustle Mr. Kendell sent the following memorable cablegram to an English newspaper editor for his guidance: "NEGOTIATIONS REFERENCE 50,000 CATS FOR EUROPE BEGUN WITH STATE DEPARTMENT." The message related only to the proposed initial shipment, which was to be headed by an aerial task force of five thousand cats. "Our plans were well laid," said Mr. Kendell. "We wanted no pets, no fancies, but hardened American short-hairs who could take it and dish it out. Several airlines were found that would fly the cats over in groups of seventeen hundred, five cats per crate, in heated DC-4 cargo planes, and the lines also agreed to lend hangar space at LaGuardia Field where the cats could be examined for health and temperament, inoculated, and registered with a serially numbered tag affixed to one ear. The cost, around a million and a half dollars for the first fifty thousand cats, I figured was to be borne by the Marshall Plan, with the trade associations of the various countries and the Society itself assisting."

The State Department, however, suggested that Mr. Kendell take up his proposal direct with the appropriate government bureaus of the Marshall Plan countries, and the scheme got entangled in red tape, from which it has yet to be extricated. Mr. Kendell was telling me that France and Italy still have the plan under favorable consideration and that he expects enthusiasm for it to pick up over all of Western Europe as soon as the red tape is cut away when the telephone rang.

Mr. Kendell answered it and carried on an animated conversation for several minutes, during which he frenziedly made pencilled notes on a piece of paper he had snatched up. Then he turned to me, breathing rapidly. There were traces of perspiration on his temples.

"That was one of the wire services!" Mr. Kendell told me excitedly. "They were relaying to me the extraordinary deed of a Dr. William Orr, a veterinarian of Minerva, Ohio, who has just miraculously saved the life of a cat that got trapped in a brick kiln out there." I had noticed that whenever Mr. Kendell talked about the misfortunes or sufferings of cats, he was inclined to lower his voice. Now he was talking almost in a whisper. "Brick kilns get frightfully hot, you know," he said. "How the cat got in this one is a mystery. But when the workers opened it to take out the baked bricks, after thirty-six hours of continuous operation at between six hundred and nine hundred degrees Fahrenheit, there was poor pussy—terribly dehydrated, its tail and paw pads scorched off, scarcely able to move. What chance did it have for survival? None, you'd say. But after almost a week of skillful medical attention and selfless, twenty-four-hour care, Dr. Orr pulled his patient through. What altruism! What an act of devotion to cats! I must notify our membership at once. I must poll our board of directors on awarding

Dr. Orr the Society's special citation for humanity. Please excuse me." The soft sound of his voice ceased, and the room was quiet except for the wind chuffing outside.

Mr. Kendell turned quickly to his typewriter, inserted some paper, and, without a preliminary pause, began hitting the keys. It was time for me to go. He seemed so absorbed that I didn't interrupt him to say goodbye. I doubt whether he was even conscious of my leaving the little room. Quietly, I closed the door behind me. Lights now burned in the other offices along the hall. Back of the glass in Mr. Kendell's door there was only the late-afternoon gloom. But through it came the thump-thump of a typewriter, hurrying as though to make up for lost time.

| 1951 |

"Today is the day I start the new me!"

CAT HOUSE

MAEVE BRENNAN

A fact with which everybody who knows cats can't help being acquainted is that their traditional sign of true devotion to human beings is bringing to them, and leaving with them, gruesome offerings, such as mice, rats, birds, that they have caught and killed. Even when the person so honored knows who the cat is, he is faced with a problem that isn't easy to solve. Well, we ran into an old-fashioned artist friend of ours the other day who lives on the top floor of an old-fashioned five-story building in the southernmost part of Greenwich Village. The building, he tells us, has long been infested by both rats and cats. The cats hold a slight edge and, conscious of their worth and function, lounge around on the stairs of the building when they're not working, and have to be stepped over by the tenants, all of whom prefer the cats to the rats. Our friend swears he has never owned one of the cats himself and hasn't even petted one or spoken to one, but somewhere in that herd is a cat who has taken a fancy to him and has been honoring him, every two or three days, by toiling all the way up to the top floor during the night with the offering that might be expected and depositing it just outside his door, where he can't help seeing it first thing in the morning. He's thought of trying to make all the cats hate him by kicking at them on the stairs, but he's a gentle chap, and besides, he says, the stairways in the building are very badly lighted. He doesn't know what to do. His attitude toward the matter leads us to suspect that any day now the poor fellow may be driven to abandon his studio and that loving, unknown cat.

| 1955 |

TOWN OF CATS

Fiction

HARUKI MURAKAMI

At Koenji Station, Tengo boarded the Chuo Line inbound rapid-service train. The car was empty. He had nothing planned that day. Wherever he went and whatever he did (or didn't do) was entirely up to him. It was ten o'clock on a windless summer morning, and the sun was beating down. The train passed Shinjuku, Yotsuya, Ochanomizu, and arrived at Tokyo Central Station, the end of the line. Everyone got off, and Tengo followed suit. Then he sat on a bench and gave some thought to where he should go. "I can go anywhere I decide to," he told himself. "It looks as if it's going to be a hot day. I could go to the seashore." He raised his head and studied the platform guide.

At that point, he realized what he had been doing all along.

He tried shaking his head a few times, but the idea that had struck him would not go away. He had probably made up his mind unconsciously the moment he boarded the Chuo Line train in Koenji. He heaved a sigh, stood up from the bench, and asked a station employee  for the fastest connection to Chikura. The man flipped through the pages of a thick volume of train schedules. He should take the 11:30 special express train to Tateyama, the man said, and transfer there to a local; he would arrive at Chikura shortly after two o'clock. Tengo bought a Tokyo–Chikura round-trip ticket. Then he went to a restaurant in the station and ordered rice and curry and a salad.

Going to see his father was a depressing prospect. He had never much liked the man, and his father had no special love for him, either. He had retired four years earlier and, soon afterward, entered a sanatorium in Chikura that specialized in patients with cognitive disorders. Tengo had visited him there no more than twice—the first time just after he had entered the facility, when a procedural problem required Tengo, as the only relative, to be there. The second visit had also involved an administrative matter. Two times: that was it.

The sanatorium stood on a large plot of land by the coast. It was an odd combination of elegant old wooden buildings and new three-story reinforced-concrete buildings. The air was fresh, however, and, aside from the roar of the surf, it was always quiet. An imposing pine grove formed a windbreak along the edge of the garden. And the medical facilities were excellent. With his health insurance, retirement bonus, savings, and pension, Tengo's father could probably spend the rest of his life there quite comfortably. He might not leave behind any sizable inheritance, but at least he would be taken care of, for which Tengo was tremendously grateful. Tengo had no intention of taking anything from him or giving anything to him. They were two separate human beings who had come from—and were heading toward—entirely different places. By chance, they had spent some years of life together—that was all. It was a shame that it had come to that, but there was absolutely nothing that Tengo could do about it.

Tengo paid his check and went to the platform to wait for the Tateyama train. His only fellow-passengers were happy-looking families heading out for a few days at the beach.

Most people think of Sunday as a day of rest. Throughout his childhood, however, Tengo had never once viewed Sunday as a day to enjoy.

For him, Sunday was like a misshapen moon that showed only its dark side. When the weekend came, his whole body began to feel sluggish and achy, and his appetite would disappear. He had even prayed for Sunday not to come, though his prayers were never answered.

When Tengo was a boy, his father was a collector of subscription fees for NHK—Japan's quasi-governmental radio and television network—and, every Sunday, he would take Tengo with him as he went door to door soliciting payment. Tengo had started going on these rounds before he entered kindergarten and continued through fifth grade without a single weekend off. He had no idea whether other NHK fee collectors worked on Sundays, but, for as long as he could remember, his father always had. If anything, his father worked with even more enthusiasm than usual, because on Sundays he could catch the people who were usually out during the week.

Tengo's father had several reasons for taking him along on his rounds. One reason was that he could not leave the boy at home alone. On weekdays and Saturdays, Tengo could go to school or to day care, but these institutions were closed on Sundays. Another reason, Tengo's father said, was that it was important for a father to show his son what kind of work he did. A child should learn early on what activity was supporting him, and he should appreciate the importance of labor. Tengo's father had been sent out to work in the fields on his father's farm, on Sunday like any other day, from the time he was old enough to understand anything. He had even been kept out of school during the busiest seasons. To him, such a life was a given.

Tengo's father's third and final reason was a more calculating one, which was why it had left the deepest scars on his son's heart. Tengo's father was well aware that having a small child with him made his job easier. Even people who were determined not to pay often ended up forking over the money when a little boy was staring up at them, which was why Tengo's father saved his most difficult routes for Sunday. Tengo sensed from the beginning that this was the role he was expected to play, and he absolutely hated it. But he also felt that he had to perform it as cleverly as he could in order to please his father. If he pleased his father, he would be treated kindly that day. He might as well have been a trained monkey.

Tengo's one consolation was that his father's beat was fairly far from home. They lived in a suburban residential district outside the city of Ichikawa, and his father's rounds were in the center of the city. At least he was able to avoid doing collections at the homes of his classmates. Occasionally, though, while walking in the downtown shopping area, he would spot a classmate on the street. When this happened, he ducked behind his father to keep from being noticed.

On Monday mornings, his school friends would talk excitedly about where they had gone and what they had done the day before. They went to amusement parks and zoos and baseball games. In the summer, they went swimming, in the winter skiing. But Tengo had nothing to talk about. From morning to evening on Sundays, he and his father rang the doorbells of strangers' houses, bowed their heads, and took money from whoever came to the door. If people didn't want to pay, his father would threaten or cajole them. If they tried to talk their way out of paying, his father would raise his voice. Sometimes he would curse at them like stray dogs. Such experiences were not the sort of thing that Tengo could share with friends. He could not help feeling like a

kind of alien in the society of middle-class children of white-collar workers. He lived a different kind of life in a different world. Luckily, his grades were outstanding, as was his athletic ability. So even though he was an alien he was never an outcast. In most circumstances, he was treated with respect. But whenever the other boys invited him to go somewhere or to visit their homes on a Sunday he had to turn them down. Soon, they stopped asking.

Born the third son of a farming family in the hardscrabble Tohoku region, Tengo's father had left home as soon as he could, joining a homesteaders' group and crossing over to Manchuria in the 1930s. He had not believed the government's claims that Manchuria was a paradise where the land was vast and rich. He knew enough to realize that "paradise" was not to be found anywhere. He was simply poor and hungry. The best he could hope for if he stayed at home was a life on the brink of starvation. In Manchuria, he and the other homesteaders were given some farming implements and small arms, and together they started cultivating the land. The soil was poor and rocky, and in winter everything froze. Sometimes stray dogs were all they had to eat. Even so, with government support for the first few years they managed to get by. Their lives were finally becoming more stable when, in August, 1945, the Soviet Union launched a full-scale invasion of Manchuria. Tengo's father had been expecting this to happen, having been secretly informed of the impending situation by a certain official, a man he had become friendly with. The minute he heard the news that the Soviets had violated the border, he mounted his horse, galloped to the local train station, and boarded the second-to-last train for Da-lien. He was the only one among his farming companions to make it back to Japan before the end of the year.

After the war, Tengo's father went to Tokyo and tried to make a living as a black marketeer and as a carpenter's apprentice, but he could barely keep himself alive. He was working as a liquor-store deliveryman in Asakusa when he bumped into his old friend the official he had known in Manchuria. When the man learned that Tengo's father was having a hard time finding a decent job, he offered to recommend him to a friend in the subscription department of NHK, and Tengo's father gladly accepted. He knew almost nothing about NHK, but he was willing to try anything that promised a steady income.

At NHK, Tengo's father carried out his duties with great gusto. His foremost strength was his perseverance in the face of adversity. To someone who had barely eaten a filling meal since birth, collecting NHK fees was not excruciating work. The most hostile curses hurled at him were nothing. Moreover, he felt satisfaction at belonging to an important organization, even as one of its lowest-ranking members. His performance and attitude were so outstanding that, after a year as a commissioned collector, he was taken directly into the ranks of the full-fledged employees, an almost unheard-of achievement at NHK. Soon, he was able to move into a corporation-owned apartment and join the company's health-care plan. It was the greatest stroke of good fortune he had ever had in his life.

Young Tengo's father never sang him lullabies, never read books to him at bedtime. Instead, he told the boy stories of his actual experiences. He was a good storyteller. His accounts of his childhood and youth were not exactly pregnant

with meaning, but the details were lively. There were funny stories, moving stories, and violent stories. If a life can be measured by the color and variety of its episodes, Tengo's father's life had been rich in its own way, perhaps. But when his stories touched on the period after he became an NHK employee they suddenly lost all vitality. He had met a woman, married her, and had a child—Tengo. A few months after Tengo was born, his mother had fallen ill and died. His father had raised him alone after that, while working hard for NHK. The End. How he happened to meet Tengo's mother and marry her, what kind of woman she was, what had caused her death, whether her death had been an easy one or she had suffered greatly—Tengo's father told him almost nothing about such matters. If he tried asking, his father just evaded the questions. Most of the time, such questions put him in a foul mood. Not a single photograph of Tengo's mother had survived.

SEDATIVE

The man who regaled us with the following episode is a Republican, but he swears that his part in it was spontaneous. "My Manx cat," he said, "who, in the circle of those that know her, is one of the more respected animals of northern Westchester, had a marked reaction the other night when the name of Harry S. Truman was mentioned in her presence at a fairly large party. She leaped to the top of the living-room mantel, sat on her haunches, and yowled uninterruptedly. There was chaos for some moments. I had an inspiration. Walking over to her, I looked her straight in the eye and said quietly but firmly, enunciating each syllable carefully, 'Dwight D. Eisenhower.' It shut her right up, and she came down from the mantel of her own accord."

| 1954 |

Tengo fundamentally disbelieved his father's story. He knew that his mother hadn't died a few months after he was born. In his only memory of her, he was a year and a half old and she was standing by his crib in the arms of a man other than his father. His mother took off her blouse, dropped the straps of her slip, and let the man who was not his father suck on her breasts. Tengo slept beside them, his breathing audible. But, at the same time, he was not asleep. He was watching his mother.

This was Tengo's photograph of his mother. The ten-second scene was burned into his brain with perfect clarity. It was the only concrete information he had about her, the one tenuous connection his mind could make with her. He and she were linked by this hypothetical umbilical cord. His father, however, had no idea that this vivid scene existed in Tengo's memory, or that, like a cow in a meadow, Tengo was endlessly regurgitating fragments of it to chew on, a cud from which he obtained essential nutrients. Father and son: each was locked in a deep, dark embrace with his own secrets.

As an adult, Tengo often wondered if the young man sucking on his mother's breasts in his vision was his biological father. This was because Tengo in no way resembled his father, the stellar NHK collections agent. Tengo was a tall, strapping man with a broad forehead, a narrow nose, and tightly balled ears. His father was short and squat and utterly unimpressive. He had a small forehead, a flat nose, and pointed ears like a horse's. Where Tengo had a relaxed and generous look, his father appeared nervous and tight-fisted. Comparing the two of them, people often openly remarked on their dissimilarity.

Still, it was not their physical features that made it difficult for Tengo to identify with his father but their psychological makeup. His father showed no sign at all of what might be called intellectual curiosity. True, having been born in poverty he had not had a decent education. Tengo felt a degree of pity for his father's circumstances. But a basic desire to obtain knowledge—which Tengo assumed to be a more or less natural urge in people—was lacking in the man. He had a certain practical wisdom that enabled him to survive, but Tengo could discern no hint of a willingness in his father to deepen himself, to view a wider, larger world. Tengo's father never seemed to suffer discomfort from the stagnant air of his cramped little life. Tengo never once saw him pick up a book. He had no interest in music or movies, and he never took a trip. The only thing that seemed to interest him was his collection route. He would make a map of the area, mark it with colored pens, and examine it whenever he had a spare moment, the way a biologist might study chromosomes.

Tengo, by contrast, was curious about everything. He absorbed knowledge from a broad range of fields with the efficiency of a power shovel scooping earth. He had been regarded as a math prodigy from early childhood, and he could solve high-school math problems by the time he was in third grade. Math was, for young Tengo, an effective means of retreat from his life with his father. In the mathematical world, he would walk down a long corridor, opening one numbered door after another. Each time a new spectacle unfolded before him, the ugly traces of the real world would simply disappear. As long as he was actively exploring that realm of infinite consistency, he was free.

While math was like a magnificent imaginary building for Tengo, literature was a vast magical forest. Math stretched infinitely upward toward the heavens, but stories spread out before him, their sturdy roots stretching deep into the earth. In this forest there were no maps, no doorways. As Tengo got older, the forest of story began to exert an even stronger pull on his heart than the world of math. Of course, reading novels was just another form of escape—as soon as he closed the book, he had to come back to the real world. But at some point he noticed that returning to reality from the world of a novel was not as devastating a blow as returning from the world of math. Why was that? After much thought, he reached a conclusion. No matter how clear things might become in the forest of story, there was never a clear-cut solution, as there was in math. The role of a story was, in the broadest terms, to transpose a problem into another form. Depending on the nature and the direction of the problem, a solution might be suggested in the narrative. Tengo would return to the real world with that suggestion in hand. It was like a piece of paper bearing the indecipherable text of a magic spell. It served no immediate practical purpose, but it contained a possibility.

The one possible solution that Tengo *was* able to decipher from his readings was this one: *My real father must be somewhere else.* Like an unfortunate child in a Dickens novel, Tengo had perhaps been led by strange circumstances to be raised by this impostor. Such a possibility was both a nightmare and a great hope.

After reading *Oliver Twist*, Tengo plowed through every Dickens volume in the library. As he travelled through Dickens's stories, he steeped himself in reimagined versions of his own life. These fantasies grew ever longer and more complex. They followed a single pattern, but with infinite variations. In all of them, Tengo would tell himself that his father's home was not where he belonged. He had been mistakenly locked in this cage, and someday his real parents would find him and rescue him. Then he would have the most beautiful, peaceful, and free Sundays imaginable.

Tengo's father prided himself on his son's excellent grades, and boasted of them to people in the neighborhood. At the same time, however,

"Have you ever wondered what would happen if a giant hair ball were to slam into the earth?"

he showed a certain displeasure with Tengo's brightness and talent. Often when Tengo was at his desk, studying, his father would interrupt him, ordering the boy to do chores or nagging him about his supposedly offensive behavior. The content of his father's nagging was always the same: here he was, running himself ragged every day, covering huge distances and enduring people's curses, while Tengo did nothing but take it easy all the time, living in comfort. "They had me working my tail off when I was your age, and my father and older brothers would beat me black and blue for anything at all. They never gave me enough food. They treated me like an animal. I don't want you thinking you're so special just because you got a few good grades."

This man is envious of me, Tengo began to think at a certain point. He's jealous, either of me as a person or of the life I'm leading. But would a father really feel jealousy toward his son? Tengo did not judge his father, but he could not help sensing a pathetic kind of meanness emanating from his words and deeds. It was not that Tengo's father hated him as a person but, rather, that he hated something *inside* Tengo, something that he could not forgive.

When the train left Tokyo Station, Tengo took out the paperback that he had brought along. It was an anthology of short stories on the theme of travel and it included a tale called "Town of Cats," a fantastical piece by a German writer with whom Tengo was not familiar. According to the book's foreword, the story had been written in the period between the two World Wars.

In the story, a young man is travelling alone with no particular destination in mind. He rides the train and gets off at any stop that arouses his interest. He takes a room, sees the sights, and stays for as long as he likes. When he has had enough, he boards another train. He spends every vacation this way.

One day, he sees a lovely river from the train window. Gentle green hills line the meandering stream, and below them lies a pretty little town with an old stone bridge. The train stops at the town's station, and the young man steps down with his bag. No one else gets off, and, as soon as he alights, the train departs.

No workers man the station, which must see very little activity. The young man crosses the bridge and walks into the town. All the shops are shuttered, the town hall deserted. No one occupies the desk at the town's only hotel. The place seems totally uninhabited. Perhaps all the people are off napping somewhere. But it is only ten-thirty in the morning, far too early for that. Perhaps something has caused all the people to abandon the town. In any case, the next train will not come until the following morning, so he has no choice but to spend the night here. He wanders around the town to kill time.

In fact, this is a town of cats. When the sun starts to go down, many cats come trooping across the bridge—cats of all different kinds and colors. They are much larger than ordinary cats, but they are still cats. The young man is shocked by this sight. He rushes into the bell tower in the center of town and climbs to the top to hide. The cats go about their business, raising the shop shutters or seating themselves at their desks to start their day's work. Soon, more cats come, crossing the bridge into town like the others. They enter the shops to buy things or go to the town hall to handle administrative matters or eat a meal at the hotel restaurant or drink beer at the tavern and sing lively cat songs. Because cats can see in the dark, they need almost no lights, but that particular night the glow of the full moon floods the town, enabling the young man to see every detail from his perch in the bell tower. When dawn approaches, the cats finish their work, close up the shops, and swarm back across the bridge.

By the time the sun comes up, the cats are gone, and the town is deserted again. The young man climbs down, picks one of the hotel beds for himself, and goes to sleep. When he gets hungry, he eats some bread and fish that have been left in the hotel kitchen. When darkness approaches, he hides in the bell tower again and observes the cats' activities until dawn. Trains stop at the station before noon and in the late afternoon. No passengers alight, and no one boards, either. Still, the trains stop at the station for exactly one minute, then pull out again. He could take one of these trains and leave the creepy cat town behind. But he doesn't. Being young, he has a lively curiosity and is ready for adventure. He wants to see more of this strange spectacle. If possible, he wants to find out when and how this place became a town of cats.

On his third night, a hubbub breaks out in the square below the bell tower. "Hey, do you smell something human?" one of the cats says. "Now that you mention it, I *thought* there was a funny smell the past few days," another chimes in, twitching his nose. "Me, too," yet another cat says. "That's weird. There shouldn't be any humans here," someone adds. "No, of course not. There's no way a human could get into this town of cats." "But that smell is definitely here."

The cats form groups and begin to search the town like bands of vigilantes. It takes them very little time to discover that the bell tower is the source of the smell. The young man hears their soft paws padding up the stairs. That's it, they've got me! he thinks. His smell seems to have roused the cats to anger. Humans are not supposed to set foot in this town. The cats have big, sharp claws and white fangs. He has no idea what terrible fate awaits him if he is discovered, but he is sure that they will not let him leave the town alive.

Three cats climb to the top of the bell tower and sniff the air. "Strange," one cat says, twitching his whiskers, "I smell a human, but there's no one here."

"It *is* strange," a second cat says. "But there really isn't anyone here. Let's go and look somewhere else."

The cats cock their heads, puzzled, then retreat down the stairs. The young man hears their footsteps fading into the dark of night. He breathes a sigh of relief, but he doesn't understand what just happened. There was no way they could have missed him. But for some reason they didn't see him. In any case, he decides that when morning comes he will go to the station and take the train out of this town. His luck can't last forever.

The next morning, however, the train does not stop at the station. He watches it pass by without slowing down. The afternoon train does the same. He can see the engineer seated at the controls. But the train shows no sign of stopping. It is as though no one can see the young man waiting for a train—or even see the station itself. Once the afternoon train disappears down the track, the place grows quieter than ever. The sun begins to sink. It is time for the cats to come. The young man knows that he is irretrievably lost. This is no town of cats, he finally realizes. It is the place where he is

PRICE $4.95

AUG. 8 & 15, 2005

THE
NEW YORKER

Sempé.

meant to be lost. It is another world, which has been prepared especially for him. And never again, for all eternity, will the train stop at this station to take him back to the world he came from.

Tengo read the story twice. The phrase "the place where he is meant to be lost" attracted his attention. He closed the book and let his eyes wander across the drab industrial scene passing by the train window. Soon afterward, he drifted off to sleep—not a long nap but a deep one. He woke covered in sweat. The train was moving along the southern coastline of the Boso Peninsula in midsummer.

One morning when he was in fifth grade, after much careful thinking, Tengo declared that he was going to stop making the rounds with his father on Sundays. He told his father that he wanted to use the time for studying and reading books and playing with other kids. He wanted to live a normal life like everybody else.

Tengo said what he needed to say, concisely and coherently.

His father, of course, blew up. He didn't give a damn what other families did, he said. "We have our own way of doing things. And don't you *dare* talk to me about a 'normal life,' Mr. Know-It-All. What do *you* know about a 'normal life'?" Tengo did not try to argue with him. He merely stared back in silence, knowing that nothing he said would get through to his father. Finally, his father told him that if he wouldn't listen then he couldn't go on feeding him. Tengo should get the hell out.

Tengo did as he was told. He had made up his mind. He was not going to be afraid. Now that he had been given permission to leave his cage, he was more relieved than anything else. But there was no way that a ten-year-old boy

could live on his own. When his class was dismissed at the end of the day, he confessed his predicament to his teacher. The teacher was a single woman in her mid-thirties, a fair-minded, warm-hearted person. She heard Tengo out with sympathy, and that evening she took him back to his father's place for a long talk.

Tengo was told to leave the room, so he was not sure what they said to each other, but finally his father had to sheathe his sword. However extreme his anger might be, he could not leave a ten-year-old boy to wander the streets alone. The duty of a parent to support his child was a matter of law.

As a result of the teacher's talk with his father, Tengo was free to spend Sundays as he pleased. This was the first tangible right that he had ever won from his father. He had taken his first step toward freedom and independence.

At the reception desk of the sanatorium, Tengo gave his name and his father's name.

The nurse asked, "Have you by any chance notified us of your intention to visit today?" There was a hard edge to her voice. A small woman, she wore metal-framed glasses, and her short hair had a touch of gray.

"No, it just occurred to me to come this morning and I hopped on a train," Tengo answered honestly.

The nurse gave him a look of mild disgust. Then she said, "Visitors are supposed to notify us before they arrive to see a patient. We have our schedules to meet, and the wishes of the patient must also be taken into account."

"I'm sorry. I didn't know."

"When was your last visit?"

"Two years ago."

"Two years ago," she said as she checked the list of visitors with a ball-point pen in hand.

"You mean to say that you have not made a single visit in two years?"

"That's right," Tengo said.

"According to our records, you are Mr. Kawana's only relative."

"That is correct."

She glanced at Tengo, but she said nothing. Her eyes were not blaming him, just checking the facts. Apparently, Tengo's case was not exceptional.

"At the moment, your father is in group rehabilitation. That will end in half an hour. You can see him then."

"How is he doing?"

"Physically, he's healthy. It's in the other area that he has his ups and downs," she said, tapping her temple with an index finger.

Tengo thanked her and went to wait in the lounge by the entrance, reading more of his book. A breeze passed through now and then, carrying the scent of the sea and the cooling sound of the pine windbreak outside. Cicadas clung to the branches of the trees, screeching their hearts out. Summer was at its height, but the cicadas seemed to know that it would not last long.

Eventually, the bespectacled nurse came to tell Tengo that he could see his father now. "I'll show you to his room," she said. Tengo got up from the sofa and, passing by a large mirror on the wall, realized for the first time what a sloppy outfit he was wearing: a Jeff Beck Japan Tour T-shirt under a faded dungaree shirt with mismatched buttons, chinos with specks of pizza sauce near one knee, a baseball cap—no way for a thirty-year-old son to dress on his first hospital visit to his father in two years. Nor did he have anything with him that might serve as a gift on such an occasion. No wonder the nurse had given him that look of disgust.

Tengo's father was in his room, sitting in a chair by the open window, his hands on his knees. A nearby table held a potted plant with several delicate yellow flowers. The floor was made of some soft material to prevent injury in case of a fall. Tengo did not realize at first that the old man seated by the window was his father. He had shrunk—"shrivelled up" might be more accurate. His hair was shorter and as white as a frost-covered lawn. His cheeks were sunken, which may have been why the hollows of his eyes looked much bigger than they had before. Three deep creases marked his forehead. His eyebrows were extremely long and thick, and his pointed ears were larger than ever; they looked like bat wings. From a distance, he seemed less like a human being than like some kind of creature, a rat or a squirrel—a creature with some cunning. He was, however, Tengo's father—or, rather, the wreckage of Tengo's father. The father that Tengo remembered was a tough, hardworking man. Introspection and imagination might have been foreign to him, but he had his own moral code and a strong sense of purpose. The man Tengo saw before him was nothing but an empty shell.

"Mr. Kawana!" the nurse said to Tengo's father in the crisp, clear tone she must have been trained to use when addressing patients. "Mr. Kawana! Look who's here! It's your son, here from Tokyo!"

Tengo's father turned in his direction. His expressionless eyes made Tengo think of two empty swallow's nests hanging from the eaves.

"Hello," Tengo said.

His father said nothing. Instead, he looked straight at Tengo as if he were reading a bulletin written in a foreign language.

"Dinner starts at six-thirty," the nurse said to Tengo. "Please feel free to stay until then."

Tengo hesitated for a moment after the nurse left, and then approached his father, sitting down in the chair opposite his—a faded, cloth-covered chair, its wooden parts scarred from long use. His father's eyes followed his movements.

"How are you?" Tengo asked.

"Fine, thank you," his father said formally.

Tengo did not know what to say after that. Toying with the third button of his dungaree shirt, he turned his gaze toward the pine trees outside and then back again to his father.

"You have come from Tokyo, is it?" his father asked.

"Yes, from Tokyo."

"You must have come by express train."

"That's right," Tengo said. "As far as Tateyama. Then I transferred to a local for the trip here to Chikura."

"You've come to swim?" his father asked.

"I'm Tengo. Tengo Kawana. Your son."

The wrinkles in his father's forehead deepened. "A lot of people tell lies because they don't want to pay their NHK subscription fee."

"Father!" Tengo called out to him. He had not spoken the word in a very long time. "I'm Tengo. Your son."

"I don't have a son," his father declared.

"You don't have a son," Tengo repeated mechanically.

His father nodded.

"So what am I?" Tengo asked.

"You're nothing," his father said with two short shakes of the head.

Tengo caught his breath. He could find no words. Nor did his father have any more to say. Each sat in silence, searching through his own tangled thoughts. Only the cicadas sang without confusion, at top volume.

He may be speaking the truth, Tengo thought. His memory may have been destroyed, but his words are probably true.

"What do you mean?" Tengo asked.

"You are nothing," his father repeated, his voice devoid of emotion. "You were nothing, you are nothing, and you will be nothing."

Tengo wanted to get up from his chair, walk to the station, and go back to Tokyo then and there. But he could not stand up. He was like the young man who travelled to the town of cats. He had curiosity. He wanted a clearer answer. There was danger lurking, of course. But if he let this opportunity escape he would have no chance to learn the secret about himself. Tengo arranged and rearranged words in his head until at last he was ready to speak them. This was the question he had wanted to ask since childhood but could never quite manage to get out: "What you're saying, then, is that you are not my biological father, correct? You are telling me that there is no blood connection between us, is that it?"

"Stealing radio waves is an unlawful act," his father said, looking into Tengo's eyes. "It is no different from stealing money or valuables, don't you think?"

"You're probably right." Tengo decided to agree for now.

"Radio waves don't come falling out of the sky for free like rain or snow," his father said.

Tengo stared at his father's hands. They were lined up neatly on his knees. Small, dark hands, they looked tanned to the bone by long years of outdoor work.

"My mother didn't really die of an illness when I was little, did she?" Tengo asked slowly.

His father did not answer. His expression did not change, and his hands did not move. His eyes focussed on Tengo as if they were observing something unfamiliar.

It seems to us that the resident who was best able to look the building strike squarely in the face was the cat of Mme. Alice Bédat, the opera singer, who lives at 156 West Seventy-fifth Street, and who long ago resolved to live independently of lifts and liftmen. The cat's name is Bo-Bo, and it has been trained to take its outings in the Bédat back yard when lowered in a basket on the end of a rope. This is the sort of trick Penrod hoped to perfect Duke in. Mme. Bédat has succeeded. Strikes may come and go; Bo-Bo is lowered regularly to the peaceful garden, strolls alone there for a brief hour, and returns obediently to the basket (which has meanwhile been hoisted aloft, baited with meat, and lowered again). The whole performance seems to us as improbable as inducing a smooth-haired fox terrier to pull a sled.

| 1936 |

"My mother left you. She left you and me behind. She went off with another man. Am I wrong?"

His father nodded. "It is not good to steal radio waves. You can't get away with it, just doing whatever you want."

This man understands my questions perfectly well. He just doesn't want to answer them directly, Tengo thought.

"Father," Tengo addressed him. "You may not actually be my father, but I'll call you that for now because I don't know what else to call you. To tell you the truth, I've never liked you. Maybe I've even hated you most of the time. You know that, don't you? But, even supposing that there is no blood connection between us, I no longer have any reason to hate you. I don't know if I can go so far as to be fond of you, but I think that at least I should be able to understand you better than I do now. I have always wanted to know the truth about who I

am and where I came from. That's all. If you will tell me the truth here and now, I won't hate you anymore. In fact, I would welcome the opportunity not to have to hate you any longer."

Tengo's father went on staring at him with expressionless eyes, but Tengo felt that he might be seeing the tiniest gleam of light somewhere deep within those empty swallow's nests.

"I am nothing," Tengo said. "You are right. I'm like someone who's been thrown into the ocean at night, floating all alone. I reach out, but no one is there. I have no connection to anything. The closest thing I have to a family is you, but you hold on to the secret. Meanwhile, your memory deteriorates day by day. Along with your memory, the truth about me is being lost. Without the aid of truth, I am nothing, and I can never be anything. You are right about that, too."

"Knowledge is a precious social asset," his father said in a monotone, though his voice was somewhat quieter than before, as if someone had reached over and turned down the volume. "It is an asset that must be amassed in abundant stockpiles and utilized with the utmost care. It must be handed down to the next generation in fruitful forms. For that reason, too, NHK needs to have all your subscription fees and—"

He cut his father short. "What kind of person was my mother? Where did she go? What happened to her?"

His father brought his incantation to a halt, his lips shut tight.

His voice softer now, Tengo went on, "A vision often comes to me—the same one, over and over. I suspect it's not so much a vision as a memory of something that actually happened.

"Miss Egan, bring me everything we have on cats."

I'm one and a half years old, and my mother is next to me. She and a young man are holding each other. The man is not you. Who he is I have no idea, but he is definitely not you."

His father said nothing, but his eyes were clearly seeing something else—something not there.

"I wonder if I might ask you to read me something," Tengo's father said in formal tones after a long pause. "My eyesight has deteriorated to the point where I can't read books anymore. That bookcase has some books. Choose any one you like."

Tengo got up to scan the spines of the volumes in the bookcase. Most of them were historical novels set in ancient times when samurai roamed the land. Tengo couldn't bring himself to read his father some musty old book full of archaic language.

"If you don't mind, I'd rather read a story about a town of cats," Tengo said. "It's in a book that I brought to read myself."

"A story about a town of cats," his father said, savoring the words. "Please read that to me, if it is not too much trouble."

Tengo looked at his watch. "It's no trouble

"Hey, let's do lunch."

they all died in an epidemic of some sort—and the cats came to live there."

His father nodded. "When a vacuum forms, something has to come along to fill it. That's what everybody does."

"That's what everybody does?"

"Exactly."

"What kind of vacuum are you filling?"

His father scowled. Then he said with a touch of sarcasm in his voice, "Don't you know?"

"I don't know," Tengo said.

His father's nostrils flared. One eyebrow rose slightly. "If you can't understand it without an explanation, you can't understand it with an explanation."

Tengo narrowed his eyes, trying to read the man's expression. Never once had his father employed such odd, suggestive language. He always spoke in concrete, practical terms.

"I see. So you are filling some kind of vacuum," Tengo said. "All right, then, who is going to fill the vacuum that you have left behind?"

"You," his father declared, raising an index finger and thrusting it straight at Tengo. "Isn't it obvious? I have been filling the vacuum that somebody else made, so you will fill the vacuum that I have made."

"The way the cats filled the town after the people were gone."

"Right," his father said. Then he stared va-

at all. I have plenty of time before my train leaves. It's an odd story. I don't know if you'll like it."

Tengo pulled out his paperback and started reading slowly, in a clear, audible voice, taking two or three breaks along the way to catch his breath. He glanced at his father whenever he stopped reading but saw no discernible reaction on his face. Was he enjoying the story? He could not tell.

"Does that town of cats have television?" his father asked when Tengo had finished.

"The story was written in Germany in the 1930s. They didn't have television yet back then. They did have radio, though."

"Did the cats build the town? Or did people build it before the cats came to live there?" his father asked, speaking as if to himself.

"I don't know," Tengo said. "But it does seem to have been built by human beings. Maybe the people left for some reason—say, cantly at his own outstretched index finger as if at some mysterious, misplaced object.

Tengo sighed. "So, then, who is my father?"

"Just a vacuum. Your mother joined her body with a vacuum and gave birth to you. I filled that vacuum."

Having said that much, his father closed his eyes and closed his mouth.

"And you raised me after she left. Is that what you're saying?"

After a ceremonious clearing of his throat, his father said, as if trying to explain a simple truth to a slow-witted child, "That is why I said, 'If you can't understand it without an explanation, you can't understand it with an explanation.'"

Tengo folded his hands in his lap and looked straight into his father's face. This man is no empty shell, he thought. He is a flesh-and-blood human being with a narrow, stubborn soul, surviving in fits and starts on this patch of land by the sea. He has no choice but to coexist with the vacuum that is slowly spreading inside him. Eventually, that vacuum will swallow up whatever memories are left. It is only a matter of time.

Tengo said goodbye to his father just before 6 P.M. While he waited for the taxi to come, they sat across from each other by the window, saying nothing. Tengo had many more questions he wanted to ask, but he knew that he would get no answers. The sight of his father's tightly clenched lips told him that. If you couldn't understand something without an explanation, you couldn't understand it with an explanation. As his father had said.

When the time for him to leave drew near, Tengo said, "You told me a lot today. It was indirect and often hard to grasp, but it was probably as honest and open as you could make it. I should be grateful for that."

Still his father said nothing, his eyes fixed on the view like a soldier on guard duty, determined not to miss the signal flare sent up by a savage tribe on a distant hill. Tengo tried looking out along his father's line of vision, but all that was out there was the pine grove, tinted by the coming sunset.

"I'm sorry to say it, but there is virtually nothing I can do for you—other than to hope that the process forming a vacuum inside you is a painless one. I'm sure you have suffered a lot. You loved my mother as deeply as you knew how. I do get that sense. But she left, and that must have been hard on you—like living in an empty town. Still, you raised me in that empty town."

A pack of crows cut across the sky, cawing. Tengo stood up, went over to his father, and put his hand on his shoulder. "Goodbye, Father. I'll come again soon."

With his hand on the doorknob, Tengo turned around one last time and was shocked to see a single tear escaping his father's eye. It shone a dull silver color under the ceiling's fluorescent light. The tear crept slowly down his cheek and fell onto his lap. Tengo opened the door and left the room. He took a cab to the station and reboarded the train that had brought him here.

(Translated, from the Japanese, by Jay Rubin.)

| 2011 |

CAT'S ROBO-CRADLE

MARGARET ATWOOD

In Ann Arbor, Michigan, there is a warehouse filled with discontinued merchandise, which has been nicknamed the Museum of Failed Products. Inside, one can learn about the line of TV dinners launched by a well-known toothpaste company, with packaging that unwisely echoed the design of the toothpaste. Other candidates for the permanent collection include the Christ Child doll (parents, it seemed, could not quite picture Baby Jesus sharing a dolly tea party with a sock monkey) and the pet-of-the-month scheme that astonished child subscribers with a regular supply of dead rodents and reptiles, sent to them through the mail.

To keep myself humble, I here recall the fact that, back in my market-research days, in 1963, I was skeptical about Pop-Tarts—those breakfast confections made of two layers of flour product glued together like clamshells, with a blob of jam in the clam position. When our testers put them in the toaster, the things exploded, spewing boiling jam over the inside of the toaster. This defect was later rectified, with well-known results.

Rome wasn't built in a day, nor were Pop-Tarts. It was decades after the invention of the sewing machine that it became commercially viable. So the inevitability of the device I am about to propose may not seem immediately obvious, though there is no doubt in my mind about the need for it.

My proposal is called the Robo-Coyote.

It would address the fact that billions of migratory birds are killed in North America every year by cats, both feral and owner-operated. When you add to that the mega-millions killed by urban high-rises whose proprietors foolishly keep the lights on all night, it's a wonder there's a bird left in the skies. And, since birds are a main predator of forest insects, their dwindling is already affecting the health of our forests. As climates change and winters warm, the situation will worsen: insects will move northward in hordes, munching as they go. What's more, the cats—millions of them—are gobbling up small rodents that are the staple fare of owls, falcons, and hawks, which may cause a further decline in those bird numbers.

What to do? No point in proposing a cat cull: the same people who love birds also love cats—I am among their number—and the animal-rights folks would be aroused in their irate thousands. Whatever is set in motion must not harm cats by a single whisker, and must be enjoyable for kittydom as well.

Hence my Robo-Coyote. With foreseen advances in robotics and 3-D soft-tissue printing, the engineering of this artificial game warden should be well within reach. The Robo-Coyote would prowl the forests, ignoring skunks, porcupines, and rabbits, attuned to feral cats alone and emitting whiffs of mating hormones and possibly some soulful howls in order to attract them. Unlike a real coyote, the Robo-Coyote would be able to shinny up  trees. Once a cat had been lured close enough, the Robo-Coyote's mouth would open wide. The cat would then enter, descend the throat, and find itself in a comfortable nook, complete with cushion and squeaky-mouse catnip toy.

Thus amused, the cat would be transported by the swiftly travelling Robo-Coyote to a cat fun fair—an enclosure within which cats would be free to chase robo-birds, robo-shrews and moles, robo-squirrels, and even robo-butterflies. A cat's hunting and playing instincts are said to be separate from its hunger cycles, so the sequestered cats need not eat the robo-prey should they manage to catch any. Food would be supplied on a contract basis by cat-food companies eager to show the world of animal- and bird-lovers that they are doing their best to tackle the migratory-bird issue, while assuring their shareholders that they are improving their bottom line: with the Robo-Coyote deployed in full force, one need not feel guilty about "owning" a cat. And the pet-food companies could even sponsor their own Robo-Coyotes, which could have advertising banners painted on their sides.

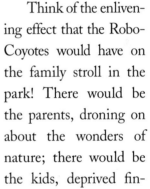

Think of the enlivening effect that the Robo-Coyotes would have on the family stroll in the park! There would be the parents, droning on about the wonders of nature; there would be the kids, deprived fingers twitching for their iPads—when, *zoom!*, across the path shoots a Robo-Coyote, yowling like a lovesick tom, stinking like a moggy in heat, and as unreal in appearance as anything in the Brotherhood of Evil Mutants. Next minute, a cat appears and is quickly inhumed. Lights flash. Beeps beep. Music sounds. What could be cooler? Something in the Museum of Failed Products, perhaps. But that is too negative a thought.

[2013]

LADY OF THE CATS

WOLCOTT GIBBS AND E. F. KINKEAD

S ince 1919, Miss Rita Ross has done her best to rid the city of half a million homeless cats which the S.P.C.A. estimates roam its streets. Almost singlehanded, during that period she has turned over more than two hundred tons of cats to the Society for painless destruction. Like the Post Office ideal, Miss Ross is deterred neither by snow, nor rain, nor heat, nor gloom of night on her round of deadly mercy. On Sundays and holidays, blown along by the high March wind or baked by August, in buildings rotten and sagging, through streets that crawl and smell, almost always among people who

are hostile or derisive, she has followed her incomprehensible star. It is a bad day when she gets only six cats; it is a good one when she gets sixteen. Once, when the S.P.C.A. recklessly provided her with one of its wagons and a driver, she bagged fifteen hundred. She has the peculiar reputation of being able to move off under her own weight in cats.

Miss Ross, though a furious and indomitable woman, is also a small one. She is five feet two and a quarter inches tall, and without equipment she weighs only a hundred and one pounds. Her face is shrewd, her glance penetrating, with a sort of birdlike fixity, her manner self-possessed and bouncy. She talks a good deal—coyly about her cats, sardonically about the enemies she has routed on a thousand battlefields. She is around thirty-seven years old.

Every morning at seven-thirty she leaves her home, a small stucco one-family house in the Bay Ridge section of Brooklyn, and takes the subway to the east end of Brooklyn Bridge. Here she alights and proceeds on foot over the bridge, gathering in cats as she goes. She works an average of fourteen hours a day, and she always keeps herself in first-class condition. Once, when a gang of hoodlums tried to deprive her of forty cats, she routed them decisively, wielding an ashcan with murderous effect.

Of the agility which makes a seven-foot billboard only a negligible obstacle in her course, she says, "I studied acrobatic dancing when I was a chorus girl and that comes in handy in climbing. I can beat any man in the S.P.C.A. up a tree except Johnny Joule of the Brooklyn Shelter. He used to be a tree pruner for the Park Department and he is wonderful at getting up a tree."

This is no empty boast. Once Miss Ross was interrupted in her customary work on the third floor of a deserted Harlem tenement by a man who came in quietly and locked the door behind him. His manner was menacing and Miss Ross did not stop to question him about his intentions. She dissolved an untidy situation by scrambling through the transom.

Miss Ross's clothes are nondescript except for an enormous cone-shaped hat, which she wears to keep cobwebs and plaster out of her hair. Her equipment is bizarre. She carries more impedimenta than the average Red Cap: a big, home-made wire trap of the cage type, an animal case, and a good-sized market basket. The trap may contain as many as ten swearing cats, the animal case up to six more. In the market basket are tins of canned salmon, catnip, tin pie plates, a can opener, a flashlight, a police whistle, a ball of twine, and five burlap sacks, used to contain an occasional overflow from the trap and the animal case. Laden with these unusual devices and proceeding at an effortless lope that eats up the miles, Miss Ross is an arresting figure. She is even more so when a vague but cheerful impulse leads her to dye her black hair red, or to wear a yellow wig.

Cat-catching on the grand scale leaves little time for other interests. Miss Ross has none of the accepted vices. She neither smokes nor drinks and if she had her choice, she says emphatically, she would rather kiss a cat than the best man who ever walked on two feet.

While Miss Ross is unquestionably the champion cat woman, there are lesser ones, and occasionally she is accompanied by a Miss Marion Kane. Miss Kane is about thirty-three, short, Celtic, and a ferocious hitter with either hand. When she and Miss Ross roam the streets of Harlem at night, prudent residents take cover, for both ladies have hasty dispositions and would not hesitate to engage an army. Most of the time, however, Miss Ross prefers to hunt alone, having, like so many gifted people, a distaste for collaboration.

Her usual hunting grounds are the bleaker, poorer parts of town. There she operates with matchless precision and technique, as relentlessly as doom. Every day she speaks to about a hundred people on the street, asking them to be on the lookout for stray cats and to communicate with her by mail when they hear of any. One ally, who modestly prefers to be known only as "The

Lady from Grantwood, N.J.," scarcely allows a day to pass without providing Miss Ross with the address of at least one underprivileged cat. Miss Ross carries the answers to these requests in her bag and they dictate roughly her course for the day. In addition, she cuts out bankruptcy notices from the papers, because small-store failures almost always result in homeless or locked-in cats. The greater part of her success, however, can be laid to simple vigilance. She penetrates sewers, elevator shafts, and cellars, and climbs to roof tops. She investigates freight yards, abattoirs, bridges, and cemeteries. She never passes a deserted building without making cat sounds, and it is a hard and cynical cat that can resist Miss Ross when she mews. She never allows any animal to be maltreated in her wide and various wanderings and can be almost as indignant about a horse whose teeth aren't clean as she can about one that is being beaten. While Miss Ross has room in her heart for the entire animal kingdom, she focusses principally on cats because she thinks they are victims of prejudice and bigotry.

"A dog has a million friends to a cat's one," she says. "Why, even *snakes* are sometimes praised!"

In a typical working day Miss Ross frequently covers between twenty-five and thirty miles, running like a flame through the Bronx, Brooklyn, Manhattan, and nearer New Jersey, stopping only reluctantly for food. In restaurants and lunchrooms her mystifying burden often arouses comment, but she is not embarrassed.

"They're just a little nervous," she says, referring to the ghostly heave and bounce of the containers at her feet.

The people among whom Miss Ross works always regard her with amazement and sometimes even with consternation, a lady so oddly possessed being a little upsetting to the simpleminded. Once, accompanied by an admiring representative of this magazine, she entered a building at 447 Lexington Avenue to call for a cat. The building was being renovated and the only occupant was a moody Negro in spectacles, hoeing mortar in a tub. Miss Ross told him she had come for the cat.

"Whut cat?" he said. "I don't know of no cat."

"Listen," said Miss Ross, and she gave her celebrated cry. They listened, and from a dark tunnel in the rear of the basement there came an answering cry, soft and dolorous.

"Why you want that cat?" asked the colored man, nervously.

Miss Ross did not reply

"This is humiliating. Couldn't you drop me a block from school?"

directly. She had put on her beehive hat and prepared a mess of salmon on a tin plate. She paused at the mouth of the aperture and looked at the colored man.

"I don't suppose you noticed whether it was a boy or girl?" she asked.

"No'm," he replied. "I don' recollect."

"Well," said Miss Ross, and disappeared, mewing softly.

When she came out, blurred with cobwebs, she was carrying a thin, exasperated cat which she thrust into her basket, already the prison of three others. Leaving the building, she spoke once more to the colored man, who had retreated behind a barrel of lime.

"If you see any more kitties, you be nice and play with them, won't you?" she said.

The uneasiness inspired by Miss Ross is by no means confined to the humble. There is no way of telling what the cats themselves think about her, though their gratitude is probably mixed with other emotions, but the S.P.C.A., that enlightened body of humanitarians, speaks of her with horror. The day in 1926 when she brought in fifteen hundred cats is still remembered as the darkest point in the Society's history, although Miss Ross dismisses her stupendous feat lightly. She had spotted colonies of cats around town too large to be handled by a lady on foot—there were eighty-seven in the basement of one deserted tenement—and she had dreamed of the day when she would be able to deal with them wholesale. The Society's wagon and driver gave her her glorious opportunity and she seized it fiercely. From dawn until deep night, driven furiously from the Battery to the Bronx, delivering fifty, sixty, a hundred cats at a clip to the stupefied officials, she accomplished the miraculous. The wagon and driver were withdrawn soon af-

terward. Miss Ross, disappointed but by no means daunted, went back to patrolling the streets on foot, and even with this handicap continued to tax the Society's facilities. She still does. Sydney Coleman, vice-president of the Society and not essentially a robust man, has barred his door against her in a pitiable effort to save his reason. The Society itself would like to have her restrained legally before it is engulfed in a living wave of cats. This, however, would mean a court suit and such an advertisement might easily be bad for the Society. Kindly people, unaware of the real nature of the crisis, would take Miss Ross's side; contributions would drop off. Last year an unofficial hearing was arranged before Magistrate Louis Brodsky in West Side Court. The judge told Miss Ross that the Society had a legal right to refuse cats in such staggering abundance. Miss Ross, with a ringing eloquence that made the representatives of the Society shudder, cried that it had no *moral* right before God or man to close its doors to sick or suffering animals. Magistrate Brodsky, a sanguine man, said in conclusion that he was satisfied that no further trouble would come up between Miss Ross and the Society. Miss Ross continued to use the Society's five borough shelters to deposit her cats.

The charge has arisen—and the Society would probably give its handsomest medal to the man who can prove it—that Miss Ross is indiscriminate in her choice of cats, that in the fever of the chase she has abducted cats whose home lives were by no means insupportable. One fall, a few years ago, the West End Fruit Market, the New Yorker Delicatessen Store, Schwartz Brothers Fruit Store, and other establishments on the upper West Side missed their cats after Miss Ross had passed that way, conceivably on a broomstick, but whether she had anything to do with these disappearances has never been proved.

To accusations of this kind Miss Ross has a firm, invariable answer. Three kinds of cats are safe from her—well-fed cats, altered cats, and nursing mothers. The first two imply ownership, the third maternity. No one can say with certainty that she has ever violated this rule.

If nobody calls for them within forty-eight hours, the cats Miss Ross brings in to the S.P.C.A. are placed in a lethal chamber and asphyxiated in fifteen seconds. That her love is deadly, her artful miaou a siren song, does not concern Miss Ross too much. The stray cat in New York, she feels, can look forward only to a life of great suffering and anxiety, a lonely and misera-ble end. The alternative is euthanasia and, since he can-not make the choice himself, she does so for him, merciful beyond pity or regret. Esti-mating that Miss Ross has seduced an average of ten cats a day for nineteen years, she has nearly seventy thousand souls on her conscience. They weigh lightly.

"It's a better death than most humans get," she says.

The police have also met Miss Ross, and they look on her with distaste mixed with a sort of stunned respect. She knows that any citizen has a right to use a patrolman's box to call the station house, and that a reported felony will bring two patrol cars; a murder, five. Several times when she has felt that things were getting a little out of hand, Miss Ross has not hesitated to shout mur-der.

Innocent patrolmen have occasionally made the mistake of summoning Miss Ross to court and charging her with disorderly conduct. Not one of them has done so twice. She has an impos-

ing courtroom presence and an astonishing legal vocabulary, so her accusers are often dismayed to learn that in the eyes of the law they have been either brutal or incompetent or both. She has even been known to bring departmental charges against patrolmen who have tried to thwart her in one way or another, and this has made the force wary, since such a charge remains on a man's record, proved or not. There are officers in New York who would not arrest Miss Ross if they caught her setting off a bomb.

Thoughtful policemen, in fact, have con-cluded that the best way to deal with Miss Ross is to do what she says, even if it in-volves situations not found in the Manual. Once she com-mandeered two patrolmen from the Borough Park Sta-tion in Brooklyn and took them to a deserted bakery which, she said, contained two cats. This was true. The cats were plainly visible and painfully emaciated but, as the policemen discovered when they had forced their way in, Miss Ross had for-gotten to mention that they were also insane. In their delirium they mistook their rescuers for ag-gressors and leapt furiously about the bakery. They were marvellously light from hunger and strain and for the better part of an hour they kept their freedom while Miss Ross and the patrol-men, all heavily floured, toiled irritably after them among the barrels. At last superior physical con-dition triumphed and the cats were captured and turned over to their nemesis. Miss Ross can be appreciative when the occasion seems to call for it. She wrote a letter of commendation to the Po-lice Commissioner himself.

Probably the most striking example of the influence Miss Ross has with the police occurred some time ago in the Williamsburg section of Brooklyn. She was chased into the subway by a gang of boys trying to rescue a rather unwieldy dog which she had been given by one of their mothers and now carried under her arm. It was her plan to conceal the dog in the ladies' room until the excitement blew over, but she was thwarted by an officious guard. Undaunted, Miss Ross reversed her field, ran up another flight of stairs, and swung down the street to a stationery store. Once inside, to the owner's amazement she slammed the door and locked it.

"Don't open that door," she said sharply as he came from behind the counter.

"But Madam, this is a place of business."

"Don't open that door," repeated Miss Ross, and gave him the dog to hold. While he held the dog uncertainly, she went to the telephone and put in a murder call. Inside thirty seconds, five radio patrol cars, commanded by a Sergeant Kelly of the Canarsie Station, had rushed to the scene. The police dispersed the crowd, and Miss Ross emerged triumphantly with the dog.

"I demand protection against these ruffians," she said, and rode majestically in Sergeant Kelly's car to the nearest police station, where she left an order for an S.P.C.A. truck to come and pick up the dog. Then, as calmly as if such stirring things happened every day, she went out cat-gathering.

Miss Ross met Sergeant Kelly just the other day in the subway.

"Remember all that excitement in the stationery store, Rita?" he asked genially.

In spite of the truce which she has forced upon the Police Department, Miss Ross is still a familiar figure in the magistrates' courts. At least six times a year she appears against people who have maltreated animals or else have insulted her or hampered her in the performance of her duty.

She is merciless with those who abuse animals. She has succeeded in having countless five-dollar fines imposed on tradesmen who beat their horses, and one Negro janitor who was convicted of burning cats alive in his furnace was sentenced to six months in jail. She has never lost a case, though sometimes the penalties have seemed to her soft and foolish beyond belief.

"My pet dislike is judges who are lenient in cruelty cases," she says, and probably only their judicial robes have saved many magistrates from the more tangible weight of her displeasure.

With those who harass her personally, she is more moderate, though no less effective. All she wants is an apology, and her courtroom manner is lucid, demure, and undoubtedly maddening to her opponents. Last summer Miss Ross summoned an Irene Mara before Magistrate Nicholas Pinto in Coney Island Court. This woman, aided and abetted by her mother, had used uncivil language in attempting to restrain Miss Ross from making off with a brood of cats. Unkind words had led to blows and in the end the embattled ladies had been separated by several patrolmen. A certain disarray in Mrs. Mara's appearance suggested that Miss Ross had had all the better of the skirmish. Nevertheless, the judge, influenced by the deceptive meekness in Miss Ross's manner, ruled that she was entitled to an apology.

COLLECTOR

"Have you missed any dish towels?" reads a notice tacked up in the entrance hall of that huge old apartment house at 142 East Eighteenth Street. "We have a cat who keeps bringing them home. Please come in and claim them. Sands, Apt. 4-A."

| 1949 |

"Me apologize to *her*!" cried Mrs. Mara incredulously, and started to flounce out of the courtroom. The judge had her brought back and, after a stern lecture, the apology was given.

"He called me a lady," Miss Ross says merrily, recalling this scene. "'You apologize to this lady,' he said. Me, a lady!"

Before the stray cats of the city so relentlessly took possession of her life, Rita Ross gave every promise of a successful career on the stage. Born Marion Garcewich, in the section of Harlem just north of 110th Street, she was the daughter of the German-Jewish proprietor of a gents' furnishing store. She attended Public School 170 in that neighborhood and eventually was graduated. In her teens, her family moved to Brooklyn. For a while she was a salesgirl for Loft's, and afterward a model for Galen Perrett, a commercial artist, from whose studio at 51 West Tenth Street her likeness emerged as the radiant face in the Bel-Ton Powder advertisements, displayed throughout the transportation systems of the city. In 1919 she got a job as a chorus girl in a road company of *So Long, Letty*.

Unfortunately for her career, it was at this time that she fell under the influence of her private daemon. Foreshadowing that remarkable pedestrianism which was later to wear down strong men, Miss Garcewich (now, for theatrical purposes, Rita Ross) used to walk across Brooklyn Bridge every day on her way to work in Manhattan. The cats of the lower East Side, degraded and mournful, attracted her strongly, and she got to picking up one or two of them and taking them to an S.P.C.A. shelter on her way uptown.

It is hard to say how this merciful habit gradually became a compulsion. It appears that one cat simply led to another. Miss Ross herself has no explanation of it except in vague, humanitarian terms. It is only clear that from a lady who could, on the whole, take a cat or leave it alone, she was suddenly translated into the most prodigious cat-catcher of our time. As her obsession grew, her other interests inevitably suffered. She was no less fetching as a chorus girl, of course, but she became a little embarrassing as an associate. In Salt Lake City, she rescued an alley cat from a vivisectionist by beating him severely over the head with her handbag. In Indianapolis, where she had gone with *The Spice of 1922* company, she was dismissed for picking up a dirty white poodle and installing it in her dressing room.

By 1926, when she was playing in *The Song of the Flame* in Chicago, her peculiarities were so generally recognized that she was warned by the management not to bring any animals into the theatre. She wrestled heroically with temptation, but the habit had her in an iron grip. One night she smuggled in two shivering kittens and hid them in shoebags below her mirror in the general dressing room. The cats, numb and grateful, remained as they were during the first number. When, however, the chorus girls came back after the second number, clawed costumes covered the floor and the wardrobe mistress panted after two hilarious cats. Miss Ross returned to New York. She remained on the stage during the run and tour of Hope Hampton's *My Princess* in 1927, but her heart wasn't in it. When it closed, she retired to devote all her time to her cats.

"I'm not sorry I stopped the stage," she

Nov. 1, 1982

Price $1.50

THE
NEW YORKER

says. "This work is much more interesting. You never know what's going to happen."

She realizes that a professional cat-catcher cannot hope to be as immaculate as Mrs. Harrison Williams, and occasionally this causes her mild distress. Last summer she passed Arthur Hammerstein in Greenwich Village. Miss Ross was in full regalia and the producer looked firmly at something else.

"My, was I embarrassed! I just slunk past."

On the whole, though, she has never regretted her choice. The average chorus girl, she feels, is at least as peculiar as she is, and not in the direction of good works, either.

Miss Ross now lives with her widowed mother, a brother, two sisters, and a nephew, all of whom regard their relative's habit of sleeping in a room crawling with cats as merely odd. These cats are transient, being

ones that she has picked up too late at night to turn over to the S.P.C.A. She maintains only one cat of her own, a deaf, toothless antique named Tibby-Wibby Simpson Ross, the gift of an amiable colored woman Miss Ross met on Lenox Avenue. In addition to the usual handicaps of age, Tibby-Wibby has another, of an embarrassing nature.

"He'll never be a daddy," Miss Ross explains delicately.

Miss Ross is given her room and some of her meals by her family, and, since she is a vegetarian and a light eater anyway, the others don't cost much. Money for her clothes, her cat-trapping equipment, and the rest of her needs comes from well-wishers. She is supported at the moment by two anonymous ladies—one in Brooklyn and one in Manhattan—who send her a total of fifteen dollars a week in care of *Variety*, which still nervously handles

"You never chase me through back yards anymore."

her mail. At various times during her career, Miss Ross's patronesses have changed, but she has always been able to find ladies, generally prominent supporters of the S.P.C.A., who were anxious to continue her good, though unusual, work. Occasionally there are windfalls from antivivisectionists or people whom she has helped to rid of a plague of cats. In all, she receives about nine hundred dollars a year, which is ample for a woman who up to now has never even been able to find time to go to a talking picture.

Singular things have happened in the course of her career. Once, when she was rearranging her cats in a ladies' room in an "L" station, a habit she has when pressed for time, another passenger, alarmed by strange, thin cries from an adjoining booth, told the ticket agent that a child had just been born, and was barely restrained from sending for an ambulance. Again, in the old New York Hospital at Fifteenth Street and Sixth Avenue, Miss Ross was forced by a series of improbable circumstances to pursue a cat up from the basement and under a bed in the psychopathic ward. Doctors and nurses, coming in to find what they imagined to be a fully dressed patient down on her hands and knees mewing, tried to get her undressed and back into bed. Things looked fairly black until somebody discovered that there actually *was* a cat under the bed. Miss Ross, however, kept her poise.

As a matter of fact, she says she has been really at a loss only once. That was when a dozen of her cats escaped three summers ago while she was riding on the Third Avenue "L." Miss Ross was sitting quietly with her eyes closed, bothering no man. Suddenly, for some unexplained reason, the lid of her animal case flew open. A stream of cats, long pent and in-

dignant, emerged and, with Miss Ross anxiously after them, leaped and gambolled down the aisle, springing over and upon the agitated passengers. When the train stopped, the cats, Miss Ross, and most of the passengers got off in a hurried flux. The passengers milled unhappily around on the platform. The cats, with Miss Ross pursuing the main body, scampered down both stairways. Baffled by their unfamiliar surroundings in the street, the cats darted perilously about in the traffic while Miss Ross sifted after them, like an image in an old moving picture cranked up to dizzy speed. In the end she got them all, but for once the situation threatened to be a little beyond her.

"I can tell you I blushed," she says, describing a vehicular chaos which must have compared very favorably with that immediately following the Wall Street explosion.

The future, like the past and present, holds for Miss Ross only a continuation of her singular crusade. The half-million cats still loose on the streets are a challenge to her genius and she cannot rest until the last one is trapped and riding to its doom. Even at her present spectacular rate, it is the work of a lifetime. She approaches it without misgiving.

| *1938* |

ARMY CATS

1.

Over by the cemetery next to the CP
you could see them in wild catmint going crazy:
I watched them roll and wriggle, paw it, lick it,
chew it, leap about, pink tongues stuck out, drooling.

Cats in the tanks' squat shadows lounging.
Or sleeping curled up under gun turrets.
Hundreds of them sniffing or licking
long hind legs stuck in the air,

great six-toed brutes fixing you with a feral,
slit-eyed stare . . . everywhere ears twitching,
twitching as the armor plate expanding
in the heat gave off piercing little pings.

Cat invasion of the mind. Cat tribes
running wild. And one big pregnant
female comes racing through weeds to pounce
between the paws of a marble dog

crouching on a grave and sharpens
her claws against his beard of moss
before she goes all silky, luxuriously
squirming right under the dog's jaws,

and rolls over to expose her swollen belly.
Picture her with gold hoop earrings
and punked-out nose ring like the cat goddess Bast,
bronze kittens at her feet, the crowd drinking wildly,

women lifting up their skirts as she floats down
the Nile, a sistrum jangling in her paw.
Then come back out of it and sniff
her ointments, Lady of Flame, Eye of Ra.

2.

Through the yard the tanks come gunning,
charioteers laughing, goggles smeared with dust
and sun, scattering the toms slinking
along the blast wall holding back the waves

from washing away white crosses on the graves,
the motors roaring through the afternoon
like a cat fuck yowling on and on.
The gun turrets revolving in the cats' eyes

swivel and shine, steel treads clanking,
sending the cats flying in an exodus
through brown brittle grass, the stalks
barely rippling as they pass.

3.

After the last car bomb killed three soldiers
the Army Web site labelled them "martyrs."
Four civilians killed at checkpoints. Three on the
    airport road.
A young woman blown up by a grenade.

Facts and more facts . . . until the dead ones
climb up out of the graves, gashes on faces
or faces blown away like sandblasted stone
that in the boarded-up museums'

fractured English "leaves the onlooker
riddled and shaken, nothing but a pathetic gaping . . ."
And then I remember the ancient archers
frozen between reverence and necessity—

who stare down the enemy, barbarians,
as it's told, who nailed sacred cats to their shields,
knowing their foes outraged in their piety
would throw down their bows and wail like kittens.

—TOM SLEIGH | 2009 |

CROUCHING TIGER, TREMBLING PENGUIN

ROBERT SULLIVAN

For the moment, the penguins at the New York Aquarium are safe. But the aquarium's staff remains concerned, and, naturally, is taking some extra precautions, because the penguins are being stalked by a pack of feral cats.

One morning last November, Paul Moylett, a seal-and-walrus keeper, was walking through the aquarium when he noticed a black cat eying the penguins, in their open-air habitat, alongside the Coney Island boardwalk. "I saw the cat in a crouched position, and its tail was flicking back and forth, so I ran into the exhibit and scared it away," he said the other day. Around the same time, Dave Rodahan, a lab technician, spotted one cat in with the penguins and a pair crouching among some yucca plants. "They were looking at me almost as if they were doing a kind of bait thing," he said. "I've never seen any cat here do that kind of behavior before."

The cats in question are abandoned pets and their offspring. They have been seen around the aquarium in small numbers for years, like feral animals all over the city. (The Bronx Zoo has begun shooting wild dogs.) Several years ago, however, a retired Wall Street precious-metals trader who lives in the neighborhood began feeding the cats, and the population exploded. Last year, about thirty cats could be seen regularly patrolling the outskirts of the penguins' poured-concrete habitat, so the aquarium hired an exterminator to trap them. This made neighborhood cat lovers mad. They complained to the *Bay News*, a local paper, about the exterminator, who

seemed evasive when he was asked how he was disposing of the strays: he told the paper that he had given some of the cats to "a person in New Jersey who takes care of animals." The aquarium fired the exterminator, and the cat problem returned.

The species of penguin being stalked is *Spheniscus demersus*, more commonly known as the black-footed penguin. It is a native of southern Africa and can reach a height of twenty-four inches. When it stands, its armlike flippers often shiver slightly, making it appear nervous. And because it emits a donkey-like braying sound, *Spheniscus demersus* is also known as the jackass penguin.

On a recent cold afternoon, several of Coney Island's jackass penguins were standing, un-stalked, in their habitat, in plain view of the Cyclone, the old Coney Island roller coaster. A pond of sixty-degree water stood between them and a clutch of Russian women wearing furs and carrying small children and Louis Vuitton bags. The rest of the penguins were in their burrows, where they were being tended by their keeper, Stephanie Mitchell, a thirty-two-year-old Massachusetts native who started at the aquarium in 1998, as a volunteer. Mitchell admitted that she had not initially been drawn to the penguins, whose reputation suffers among aquarium keepers because of their intense, ammonialike smell; she had hoped to be a dolphin keeper. "Obviously, I was one of those persons who was, like, *dolphin, dolphin, dolphin*," she said. "But I'm really, really happy. I love these guys."

Mitchell was wearing khakis and a blue jacket smeared with penguin guano. She said that the aquarium is home to twenty-two male penguins, eleven female penguins, and four penguins whose gender is not yet known. The names of some of the penguins are Giovanni, Curly, Bert, Moni, Willow, Cinders, Old Man, and Roxette. Carmine is the oldest penguin; he has lived in Coney Island for about twenty-two years. Penguins are monogamous, but, because there are more males than females at the aquarium just now, relationships in the colony are in flux. "We have some females doing some shopping," Mitchell said.

As she set out to feed her charges, Mitchell talked about the likelihood of a feral cat's killing a jackass penguin, whose only predators in the wild are Cape fur seals, skuas, and great white sharks. "Penguins are fast, but not that fast—though they could just jump in the water," she said. "I am constantly worried about Willow, because he's a small bird. If anybody's gonna get caught by a cat, he's the one. But there's no way a cat's going to get them out of their burrows. Sometimes *I* can't get them out of the burrows."

Mitchell crept carefully out onto the simulated concrete rocks with a bucket of fish in her hand, and a little crowd of penguins waddled up to her. She was tossing fish and chatting with the penguins, complimenting them, when suddenly she sensed something behind her. She turned slowly. It was only a seagull. She shooed it away.

"They're not gone," Mitchell said ominously, referring to the wild cats. "They've just gone underground."

| 2001 |

HOW TO MAKE A CAT TRAP

E. B. WHITE

Anyone who can use a square, a saw, and a hammer can make a cat trap. It is well, however, to have a blueprint to go by, and if possible a particular cat in mind that you want to trap; for if you were to make a trap that didn't work, or even made a trap that worked and caught a cat you didn't want, I can't see that there would be anything gained on either side.

The following materials are necessary for building the trap: one twelve-inch board fourteen feet long, one one-and-a-half-inch strip seven feet long, one three-quarter-inch strip two feet long, twenty inches of No. 3 gage wire, two small screw-eyes, one piece of wire netting six inches square, and a little piece of fresh fish.

*The trap
from the rear*

Cut the twelve-inch board to make the following pieces: one bottom board thirty inches long, one top board twenty-eight and a half inches long, two side boards twenty-nine and a quarter inches long, one treadle board twenty-seven inches long, one drop board thirteen and a half inches long, one end board ten and a half inches long. Now put the little piece of fresh fish away in the icebox, sweep up the sawdust, and look what you've done to the floor already.

Cut the one-and-one-half-inch strip to make the following

pieces: two drop-door guides twenty-four inches long, two drop-door guides eleven and one-fourth inches long, one fulcrum piece for treadle ten and one-half inches long.

Cut or plane a quarter of an inch from the edge of the treadle board so that it will move freely inside the trap without binding. Cut a V-shaped groove about a quarter of an inch deep across the treadle at right angles and thirteen and one-half inches from the front end to fit over the top of the fulcrum. If you are unable, or unwilling, to cut a V-shaped groove, cut an S-shaped, or even an R-shaped groove. It will be all one to the people who live in the same building.

Except for the fulcrum, which is impossible to construct, nothing is so difficult to construct in the cat trap as the door guides. They are very hard. Cut or plane the fulcrum piece to a ridge one inch high, to fit into the groove in the treadle. Cut or plane the edges of the drop door so that it will slide freely in the guides after the cat is in. (Incidentally, you ought to begin looking around for a cat—the disappointment of building a cat trap and having no use for it is real.) Now then, cut an opening four by five inches in the centre of the rear-end board and tack a piece of wire netting over it to provide ventilation. A stuffy cat trap is worse than no cat trap! Nail the bottom, sides, top, and end in position to form the box. Screw one screw-eye into the top of the treadle half an inch from the right side and seventeen and

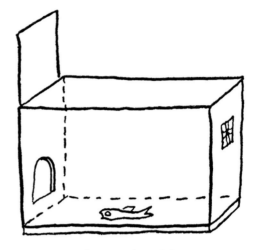

Cross section of the completed trap

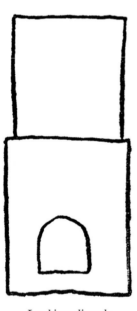

Looking directly at the trap

one-half inches from the front end. Screw the second screw-eye into the piano for all I care. The trap should be given two coats of paint inside and out, and the apartment should be completely done over, walls, floors, and ceilings. While the paint is drying, a good way to utilize your time is to cook the little piece of fish and eat it.

The simplest and most humane way of disposing of the trapped cat is to gas it. Insert into the trap a tablespoonful of calcium cyanide or a wad of cotton saturated with one ounce of carbon disulphide or chloroform. A heavy blanket thrown over the trap will assist in keeping the gas confined and will ruin the blanket. CAUTION: Carbon disulphide is highly explosive and inflammable and calcium cyanide and its fumes are extremely toxic; but if you're going to trap cats you've got to expect a few hard knocks.

Some people prefer to shoot a cat rather than trap it. To such people I have nothing to say, but I have usually found that they didn't know how to use tools.

| 1930 |

THE CAT-SAVERS

WALLACE WHITE

A fat white cat leaped from behind a vertically propped bedspring, flew to a dusty table, and headed for a grille-covered window. "Get him! Have you got him? Emily, quick!" a slim girl with long tawny hair shouted. The cat soared from the table to the windowsill and then out through the window and its grille, and, with great agility, dashed past the outstretched hands of two people standing on the sidewalk and vanished down the street.

"He just left town," said an attractive woman with dark-blond hair who was standing outside the building. "Did you see anybody else?"

"I saw a tabby upstairs, Judy—I'm sure I did," the slim girl replied, stepping through a pile of debris that sent up a puff of dust around her ankles, which were encased in plaid trousers. "Is there any more food out there?"

It was a Sunday afternoon, and we were standing with three other people inside a deserted building—one of several tenements in the West Nineties that were about to be razed. The people around us—the two outside as well as the three inside—were members of the Save A Cat League, an organization whose main function is the rescuing of homeless cats, many of which, like the ones that were being sought in this neighborhood, are left behind when their owners move. After a stray cat has been res-cued, the League takes it to a veterinarian for a checkup, and then places it in a tempo-rary home while putting it up for adoption. "You do it because it's got to be done and nobody else is doing it," we had been told earlier by the attractive dark-blond woman, who was Mrs. Judith Scofield, the League's founder and president. "You can't live with yourself if you don't."

Now, inside the building, an auburn-haired woman said as she stepped over a fallen chair, "I'm going back upstairs. That tabby can't have got away." She was Emily Cobb, an actress and a member of the League's Canine Auxiliary, which does roughly the same thing for dogs that the parent organization does for cats.

"The tabby might have run off over the roofs," said a strongly built man in a green parka, who had been introduced to us as Gil McKean, an advertising copywriter.

"There's all kinds of furniture in here!"

the slim girl, whose name was Susan Neher, called to those outside. "Anybody want a cane chair? A bathtub?"

As the two young women and Mr. McKean plodded around broken furniture and unidentifiable artifacts on their way to the building's staircase, we made our way out to the sidewalk. It was about two o'clock, and a drizzling rain had begun to fall. Mrs. Scofield turned to her companion, a man named Mack Shopnick, and said, "We'll try that building across the street, and then go see the little girl who wrote to us." On the sidewalk were five or six cat-carriers—large, perforated cases with suitcase handles—and a cardboard carton containing perhaps a dozen cans of cat food.

After about five minutes, the three searchers emerged from the building empty-handed. Mr. McKean was panting, and Miss Cobb looked a bit dishevelled.

Miss Neher, who we had learned was a secretary for The Players, picked up one of the cat-carriers and started across the street. Other League members picked up carriers and followed her toward a bleak-looking tenement whose windows had been boarded up. Mr. McKean managed to open a basement door, and a party of four (Mrs. Scofield and Miss Neher stayed behind), armed with flashlights, advanced into the gloomy interior. They returned several minutes later and reported that they had found nothing but a dead kitten. Miss Neher looked stricken, but Mrs. Scofield bore the news stoically and suggested that the group move on.

With Mrs. Scofield and Mr. Shop-nick, who is an arranger and conductor of music for radio and television commercials, we got into a gray sedan and began driving west. The others followed in Miss Cobb's car. "No, turn there, Mack," Mrs. Scofield said. "No. No, *left!*" She glanced at us and said, "The rain's going to make it difficult. The cats aren't out. They're all hiding inside somewhere. Quite a few people write us or call us when they learn of cats that have been abandoned. You'd be surprised how many people move out and leave their pets to fend for themselves. I just wish the owners would call us, instead of deserting the animals. People can be so intolerably cruel. We got a call a while ago to come down to West Twenty-second Street. A bunch of boys were taking stray cats up onto the roof of a building and throwing them off." Mrs. Scofield said this with an equanimity that, we guessed, stemmed from years of dealing with such grisly matters. She began rescuing homeless cats, as a personal venture, in 1942, and she founded the League in 1956. She has continued to run the organization while working as an insurance broker. The League, which now has about two hundred and fifty members, devotes much of its energy to placing rescued animals with adoptive families. It also helps arrange cat-boarding and sitting services, and distributes free cat food to people known as "feeders," who attempt to care for the strays in their neighborhoods.

Mr. Shopnick pulled up before a nondescript gray stone building, and we accompanied Mrs. Scofield to its door. In a minute or so, she and we were standing inside the apartment of the building superintendent, whose daughter, a pretty girl of about ten, had written to Mrs. Scofield about a demolition area where ownerless cats were reported to be roaming.

"Now, where did you see them?" asked Mrs. Scofield.

"Well, I know the lady who can take you to them," the little girl replied. She gave Mrs. Scofield a name and address, and Mrs. Scofield returned to the car and directed Mr. Shopnick to drive on for several blocks. The building they were seeking turned out to be the most dilapidated of the day. A dingy tenement, it stood alone on a corner, with rubble-covered lots stretching away from it in two directions. We went inside with Mrs. Scofield, and followed her down a hallway whose faint lights illuminated crayon-scrawled walls and up two creaking flights of stairs. Mrs. Scofield pushed a button outside a third-floor apartment several times, and at last the door opened, revealing a very small, very old woman with a black kerchief on her head.

Mrs. Scofield said, "Does Mrs. Hernandez live here?"

"I'm Mrs. Hernandez," the woman said in a tiny, childlike voice.

Mrs. Scofield explained her mission, and Mrs. Hernandez disappeared into the apartment. In a few moments, she reappeared and, moving slowly, escorted Mrs. Scofield down the stairs and out of the building. We followed as the entire group advanced across some rugged, obstacle-strewn terrain. It was still drizzling, and the earth was beginning to turn to mud. At a point where the vacant lots ended and the back yards of two buildings that faced on parallel streets began, Mrs. Hernandez pointed vaguely toward the buildings and said, "There. They live in there."

With cat-carriers in each hand, Miss Cobb, Miss Neher, and Mr. McKean began picking their way across broken bricks and nail-studded timbers toward the back yards. High in a neighboring building, a window flew open and a man stuck out his head and yelled, "You looking for the cats?"

"Don't talk to him!" Mrs. Hernandez piped in her small voice. "He hates cats!"

The cat-savers ignored the cat-hater and pressed on with their search.

"Where's the food?" Miss Cobb called. "Have you got the Friskies?"

"I'm coming with them!" Mr. McKean called back.

Below a pile of wreckage, Miss Cobb made a gingerly descent into one of the back yards. She emptied a can of cat food onto a paper plate, crushed the empty can with one foot, and drew back. In a few minutes, a tiger-striped gray cat emerged from the shadow of a fence and crept cautiously toward the food. "Oh, he's a saint!" Miss Cobb whispered.

Mrs. Hernandez cried, "Oh, no! That's one of Mrs. Miller's cats!"

The League members looked disappointed.

At intervals of several minutes, a calico cat, an all-gray cat, and a black-and-white cat emerged from the shadows and crept toward the food. As each cat appeared, Mrs. Hernandez cried, "No! No! That's one of Mrs. Miller's cats!"

The group looked very discouraged.

Rain was coming down hard now, and Mrs. Scofield decided to terminate the search. "If it weren't for the rain, we'd have had them," she said as we accompanied her back toward the cars. "The last time we went out on one of these hunts, we got thirty cats, just like that! Why, some of them practically walked right up and said, 'Take me.'"

Having arranged, this time, to ride in Miss Cobb's car, we got into its front seat—Miss Neher was in the back—and Miss Cobb drove along an eastbound street. When we reached Central Park West, she came to a sudden halt. "That dog!" she exclaimed. "Quick! Somebody get him! He's a stray! Quick! Oh!" She sprang from the car, which was in the middle of the intersection, and ran toward the Park. The dog, a young brown mongrel that looked to be part German shepherd, fled through the rain along the edge of the Park. We watched the flight and pursuit in numbed fascination.

Three minutes later, the wet dog climbed docilely into the back seat, shook itself, and began to munch on a dried dog-burger. "He's a stray. See? No license," Miss Cobb said as she slid behind the wheel. "Oh, what a prize, what a beauty! I can hardly wait to get him to a vet. I just can't wait. Anybody would be a fool not to take him. Just look at him! A saint!"

"Emily's heart really belongs to dogs. There's no getting around it," Miss Neher said. "We'll get our cats the next time." She reached down and patted the dog on the head, and it looked about as pleased as a dog can look.

| 1967 |

BOOTH

A DULL, ORDINARY, NORMAL LIFE IN MANHATTAN

Fiction

BERNARD TAPER

An incident that occurred the other day has started me thinking once more about moving out to the suburbs, or the exurbs, or, if possible, even farther away than that from this crazy city. One of my children once observed, when my wife and I were having an inconclusive discussion about the ideal place to live, "Well, there are more advantages to living in the city, but there are fewer *dis*advantages to living in the suburbs"—a remark that struck me as prattle at the time but that I now think sums up the matter compendiously.

My wife sees only the advantages in city living. Manhattan is still an adventure to her. She goes out to take the wash to the laundry or buy a loaf of bread, and she comes back to the apartment all aglow, looking like someone who has just made an exhilarating ski run. With me, the disadvantages loom larger, and there are times when the complications attendant on trying to live just a dull, ordinary, normal life here are more than I can contemplate.

We live on the eighth floor of a fifteen-story apartment house—my wife, myself, our two sons, and a cat, of whom the children are inordinately fond. The incident I mention involved the cat—or, I should say, it involved us all, but it started with the cat. As I was about to leave for work one morning, my older son, Philip, who is eleven, came up to me with a worried look, saying that he could hear the cat crying but couldn't find her anywhere in the apartment and was afraid she had got out and was stuck somewhere.

"Oh, damn!" I said. "Who left the window open?"

You have to concern yourself with trifling problems if you live in

Manhattan, such as how to get an adequate supply of soot-laden air into your apartment without providing an aperture large enough to tempt a cat.

"Mother thinks you did," Philip replied.

"Well, never mind," I said briskly. "We'll find her."

I went out, searched the back stairs up to the top floor, looked behind the chimneys on the roof, and then went down to the courtyard, where I found my wife, our six-year-old son, Mark, a couple of women I didn't recognize but supposed were fellow-tenants, and the building's handyman. One of the women had her hands cupped behind her ears and was rotating slowly on her axis, as if she were a radar station. "The cat may be in the basement," she said thoughtfully.

"I already looked there," the handyman said.

"To me, it comes from up high," said the other woman, in a Middle European accent, and, tilting her head back and stretching her neck, she called sternly, "Kidt, kidt, vere are you?"

I have long suspected that cats are natural ventriloquists. As far as I could tell, the sound of our cat's crying, which had now become very loud and piteous, might have been coming from any direction. My child, baffled, continued to look high and low, and to rush about helplessly whenever the cat wailed. My wife asked me, "Why don't you go up to the roof again and see if you can spot it by looking over the edge?"

I said I would. On the way up I stopped off at our apartment to phone my office and leave word that I would be late for an appointment. "Just say I've been detained," I told the receptionist.

When I emerged on the roof a few minutes later, I saw our mailman. He was strolling along by the edge of the roof, smoking a pipe, his mail sack over his shoulder. Surprised, I asked him what he was doing.

"Looking for a cat," he answered.

"*Our* cat," I said.

"Oh, it's yours, is it? I wondered," he said.

We deployed, the mailman on one wing of the building and I on the other, walking along the rim of the roof and peering down. The courtyard group, I could see, had been augmented, and there were also a couple of heads protruding from apartment windows. The search for our cat was becoming a public spectacle. After a while, the mailman called out triumphantly "There it is!" and, going over to him and sighting along his pipe, with which he was pointing, I saw the cat crouched shivering on a window sill two stories below. "It's at 13-E," the mailman said. Then he added, "They're away on vacation, 13-E."

Someone in the courtyard must also have spied the cat about then, for there was a sudden hubbub and arm-waving down there, and I heard somebody call, "Go down the fire escape!" Well, that was obviously the thing to do, all right—the fire escape went within a foot or two of the cat's perch—and I was obviously the one expected to

"*Yeah, I was into the pet thing for a while, but that scene wasn't for me.*"

do it, so I stepped awkwardly over the edge of the roof and started down, clutching the railings of the fire escape fiercely.

I happen to be somewhat vertiginous—not to a medically significant degree, but enough to make high places seem pretty unpleasant to me. For one thing, they inflame my imagination. The moment I stepped off the roof, lurid pictures flashed into my mind. First, I had a vision of the fire escape collapsing into the courtyard in an avalanche of ironwork, bringing destruction to all. I had read newspaper accounts of just such catastrophes, usually with some building inspector being quoted as saying, "We inspected that escape only a week ago. The bolts must have been rusted clear through." Then, as the fire escape held firm under my full weight, that vision was supplanted by a more poignant one. I saw myself losing my hold on the railings (because of the buffeting of the wind, perhaps, or a missed step, or a momentary dizziness; all three possibilities presented themselves) and plummeting down through space, paying, like Icarus, the penalty for

CAT GODDESSES

A perverse habit of cat goddesses—
Even the blackest of them, black as coals
Save for a new moon blazing on each breast,
With coral tongues and beryl eyes like lamps,
Long-leggèd, pacing three by three in nines—
This obstinate habit is to yield themselves,
In verisimilar love ecstasies,
To tatter-eared and slinking alley toms
No less below the common run of cats
Than they above it—which they do for spite,
To provoke jealousy, not the least abashed
By such gross-headed, rabbit-colored litters
As soon they will be happy to desert.

—ROBERT GRAVES | 1953 |

having presumed to venture too high. Then, wistfully, as from a great spiritual distance, I contemplated the ensuing tableau: my crumpled body in the courtyard, the horrified crowd of onlookers, my children standing pale and silent, unable to comprehend what had happened, my wife weeping heartrendingly, and all the time—a gruesome but effective touch—the cat, trivial cause of the tragedy, keening away on its ledge, still preoccupied only with its own precious plight.

But during those moments when I was mourning myself so sincerely my wife was not sharing the full pathos of the situation. She was standing in the courtyard watching my progress and, as she has since confessed, laughing helplessly. She insists that she couldn't successfully worry about me, because the fire escape is broad, solid enough to support a battalion, and pitched no steeper than an ordinary staircase. She says that the sight of me inching backward down this substantial stairway, spread-eagled, holding on to both railings for dear life, and feeling timorously for each step with my foot, was one of the funniest performances she has ever seen.

Be that as it may, I was immensely relieved when, at last, I found that I had worked my way down to the cat's level. I looked forward hopefully to winding up the extravaganza shortly and going about my normal business. Reaching toward the trembling cat, I crooned, "There, there, kitty. Everything's going to be all right," to which the cat responded in a way familiar to would-be cat rescuers ever since cats first domesticated unwary mankind. With rescue at hand, the cat became transformed. It ceased to shiver and wail. It stretched, yawned, rose languorously to its feet, blinked once or twice at me, as if to show surprise but no great interest at seeing me there, eyed my importunate fingers with light disdain, and then, the window beside her being open a few inches,

slid gracefully into Apartment 13-E. There, on what I now saw was the bathroom floor, she settled down to licking delicately at the handsome streak of white fur on her sleek gray chest.

Deeply regretting that the apartment's tenants had not seen fit to close their windows before they went on vacation, I pushed the window up and leaned over the sill, murmuring such blandishments as "Come please, kitty, goddammit."

The cat didn't even bother to look at me. I threw one leg over the sill and made a quick grab at her. She drew back out of reach. I brought the other leg over and rushed at her. That was a mistake. She darted out of the room. I hesitated a moment, then—not knowing what better to do—dashed after her, finding myself in a bedroom, where I caught a glimpse of the cat's tail whisking out through a door on the far side. That door, I discovered, opened into the foyer of the apartment. The living room was on one side of it and the dining room on the other. All the furniture in both rooms was covered with sheets and dropcloths. The cat was not to be seen.

I paused in the foyer, feeling increasingly uneasy about having let myself be lured into a strange apartment, and wondering what to do now. As I stood there, to my consternation I saw the front door slowly open. A man and a woman came through it. They were talking earnestly, and they obviously belonged there. They could only be the apartment's tenants, returned, at this moment, of all moments, from their vacation.

A small eternity—several seconds, perhaps—passed before they noticed me. If I had been able to move, I would have fled back through the bedroom and out the bathroom window, braving all the perils of the fire escape, but I could not stir. When, at last, they became aware of me, they merely stared at me, immobilized, and said

nothing. "I live in Apartment 8-E," I said, trying for a light conversational tone, "and I'm trying to find our cat."

"Cat?" the man said. He was a large man with rumpled blond hair and a harassed expression.

"It's here somewhere," I said. "It must have crawled under the couch. I *know* it's here."

The man had a telegram in his hand, and its contents must have been on his mind, preventing him from adjusting at once to the presence in his apartment of a stranger who claimed to be hunting a cat. He kept looking from the telegram to me, and then, still speechless, blankly about him. Here, things become somewhat blurred for me. Suddenly the apartment was full of people—mostly women, one of them my wife—rushing about, poking under the furniture, and calling, "Here, kitty, kitty!"

Having seen the cat and me vanish into 13-E, my wife had scooped up a posse in the courtyard and led it upstairs. When the posse arrived at the apartment, the tenants had dazedly invited them in to help in the search. And now the women were all over the place, like a pack of hounds running down a fox. The harassed blond man and his wife stood in the middle of it all, trying to consult about the telegram. Every few minutes, the man would mop his brow, run distractedly about, adding his own cry of "Kitty, kitty!" to those of the pack, and then, circling back to his wife, resume his efforts to cope with whatever urgent matter the telegram had announced. I decided that I had better get out of there, before hysteria set in, and murmuring to no one in particular, "I guess there's nothing more that I can do," stole away and went shakily to my office.

I didn't get much work done the rest of that day, but I did spend a good deal of time thinking how simple and beautiful life could be anywhere but in Manhattan. Late in the morning, I received a report from my wife, by telephone, that the cat had eventually been found behind the stove of 13-E. And when I got home that evening, I felt that surely, after the day's experience, my wife would be ready to discuss tolerantly the idea of moving to the suburbs.

To my surprise, I discovered that she was nothing of the sort. She seemed, instead, quite inspired by the events of the morning. She kept saying how helpful everybody had been, even the mailman. That was the great thing about Manhattan, she said—that people could be helpful there without having to be perpetual friends. "It's not like Greenwich or Larchmont," she said, pronouncing these names with repulsion. "Or any of those other cozy places. Why, the people who helped us today probably won't even say hello if they meet us in the elevator tomorrow." With a laugh, she added, "By the way, the tenants in 13-E said they never for a moment thought you were a burglar. They thought you must be a building inspector, or something. I guess they thought that because you were wearing a suit."

Not to be deflected, I said, "You have to admit this couldn't even have happened in Larchmont."

My wife gazed at me with real surprise. "Why!" she said. "If you'd broken into the house of one of those property-conscious Larchmont people the way you did into 13-E, you wouldn't have got off so easily, I can tell you. Larchmont isn't Manhattan. They've all got guns in those places. They'd have shot you dead."

| 1958 |

WHO'S REALLY RUNNING THE CITY

PRICE $4.99

THE

NEW YORKER

JAN. 23 & 30, 2006

CAT FANCIERS

TIGER IN THE SNOW

PETER MATTHIESSEN

In early April of 1996, I went to the zoo in Indianapolis to pay my respects to a young Amur tiger, which I found stretched gracefully on a sunny ledge, the highest and most isolated point in an outside enclosure she shares with two other Amur tigers, another young female and an adult male. She peered at me—or, rather, past me, in the cat's indifferent manner—through the slanted ellipses of gold-amber eyes. Unlike her companions—and unlike most zoo tigers—this beautiful creature was born in the wild, and, as it happened, I had recently returned from southeastern Siberia, where I had visited the alder wood on a snowy ridge on which she had been captured four years earlier, as an unweaned, orphaned cub.

According to her keepers, the young tigress remains rather shy and apprehensive around strangers, owing to the traumatic circumstances surrounding her capture; a young zoo-bred tigress, who is more gregarious, was placed in her enclosure as a "surrogate sibling," to help acclimate her to captivity and calm her down. The Siberian tigress is beautiful and healthy, at about two hundred and fifty pounds, and is exceptionally valuable because of her genes, which promise a welcome infusion of new blood into captive-tiger-breeding programs all over the country. This month, she is scheduled to be bred with a genetically suitable male from the Minnesota Zoo—one whose genes are not already widespread in American zoo populations. Her cubs would be exponentially more valuable in maintaining the small tiger population in the wild, but that is not her story.

The remote and beautiful Primorski Krai, or Maritime Province, in eastern Siberia, is best known to the outside world through an enchanting book called *Dersu the Trapper* (the source of the fine 1975 Kurosawa film *Dersu Uzala*), which filled me with yearning to travel to that remote region ever since I first read it, back in the sixties. Its author, V. K. Arseniev, was a young Russian Army geographer, ethnographer, and naturalist who between 1902 and 1907 made three expeditions on horse and on foot to map the still unknown Maritime Province; his guide was Dersu, a local hunter, who had survived a terrible mauling by a tiger. Known to the local Chinese as Hu Lin, the King, and to the Tungus tribes as Amba, Protector of the Forest, the tiger pervades Arseniev's accounts. To indigenous people such as Dersu, it was the very spirit of the great Old World forest known as the taiga.

In late June of 1992, I made my first visit to Primorski Krai, which curves south along the Sea of Japan like a great claw to its borders with northeastern China and North Korea. My destination was the Sikhote-Alin International Biosphere Reserve, the largest wildlife sanctuary in the Far East, consisting of a thousand three hundred and fifty square miles of forested mountains, clear silver torrents, and

WINTER QUARTERS

Since the advent of the cold weather, a large, handsome, and extremely dirty cat has taken up residence in a parking lot on East Thirty-sixth Street. When a car arrives, it hops onto the hood, nestles there until the radiator cools off, then transfers to a newer and warmer arrival.

| 1951 |

unbroken coast. Here the brown bear and lynx, wolf and salmon of the north share their range with the tiger and leopard and subtropical flycatchers in a remarkable faunal region, unlike any other wilderness on earth.

The Sikhote-Alin Mountains are the last stronghold of *Panthera tigris altaica*, the so-called Siberian, or Manchurian, tiger, which as recently as the last century was common not only in Siberia but throughout northeastern China and the Korean Peninsula, and ranged west perhaps as far as Mongolia and Lake Baikal. Yet the heart of the tiger's range has always been the watershed of the mighty Amur River and its main tributary, the Ussuri, which form the eastern boundary of Russia and China. Known more precisely as the Amur tiger, it resembles the Indian, or Bengal, race in its general aspect, but there is more white in the striking patterns of the head and also on the underbelly, and the flame color is less intense—less fire orange than old gold. Although only slightly taller, the Amur race in its longhaired winter coat appears more massive than the Bengal—the only one of the five surviving tiger races or subspecies which compares to it in size—and captive males have approached a weight of a thousand pounds.

This largest of the earth's great cats is already effectively extinct in China and the Koreas, and the few hundred surviving in Russia were in mortal danger, when, in 1989, Russian tiger authorities and American wildlife biologists first discussed an international research program to study the ecology and range and habitat requirements of *P. t. altaica* as the basis for a comprehensive plan that would try to save it. In January of 1992, the Siberian Tiger Project was set up at Terney, a fishing port about two hundred miles northeast of Vladivostok, which is surrounded by the Sikhote-Alin Reserve. The American co-directors of the project, Dr. Maurice Hornocker and Dr. Howard Quigley, of the Hornocker Wildlife Institute, which is affiliated with the University of Idaho, were pioneers in the use of radio telemetry to conduct field studies of cougars and jaguars: after immobilizing the animal with drugs by means of a rifle-fired dart, they would take its measurements and blood samples, then fit it with a radio collar that permitted scientists to monitor the animal's movements and arrive at a better understanding of its ecology and range.

I was eager to observe field operations, but, as it happened, I arrived two days too late to witness the capture and release of a large tigress nicknamed Lena, only the second study animal caught since the project had begun. At Terney, Hornocker, a rangy, well-weathered wildlife biologist in his early sixties, and a foremost authority on the great cats, introduced me to three of his associates: a husky young American, Dr. Dale Miquelle, and two of their Russian colleagues—Igor Nikolaiev and Evgeny Smirnov—who, before the arrival of radio telemetry, had done most of their extensive research by tracking the animals on foot in winter. The researchers told me that Lena's signals were still coming from a wooded drainage area known as the Kunalaika in the southern part of the reserve, very close to the site of her capture two days earlier. Though full recovery from the immobilization drug might take two or three days, they were concerned that Lena had not recovered faster and wandered farther.

The next day, in the hope of monitoring the tiger's signals more precisely, we trekked into the forest, following a creek upstream for several miles through hardwood taiga of oak and birch, cottonwood and maple, poplar, ash, and elm, with scattered pines. On a dim old trail, all but closed by ferns, were big, raw pugmarks, or footprints. Perhaps these had been made by Lena, perhaps not. Farther on were deep-scratched trees where a tiger had sharpened its claws. Eventually, we arrived at the site where Lena had been snared—a large cottonwood where the ground was torn up all around and a strong sapling as thick as a man's arm had been snapped off clean. Lena's captors spoke with quiet awe of the terrible roars and lunging, the ferocity, with which this young female had made three swift charges on the cable of her snare before Hornocker and Nikolaiev were able to tranquillize her with two rifle-fired darts. Since then, Lena had moved less than a mile upstream. Using some rough triangulation to fix her precise location, we paused at a point estimated by Hornocker to be approximately a hundred yards from the tiger. Over the receiver came more rapid beepings, indicating that Lena was up and moving and had us located, too. She did not roar, but nobody believed that she was in a good temper. I envisioned her with her head raised and alert, her small, round white-spotted ears twitching in the greenish sunlight. In the fragmented sun shafts of the woodland, the head would be camouflaged by bold black calligraphic lines inscribed on frost-bright brows and beard and ruff, in a beautiful and terrifying mask of snow and fire.

In *Dersu the Trapper* Arseniev translates an inscription he had found in a Chinese joss house in Primorski Krai: "To the Lord Tiger who dwelleth in the Forest and the Mountains. In ancient days . . . he saved the state. Today his Spirit brings happiness to man." Considering the menace of the tiger, I had originally found the word "happiness" rather curious. But on that day in the Kunalaika forest while Lena observed us from her place of hiding I felt a kindled exaltation very close to what the poet Elizabeth Bishop felt when confronted with the enigma of a roadside moose:

> Why, why do we feel
> (we all feel) this sweet
> sensation of joy?

In late summer, Dr. Hornocker wrote me to say that Lena had resumed hunting in a normal manner. Also, a third female had been snared and collared, and in October, in the northern part of the Sikhote-Alin, a fourth female and two half-grown cubs were caught, making six "marked" animals all together. More exciting still was a discovery in the next month that Lena had produced a litter of four cubs. Elated, Hornocker suggested that I pay a return visit to Primorski Krai in winter, when I might hope to see a tiger in the snow. But in November he sent the terrible news that Dale Miquelle had found Lena's radio collar slashed from her neck and tossed into the snow. Apparently, she had been killed by poachers on a road edge. Of her cubs there was no sign whatsoever.

Because Lena had been the first "marked" animal to produce a litter, and was therefore of critical importance to many aspects of the tiger study, her loss was devastating. The heartbroken and enraged Miquelle had rushed back to Terney to report what had happened. Evgeny Smirnov and the reserve director, Anatoli Astafiev, accompanied by a forest guard and a police officer, returned with him to investigate the poaching site. While they were standing on the road, Smirnov glimpsed a movement in the bushes, and a moment later four tiger cubs were seen floundering uphill through the snow and alders. Though Miquelle tore off in pursuit, he was unable to catch them, yet it was clear that the unweaned and famished cubs, still awaiting their mother after a week or more, had kept circling back toward the killing place. (Though only a few months old, they were already the size of bobcats.) Realizing that they would not stray far, the men had returned to Terney and organized a capture party.

The next morning, the forest guard came upon two hiding cubs. Seizing one up against his chest and shouting for help, he stumbled along in pursuit of the other. By now, Astafiev and his party had come across the third and fourth, backed into a hollow tree. They were duly extricated, with precocious roars and snarl-

"Honey, I'm home!"

ing, and the capture of the four cubs left everyone in the party either scratched or bitten. Two of the cubs died of natural causes shortly after capture, but a month later, in January, 1993, the two survivors were sent off on a five-thousand-mile journey to the United States, accompanied by Howard Quigley and his wife, Kathy, the project veterinarian. At the Omaha zoo, the cubs were placed in a captive-breeding program for endangered species, and a few months later one was transferred to Indianapolis, where the zoo staff, to commemorate her mother, named her Lena.

On January 18, 1996, when I returned to Primorski Krai, I was met at the Vladivostok airport by two of the wildlife biologists—Quigley, tall, trim-bearded, and soft-spoken, and the bearish Miquelle, now project field director. The Amur tiger, they told me, was more seriously endangered than ever. As a result of epidemic poaching, more than a third of the wild tigers were thought to have been destroyed since my last visit. Foreign enterprises—mining and timber interests in particular—had reportedly paid off officials for the right to ravage eastern Siberia. An assault on tiger country north of the reserve was under way, especially in the wild region of the Bikin River. However, neither Quigley nor Miquelle had given up hope for the tiger, or lost enthusiasm for the project. At present, they said, the Sikhote-Alin Reserve was being used as a significant part of their territory by twenty to twenty-five tigers. Most of the tigers, however, lived outside the reserve, and they had to be given protection if the Amur race was to survive. Besides helping the local government improve public education about tigers, the project was encouraging the acquisition of wild land by the reserve and the

establishment of woodland corridors between the scattered sanctuaries to allow young animals dispersing from a litter to encounter other tigers all the way south from the roadless region of the Bikin River to the Lazovsky Reserve, northeast of Vladivostok.

The following morning, we flew with Anatoli Astafiev up the icebound coast to a new timber-export facility at Plastun, and from there we continued north to Terney on the coast road. Terney, a village of small wooden houses painted zinc green or faded blue, of gardens and picket fences, outhouses, and trim woodpiles, and of twisting birch-shaded mud lanes climbing uphill and inland, looked much as it had on my first visit, but its seeming tranquillity disguised some disturbing changes. In Soviet days, guns and travel, not to speak of commerce, had been severely restricted—a circumstance that helped spare the beleaguered tigers. But, with the advent of capitalism and a free market, everything had been put up for sale, including the forests and their wildlife. Soon what had been iron borders were laid wide open to international trade, and local hunters turned poachers and smugglers made the most of their opportunity to supply tiger parts for traditional medicines to the Chinas and Koreas. The mainland Chinese, in particular, were willing to pay as much as ten thousand dollars for a single tiger—more than a local man might hope to make in five years' work—and were encouraging poaching in other tiger countries, especially India and Russia. They paid well not only for the beautiful striped pelt but for "medicine bones"—sinews, organs, glands, and even whiskers, which typically are ground to powder and consumed in the hope of curing mankind's afflictions, and also of acquiring the tiger's strength and its legendary potency, which permits it to mate vigorously over several days.

Thirteen tigers that had been collared and released since 1992 were being monitored bi-weekly from the air, and one morning, as the biplane used in project surveys crisscrossed an open valley and made a slow, grinding turn over a logging road, I saw the first wild tiger of my life, bounding swiftly across open ground through two feet of powder snow and whisking out of sight beneath a great lone spruce. Alerted, the pilot circled the spruce tighter and tighter. On that first sighting, with the low winter sun glancing off the snow, all I had seen was a leaping black silhouette, an emblematic tiger. (The image evoked a Tungus belief that stalking tigers use the sun to blind their prey, by springing out of the dawn light or the sunset like a spurt of flame.) But as the plane made a turn over the treetops, the tiger abandoned the lone tree and headed for a grove of pines nearby. I glimpsed a flash of bold color in the shifting greens, then the sunlit burnt orange and golden brown of a splendid creature moving purposefully but without haste over the snow; sheltered by the trees, it did not bound or hide but advanced unhurriedly down a sparkling white corridor between the pines.

The next day, with Quigley and Miquelle, I accompanied Anatoli Astafiev by car to the high-country logging village of Melnichnoye, where livelihoods were bound to be affected by a new western extension of the reserve.

At seven, the coast range was still locked in bitter darkness, and an hour later, though the sun had risen from the sea, the air remained transfixed by Arctic cold. At the Djigit River, a road led west over the mountains, following the southwestern boundary of the reserve in a gradual ascent into

higher, colder country. Drab winter finches flitted across the white road and the ice-choked river like blown chips of bark, and a gray squirrel with handsome ear tassels cavorted up onto a snowbank and whisked down again. Twisting the bright-orange cones among white snow caps on the fir tops was a flock of crossbills, the males fire red and black, the females a flame yellow.

On the four-hour journey there were no settlements, and the only traffic on the roads were the great logging trucks bound east from Melnichnoye to Plastun. In midmorning, we crossed a high divide and headed out across Sikhote-Alin's central plateaus, where the mountain air bit at the face like an ice tiger. Elk tracks wandered everywhere among snowy firs and bone-white birches, and we chased from the roadside a young elk, woolly brown in its thick winter coat: it struggled away over a rocky knoll, up to its brisket in the snow. Farther on, Astafiev pointed with pride at mountain landmarks of the new reserve addition. Soon the road crossed the Kolumbey River, which traverses a high plain before descending west to the Ussuri.

When Arseniev rode through here almost a century ago, Melnichnoye (then called Tsidatun, which is Chinese for "windy valley") was a settlement of native Udege, a Tungus people. The community's head forester, Nikolai Kosichko, an iron-haired man with melancholy eyes who welcomed us into his small house at the west end of town, told us that until 1971 the scattering of peasant cottages and sheds had remained "a pure forest village, and everybody was a hunter and trapper, with scarcely a hundred and fifty people all together." Then logging arrived, at that time a state-run enterprise but now taken over by a private timber company. By 1985, the village population had become five times its former size, and today it shelters about a thousand souls.

"Most of our timber is shipped out through Plastun, and almost nothing comes back into our community," Kosichko said. "We are supposed to receive thirty percent of any profit, but the federal government takes eighty percent and local officials take the other twenty. We can't expect help from those officials, who have plenty of problems of their own—that is to say, no money."

As we talked, men and women came in to hear the conversation. A forest guard named Vladimir Sharov, a handsome man in a green camouflage uniform who had bushy eyebrows, sideburns, and a black beard that gave him a slight resemblance to Fidel Castro, said that local sentiment ran strongly against the reserve and its new extension, and against him, as a consequence. Saying this, he offered a fine metallic smile. "Life is very different now," he said. "It's not just the economy. People are all living for the moment, and looking out only for themselves. Our life is out of control—it's chaos." This refrain is heard repeatedly in the new Russia. Before their world changed, there was an environmental-education program in the village, and tree planting, too, the guard recalled. "That's all gone now. Before, the people volunteered to help, out of enthusiasm. Today, nobody will lift a finger except for money."

"If the Japanese ask for our Korean pine, we cut our pine, and if the Chinese want tiger bones we shoot our tigers," Kosichko said ironically. "It's not our fault!" And Sharov's wife, Nina, cried in laughter and regret, "We have a democracy in Russia now! No rules at all!"

Miquelle had told me that tigers in Primorski Krai take about one human life each year, a fact that lends a certain edge to walking in the taiga. Last year, he said, a Melnichnoye trapper named Sergei Denisov was killed in the forest by a tiger, leaving a widow and two children. No, he had not made a mistake, said Sharov, who had been the dead man's friend. "There is a critical distance with a tiger. He walked within it—that was that. Sergei did not intend to harm the tiger, therefore he made no mistake." Anyway, he was not Melnichnoye's first and only tiger victim. In 1958—the villagers consulted on this date—the head of the local weather station had been taken.

In Dersu's time, the tiger was revered as "the True Spirit of the Mountains," a wilderness god and the protector of the precious ginseng root from mankind. The word *amba* is no longer used, nor have the villagers retained any Udege myths about the forest. "We have the Russian outlook now," Kosichko said.

When I asked if there was any feeling that the community would be better off if the last tigers were exterminated, the villagers gave a heartfelt groan of assent. But almost immediately Sharov protested that the reserve would be "boring" without tigers, and Kosichko's assistant, Sergei Zinoviev, a balding, bearded man with a sly humor, strongly agreed, but he granted that fewer tigers might be better, since the game animals they killed were needed by the community. "For me," he asserted, "life is more interesting with tigers around, but most people here would never miss them." Even the women present discounted any threat to village life, although ten years earlier—the same hard winter during which a tiger was killed at a Vladivostok trolley station—a tiger had entered the dirt lanes between rows of cottages, killed a dog, and mauled a colt. As for the reserve, Zinoviev said, local gatherers of ginseng and other wild foods walked the forest all summer without guns. A man should not go there if he was afraid.

Nowadays, I was informed, the fine for shooting a tiger was a million rubles, or two hundred times the state minimum salary, and half of that again was the fine for selling their parts. However, a man would not be sent to prison for failure to pay the fine; he would only have most of his belongings confiscated.

"If you're going to save tigers, you have to have stiffer penalties or provide a better life," Zinoviev said. "If people could make a decent living, they would not shoot tigers." These days, he went on to say, the tiger was poached less often for its hide and bones, because the trade in tiger parts was being closed down by the anti-poaching patrol on the Plastun road—formerly a favorite haunt of gun traders and hunters—and by replacement of corrupt customs officials on the borders. He then astonished us by adding that tigers were sometimes killed these days for food. "A third of the people here have eaten tiger, though they might not admit it," he said. He pointed toward a ridge north of the village. "A tiger used to travel along that hillside. Somebody saw him every year. But we don't see him anymore, because we ate him." Tiger meat was like pork, he said, but leaner, lighter. "Want to try some?" he asked, and everybody laughed.

Later, I asked Astafiev if this sly fellow was fooling us. Astafiev shook his head. Maybe Zinoviev had exaggerated—tiger was not to everybody's taste—but, yes, some people ate tiger, that was true.

When the meeting broke up, Sharov led us to the house of the late Sergei Denisov's hunting partner, a woolly-headed young man with a muffled voice, introduced as Sasha. He described how he and Denisov and Denisov's brother-in-law Sergei Polishuk had been hunting and trapping on a tributary of the Kolumbey River. On the fourteenth of February in 1995,

Denisov, who had gone upstream to check his sable traps, failed to return. On the sixteenth, Polishuk went to look for him, and that same day Sharov came through on his patrol, staying overnight in the trappers' cabin. Returning on the seventeenth, Polishuk told them that all he'd found were a pair of legs and a few red traces in the snow, surrounded by the pugmarks of a tigress. A few days later, the tiger researcher Igor Nikolaiev came to investigate, accompanied by Dale Miquelle. Though the original tracks were by then quite old, and had been obscured by light fresh snow and also by the tracks of a second tiger, Nikolaiev went to work with a spruce whisk, uncovering sign. He soon concluded that the man-eater had been half starved, for not only had she attacked a man but the whitish color of her scat denoted an animal that had eaten insufficiently for a long time. The tigress had lain in a sheltered bed under the base of a fallen tree and had gathered herself for an attack when she heard something coming. Had Denisov seen the tigress, he would probably have stood his ground and shouted aggressively, and perhaps fired off his gun, and in all likelihood this would have saved his life, but to the end he remained unaware of her, to judge from the absence of any signs of flight or struggle. The chances are that, except for one blow of wild pain and terror in the impact, he never realized that his life was ending.

Denisov's hunting partner nurtured no resentment against the reserve and its new addition—"Let it stay," he said. Nor did he express either fear or bitterness about the presence of the tigers. He shrugged, fatalistic. "Let them be," he said. As far as he knew, Denisov's brother-in-law felt the same way, for on this frozen day in the high mountains Sergei Polishuk was "out in the forest," where he belonged.

THE AMAZING ADVENTURES OF WONDERCAT

Before leaving Melnichnoye, we enjoyed a fine elk feast, prepared by the local women, then returned to Terney, arriving about midnight. The following day, in the afternoon, we stopped again on the icebound empty road where Lena's collar had been found—not to commemorate Lena but because a tigress, Katia, which had taken over Lena's territory two years earlier and was thought to have cubs, had adopted Lena's troubling habit of hiding her litter in a den east of the road and crossing the road to hunt in the Kunalaika. Not fifty yards from where Lena had been killed—and this seemed eerie—we found Katia's tracks in the deep snow where she had come down the ridge and crossed the road to make her way to the elk bottoms. Her radio signal—a pulsing beat, like the hard chipping of a bird, or like the rubbing of two stones together—was loud and fast, but that might mean only that her collar was rubbing on a frozen kill.

To verify the existence of the litter, we wanted to check the tiger tracks around the kill. While Katia was present we could not go down there, for the sake of the tiger and her cubs as well as for our own sake. But that same evening, toward dusk, according to a reserve assistant, Alyosha Kostnya, Katia recrossed the road and climbed the eastern ridge, apparently on her way back to her litter. (As it turned out, she had just one cub, and she brought it across the road a few days later.) The following day, her signal, still coming from the east, indicated that she was resting, which is usual in the middle of the day, and so we descended through the hillside woods to find her kill.

The snow in the woods was two feet deep and fluffy with dry cold. In the deep frost, a pea-green moth cocoon suspended from a twig was the solitary note of green. In the bottoms we followed the smooth white surface of the Kunalaika, which in this place might have been forty feet across. On the river ice, the snow left by the wind was light, and Katia's pugmarks were sharp, as if

BRONX - ZOO

incised in steel. In one place, the tigress had lain down and stretched, leaving a ghostly outline of the True Spirit of the Mountains, even to the great head and long tail, the leg crook, and the big, floppy paws—so clear that one could almost see the stripes.

Her ambush site was a river island of small, bent black saplings against snow—uncanny camouflage for the white accents of her mask and her vertical black markings. Not far away, the heart-shaped prints of a young elk broke the ice glaze on an oxbow off the river, and from the snow evidence we were able to reconstruct what had happened. The fore-prints came together where the elk stopped short, in a place of elms and cottonwoods, some seventy yards from the crouched tiger. Perhaps the elk listened, sniffed, and trembled for a moment, big dark eyes round. From this taut point, it suddenly sprang sidewise, attaining the far bank in one scared bound, as the tigress launched herself from hiding and cut across her quarry's route in ten-foot leaps, leaving

silent round explosions in the snow. Shooting through the dark riverine trees like a tongue of fire, she overtook the big deer and hauled it down in a wood of birch and poplar about thirty-seven yards (Miquelle paced it off) from where she'd started. Striking from behind, she'd grasped the throat, to suffocate her prey, for there was little blood—only the arcs of a bony elk leg sweeping weakly on the surface of the snow, and a last, sad spasm of the creature's urine.

With logging trucks howling past perhaps sixty yards up the steep slope, this wood was much too close to the road. The tigress had dragged the elk some ninety yards farther back, across the oxbow and the swamp island to the western bank, where she had lain in hiding. And seeing the smooth drag mark, with its spots of blood, one unwillingly imagined the similar track left by the body of poor Sergei Denisov, who must have been close to the size and weight of this young carcass, with the same astonishment in his wide eyes.

The elk's carcass was dropped beneath a thick-trunked alder with dry catkins. Here the tigress fed before moving the elk to a wiry thicket at the edge of a swampy meadow.

Of the elk, all that remained were the legs, the head, and the stiff, coarse hide, which are usually abandoned by the tiger. There was no meat left on the twisted carcass. The eyes were frozen to blue ice, too hard even for ravens. Nearby, along the dragging track, were the tigress's redoubtable defecations, and Miquelle, delighted by what he called the clearest and most classic kill among a hundred-odd that he had seen, pointed out that she had hardly left her lair except to go relieve herself, which was why no detail of this ambush, kill, or feeding was obscured. "Can you imagine," he exclaimed, "what this place would look like if a human hunter had lived here for four days, coming and going!" Having seen this clear place in the winter forest, I understood much better how the Russian researchers, before the advent of radio telemetry here in Primorski Krai, had learned so much about *P. t. altaica* by reading the signs of life and death in the winter taiga.

At the end of January, in Vladivostok, we dined at the apartment of a project consultant, Dr. Dimitri Pikunov, who told us that on January 22nd—the same bitter-cold day we heard the tale of Sergei Denisov at Melnichnoye—a tiger had attacked and mauled a woman who was following her husband through the forest toward a rural train station outside the town of Partizansk, northeast of Vladivostok, then had turned

and killed the courageous man when he ran up and struck it with a flashlight, yelling at his wife to make a run for it. Several hours later, after it had fed on the man's entrails and rib cage, the tiger—a male—was tracked and killed by hunters and militia.

A month later, returning home to the United States, I found a letter from Dale Miquelle, who said that after my departure there had been reports of two other human deaths caused by tigers. Unlike the attacks near Melnichnoye and Partizansk, which were apparently unprovoked, "all evidence indicated that hunters had stalked and fired at these tigers, which then turned and killed them." In one case, the tiger did not even bite the poacher but simply swatted him to the ground and ran

"Do you have this in a cat?"

away; apparently the man died of shock and cold. Four human fatalities in just over a year was unusually high in this sparsely populated region. Though one might argue that the poaching of hoofed animals, which the tiger requires for survival, was a critical factor in these cases, the shooting of game was unlikely to stop in this era of hard times in the new Russia. Human needs come first, and I feared that the human mortalities would inevitably lead to widespread condemnation of the tiger.

In February, Pikunov and Miquelle had organized the most comprehensive tiger census ever made, involving some six hundred trackers. After months of analysis of the data, the results were announced: the tiger population was estimated at three hundred and fifty adults—give or take twenty or thirty—accompanied by a hundred and one sub-adults. This was at the high end of projections, and Howard Quigley, who conveyed the results to me, was elated. "The tigers took an awful hammering in the early nineties," he said, "but, given a little breathing room, tigers know how to survive."

In arguing for protective measures on behalf of the tiger, one could cite the critical importance of biodiversity and the interdependence of all life. Quigley points out, for example, how many attributes of the tiger's prey species—the astonishing alertness, keen senses, speed, and strength of the deer and the wild boar—might never have evolved without the tensions imposed on their ecology by this great predator. But, in the end, these abstractions seem less vital than our humane instinct that the spiritual and mythic resonance of a creature as splendid as any on our earth can only be removed from man's environment at a terrible cost.

One cannot speak for those who live in tiger country, but, for my part, the spirit and the mystery of Hu Lin the King—merely knowing that His Lordship is there twitching his white brows in the snowing taiga—bring me deep happiness. That winter afternoon in the Kunalaika, the low sunlight in the south glancing off black silhouetted ridges and shattered into frozen blades by the black trees, the ringing clarity of the cat tracks on the ice, the blood trace and stark signs of the elk's passage—that was pure joy. As Howard Quigley once observed, "Life would be less without the tiger."

| 1997 |

"You know, I've never seen you without your whiskers before."

May 16, 1964　THE　Price 25 cents

NEW YORKER

STEINBERG

WHERE I LIVE

AMY OZOLS

Welcome to my apartment. Can I take your coat? Please make yourself at home.

This is my cat.

It's a studio apartment, so there's not much to see, but let me give you a quick tour anyway. Here's the kitchen. It's not very big, but there's a ton of cabinet space, which is nice. Here's my desk, where I do most of my writing, and that's the bathroom over there.

Here is another cat.

This is a picture of my family from last Thanksgiving. Here's my mom—she's a real pistol. I think that's where I get my sense of humor. These are my sisters. My dad's the tall guy in the back. And that's my grandmother, with a cat on her lap. And that animal crouched menacingly on top of the picture frame—that's an actual cat, far more knowledgeable and terrifying than the cat in the picture.

This is my couch, where we can sit and watch a movie later, and then maybe make out awkwardly while three to six cats stare at us.

This cat over here—the one burrowing into your overcoat—belongs to my neighbor. But he comes over a lot, so I feed him and buy him toys and take him to the vet and stuff like that. He's a pretty great cat, so I sort of just let him live here and systematically destroy my clothing and furniture.

This is an antique gramophone I inherited from my grandmother. It's worth a lot of money, but I'm never going to sell it, on account of how much it means to my family.

I'm kidding, of course. It's not really an antique. Or a gramophone. It's a cat.

Do you want a drink? I think I have some beer, or there's a pitcher of water in the fridge. It's tap water, but it's filtered through one of those Brita things, so it tastes pretty good. I also have some bottled water, which I save for the cats, but you're totally welcome to one of the bottled waters, if you want to be a dick about it.

You can probably tell that I'm more of a cat person than a dog person. I'm more of an "all animals" person, actually. I like animals way better than people, because they're friendly and they don't eat very much, and they don't tend to fuck twenty-six-year-old flight attendants under adulterous circumstances, the way humans do.

Are you allergic? There's some stuff coming out of your nose. Don't be embarrassed; it happens to me all the time. In fact, if I'm being totally honest here—and, let's face it, I'm being totally honest here, perhaps unsettlingly so—I haven't breathed freely since the Clinton Administration. But it's a small price to pay, considering how much joy these cats bring into my life. These watchful, almost eerily numerous cats.

I'm sorry about the smell—that's sort of a litter-box issue. It's tough to have eight cats in a studio apartment, but I think while you're spending the night here—the first of many, many passion-filled nights you'll undoubtedly wish to spend here—you'll find that it's well worth the smell to have the selfless companionship of these seventeen reeking, dander-encrusted ani-mals. I said "eight" before when I meant to say "seventeen." That's the number of cats that I have.

I understand that you need to step out for some Claritin, but I'm really looking forward to your coming back. I think we're going to have a lot of fun, you and I, watching movies and eating popcorn and having workmanlike intercourse on the fold-out sofa—all under the penetrating gaze of the vile feline minions with which I have inexplicably chosen to share my home.

I am begging you: please do not tell them I said that. Should they deem it distasteful, we would have zero chance of survival.

Anyway, I'll see you soon. And thanks again for coming over. It's always such a treat to have guests.

| *2011* |

INTERCAT

HENDRIK HERTZBERG

We're happy to report that the First International Cat Film Festival, which we attended the other afternoon, was one heck of a nice film festival. Intercat '69, as the festival was also called (inevitably), took place at the Elgin Theatre, on Eighth Avenue at Nineteenth Street, and it consisted of four solid hours of cat movies—professional and amateur, underground and overground, happy and sad, ranging in length from ninety seconds to twenty-eight minutes and in style from traditionally cute animation to paw-held *auteur* cinema.

One doesn't just walk into an event of this kind without some background information, and before the show we had a word with its organizer, Pola Chapelle. Miss Chapelle, a pretty brunette who used to be a night-club singer, told us she had put the festival together because she loves cats and because she herself had made a cat movie and wanted to show it before an audience capable of appreciating it. "My original idea was that this would separate the real cat lovers from the fair-weather friends," she said. "After four hours, I figured, there wouldn't be anybody left but the hard core. But the other day a friend of mine called and said, 'Pola, how can you *do* this? You *know* I can't leave my cats alone for four hours.' So now I'm not sure."

We asked Miss Chapelle what she planned to do with the box-office receipts.

"Intercat '69 is a benefit for needy cats," she said. "We're going to give the money to free-lancers, though—not to organizations. For instance, there's a man who lives across from me who must spend ten dollars a week on cat food. He's an unsentimental-seeming fellow—rather gruff, actually—but he feeds all the stray cats in the neighborhood. And there's a lady on a Hundred and Third Street who has something like two dozen formerly homeless cats living in her apartment. If you hear of anybody like that, by the way, let me know."

We said we would, and headed for the balcony, where we sat for the next four hours. (We're hard-core, and our cat doesn't mind being left alone for a while.) The theatre was nearly full, and the audience included plenty of old folks and families with small children, in addition to the young and unattached who generally frequent film festivals. A lady on our right, in a spirit of self-reliance that was almost feline, had brought along a thermos of coffee, and two girls on our left seemed continually amazed at how closely this or that cat on the screen resembled their own. We had been foolish enough to imagine that the cat movie, as a genre, would prove to be rather limited. We were soon relieved of this notion. The influence of the great directors was emphatically there. James Langlois's *Fore-Footage,* for example, depicted a Vermont-bred cat giving himself a bath with unrelenting, Rossellini-like realism. The birth scene in Maya Deren's and Alexander Hammid's *The Private Life of a Cat* recalled Ingmar Bergman's little-known but excellent *Brink of Life,* and Peter Knuppel's *Oma,* in which an old woman plays with her kitten in a cemetery, muttering to herself in German the while, brought to mind the Swedish master's darker visions. Joyce Wieland's *Catfood,* in which a tabby cat eats five large fish in succession, was as uncompromisingly didactic as anything by Godard. *Sausalito Cat,* by Viva, represented the Warhol school; it consisted of painfully out-of-focus shots of the Sausalito waterfront interspersed with footage of a black cat standing in a doorway. Miss Chapelle's film, dramatically titled *Fishes in Screaming Water,* showed a marmalade-colored cat working to get some rosebuds out of its water dish with all the oblivious determination of Chaplin's little tramp. The film's

star, an animal named Mamacat, wrote the music herself by walking around on a piano, and we remembered with approval that Chaplin, too, had scored his own movies. Elsie Esposito's *Tony* featured a series of kittens in thirties-style getups performing in Busby Berkeley fashion, and Walter Gutman's *Orpheus and Vikanna,* in which a cat is petted by a scantily clad exotic dancer, owed much to the sensitivity of Russ Meyer.

Carroll Ballard's *The Perils of Priscilla,* a thriller about a Siamese left home alone, makes ample use of the low camera angles pioneered by Welles. The documentary short *Hickory Hill,* in which George Plimpton leads the viewer on a tour of a pet show on the grounds of Mrs. Robert F. Kennedy's home, had the grainy authenticity of a Leacock Pennebaker film. In fact, as we discovered when the credits were shown, it *was* a Leacock Pennebaker film.

Our favorite, though, was a classic (1941) "instructional film for the primary grades" called *Fluffy the Kitten,* which had been lent by the Museum of Modern Art Film Library. In it a very small kitten goes through its daily routine of fun and mischief. Title cards saying things like "I am looking for a little mouse" and "Yum, yum!" more than made up for the lack of a sound track. When the final title ("Now I will look pretty to say goodbye. I hope you liked me") flashed on the screen, the audience cheered. Even the Supreme Soviet has never applauded more stormily.

| 1970 |

THE LAST MEOW

BURKHARD BILGER

She arrived in Manhattan looking ravaged and ravishing, like a queen of silent film with one last swoon left in her. Her sleek ermine coat was matted and worn, her long neck so weak that it drooped to her chest. For months she had managed to hide her condition, eating full meals yet still losing weight. Now she was days away from dying, but her pale-green eyes didn't show it.

Shawn Levering glanced down at his cat, Lady, then cast a bewildered look around the waiting room of the Animal Medical Center, on New York's Upper East Side. He had on scuffed bluejeans and a faded Wheels of Time T-shirt, silk-screened with a picture of a custom Cadillac. His face was freckled and ruddy, his forearms thickly cabled. Standing in the middle of the room, his feet spread wide, he had the specific gravity of a man who knows exactly where to reach for his tools. Back home, in Wilmington, Delaware, Levering liked to work on old cars, taking rusted wrecks and transforming them into street rods. But this cat and her problems, and the city to which he'd been compelled to take her, were beyond him. "This place is crazy," he said. "The taxi-drivers are like demolition experts. I just hope we can find our way out again."

Beside him, the veterinarian, Cathy Langston, nodded, her eyes on Lady. The cat was in the throes of chronic renal failure, she said. Her kidneys weren't filtering out the toxins in her blood anymore. "I think she would definitely benefit from dialysis. It won't make her kidneys better, but it will buy her time to see if she's a good candidate for a transplant." There were risks: clotting, internal bleeding, dangerous

PROPINQUITY

is the province of cats. Living by accident,
lapping the food at hand, or sleeking down
in an adjacent lap when sleep occurs to them,
never aspiring to consistency
in homes or partners, unaware of property,
cats take their chances, love by need and nearness
as long as the need lasts, as long as the nearness
is near enough. The code of cats is simply
to take what comes. And those poor souls who claim
to own a cat, who long to recognize
in bland and narrowing eyes a look like love,
are bound to suffer should they expect
cats to come purring punctually home.
Home is only where the food and the fire are,
but might be anywhere. Cats fall on their feet,
nurse their own wounds, attend to their own laundry,
and purr at appropriate times. O folly, folly
to love a cat, and yet
we dress with love the distance that they keep,
the hair-raising way they have, and easily blame
all the abandoned litters and torn ears
on some marauding tiger. Well, no matter;
cats do not care.

      Yet part of us is cat. Confess—
love turns on accident, and needs
nearness; and the various selves we have
all come from our cat-wanderings, our chance
crossings. Imagination prowls at night,
cat-like among odd possibilities.
Only our dog-sense brings us faithfully homeward,
makes meaning out of accident, keeps faith,
and, cat-and-dog, the arguments go at it.
But every night, outside, cat-voices call
us out to take a chance, to leave
the safety of our baskets, and to let
what happens, happen. "Live, live!" they catcall.
"Each moment is your next! Propinquity,
propinquity is all!"

                —ALASTAIR REID | 1961 |

drops in blood pressure. More than a quarter of Lady's blood would be taken out of her body each time and filtered artificially. If the dialysis was done too quickly, it could cause seizures or even a coma, but the alternative was certain death. "I've got the whole team on standby," Langston said. "We can whisk her back, put in a catheter, and take a biopsy today. If she passes all the tests, we could have her ready for transplant by next week."

Like many of the center's eighty-five veterinarians, Langston is a specialist. "Everyone has to have a passion, and the kidneys are mine," she says. But such passions are relatively new in her field. Little more than twenty years ago, all vets were general practitioners, and neutering and spaying were among the most elaborate procedures they performed. Now the American Veterinary Medical Association has more than seven thousand specialists in thirty-nine fields, including cardiology, radiology, ophthalmology, and oncology. As the director of the center's quarter-million-dollar kidney unit, Langston usually has one or two patients in dialysis at any given time. Some owners have chartered planes for their animals, then stayed at nearby hotels during the treatment. But not all her clients are wealthy.

"We're looking at spending a thousand dollars in the next twenty-four hours and between three and four thousand in the next week," Langston told Levering. If the dialysis was successful, Lady would have to be transferred to the University of Pennsylvania, where her condition was first diagnosed. (The university's veterinary hospital didn't yet have a dialysis unit, but its vets were more experienced in performing transplants, and Lady was a high-risk patient.) The total cost would be more than fifteen thousand dollars.

Levering sighed and shook his head. Lady

was already anemic, asthmatic, and congenitally blind. She had been born on the streets of Wilmington four years earlier, and dropped at a local animal clinic at the age of six months. Soon after Levering and his wife adopted her, she became allergic to her own tooth enamel. "That was a weird thing," Levering said. "Never heard of that before." But he had willingly paid four hundred dollars to have all her teeth pulled. In retrospect, it seemed like a bargain.

"I don't know. If it was up to me, I might not go through with it," he said. He was recovering from a bout of Lyme disease and from carpal tunnel syndrome, and he had recently had sinus surgery. His wife had been laid up for three years with back injuries, and was only now going back to work. If they were willing to go this far for a cat, it was partly out of a sense of shared misfortune. But mostly it was a matter of love. "My wife is totally wiped out about this," he said.

A nurse in blue scrubs came over and carefully took the cat from Levering. As she turned to go, he reached over and laid his hand on Lady's head. Then he watched as she was borne away in the nurse's arms, through a pair of swinging doors, and into another world.

The Animal Medical Center and the University of Pennsylvania veterinary hospital are the Mayo Clinic and the Mass General of their field. One is perhaps the world's largest private animal hospital; the other is the world's largest university veterinary center. The A.M.C. occupies an eight-story concrete tower at the corner of Sixty-second Street and York Avenue, overlooking the East River, and in an average year admits sixty-five thousand patients. The center has its own oncology, dentistry, and dermatology departments, as well as the usual surgery, emergency, and recovery wards. To insure that there is

a steady supply of blood flowing to surgical patients, it keeps thirteen donor greyhounds, twenty-six donor cats (some of them inherited from an elderly woman who kept seventy in her apartment), and three donor ferrets. The ferrets are called Larry, Mo, and Curly.

New Yorkers, with their dog-averse landlords, have an unusual number and variety of exotic pets. Throughout the years, the city has been swept by vogues for potbellied pigs, Day-Glo anole lizards, and sugar gliders—a nectar-eating Australian marsupial. Most owners don't really know how to care for these animals (sugar gliders, for instance, are prone to osteoporosis in captivity), so the A.M.C. sees a steady circus parade of patients. On a recent day, the exotics unit treated a ferret with a hair ball, an anorexic bearded dragon, a pigeon with a fracture, two wild Canada geese that had got tangled in fishing line, a four-year-old guinea pig awaiting a five-thousand-dollar surgery on a ureteral stone, and a hummingbird with a broken wing. Two X-rays hung on a light board on a wall in the corridor. One was of a duck called Nip-Nip, who had swallowed a metallic object. The other showed a long, elegant spine strung with eight perfect ovals: a corn snake with a clutch of eggs stuck in her birth canal.

In 1910, when the A.M.C. was founded, animal welfare was a relative term. Officers with the American Society for the Prevention of Cruelty to Animals carried guns with which to dispatch horses, several hundred of which collapsed from heat and exhaustion in the city every summer. It was considered unladylike to bear firearms, so the women's auxiliary to the A.S.P.C.A. founded the New York Women's League for Animals, and opened a clinic. Situated on the Lower East Side, the clinic was devoted to the city's strays and to the pets of poor immigrants, and funded by charitable donations. Its first patient, carried across the Brooklyn Bridge by a young girl, was a cat whose tail had been caught in a door.

In 1962, when the clinic moved to the Upper East Side, veterinarians were still a utilitarian breed and more than 90 percent of them were men. Much of their work was of the kind made famous by James Herriot in *All Creatures Great and Small:* dosing sheep, midwifing cattle. Then, gradually, women began to enter vet schools. By 1975, they represented half of all students; by 2000, nearly three-quarters—and most of them wanted to treat pets. Hospitals sold vets their outdated CAT scanners and MRI machines, making high-tech medicine more affordable. And, as the birth rate dropped, pets came to take the place of children in some families.

Between 1980 and 2001 alone, the number of dogs and cats in the United States grew from ninety-eight million to a hundred and thirty million. Two generations ago, fathers still gave their sons sacks of kittens to drown in the river. Today, according to a recent survey by the American Animal Hospital Association, 63 percent of pet owners say "I love you" to their pets every day. Eighty-three percent refer to themselves as their pet's mom or dad.

The current director of the A.M.C., Guy Pidgeon, has lived through both halves of this history. He was born on a farm in western Nebraska in 1947—though you'd never guess it from the stout, Friar Tuck–ish figure he now is—and went to the Colorado State University veterinary school, intent on becoming a country vet. "Then, at some point, I began to see an incredible dichotomy between agricultural and veterinary medicine," he told me. "One was driven by economics, the other by emotion." A sick cow could merit only a few shots before it was sent to the slaughterhouse; a sick hamster could motivate a

six-hour surgery. To a veterinarian interested in cutting-edge medicine, the future lay with pets.

"My staff likes to tease me about the time my father came here for a visit," Pidgeon said. "He's eighty-six now and still lives on the farm. He tries to maintain a sense of humor about what I do, but he doesn't really understand it." The poodles getting root canals, the rabbits in radiation wards, were strange enough; but the crowning absurdity was the sight of two prairie dogs in the intensive-care unit. Members of the latest exotic pet craze, they had contracted pneumonia and were having trouble breathing. "If you're a farmer in Nebraska, you've been waging holy war against prairie dogs all your life," Pidgeon said. "And here I was giving them oxygen therapy."

Before I visited the A.M.C., I had a certain cartoonish image of its clientele: the dragon lady from Carnegie Hill kissing her lapdogs on the lips; the Wall Street power broker sending his wolfhounds to have their teeth cleaned. I thought of the German countess Carlotta Liebenstein, who in 1991 bequeathed her eighty-million-dollar estate to her dog Gunther. Of J. Paul Getty, who refused to return from Europe when his twelve-year-old son died of a brain tumor but had a vet flown in when his dog developed cancer. When the disease proved fatal, he spent three days weeping in the dog's room.

Lady's owners were different. Like many of the rumpled, red-eyed people I sat with in the A.M.C. waiting room, they could scarcely afford their sympathies. Shawn Levering works with mentally disabled adults, finding them jobs and visiting them weekly at their workplaces. He recently turned forty and makes twenty-seven thousand dollars a year. His wife, Karen, who is thirty-four, is the caregiver for a disabled teenager and is earning a degree in child psychology. They

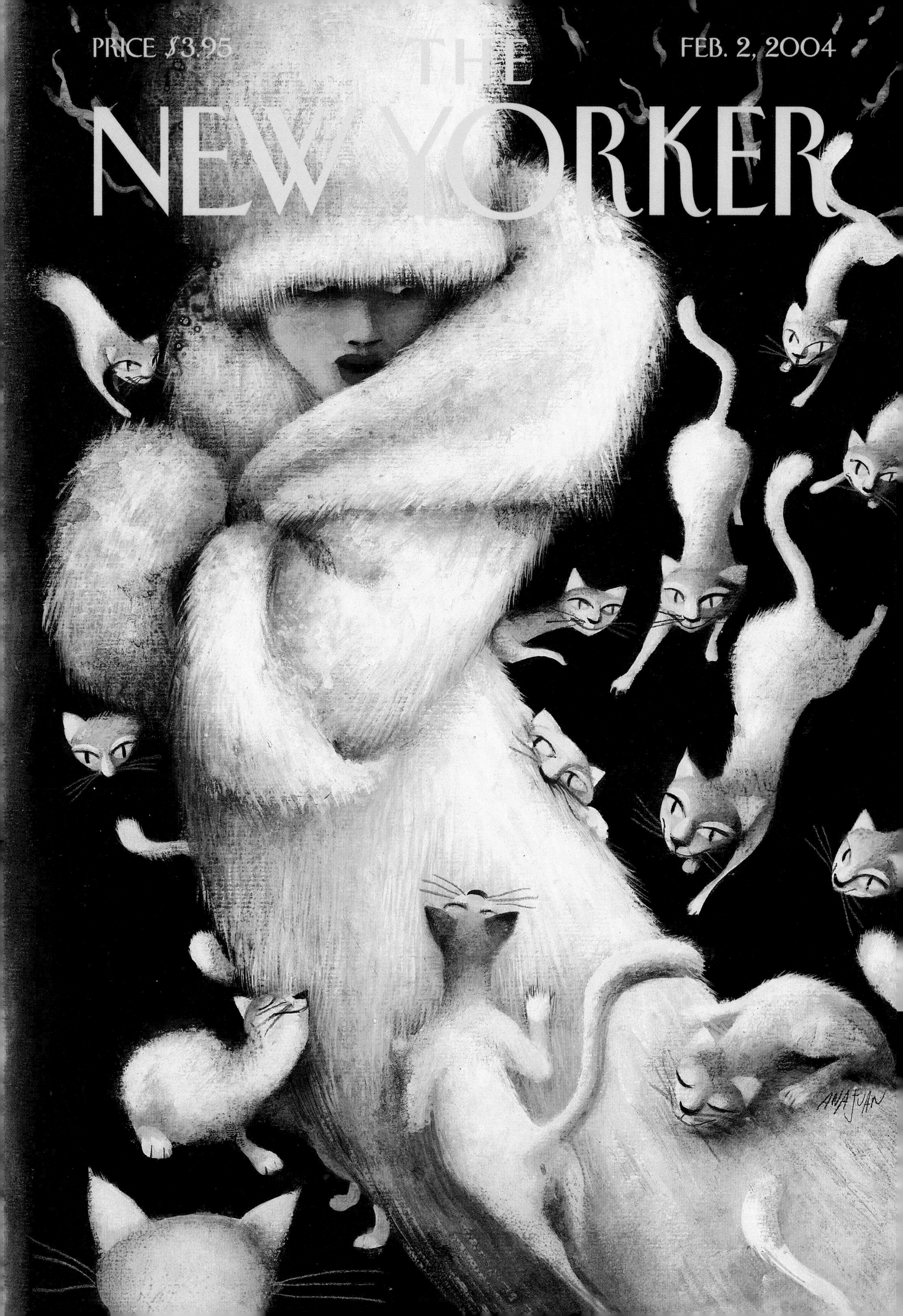
PRICE $3.95
THE NEW YORKER
FEB. 2, 2004
ANA JUAN

live in a three-room apartment in a plain brick building on the outskirts of Wilmington. At night, trains rumble in and out of the nearby Saturn car factory, delivering parts, and you can hear the thrum of Interstate 95 half a mile away.

When I visited them at home, on a Wednesday evening, Lady was scheduled for a transplant the next morning. She had made it through the dialysis treatment at the A.M.C. and had been transferred to the University of Pennsylvania. Karen had been to Philadelphia that morning to see the kidney donor. The hospital maintains a pool of cats for the purpose, often taken from local shelters and research labs. The surgery seems to have no ill effect on the donor cats' health, and it solves the problem of having to put them to sleep: the owners of the transplantee have to agree to adopt the donor. In the Leverings' case, the new cat would bring their feline population to four.

As we talked, Jimmy, a fat brown tabby with a cream belly, slinked warily past Bogart, a scruffy white tom lounging on the couch. Karen had found Bogart starving in front of a 7-Eleven one night and brought him home, only to find that the cat was stone deaf and deeply irritable. The first time Shawn tried to pull Bogart and Jimmy apart, he was bitten so deeply that he had to go to the emergency room. The second time, he had to take a round of antibiotics and get a tetanus shot. Karen's asthma flared up so badly, with all the dander in the air, that she had to use her albuterol inhaler repeatedly. "But I really think my system has adjusted to them," she said.

Karen has strawberry-blond hair and a moon-shaped face unmarked by her relentless bad luck. When she met Shawn, in 1997, through a dating service on the local radio station, she was a teacher at a Christian school. A month before their wedding, her car was rear-ended when she stopped at a yield sign. Her injuries were serious enough to warrant visits to a chiropractor during her honeymoon, and they were compounded, three months later, when she was rear-ended again. With a fractured vertebra and several torn disks in her spine, she couldn't stand in front of a classroom anymore, so she stayed home, on constant medication. When she tried to start a family, she couldn't get pregnant.

"I don't know what I would have done without the cats," she said. "Shawn was working long hours, and the pain was so extreme sometimes that I would just go to the bathroom and cry." Lady seemed to sense her moods. She would leap onto the bed at night and

"You look just like your profile picture."

nestle on her chest. Karen had studied enough psychology to suspect that her feelings for Lady were partly misplaced mothering instincts, but she also knew that relationships like theirs could have a particular intensity. In the early 1970s, for instance, the biologist Erika Friedmann, of Brooklyn College, studied how heart-attack patients respond to social support. Patients who had a dog or cat, she found, were more than four times as likely to survive a year after a heart attack than those who didn't have a pet.

Research like Friedmann's has since spawned its own scholarly journal, *Anthrozoös*, and a "prescribe-a-pet" movement has sprung up among some therapists. Three years ago, Karen Allen, a psychologist at the State University of New York at Buffalo, studied two groups of hypertensive stockbrokers from Wall Street. One group was given drugs and a pet, while the other received only drugs. Six months later, the brokers took a stress test. They were asked to appease a client who pretended to have just lost eighty-six thousand dollars, thanks to their advice. Everyone's blood pressure rose, but for those with pets it rose half as much. Allen later ran another series of tests on pet owners. This time, she had them perform stressful activities alone, in the presence of their pets, and in the presence of their spouses. The results were unequivocal: pets made people's blood pressure drop; spouses made it shoot up.

Sitting side by side on the love seat in their living room, Karen and Shawn could have passed for two of the pet lovers in Allen's study. Karen argued that her cats deserve "the respect of life." She described the prayer group that she belonged to at a Methodist church and said that the other members would be sending their blessings to Lady the next morning. Shawn reminded her that they were already in debt—"We've gone from getting by to barely scraping." He said the

There's a cat on the payroll of the New Yorker Delicatessen at Madison and Thirty-sixth Street who has learned to sit on the green bananas and ripen them.

| 1944 |

first time she mentioned a transplant he was tempted to have her sanity checked. The cats wound their way between them, filling the silences with their purring.

Late that night, Shawn and I took a drive through the deserted streets of Wilmington, past strip malls and sandwich shops to the garage where he works on his street rods. Inside, a 1940 Ford truck lay on blocks, its body sanded and primed, waiting for parts from the crippled car beside it. Shawn and his friend Eddie had bolted the truck's body to a Chevy S-10 frame. They had chopped five inches from the frame, dropped in a burly 305, and laid in a steering column and brakes from a 1987 Monte Carlo. Then the money ran out.

"Before Karen and I got married, I was hoping to have this car done in two years," Shawn said. He glanced around the garage and chuckled. No, he said, he wasn't imagining what fifteen thousand dollars could buy. He, too, had come to depend on Lady's company. "I can't say I haven't compared this transplant to a down payment on a house," he said. "But you can't go too far down that road. If Lady comes through this thing alive, I won't think about it twice."

I was reminded of the two trucks the next morning, in the operating room at the University of Pennsylvania. The donor cat, Jasper, was lying on one table, his kidney stripped out and strung from its blood vessels like an old transmission. Beside him, Lady, covered with surgical drapes, was awaiting her replacement part. An oxygenation monitor had been clipped to her tongue, an anesthesia tube was pumping Isoflurane gas down her throat, and nylon cords anchored her limbs to the corners of the table. As soon as one team of surgeons cut her open and located her renal blood vessels, aorta, and vena cava, another team would cut Jasper's kidney free. Then the transplant would begin.

Lillian Aronson, the head surgeon, strode in with her forearms scrubbed and dripping, her face set in an uneasy grin. She'd begun the day in good spirits, joining the nurses in the kidney chant they had made up: "K-I-D-N-E-Y, You can do it if you try! Kidney! Kidney! Kidney!" Then things began to go wrong. Every cat has two kidneys, though it needs only one to survive, but not every kidney is fit for a transplant. Jasper was Lady's second donor. The first donor, Jack, seemed to have an ideal kidney: a CT scan showed that it was neither too big nor too small, and that there was a single artery and vein servicing it. But when Aronson opened the cat up, she found a second artery tucked behind the first. This artery would have to be sacrificed in a transplant, depriving part of the organ of blood. Luckily, Jasper—Jack's littermate—was available for surgery, and his blood type was a match for Lady's.

"It's all very scary," Aronson said, putting on her surgical gloves. "I ought to just open up a bed-and-breakfast and hang a 'No Vacancy' sign." Aronson, who is thirty-six, has been transplanting kidneys for ten years. Though her success rate is high—94 percent of her patients leave the hospital, and more than half are alive after four years—the procedure still fills her with a pleasurable dread. The night before, I'd watched her practice in this room, sewing stitches into a sliced rubber glove. A cat's renal artery is only about two millimeters thick. To stitch it to another artery of the same size, Aronson has to use an enormous sur-

gical microscope suspended above the patient's open belly, with dual eyepieces for the surgeon and for her assistant. That brings the sutures into view but throws her eye-hand coordination out of synch. Seen through the eyepiece, the most delicate forceps loom like pliers.

As Aronson took a scalpel and placed the tip on Lady's belly, I could see her bracing for the start as if for a pistol shot at a racetrack. Animal lovers are often accused of anthropomorphism, but after you've spent a few weeks in a veterinary hospital it's hard to resist the opposite urge: the doctors all begin to look like their patients. Aronson is unmistakably a greyhound: lean and tightly wound, with dark, downturned eyes and a disarmingly sweet nature for someone who is so single-minded. She runs marathons regularly with her husband, and has wanted to be a vet almost from the time she could talk. When her oldest brother, a physicist, first heard about her transplanting a cat's kidneys, his only comment was "Why not just perform a collar transplant instead?"

Aronson needed only a few minutes to open Lady's belly, clamp the aorta and the vena cava, and bring over Jasper's kidney. "This cat has issues," she had warned me before the surgery. "With that asthma, I'm not sure how she'll hold up under anesthesia." So far, though, Lady's breathing was deep and even, her blood pressure steady. Using a foot pedal, Aronson steered the motorized microscope into position. She grasped the cut end of Jasper's renal artery with forceps and pressed it against a tiny hole that she had cut in Lady's aorta, like a T-joint in a pipe. For the next ten minutes, she sutured the joint together. Then, just as she was putting in the final stitch, her needle caught the back wall of the artery. As she drew in the thread, it pinched the vessel partially shut. Blood could still flow through it, but there was the possibility of a blood clot.

"All you really need in life is the love of a good cat."

BOOTH

Aronson glanced up at her assistants, her features thrown into shadow by the overhead lamp. "Can anything else go wrong today?" she said. She had no choice but to take out the thread and re-stitch the joint, but that could irritate the arterial wall, again increasing the chance of a clot. "Her potassium level is going up," a technician called out beside her. Aronson shook her head. "I'm worried about that artery," she said. "Very worried. I'm telling you right now this may not work."

The dire choices that define a veterinarian's day aren't particularly well compensated. The average American vet makes around sixty thousand dollars a year—a hundred thousand less than the average physician, though veterinary training can be just as rigorous and costly as medical school. If

vet schools still have to turn applicants away, it's partly because people love to work with animals and partly because they're put off by the tortured ethics of human medicine. Whatever dramas veterinarians have to face, they know that malpractice suits are rare and relatively inexpensive, and that euthanasia is always an option.

But that may be changing. The law has long treated pets as property, no different from a Teddy bear or a windup toy. If an owner sues for the wrongful death of his cat, the most he can demand is the cost of replacing the animal. Recently, though, lawyers have begun to demand more. Two years ago in Oregon, a retired football player named Stan Brock filed a lawsuit against a man who had shot his two Labrador retrievers with arrows. (The man claimed that the dogs had

"Before Prozac, she loathed company."

been threatening stray cats near his house.) Replacing the dogs would have cost, at most, a few hundred dollars, but Brock sued for three hundred thousand dollars. "Pets don't depreciate; they appreciate," his attorney, Geordie Duckler, argued in court. "That's very different from what you can say about a purse or a car." The trial judge agreed.

Brock eventually settled out of court for an undisclosed sum, but Duckler expects a number of similar cases in coming years. In Tennessee, he says, a law that was recently passed allows owners to sue for up to four thousand dollars in emotional damages if their pet is killed by a negligent pet owner's dog, and several other states have comparable bills on the docket. In New York, in 1999, a housing court forced a landlord to let a woman keep a puppy in her Queens apartment when she cited research on the health benefits of pets. Elsewhere, a group called In Defense of Animals has lobbied communities to define peo-

ple as "guardians" rather than owners of their pets. Seven cities and the state of Rhode Island have adopted at least a variation of the ordinance.

"The more people spend on their pets, the more that cost is going to be reflected in the law," Duckler says, which means that veterinarians could face million-dollar malpractice suits in the future. Each time they introduce an expensive new procedure—radiation therapy in the 1980s, MRIs in the 1990s, experimental cancer vaccines in the new millennium—they implicitly raise the value of their patients. Many vets, like doctors, are now on call at night and on weekends. When they sit at kitchen tables at four in the morning, listening patiently to owners describing their dogs' stool consistency, they suggest that a pet is worth almost any effort, any cost.

Vets say that rising malpractice awards will hurt both sides. "They'll just bring the insanity of the human side of the business into my profession," Guy Pidgeon told me at the A.M.C. "And all those costs will be passed on to the client." But pet owners have already begun to prepare for those costs. Nearly four hundred thousand pets are now covered by medical insurance policies in the United States, and that number is expected to grow to two and a half million in the next five years.

Not long ago, at an all-day symposium at Harvard Law School, Jane Goodall, Alan Dershowitz, and others tried to sort out the legal and ethical principles behind these issues. Should courts grant animals some human rights? If so, which animals and which rights? There was much talk of I.Q. and the theory of mind, of gorillas that can communicate in sign language and parrots that can do arithmetic. Steven Wise, an animal-rights attorney and the author of the book *Drawing the Line,* divided the animal world into four categories, based on ascending levels of intelligence. At the bottom were earthworms, bacteria, and other creatures that are notably lacking in self-knowledge or the power of deductive reasoning. At the top were the great apes, dolphins, and a few clever birds. Only this last group, Wise argued, could claim "legal personhood." Dogs, cats, and most other pets hovered somewhere in category three: just a little too dim—or poorly understood—to earn our highest regard.

Wise knows that his categories won't convince most people. An adult chimpanzee may be smarter than most two-year-old boys, but that won't get it into day care. The rights we grant animals are, first and foremost, a function of empathy—and, on that count, no ape can compete with a pet. "The chimp is amazingly similar to us in brain structure, DNA, and behavior," Jane Goodall told me during an intermission. "But a dog can be a better friend to you than anyone else." Goodall has spent most of her life living with chimpanzees, but it was her childhood dog, Rusty, who first taught her that animals have personalities, intelligence, and feelings. If one research facility was being cruel to dogs and another was abusing primates, she said, she knew which one she would shut down first: "I'd choose the dogs."

The missing voice in this debate, of course, is that of the animals. Is the agony of chemotherapy worth an extra six months of life to a dachshund? Does a parrot really want legal autonomy? Veterinarians like to talk about a pet's quality of life, but no one really knows what they

mean. Injured animals no doubt experience fear and pain: the parts of their brains that process those feelings (the amygdala, the thalamus, and the hypothalamus) are similar to ours, and animals often have keener senses. Do they also feel enough pleasure—enough joy in the sheer fact of existence—to make surviving worthwhile?

Two weeks before Lady's transplant, I saw a mastiff named Taberia in the intensive-care unit at the A.M.C. The dog was eleven years old—ancient for her breed—and barely able to stand. Her eyes were rimmed with red, and her skin draped over her bones like an old rug. She had a grapefruit-size growth hanging from her belly and a bleeding tumor on her spleen that seemed to have spread to her liver. "Surgery will probably just prolong the inevitable," a resident said. "Dogs with this kind of cancer don't respond well to chemo." The doctor gently suggested putting the dog to sleep, but the owner seemed not to have heard him. She was a bartender at Red Rock West, in Manhattan, with a pale, defiant face and a voice gone smoky from years of screaming above crowds. She crouched inside the mastiff's cage and cradled its head. "Taberia used to love hanging out at the bar," she said. "I've always thought she must have been a drunken ballerina in her last life."

Euthanasia is one of the last dividing lines between human and animal medicine, but it has been blurred in recent years. Although Oregon legalized assisted suicide in 1997, and Jack Kevorkian and others have championed the practice for the terminally ill, veterinarians have grown more wary of the procedure. Less than twenty years ago, a pet owner could still have a healthy animal put down. Now most vets will euthanize only the very sick, and their standards continue to rise as their medicine improves. "Sometimes, in all the hoopla over what we can do, we lose sight of the fact that there are people who don't want to go that far," Pidgeon said. "And sometimes we think the pet is being forced to endure more than it should." Owners can still weigh the costs and benefits of saving a pet's life. But the more pets are treated like surrogate children, the more complicated the equation becomes.

In Taberia's case, under the surgical lights the doctors found exactly what they had expected: the abdomen full of blood, the spleen and the liver so engorged with purplish cancer cells that they had burst open. Even then, the owner wanted the dog sewn back up and sent home. If Taberia could just live for a few more weeks, she thought, she might be able to cure her holistically.

The surgeons eventually persuaded Taberia's owner to let them put the mastiff to sleep. When I asked her what she planned for the body, she said that she was going to buy Taberia a plot in Hartsdale, New York, in the country's oldest and most prestigious pet cemetery. "When someone buries a dog there, you know they must have loved it to death," she said.

It had been six hours since Lady's first donor was cut open. For the past twenty minutes, a brittle silence had fallen over the room. Aronson shuttled from one side of the surgical table to the other, getting the best angle on her final stitches. The replacement kidney had been without blood for about forty-five minutes. Most organs can survive that long and still function, but Aronson could never be sure. She gave her assistants a weak smile. "Pray to the urine gods," she said.

When the clamps came off, the renal artery and vein hung limply at first, like guy wires from a deflating zeppelin. Then, little by little, they began to stiffen. Their pale white walls stretched and expanded, until a delicate tremor ran down their length: the beating of Lady's heart. "Unbelievable," Aronson said. The sutures were hold-

ing, and the weakened artery showed no signs of collapse. Now she just had to attach the ureter: the vessel, even thinner than the artery, that carried urine from the kidney to the bladder.

Aronson sliced open the bladder, flipped it inside out, and cut a small hole in the side. She threaded the ureter through the hole and was preparing to attach it with a crown stitch when her hand suddenly froze. "Will you look at that?" she said. Her assistants crowded around, craning their necks. A thin stream of clear fluid was trickling from the ureter's open end. "A new kidney making urine," Aronson said, as everyone whooped and cheered around her. "There's nothing better than that."

Afterward, when the bladder had been stitched shut and injected with salt water to insure that it was watertight, and the kidney had been sewn to the side wall of her belly to prevent it from drifting, Aronson closed up Lady's belly and rolled her to the intensive-care unit. She gave the nurse on duty the rundown: "She's blind, she's toothless, she has renal disease, and she's really sweet." Then she went out to get a Diet Coke—her first meal in more than twenty hours. Lady lay on the table, immobile. After a few minutes, she opened a single eye.

Americans now spend nineteen billion dollars a year on veterinary care, up from eleven billion just seven years ago. Add to that the cost of pet food and other supplies and the number rises to forty-seven billion, nearly three times as much as the federal government spends on welfare grants. The figures fill even some pet owners with dismay. If society could give up on goldfish alone, the sentiment suggests, it could fund a few dozen more Head Start programs. Cure the addiction to dogs and cats, and millions of families might be lifted out of poverty. Pets, as George

"You needn't feel guilty. You earned the fortune you inherited by giving her great happiness while she was alive."

Bernard Shaw wrote, "bear more than their natural burden of human love."

But, of course, it's not that simple. Our feelings for animals aren't easily transferred, a fact best illustrated by our treatment of the pets we don't own. When Lady was recovering from her transplant, a kitten was being treated next door. His mother had died after giving birth, and his littermates, hungry for milk, had mistaken their brother's penis for a nipple, eventually giving him a bladder infection. The kitten's owners had driven in from western Pennsylvania and were paying hundreds of dollars for his treatment. Yet they could have got another kitten for free in any shelter. Every year, while pets like theirs are saved by the most elaborate means, some six million strays are put to sleep.

Americans are no more inconstant than other nationalities. The Chinese pamper their Pekingese and stir-fry other breeds. Polynesians used to slaughter some puppies and breastfeed others. The Inca kept hairy dogs as hunters, and hairless ones as bed warmers, shielding the latter from sunburn in rooms filled with orchids. Modern veterinary medicine is either the natural culmination of these ancient relationships or their crowning folly. Spending fifteen thousand dollars on a cat is an outrage, some say, yet they gladly spend four times more on a BMW.

The last time I saw the Leverings, Lady had been back from the hospital for a week and had a bedroom to herself. The first days of recovery are a dangerous time, Aronson says. One of her other clients tried to keep her cat from jumping down from the couch not long after its transplant. The cat shook itself free, ran downstairs, and fell over dead—its renal artery having torn free in the tussle. Even if Lady avoids such mishaps, she will have to take steroids and immunosuppressants for the rest of her life to keep her body from rejecting the new kidney. The drugs will cost about five hundred dollars a year, not counting veterinary fees for trimonthly visits, and will leave Lady prone to infections, cancers, and diabetes.

Karen showed me how she prepared the doses twice a day, injecting amber cyclosporine into clear-gel capsules. Two days earlier, she said, she had locked herself out of the house when it was time for the afternoon dose and had to use a rock to break in through the kitchen window. Otherwise, it had been a smooth transition. Jack, the failed kidney donor, was being adopted by a vet at the hospital. Jasper had developed a toe infection and an allergy to his plastic food bowl, but he had taken to the other cats immediately.

Halfway through the conversation, Shawn came back from church, propping up an elderly man with an enormous, lopsided grin. His name was Don and he worked at an auto-parts factory, and sometimes helped out in the garage on weekends. He and Shawn settled on the couch across from Karen and talked about streets rods for a while. Lady padded in from her room, picking her way around the furniture by memory, and joined Bogart and Jasper on the carpet. They were an oddly harmonious trio—one blind, one deaf, one allergic to plastic and missing a kidney—not unlike the people around them. Gathered there in the living room, they kept an eye on one another, the cats and the people. "It would have been hard not to have Lady around," Shawn said. The cats, as always, didn't say a word.

| 2003 |

From: Karen Smith-Levering

Date: Sat, 9 Aug 2008 22:27:52 -0400

To: themail@newyorker.com

Subject: More than just a response . . . "Thank you, Burkhard Bilger"

We are writing in hopes that this letter will reach our friend, Burkhard Bilger. In September, 2003, he wrote an article including details concerning our cat, Lady: The Last Meow. We just were hoping to inform Mr. Bilger that Lady enjoyed 6 wonderful years within our family, post-transplant. We felt that Mr. Bilger's article captured Lady's "character" very well. We also felt that Mr. Bilger shared a significant experience with our family. We thought he may like to hear of the outcome, success of the transplant. We also want to thank him for contributing to the dignity of "our little girls" life.

Sincerely,
Shawn and Karen Levering

THE CATTERY

HENRY S. F. COOPER

According to Milan J. Greer, the burly proprietor of an establishment at Lexington Avenue and Twenty-ninth Street that is known, all too alliteratively, as Fabulous Felines and can be summed up as the world's largest pedigreed cattery, with a hundred and twenty-five aristocratic cats in residence and a couple of thousand graduate aristocrats scattered throughout the city and environs, this country is currently riding the crest of the greatest cat wave in history. Mr. Greer, who buys, sells, and breeds cats, told us, in the course of a visit we recently paid to F.F., that there are seven hundred thousand more cats than dogs in the United States and that the postmark of F.F.—"Dogs Are Passé"—is turning from prophecy into fact. "All this 'man's best friend' stuff is garbage," Mr. Greer growled. (If there is any feline that Mr. Greer resembles, it's a grumpy lion.) "A dog is simply a very insecure animal. Loyalty and affection? Bosh! A dog has to ingratiate himself with people or he'd starve to death. If a dog has a personality, it's the personality of a human being you wouldn't want to know. Cats, on the other hand, make no pretense of affection. If you treat them right, they'll respect you, but they won't come a step closer than that."

Mr. Greer grumpily went on to say that he had made Fabulous Felines a fairly formidable place to enter, because he was determined to keep his cats from being indiscriminately doted on. "If I spot somebody who wants a cat to lavish affection on, I hurry him straight out of here," Greer said. "A pedigreed cat is nothing less than an animated objet d'art, and to consider it in any other light is crueler than tying a can to its tail. Cats have gained a bad reputation in some quarters because they've been pampered and have become neurotic. Cats like to be treated rough. That's one reason men make better cat owners than women do." Greer took a swipe at a red Persian, which skillfully eluded him. "My first duty to my cats is to find customers suited to them," he continued. "The basic quality that I look for in a customer is a very strong ego. If a man's ego is fragile, a smart cat will make him feel pretty silly. People who lack confidence are better off with dogs, or even with other people. Once I'm satisfied with the size of a customer's ego, I face the next question, which is whether the customer is a Siamese type or a Persian type. A few weeks in the wrong sort of home will turn even the best-behaved cat into a J.D."

Mr. Greer guarantees the health of his cats up to the age of eight and a half months. "This guarantee turns me into a sort of walking Blue Cross for cats," he said. "Certain health problems for cats in a big city are easily predicted. One problem that you mightn't predict is that cats have very poor depth perception and often fall off apartment balconies and other high places. A cat has a good chance to survive a fall of as much as ten stories." He introduced us, in a gruff, offhand fashion, to three sleek blue cats with green eyes; one was named Serge, and the others—Serge's kittens by a cat named Natasha—were Jarmilla and Maruska. "Serge and Natasha are the only Russian Archangel cats ever to leave the Soviet Union," Greer said. "Archangels are the traditional cats of the Czars. The breed is at least a thousand years old. I recently sold Natasha for a thousand dollars—the highest price ever brought by a cat. I'm hoping to get four thousand for Serge."

The most popular breed of cat sold at F.F. is the Siamese, a good specimen of which brings about sixty-five dollars. Curiously, the breed has fallen on hard times back in its homeland, and Mr. Greer has just arranged to ship a Siamese to the King of Siam—Thailand, that is—for the purpose of improving the stock out there. F.F. is the world's biggest breeder of Burmese cats, which come in beautiful shades of brown and have golden eyes. "About the only important species we don't carry is Manx," Greer said. "I used to carry them, but a neighbor turned me in to the A.S.P.C.A., thinking that I was catching alley cats and cutting off their tails. I didn't want to be bothered with that kind of thing. Next to Archangels, our most expensive cats are Abyssinians, which start at a hundred and seventy-five dollars. My partners—Miss Bobbi Thompson and my wife, Eileen—and I are trying to breed a variety of long-haired Burmese. It won't be ready for another three years. We *have* developed the Golden Siamese, a cross between a Siamese and a Burmese. It's a fearfully intelligent animal—it will bring you a leash when it wants to go out—but it isn't pedigreed yet. We've bred it successfully for five generations, and we need seven before we can register it. We're also working on a miniature Siamese, which will weigh a pound when fully grown. We've got it down to four pounds already, and all of our expected four-pounders are sold out until 1963. Cats never play and have no sense of humor. All their antics are premeditated. They're always in training, and they are very serious about it. The only toy I approve of for a cat is a rabbit's foot. No cat goes out of here without one. Sometimes I sell a cricket in a cage with a cat—a pet for a pet, as it were. Crickets give a cat the same kind of rapture that catnip does, or scratching. Purring doesn't necessarily mean that a cat's happy. A purring cat died in my arms once, and I know *he* wasn't happy."

| 1961 |

THE LADY AND THE TIGERS

SUSAN ORLEAN

On January 27, 1999, a tiger went walking through the township of Jackson, New Jersey. According to the Tiger Information Center, a tiger's natural requirements are "some form of dense vegetative cover, sufficient large ungulate prey, and access to water." By those measures, Jackson is really not a bad place to be a tiger. The town is halfway between Manhattan and Philadelphia, in a corner of Ocean County—an easy commute to Trenton and Newark, but still a green respite from the silvery sweep of electric towers and petroleum tanks to the north, and the bricked-in cities and mills farther south. Only forty-three thousand people live in Jackson, but it is a huge town, a bit more than a hundred square miles, all of it as flat as a tabletop and splattered with ponds and little lakes. A lot of Jackson is built up with subdivisions and Wawa food markets, or soon will be, but the rest is still primordial New Jersey pinelands of broom sedge and pitch pine and sheep laurel and peewee white oaks, as dense a vegetative cover as you could find anywhere. The local ungulates may not be up to what a tiger would find in more typical habitats, like Siberia or Madhya Pradesh—there are just the usual ornery and overfed pet ponies, panhandling herds of white-tailed deer, and a milk cow or two—unless you include Jackson's Six Flags Wild Safari, which is stocked with zebras and giraffes and antelopes and gazelles and the beloved but inedible animal characters from Looney Tunes.

Nevertheless, the Jackson tiger wasn't long for this world. A local woman preparing lunch saw him out her kitchen window, announced the sighting to her husband, and then called the police. The tiger

slipped into the woods. At around five that afternoon, a workman at the Dawson Corporation complained about a tiger in the company parking lot. By seven, the tiger had circled the nearby houses. When he later returned to the Dawson property, he was being followed by the Jackson police, wildlife officials, and an airplane with an infrared scope. He picked his way through a few more back yards and the scrubby fields near Interstate 195, and then, unfazed by tranquillizer darts fired at him by a veterinarian, headed in the general direction of a middle school; one witness described seeing an "orange blur." At around nine that night, the tiger was shot dead by a wildlife official, after the authorities had given up on capturing him alive. A pathologist determined that he was a young Bengal tiger, nine feet long and more than four hundred pounds. Nothing on the tiger indicated where he had come from, however, and there were no callers to the Jackson police reporting a tiger who had left home. Everyone in town knew that there were tigers in Jackson—that is, everyone knew about the fifteen tigers at Six Flags Wild Safari. But not everyone knew that there were other tigers in Jackson, as many as two dozen of them, belonging to a woman named Joan Byron-Marasek. In fact, Jackson has one of the highest concentrations of tigers per square mile anywhere in the world.

Byron-Marasek is famously and purposely mysterious. She rarely leaves the compound where she lives with her tigers, her husband, Jan Marasek, and scores of dogs, except to go to court. On videotapes made of her by the New Jersey Department of Environmental Protection, she looks petite and unnaturally blond, with a snub nose and a small mouth and a startled expression. She is either an oldish-looking young person or a youngish-looking old person; evidently, she has no Social Security number, which makes her actual age difficult to establish. She has testified that she was born in 1955 and was enrolled in New York University in 1968; when it was once pointed out that this would have made her a thirteen-year-old college freshman, she allowed as how she wasn't very good with dates. She worked for a while as an actress and was rumored to have appeared on Broadway in Tom Stoppard's play *Jumpers*, swinging naked from a chandelier. A brochure for her tiger preserve shows her wearing silver boots and holding a long whip and feeding one of her tigers, Jaipur, from a baby bottle. On an application for a wildlife permit, Byron-Marasek stated that she had been an assistant tiger trainer and a trapeze artist with Ringling Brothers and L. N. Fleckles; had trained with Doc Henderson, the illustrious circus veterinarian; and had read, among other books, *The Manchurian Tiger, The World of the Tiger, Wild Beasts and Their Ways, My Wild Life, They Never Talk Back,* and *Thank You, I Prefer Lions.*

The Maraseks moved to Jackson in 1976, with Bombay, Chinta, Iman, Jaipur, and Maya, five tigers they had got from an animal trainer named David McMillan. They bought land in a featureless and barely populated part of town near Holmeson's Corner, where Monmouth Road and Millstone Road intersect. It was a good place to raise tigers. There was not much nearby except for a church and a few houses. One neighbor was a Russian Orthodox priest who ran a Christmas-tree farm next to his house; another lived in a gloomy bungalow with a rotting cabin cruiser on cement blocks in the front yard.

For a long time, there were no restrictions in New Jersey on owning wildlife. But beginning in 1971, after regular reports of monkey bites and tiger maulings, exotic-animal owners had to register with the state. Dangerous exotic animals were permitted only if it could be shown that they were needed for education or performance or research. Byron-Marasek held both the necessary New Jersey permit and an exhibitor's license from the United States Department of Agriculture, which supervises animal welfare nationally.

After arriving in Jackson, Byron-Marasek got six more tigers—Bengal, Hassan, Madras, Marco, Royal, and Kizmet—from McMillan and from Ringling Brothers. The next batch—Kirin, Kopan, Bali, Brunei, Brahma, and Burma—were born in the back yard after Byron-Marasek allowed her male and female tigers to commingle. More cubs were born, and more tigers were obtained, and the tiger population of Holmeson's Corner steadily increased. Byron-Marasek called her operation the Tigers Only Preservation Society. Its stated mission was, among other things, to conserve all tiger species, to return captive tigers to the wild, and "to resolve the human/tiger conflict and create a resolution."

"I eat, sleep, and breathe tigers," Byron-Marasek told a local reporter. "I never take vacations. This is my love, my passion." A friend of hers told another reporter, "She walks among her tigers just like Tarzan. She told me, 'I have scratches all along the sides of my rib cage and both my arms have been cut open, but they're just playing.' Now, that's love."

You know how it is—you start with one tiger, then you get another and another, then a few are born and a few die, and you start to lose track of details like exactly how many tigers you actually have. As soon as reports of the loose tiger came in, the police asked everyone in Jackson who had tigers to make sure that all of them were accounted for. Six Flags Wild Safari had a permit for fifteen and could account for all fifteen. At the Maraseks', the counting was done by a group of police and state wildlife officers, who spent more than nine hours peering around tumbledown fences, crates, and sheds in the back yard. Byron-Marasek's permit was for twenty-three tigers, but the wildlife officers could find only seventeen.

Over the years, some of her tigers had died. A few had succumbed to old age. Muji had an allergic reaction to an injection. Diamond had to be euthanized after Marco tore off one of his legs. Marco also killed Hassan in a fight in 1997, on Christmas Eve. Two other tigers died after eating road-killed deer that Byron-Marasek now thinks might have been contaminated with antifreeze. But that still left a handful of tigers unaccounted for.

The officers filmed the visit:

"Joan, I have to entertain the notion that there are five cats loose in town, not just one," an officer says on the videotape.

Byron-Marasek's lawyer, Valter Must, explains to the group that there was some sloppy math when she filed for the most recent permit.

The officers shift impatiently and make a few notes.

"For instance, I don't always count my kids, but I know when they're all home," Must says.

"You don't have twenty-three of them," one of the officers says.

"Exactly," Must says.

"You'd probably know if there were six missing," the officer adds.

"I would agree," Must says.

On the tape, Byron-Marasek insists that no matter how suspicious the discrepancy between her permit and the tiger count appears, the loose tiger was not hers. No, she does not know whom it might have belonged to, either. And, gentlemen, don't stick your fingers into anything, please: I'm not going to tell you again.

The officers ask to see Byron-Marasek's paperwork. She tells them that she is embarrassed to take them into her house because it is a mess. The tiger quarters look cheerless and bare, with dirt floors and chain-link fences and blue plastic tarps flapping in the January wind, as forlorn as a bankrupt construction site. During the inspection, a ruckus starts up in one of the tiger pens. Byron-Marasek, who represents herself as one of the world's foremost tiger authorities, runs to see what it is, and reappears, wild-eyed and frantic, yelling, "Help me! Help! They're going to . . . they're going to kill each other!" The officers head toward the tiger fight, but then Byron-Marasek waves to stop them and screams, "No, just Larry! Just Larry!"—meaning Larry Herrighty, the head of the permit division, about whom she will later say, in an interview, "The tigers hate him."

The day of the tiger count was the first time that the state had inspected the Maraseks' property in years. New Jersey pays some attention to animal welfare—for instance, it closed the Scotch Plains Zoo in 1997 because of substandard conditions—but it doesn't have the resources to monitor all its permit holders. There had been a few complaints about the tigers: in 1983, someone reported that the Maraseks played recordings of jungle drums over a public-address system between 4 and 6 A.M., inciting their tigers to roar. The State Office of Noise Control responded by measuring the noise level outside the compound one night, and Byron-Marasek was warned that there would be monitoring in the future, although it doesn't appear that anyone ever came back. Other complaints, about strange odors, were never investigated. Her permit was renewed annually, even as the number of animals increased.

Anyone with the type of permit Byron-Marasek had must file information about the animals' work schedule, but the state discovered that it had no records indicating that her tigers had ever performed, or that anyone had attended an educational program at Tigers Only. The one tiger with a public profile was Jaipur, who weighed more than a thousand pounds, and who, according to his owner, was listed in the *Guinness World Records* as the largest Siberian tiger in captivity. Later, in court, Byron-Marasek also described Marco as "a great exhibit cat"—this was by way of explaining why she doted on him, even though he had killed Diamond and Hassan—but, as far as

anyone could tell, Marco had never been exhibited.

Now the state was paying attention to the Tigers Only Preservation Society, and it wasn't happy with what it found. In court papers, D.E.P. investigators noted, "The applicant's tiger facility was a ramshackle arrangement with yards (compounds), chutes, runs, and shift cages . . . some of which were covered by deteriorating plywood, stockade fencing and tarps, etc. . . . The periphery fence (along the border of the property), intended to keep out

THE CLOISTER

The last light of a July evening drained
into the streets below. My love and I had hard
things to say and hear and we sat over
wine, faltering, picking our words carefully.

The afternoon before I had lain across
my bed and my cat leapt up to lie
alongside me, purring and slowly
growing dozy. By this ritual I can

clear some clutter from my baroque brain.
And into that brief vacancy the image
of a horse cantered, coming straight to me,
and I knew it brought hard talk and hurt

and fear. How did we do? A medium job,
which is well above average. But because
she had opened her heart to me as far
as she did, I saw her fierce privacy,

like a gnarled, luxuriant tree all hung
with disappointments, and I knew
that to love her I must love the tree
and the nothing it cares for me.

—WILLIAM MATTHEWS | 1998 |

CAN I GET YOU ANYTHING?

NEW, IMPROVED CAT

troublemakers, was down in several places. There was standing water and mud in the compound. There was mud on the applicant's tigers." There were deer carcasses scattered around the property, rat burrows, and a lot of large, angry dogs in separate pens near the tigers. Suddenly, one wandering tiger seemed relatively inconsequential; the inspectors were much more concerned about the fact that Byron-Marasek had at least seventeen tigers living in what they considered sorry conditions, and that the animals were being kept not for theatrical or educational purposes but as illegal pets. Byron-Marasek, for her part, was furious about the state's inspections. "The humiliation we were forced to suffer is beyond description," she said later, reading from a prepared statement at a press conference outside her compound. "Not only did they seriously endanger the lives of our tigers—they also intentionally attempted to cut off their food supply."

The one suspicion that the state couldn't confirm was that the loose tiger had belonged to Joan Byron-Marasek. DNA tests and an autopsy were inconclusive. Maybe he had been a drug dealer's guard animal, or a pet that had got out of hand and was dropped off in Jackson in the hope that the Tiger Lady would take him in. And then there were the conspiracy theorists in town who believed that the tiger had belonged to Six Flags, and that his escape was covered up because the park is the biggest employer and the primary attraction in town. In the end, however, the tiger was simply relegated to the annals of suburban oddities—a lost soul, doomed to an unhappy end, whose provenance will never be known.

It is not hard to buy a tiger. Only eight states prohibit the ownership of wild animals; three states have no restrictions whatsoever, and the rest have regulations that range from trivial to modest and are barely enforced. Exotic-animal auction houses and animal markets thrive in the Midwest and the Southeast, where wildlife laws are the most relaxed. In the last few years, dealers have also begun using the Internet. One recent afternoon, I browsed the Hunts Exotics Web site, where I could have placed an order for baby spider monkeys ($6,500 each, including delivery); an adult female two-toed sloth ($2,200); a Northern cougar female with blue eyes, who was advertised as "tame on bottle"; a black-capped capuchin monkey, needing dental work ($1,500); an agouti paca; a porcupine; or two baby tigers "with white genes" ($1,800 each). From there I was linked to more tiger sites—Mainely Felids and Wildcat Hide-away and NOAH Feline Conservation Center—and to pages for prospective owners titled "I Want a Cougar!" and "Are You Sure You Want a Monkey?" It is so easy to get a tiger, in fact, that wildlife experts estimate that there are at least fifteen thousand pet tigers in the country—more than seven times the number of registered Irish setters or Dalmatians.

One reason that tigers are readily available is that they breed easily in captivity. There are only about six thousand wild tigers left in the world, and three subspecies have become extinct just in the last sixty years. In zoos, though, tigers have babies all the time. The result is thousands of "surplus tigers"—in the zoo economy, these are animals no longer worth keeping, because there are too many of them, or because they're old and zoo visitors prefer baby animals to mature ones. In fact, many zoos began breeding excessively during the seventies and eighties when they realized that baby animals drew big crowds. The trade in exotic pets expanded as animals were sold to dealers and game ranches and unaccredited zoos once they were no longer cute. In 1999, the San Jose *Mercury News* reported that many of the best zoos in the country, including the San Diego Zoo and the Denver Zoological Gardens, regularly disposed of their surplus animals through dealers. Some zoo directors were so disturbed by the practice that they euthanized their surplus animals: according to the *Mercury News*, the director of the Detroit Zoo put two healthy Siberian tigers to sleep, rather than risk their ending up as mistreated pets or on hunting ranches. Sometimes dealers buy surplus animals just for butchering. An adult tiger, alive, costs between two hundred and three hundred dollars. A tiger pelt sells for two thousand dollars, and body parts from a large animal, which are commonly used in aphrodisiacs, can bring five times as much.

Between 1990 and 2000, Jackson's population increased by almost a third, and cranberry farms and chicken farms began yielding to condominiums and center-hall Colonials. It was probably inevitable that something would come to limn the town's changing character, its passage from a rural place to something different—a bedroom community attached to nowhere in particular, with clots of crowdedness amid a sort of essential emptiness; a place practically exploding with new people and new roads that didn't connect to anything, and fresh, clean sidewalks of cement that still looked damp; the kind of place made possible by highways and telecommuting, and made necessary by the high cost of living in bigger

A CAT'S DINNER

On the Seventh Avenue I.R.T. the other day, an ordinary-looking man in a raincoat and fedora was chatting with his ordinary-looking seatmate. He lived alone, he said, with his cat.

"Oh," said his seatmate. "What kind of cat?"

"A big one," replied the man, indicating with his hands something four feet long and three feet high, and adding, with matter-of-fact pride, that occasionally the cat got loose in the streets and had knocked down many old ladies and one policeman.

The seatmate peered distractedly about the subway car and then asked the man what he fed this cat.

"Hot dogs and coffee," said the man. "Nothing else. Just plenty of hot dogs and coffee."

| 1975 |

cities, and made desirable, ironically, by the area's quickly vanishing rural character. A tiger in town had, in a roundabout way, made all of this clear.

In 1997, a model house was built on the land immediately east of the Maraseks' compound, and in the next two years thirty more houses went up. The land had been dense, brambly woods. It was wiped clean before the building started, so the new landscaping trees were barely toothpicks, held in place with rubber collars and guy wires, and the houses looked as if they'd just been unwrapped and set out, like lawn ornaments. The development was named The Preserve. The houses were airy and tall and had showy entrances and double-car garages and fancy amenities like Jacuzzis and wet bars and recessed lighting and cost around three hundred thousand dollars. They were the kind of houses that betokened a certain amount of achievement—promotion to company vice-president, say—and they were owned by people who were disconcerted to note that on certain mornings, as they stood outside playing catch with their kids or pampering their lawns, there were dozens of buzzards lined up on their roofs, staring hungrily at the Maraseks' back yard.

"If someone had told me there were tigers here, I would have never bought the house," one neighbor said not long ago. His name is Kevin Wingler, and where his lawn ends, the Maraseks' property begins. He is a car collector, and he was in his garage at the time, tinkering with a classic red Corvette he had just bought. "I love animals," he said. "We get season passes every year for the Six Flags safari, and whenever I'm out I always pet all the cows and all the pigs, and I think tigers are majestic and beautiful and everything. But we broke our ass to build this house, and it's just not right. I could have bought in any development! I even had a contract elsewhere, but the builder coaxed me into buying this." He licked his finger and dabbed at a spot on the dashboard and laughed. "This is just so weird," he said. "You'd think this would be happening in Arkansas, or something."

I drove through The Preserve and then out to a road on the other side of the Maraseks' land. This was an old road, one of the few that had been there when the Maraseks moved in, and the houses were forty or fifty years old and weathered. The one near the corner belonged to the owner of a small trucking company. He said that he had helped Joan Byron-Marasek clean up her facilities after the state inspection. "I knew she was here when I moved here fifteen years ago," he said. "Tigers nearby? I don't care. You hear a roar here and there. It's not a big concern of mine to hear a roar now and then. The stench in the summer was unbearable, though." He said he didn't think that the wandering tiger was one of Byron-Marasek's, because her tigers were so dirty and the tiger that was shot looked clean and fit. He said that, a few years before, Byron-Marasek had come by his house with a petition to stop the housing development. He didn't sign it. "The new neighbors, they're not very neighborly," he said. "They're over there in their fancy houses. She's been here a lot longer than they have." Still, he didn't want to get involved. "Those are Joan's own private kitty cats," he said, lighting a cigarette. "That's her business. I've got my life to worry about."

The tiger that had walked through Jackson for less than eight hours had been an inscrutable and unaccountable visitor, and, like many such visitors, he disturbed things. A

meeting was held at City Hall soon after he was shot. More than a hundred people showed up. A number of them came dressed in tiger costumes. They demanded to know why the roving tiger had been killed rather than captured, and what the fate of Byron-Marasek's tigers would be. Somehow the meeting devolved into a shouting match between people from the new Jackson, who insisted that Byron-Marasek's tigers be removed immediately, and the Old Guard, who suggested that anyone who knew the town—by implication, the only people who really deserved to be living there—knew that there were tigers in Holmeson's Corner. If the tigers bothered the residents in The Preserve so much, why had they been stupid enough to move in? Soon after the meeting, the state refused to renew Byron-Marasek's wildlife permit, citing inadequate animal husbandry, failure to show theatrical or educational grounds for possessing potentially dangerous wildlife, and grievously flawed record-keeping. The township invoked its domestic-animals ordinances, demanding that Byron-Marasek get rid of some of her thirty-odd dogs or else apply for a formal kennel license. The homeowners in The Preserve banded together and sued the developer for consumer fraud, claiming that he had withheld information about the tigers in his off-site disclosure statement, which notifies prospective buyers of things like toxic-waste dumps and prisons which might affect the resale value of a house. The neighborhood group also sued Byron-Marasek for creating a nuisance with both her tigers and her dogs.

Here was where the circus began—not the circus where Joan Byron-Marasek had worked and where she had developed the recipe for "Joan's Circus Secret," which is what she feeds her tigers, but the legal circus, the amazing three-ring spectacle that has been going on now for several years. Once the state denied Byron-Marasek's request to renew her permit, she could no longer legally keep her tigers. She requested an administrative review, but the permit denial was upheld. She appealed to a higher court. She was ordered to get rid of the animals while awaiting the results of her appeal of the permit case. She appealed that order. "Tigers are extremely fragile animals," she said at a press conference. "Tigers will die if removed by someone else. If they are allowed to take our tigers, this will be a tiger holocaust." Byron-Marasek won that argument, which allowed her to keep the tigers during her permit appeal, as long as she agreed to certain conditions, including preventing the tigers from breeding. During the next couple of years, two of her tigers had cubs, which she hid from state inspectors for several weeks. She declared that the state was trying to destroy her life's work. Through her Tigers Only Web site, she supplied form letters for her supporters to send to state officials and to the D.E.P.:

DEAR SENATOR:

I am a supporter of the Tigers Only Preservation Society and Ms. Joan Byron-Marasek in her fight to keep her beautiful tigers in their safe haven in Jackson, New Jersey. . . . We should all be delighted with the fact that these tigers live together in peaceful harmony with their environment and one another right here in New Jersey. If anything, the T.O.P.S. tigers should be revered as a State treasure, and as such, we citizens of New Jersey should all proudly and enthusiastically participate in this

State-wide endeavor to keep the T.O.P.S. tigers in New Jersey.

If we are successful . . . future generations of constituents will be eternally grateful for your efforts in keeping these magnificent creatures living happily in our midst for all to enjoy.

In the meantime, legal proceedings dragged on while she changed attorneys five times. Her case moved up the legal chain until it reached the state's appellate court. There, in December, 2001, the original verdict was finally and conclusively upheld—in other words, Byron-Marasek was denied, once and for all, the right to keep tigers in New Jersey.

The Byron-Marasek case reminded some people of the 1995 landmark lawsuit in Oregon against Vickie Kittles, who had a hundred and fifteen dogs living with her in a school bus. Wherever Kittles stopped with her wretched menagerie, she was given a tank of gas and directions to get out of town. She ended up in Oregon, where she was finally arrested. There she faced a district attorney named Joshua Marquis, who had made his name prosecuting the killer of Victor the Lobster, the twenty-five-pound mascot of Oregon's Seaside Aquarium who had been abducted from his tank. When the thief was apprehended, he threw Victor to the ground, breaking his shell; no lobster veterinarian could be found and Victor died three days later. Marquis was able to persuade a jury that the man was guilty of theft and criminal mischief. He decided to prosecute Kittles on grounds of animal neglect. Kittles contended that she had the right to live with her dogs in any way she chose. Marquis argued that the dogs, which got no

"Cat, anyone?"

exercise and no veterinary care and were evidently miserable, did not choose to live in a school bus. Vickie Kittles was convicted, and her dogs were sent to foster homes around the country.

The Kittles case was the first prominent suit against an "animal hoarder"—a person who engages in the pathological collecting of animals. Tiger Ladies are somewhat rare, but there are Cat Ladies and Bird Men all over the country, and often they end up in headlines like "201 CATS PULLED FROM HOME" and "PETS SAVED FROM HORROR HOME" and "CAT LOVER'S NEIGHBORS TIRED OF FELINE FIASCO." A study published by the Hoarding of Animals Research Consortium says that more than two-thirds of hoarders are females, and most often they hoard cats, although dogs, birds, farm animals, and, in one case, beavers, are hoarded as well. The median number of animals is thirty-nine, but many hoarders have more than a hundred. Hoarders, according to the consortium, "may have problems concentrating and staying on track with any management plan."

On the other hand, animal hoarders may have boundless energy and focus when it comes to fighting in court. Even after Byron-Marasek lost her final appeal, she devised another way to frustrate the state's efforts to remove her tigers. The Department of Environmental Protection had found homes for the tigers at the Wild Animal Orphanage in San Antonio, Texas, and come up with a plan for moving the tigers there on the orphanage's Humane Train. In early January, the superior-court judge Eugene Serpentelli held a hearing on the matter. The Tiger Lady came to court wearing a dark-green pants suit and square-toed shoes and carrying a heavy black briefcase. She was edgy and preoccupied and waved off anyone who approached her except for a local radio host who had trumpeted her cause on his show and a slim young man who huddled with her during breaks. The young man was as circumspect as she was, politely declining to say whether he was a contributor to the Tigers Only Preservation Society or a fellow tiger owner or perhaps someone with his own beef with the D.E.P.

Throughout the hearing, Byron-Marasek dipped into her briefcase and pulled out sheets of paper and handwritten notes and pages

"We want to register a domestic partnership."

downloaded from the Internet, and passed them to her latest lawyer, who had been retained the day before. The material documented infractions for which the Wild Animal Orphanage had been cited by the U.S.D.A. over the years—storing outdated bags of Monkey Chow in an unair-conditioned shed, for instance, and placing the carcass of a tiger in a meat freezer until its eventual necropsy and disposal. None of the infractions were serious and none remained unresolved, but they raised enough questions to delay the inevitable once again, and Judge Serpentelli adjourned to allow Byron-Marasek more time to present an alternate plan. "Throughout this period of time, I've made it clear that the court had no desire to inflict on Mrs. Marasek or the tigers any hardship," the Judge announced. "But the tigers must be removed. I have no discretion on the question of whether they should be removed, just how."

Before the state acts, however, there is a good chance that the Tiger Lady will have taken matters into her own hands. Last fall, in an interview with the Asbury Park *Press*, she said that she was in the process of "buying land elsewhere"—she seemed to think it unwise to name the state—and suggested that she and her dogs and her tigers might be leaving New Jersey for good. Typically, people who have disputes with the authorities about their animal collections move from one jurisdiction to another as they run into legal difficulties. If they do eventually lose their animals, they almost always resurface somewhere else with new ones: recidivism among hoarders is close to a hundred percent. In the not too distant future, in some other still-rural corner of America, people may begin to wonder what smells so strange when the wind blows from a certain direction, and whether they actually could have heard a roar in the middle of the night, and whether there could be any truth to the rumors about a lady with a bunch of tigers in town.

I had been to Jackson countless times, circled the Maraseks' property, and walked up and down the sidewalks in The Preserve, but I had never seen a single tiger. I had even driven up to the Maraseks' front gate a couple of times and peered through it, and I could see some woolly white dogs scuffing behind a wire fence, and I could see tarps and building materials scattered around the house, but no tigers, no flash of orange fur, nothing. I wanted to see one of the animals, to assure myself that they really existed.

One afternoon, I parked across from the Winglers' and walked past their garage, where Kevin was still monkeying around with his Corvette, and then across their backyard and beyond where their lawn ended, where the woods thickened and the ground was springy from all the decades' worth of pine needles that have rained down, and I followed the tangy, slightly sour smell that I guessed was tiger, although I don't think I'd ever smelled tigers before. There was a chain-link fence up ahead. I stopped and waited. A minute passed and nothing happened. A minute more, and then a tiger walked past on the other side of the fence, its huge head lowered and its tail barely twitching, the black stripes of its coat crisscrossed with late-day light, its slow, heavy tread making no sound at all. It reached the end of the fence and paused, and turned back the other way, and then it was gone.

| 2002 |

CAT FANTASIA

THOMAS BELLER

For several hours one afternoon last week, the unremarkable interior of the Southgate Tower Hotel, in midtown, was transformed into a kind of cat fantasia for the nineties, previewing some of the more exotic and genetically up-to-date entries in the ninth annual International Cat Show, which was held at Madison Square Garden this past weekend. Cats were perched on chairs and couches and windowsills, and a few even deigned to step on the floor. Their owners mostly stood over them, fawning, and some waved what appeared to be feather dusters lined with sparkly sequins while the cats jumped up, stared inquisitively, or assumed some other quintessential cat pose provoked by this mystery object, referred to, appropriately, as a "cat tease."

Though beautiful, most of the cats present would not be mistaken for regular house pets. One, named Battle Hymn, a Persian that had been groomed to resemble a lion (or a poodle), spent the afternoon resting languorously on its own divan, which was decorated in a cheetah pattern—a pattern that matched a bow tie around its neck and also the skirt, bracelet, and earrings of its owner, Lise Girard. On a windowsill, nestled in a cat-size playpen lined with pink fur, a father and son Sphynx team curled up,

the father diligently licking the wrinkly infant. The Sphynx differs conspicuously from most breeds of cat; indeed, one is likely to pause a moment before deciding that it is a cat at all. Their owner described the Sphynx as "a cat with no clothes on," the fact being that the Sphynx has no hair, only a stubble so faint that any skinhead could be proud of it, and a worried face. The Sphynxes' owner suggests that in order to best appreciate their beauty you might "think of them as Yoda or E.T."

The stars of the unusual cat sweepstakes, however, were Maxwell and Cotton, which belong to a breed that was making its début at this year's cat show. The Longhaired Munchkin is a breed that owes its existence in large part to Dr. Solveig Pflueger, a geneticist who counsels "both humans and cats." The Munchkin's major distinction is that it has very short legs. "It's the cat equivalent of a dachshund," Dr. Pflueger said as she twirled her cat tease above Maxwell while he vainly tried to leap up after it. Dr. Pflueger suggested that, because the Longhaired Munchkin had legs too short for jumping, it would be ideal for someone who didn't want to own a cat that would leap up on counters and sofas. Joan Rivers has dubbed the Munchkin, for reasons that are unclear, the Dr. Ruth cat.

Some of the cats fit a more conventional definition of beauty. Victoria Garvin, an administrator in the Paintings and Sculpture Department of the Museum of Modern Art, is the owner of Ursa Minor, an Ocie, whose main distinction, in addition to a lithe, sleek body, is a spotted coat closely resembling that of an ocelot. Ms. Garvin, who lives in a house in northern New Jersey with eight cats and a brother, suggested that the "jungle look" was enjoying a bit of a vogue among cats.

Perhaps the most low-key cat/owner pair was Fred Andrews and Hermes. Mr. Andrews, who happened to be the only male owner present, sat quietly in an armchair throughout the afternoon. He was wearing a purple crewneck sweater, and Hermes, an ash-gray Chartreux, huddled against his purple stomach, which provided a bit of a perch. "He's terrified," Mr. Andrews said of his cat. "It's his first show."

The Chartreux is a rare breed in America; it apparently originated in France centuries ago, and the first Chartreux didn't arrive here until 1970. Mr. Andrews, a thirty-one-year-old native of Staten Island, entered the world of pedigree cats in 1989. After consulting *Simon & Schuster's Guide to Cats*, he settled on the Chartreux because it was beautiful and also "because that was the one that looked the most normal," he said. "I wasn't interested in any of the funky-looking cats."

The Chartreux is so rare that those wishing to acquire one usually have a six-month wait, and kittens can cost as much as a thousand dollars each. Mr. Andrews now has nine Chartreux. They live with him, uncaged, in a two-bedroom apartment. The one male Chartreux has the other bedroom.

| 1993 |

CAT-SITTING

JOHN BROOKS

Mrs. Dorothy Wilde Browne, a lady who lives on West Eleventh Street, has set up a profitable business as a cat-sitter. As a matter of fact, Mrs. Browne has become something of a cat-sitting operator, since she has subsidiary sitters working out of Yonkers, Bronxville, Sutton Place, Thirty-third Street, Twenty-third Street, Maspeth, and other points too far from West Eleventh Street for her to handle personally. We stopped in to see Mrs. Browne recently and found her sparring with a fat Siamese cat, whom she addressed as Zebeard. Zebeard, she said, was a temporary boarder, and she went on to explain that she takes a few animals into her apartment while their owners are off on vacation, but most cats become unhappy when moved away from their familiar surroundings, and therefore have to be sat with at home. "Here's how I happened to get into the cat-sitting line," said Mrs. Browne. "I found myself with some rather heavy medical bills to pay, so I wanted some work, but at the same time I didn't want to go to an office. Three of my children still live at home. I didn't want to do baby-sitting, either, because I've brought up four children and that's enough of *that*. Nevertheless, the idea of baby-sitting led to the idea of cat-sitting. I've had pets all my life and I've often been faced with the problem of what to do with them when I went off on a vacation. I put an ad in the *Villager*, and the response was instantaneous and overwhelming, and practically overnight I had more business than I could handle."

Mrs. Browne dragged Zebeard off an upholstered seat that he was trying to eviscerate. "I believe the name Zebeard means absolutely nothing," she remarked. She then went on to explain her *modus operandi* as a cat-sitter. Clients, on leaving for vacation, give her their apartment keys; she makes the rounds of client cats twice a day—morning and evening—feeding, brushing, and conversing with each one. "Loneliness isn't much of a problem with most cats, but they do like their comforts," she said. As the project snowballed, she went on, she began to get requests for service from points farther and farther afield. She decreed that she would not sit south of Vandam Street or north of Seventeenth; she makes her rounds on foot, and lines had to be drawn somewhere. A little while later, she began recruiting helpers, partly through newspaper ads and partly through the Fifteenth Street Quaker Meeting, of which she is a member. "Altogether I have forty-two helpers listed," she told us. "I serve as a clearing house for jobs, but I don't take a cut. The worst sitting job I've had was with a Siamese near Gramercy Park, named Mitzi. That little hellion arched her back like a puffball, and I never dared approach her without a full watering can."

Mrs. Browne, who told us, in passing, that she is a first cousin twice removed of Oscar Wilde, began by charging a dollar a day per cat, but she found out that kennels charge ten a week, on the average, just for boarding a cat or dog in a small cage, and now she has doubled her price. She will not sit for any animals except cats, but for the living-in-her-apartment part of the operation she has accepted dogs, monkeys, and a myna bird, which kept asking her, "Going out with the boys?" An armadillo is coming to board with her late in September; she has never been asked to go and sit with an armadillo, and if she were, she wouldn't. Mrs. Browne told us that business booms in the late fall, when people begin going off to Bermuda, Nassau, and Florida. "One advantage cat-sitting has over baby-sitting is that the owners are generally so far away they can't call up and pester you," she said.

| 1954 |

MYSELF WITH CATS

Hanging out the wash, I visit the cats.
"I don't belong to nobody," Yin insists vulgarly.
"Yin," I reply, "you don't know nothing."
Yang, an orange tabby, agrees
but puts kindness ahead of rigid truth.
I admire her but wish she wouldn't idolize
the one who bullies her. I once did that.
Her silence speaks needles when Yang thrusts
his ugly tortoiseshell body against hers,
sprawled in my cosmos. "Really, I don't mind,"
she purrs—her eyes horizontal, her mouth
an Ionian smile, her legs crossed nobly
in front of her, a model of cat Nirvana—
"withholding his affection, he made me stronger."

—HENRI COLE | 2001 |

Poet with Cats

Hanging out the wash, I talk ~~with~~ to the cats.
Yin, a ~~grumpy fat maggot~~ ~~an ugly~~ tortoise shell, ~~begins~~ ~~says~~ says, "I don't belong
to nobody." I ~~say~~ reply, ~~usually~~ vulgarly "Yin, you don't know nothing."
Yang, an orange tabby, is hurt but agrees.
She puts kindness ahead of rigid truth.
I admire her, ~~But~~ though I wish she wouldn't idolize
the one who bullies her. I once did that.
Her silence speaks needles | when Yang is thirsty
his body against hers, sprawled in my cosmos —
her eyes horizontal, her mouth an Ionian smile,
her legs crossed in front of her, — her head inclined nobly
she's a model of
in some kind of cat-nirvana ⊙ — I don't mind
no ugliness
~~a good life~~ about her. "I don't mind," she ~~says~~
she purrs, who any ugliness about her.
"Withholding his affection, he made me stronger."
a little but amused & embarrassed

explains

from CAT MAN

GEORGE STEINER

This review ought to be about a cat, the most illustrious, compelling cat in the history of literature. Bébert was a Montparnasse tabby, born probably in 1935. He met his second master in occupied Paris in late 1942. "Magic itself, tact by wavelength," as his master described him, Bébert was to be left behind when the master and his wife, Lucette, decamped for Germany in the dread spring of '44. Bébert refused separation. He was carried in the travelling sack. The voyage led through lunar bomb craters, strafed rail lines, and cities burning like mad torches. Under bombardment, Bébert, almost starving, became lost, but rediscovered his master and Madame. The trio crossed and recrossed the collapsing Reich. In a last, despairing lunge, they reached Copenhagen. When the Danish police came to arrest the unwelcome guests, Bébert slipped out across a roof. Caught, the legendary beast was caged in a pound at a veterinary clinic. When his master was released from jail and was recuperating, Bébert had to be operated on for a cancerous tumor. "But the Montmartre tom had been around the block. He withstood the trauma and made a speedy recovery, with the slower and wiser serenity of aging cats, faithful, silent, and enigmatic." Amnestied, Bébert's *patron* headed for home at the end of June, 1951. Four lesser cats—Thomine, Poupine, Mouchette, and Flûte—accompanied them on the voyage. Sphinxlike in years, Bébert, the secret sharer, died in a suburb of Paris at the end of 1952. "After many an adventure, jail, bivouac, ashes, all of Europe . . . he died agile and graceful, impeccably, he had jumped out the window that very morning. . . . We, who are born old, look ridiculous in comparison!" So wrote his grieving master, Louis-Ferdinand Destouches, physician, champion of social hygiene among the destitute, wanderer in Africa and the United States, manic crank.

It is Bébert I want to write about—Bébert the arch-survivor and the incarnation of French cunning. But it is a voluminous biography of his wretched owner that I have before me—of that mad doctor who, under the name Céline (taken from his grandmother), produced some of the greatest fiction and documentary "fact-fiction" not only in this century but in the history of Western literature. Bébert would be a joy to report on. Céline is not.

| 1992 |

THE PET

Fiction

SALLY BENSON

Morton Hyde's drugstore opened at eight o'clock every morning. By that time, the man from the bakery had delivered the daily supply of jelly doughnuts, English muffins, and Danish pastry, and Mr. Hyde had started the coffee in the Silex on the electric stove behind the counter. Since he was an old-fashioned man and thought that drugstores should sell only drugs and medicines, he hated this part of his day. But the boy who worked at the soda fountain didn't come on until ten o'clock, and Mr. Hyde reluctantly filled in for him until then. Mr. Hyde also hated the cosmetics he had stocked to meet the competition of the chain drugstore two blocks down the street, and he still remembered with distaste the first dozen boxes of Djer-Kiss powder he had put on sale. He felt that the cosmetics stank up the store and drowned out the bitter, therapeutic smell of the ingredients that went into prescriptions.

One morning, at about five minutes of eight, there was a knock on the door. Turning around, he saw Ed Davis standing outside, his shoulders hunched and his felt hat pulled down over his eyes. Mr. Hyde switched the electric burner under the Silex to "Low" and went to let him in. "Morning, Ed," he said as he opened the door. "Something wrong?"

Ed Davis went to the counter and sat down on a high stool, pushing his hat back on his head with a tired gesture. "I been up all night," he said. "I don't ever want to put in a night like last night again."

Mr. Hyde switched on the neon lights, which flickered once or twice before they filled the store with a hard, uncompromising glare. "What happened?" he asked.

"God-damnedest night I ever had." Ed fished in his pocket and brought out a piece of paper, which he put on the counter. "We almost lost Midge."

"Midge?" Mr. Hyde repeated.

"Our cat," Ed explained. He shoved the paper toward Mr. Hyde. "I got a prescription for her. She almost died. I've had her to the vet's."

Mr. Hyde picked up the prescription and read it. "You want to wait?" he asked.

"Do I want to wait?" Ed said. "After all I been through, waiting don't seem nothing to me. I been waiting all night. That cat started in about nine o'clock—just when Milton Berle was signing off—and she kept it up until I got her to that vet in Middletown, about 6 A.M."

"Kept what up?" Mr. Hyde asked.

"Throwing herself around," Ed said. "I never saw nothing like it. The Missis couldn't handle her, and neither could I. You wouldn't think an old cat like Midge would have the strength to throw herself around like that. I think you'd better give me a cup of coffee. I ain't had a bite of breakfast."

Mr. Hyde went behind the counter and, setting a cup and saucer on the counter, filled the cup with coffee and pushed a pitcher of cream and a bowl of sugar toward Ed. "Animals can be a great responsibility," he said.

"Midge ain't an animal, exactly," Ed said, putting three heaping spoons of sugar in his coffee. "She's more like a human. All the time she was throwing herself around, you could tell she was ashamed of herself. She'd fly around and then look at me like she was asking me to excuse her. But she couldn't stop. It was pitiful. Do you know that vet over in Middletown?"

"No," Mr. Hyde said. "Will you have something to eat?"

"My stomach's still turning over," Ed

said. "You don't know whether that vet's a crook or not, then?"

"What makes you think he's a crook?" Mr. Hyde asked.

"He charged me seven bucks. And do you know how much that crook Jenks socked me to drive to Middletown and back? Nine dollars each way! Eighteen dollars!"

"That's a lot of money," Mr. Hyde said. "Eighteen dollars plus seven and two dollars for this prescription comes to twenty-seven dollars. You could have bought a new cat."

DOOR

The cat cries for me from the other side.
It is beyond her to work this device
That I open and cross and close
With such ease when I mean to work.

Its four panels form a cross—the rood,
Sign of suffering and redemption.
The rod, a dividing pike or pale
Mounted and hinged to swing between

One way or place and another, meow.
Between the January vulva of birth
And the January of death's door
There are so many to negotiate,

Closed or flung open or ajar, valves
Of attention. O kitty, if the doors
Of perception were cleansed
All things would appear as they are,

Infinite. Come in, darling, drowse
Comfortably near my feet, I will click
The barrier closed again behind you, O
Sister will, fellow-mortal, here we are.

—ROBERT PINSKY | 2001 |

Ed Davis set his cup down in the saucer so hard that the coffee slopped over. "I could have *what*?" he asked.

"You could have bought a new cat," Mr. Hyde repeated.

"That's a hell of a thing to say." Ed looked down at his hands; they were scrubbed clean but were callused from work. "A hell of a thing," he said. "People ain't got hearts. They got holes where their heart is supposed to be."

"I've got a heart," Mr. Hyde said, irritated. "But I see a lot of sickness in this business, and I can't get het up over a cat."

"People are skunks," Ed said. "They got no feelings. They're crooks and skunks."

"I wouldn't say that, Ed. That's a pretty sweeping statement to make," Mr. Hyde said.

"By the way, I've ordered a cat."

"You've got to admit an animal isn't a human. I mean, when you first got this cat, what did you get her *for*?"

"We got her when she was eight weeks old. She was as pretty as a picture on a calendar," Ed said. "We had field mice in the cellar."

"Exactly," Mr. Hyde said. "You got her to kill field mice. You got her for a *reason*. And now she's old. How old is she?"

"Eight," Ed said.

"Eight," Mr. Hyde repeated. "That's old for a cat. She's outlived her usefulness."

"Like hell she has," Ed said. "She acts like a kitten. And if you'd have seen her last night, you wouldn't say she was old. Up the curtains and down again—around the sofa and back. All over the damned place."

"Maybe," Mr. Hyde said. "But does she still catch mice?"

"Mice don't come into the picture no more," Ed said. "I don't give a damn if she never catches another mouse. Mice ain't the point. She ain't caught a mouse in years."

"Then what do you keep her for?" Mr. Hyde asked.

Ed Davis banged his fist on the counter. "What do we keep her for?" he said loudly. "What do you keep that boy of yours for?"

"Rich is my son," Mr. Hyde said.

"What does he do?" Ed asked. "Catch mice?" He laughed sarcastically. "No, *he* don't even catch mice, and never did. He don't do nothing—just fools around."

"Look, Ed, Rich is a boy and your cat is a cat," Mr. Hyde said. "You say she's eight years old and having fits. Maybe it would be kinder to have her put out of the way."

Ed Davis slumped on the stool and put his head down on his hands. "Now I've heard everything," he said.

"I'm trying to tell you that you haven't got the kind of money to throw away on a sick cat," Mr. Hyde said. "Twenty-seven dollars doesn't grow on trees."

"Look," Ed said wearily. "You don't get the point. It ain't the mice and it ain't the money. It's Midge. She's our cat."

Mr. Hyde walked toward the back of the store. "You want this prescription filled?" he asked.

"That's what I come for," Ed said. "The vet knocked her out, but I want this for when she comes to."

"It'll take about ten minutes," Mr. Hyde said. "You can charge it if you want to. But if I were you— Well, there's a new litter of kittens at Holbrooks' place."

"Don't give me no more arguments," Ed said. He pushed his coffee away. It had got cold. "Midge is our cat. Money don't mean a thing."

"O.K.," Mr. Hyde said. "If that's the way you feel. I told you you could charge it."

Ed Davis rubbed the rough place on one of his hands. "No, thanks," he said. "The way things stand, I'd rather pay cash."

| 1955 |

ON THE DEATH OF A CAT

In life, death
was nothing
to you: I am

willing to wager
my soul that it
simply never occurred

to your nightmareless
mind, while sleep
was everything

(see it raised
to an infinite
power and perfection)—no death

in you then, so now
how even less. Dear stealth
of innocence

licked polished
to an evil
lustre, little

milk fang, whiskered
night
friend—

go.

—FRANZ WRIGHT | 2003 |

ATTENTION: LOST CAT

PATRICIA MARX

Reward if you find my cat, Sally. Sally is eleven, but she has the face of a cat much younger. She is taffy-colored and has no distinguishing features except for the spot on her lung. Sally understands eight commands. Nine, if you count "Drop it! Drop the baby!" Sally loves a good steak but will gladly have whatever you are having. If she seems to have trouble swallowing, call Dr. Sidarsky, at (570) 555-1212. Dr. Sidarsky calls every day to ask if Sally is back. Once, Dr. Sidarsky invited me to a tennis match where a little girl who could not speak English beat the defending champion. If you ask me, Dr. Sidarsky has a crush on me. Before Sally was lost, Dr. Sidarsky nominated me for Pet Owner of the Year. When the judges came to our house, Sally would not come down from the breezeway. I'm not saying that was the reason I lost the title, but it cost me points.

Sally was last seen in Kansas, where she fell out of my car—a 1998 yellow Toyota Corolla, Indiana license plate FJ3-JR57. To tell you the truth, Sally didn't actually fall. My ex-husband was trying to push me and my suitcases out of the car and Sally was in the way. I'd opened the door to throw out a pair of pants and some other garbage of my ex-husband's. I hate a messy car. My ex-

husband says he was leaning over to close the door, but I definitely felt a nudge. Sally and the gourmet-cooking cassettes that I had taken out of the library landed all over Route 23 in Kansas. Sally ran toward Nebraska. We were on the ramp toward Missouri. My ex-husband's sister Sugar lives in Nebraska. I don't like Sugar and I know Sugar does not like me. She sent me a bathroom scale as a wedding gift. Normally, I have nothing to do with Sugar, but I called her just in case Sally had turned up there. Sometimes animals have a sixth sense about knowing who your relatives are and how to get in touch. As usual, Sugar was unpleasant. She said I sounded like I had gained weight.

Sally has been missing for more than a year, and I am losing hope. Her mother belonged to my grandfather, and now my grandfather is dead. Sally is my last link to my grandfather. If you find Sally and she is dead, send her back anyway. My parents are dead, but I have their steak knives. Once, I had a locket of my grandmother's. I gave it to my daughter for Christmas, since my daughter was named after my grandmother, who was named after her grandmother, who was named after Sally, but not that Sally. When I lost my daughter in the custody suit, I lost the locket, too. I lost everything. Well, not all of the steak knives. Or the weight—I didn't lose that, either.

In spite of what the judge said, my ex-husband is not fit to care for my daughter, pony or no pony. The only things my ex-husband can cook are Texas Tommies. My ex-husband's girlfriend cannot cook, either, but I have to admit, she knows good food.

If I still had Sally, I think the judge would have let me keep my daughter. Pets are a sign of a loving home life. I know the judge would have been impressed if I had been Pet Owner of the Year. I might have gone into politics if I had been Pet Owner of the Year, maybe alderman. I am not too old to get into politics, and I have a lot of ideas. Let's not forget that after the Russian Revolution they turned the stock exchange into an aquarium. For the people! We could do something like that. If Sally came back, I would take a picture of me holding her and use that on my campaign poster. And if she didn't my slogan could be "Help me help you find my cat!" Even if you don't find Sally, please send cash. It's not the same thing as a cat, but it is a consolation.

| 2003 |

"I'm sorry, but I think it's uncatlike."

THE CAT LADY

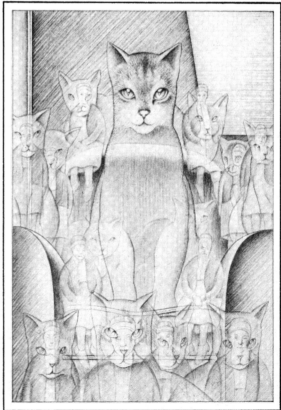

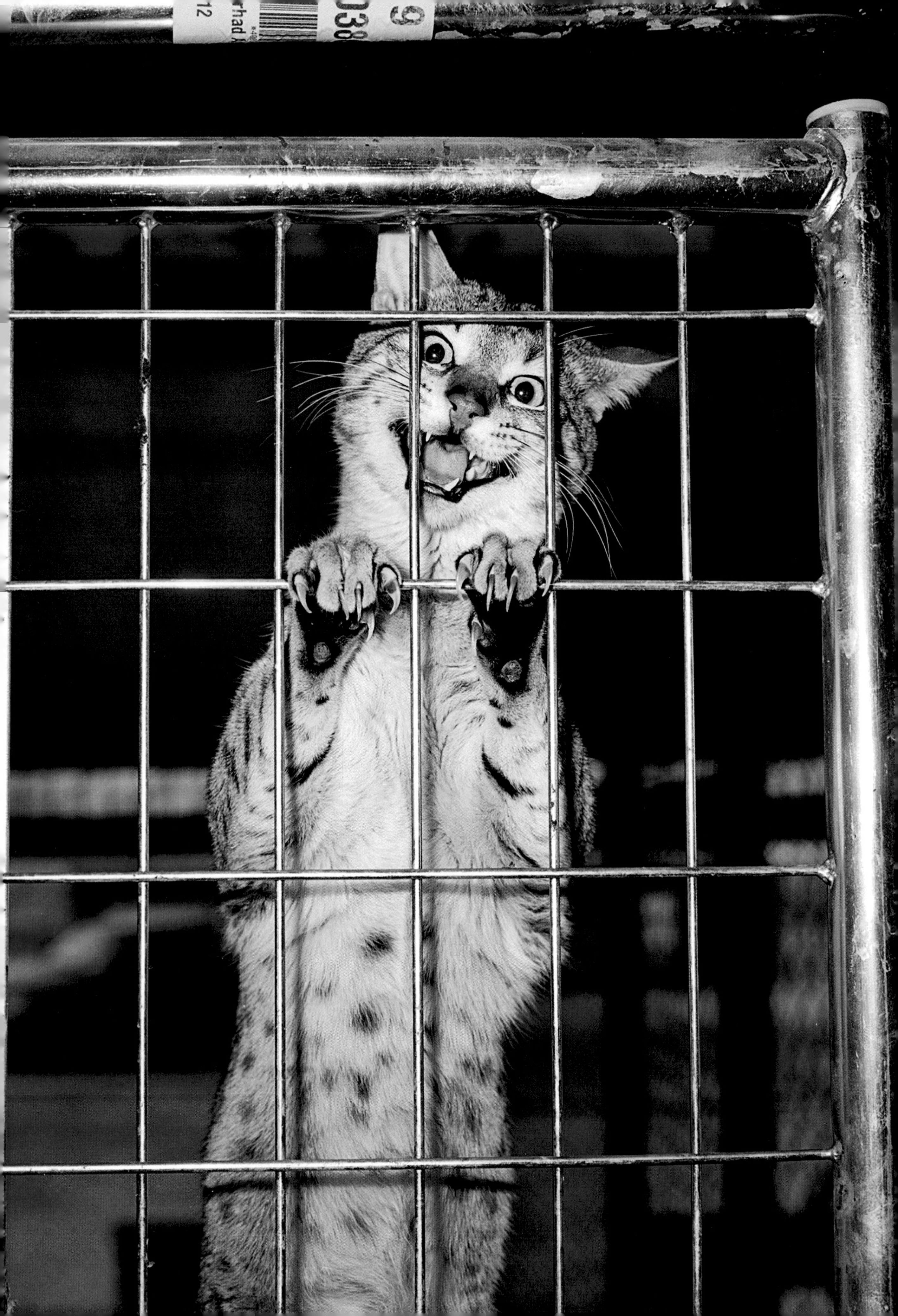

LIVING ROOM LEOPARDS

ARIEL LEVY

When Anthony Hutcherson was a little boy, what he wanted most was something wild. But he was growing up in a very tame place: Helen, Maryland, a small farming community named after the mailman's daughter. "I wanted a kinkajou and a monkey and a skunk, a pet leopard," he recalled—something unlike the cows and sheep out in the meadows nearby. One day, when he was ten years old, waiting with his mother to check out at the grocery store, he saw something that thrilled him. It was a picture in *Cat Fancy* of a pretty woman in California, holding an exotic golden cat that she'd bred by crossing a domestic shorthair with an Asian leopard cat—a foul-tempered little beast with a gorgeous spotted coat. She called the result the Bengal, and touted it as "a living room leopard."

His family didn't understand his passion, he told me one recent afternoon. Hutcherson, who is African-American, offered a cultural explanation: "Generally, black people don't like cats." So he wrote to the woman in California, Jean Mill, and, to his delight, she wrote back. They have been friends and collaborators ever since. Hutcherson, now thirty-eight, is the chairman of the International Cat Association's Bengal Breed Committee and a past president of the International Bengal Cat Society. He and Mill, like many of their colleagues, share a dream: to breed a cat that "looks like it just walked out of the jungle."

We were sitting in Hutcherson's living room, in Aquasco, Maryland, across from a glass cage where his kinkajou, a ferret-like nocturnal creature, was sleeping under a blanket. Hutcherson works as an event producer, and also runs a cattery, called JungleTrax, out of his house. When I visited, he had half a dozen sleek Bengal kittens, coppery creatures with well-defined dark spots— "rosettes," in cat-fancier parlance. As we talked, he flung a cat toy in the air, and they leaped after it with astounding speed. Several times, they scratched us as they went by. Hutcherson decided to trim their nails, holding the scruff of their neck in his mouth while he clipped. "When I'm gardening or mowing the grass, they all come outside with me," he said. "And they really do look like little leopards. It's really rewarding and humbling when you forget the bead of time, and you are watching a cat chase a bug up a tree—two thousand years ago, somebody probably watched a cat that looked like a leopard chase a bug. It is beautiful and transcendent."

But two thousand years ago anyone who saw a cat that looked like a leopard would have immediately run for shelter, or for a spear. The big cats that enchant breeders, with their dazzling coats, stalking gait, and ferocious reflexes, were our predators. For the first time in history, humans are trying to reverse, at least aesthetically, the process of domestication. The result has been voguish hybrids like the Savannah cat, a cross between a domestic and a serval, an African native that preys on gazelles and springbok.

Exotic cats have become a particular kind of status symbol (in a recent Rick Ross video, a scantily clad woman alternately fondles hundred-dollar bills and a spotted cub), and people pay as much as thirty thousand dollars for the privilege of owning a hybrid that looks as if it could prowl the wilderness. Natalie Fraser, who runs a business in Oklahoma installing central-vacuum systems, bought her first

Bengal when she was just finishing college. "It was definitely the exotic look" that enticed her, she said. She has since bought a second one, and a Savannah: "They look like something you'd find in Africa." A half-wild cat is like a feline S.U.V.—an indicator that its owner is rugged and adventurous, if only in her habits of consumption.

Before Hutcherson started breeding Bengals, he had some truly wild cats, and "it didn't work out so well." In high school, he worked a summer job as a veterinary technician and saved up eight hundred dollars to buy a jungle cat, a native of Southeast and Central Asia. "It was friendly, but it pooped all over the house. My parents were, like, Cat's gotta go." His next cat was a caracal, an African lynx. "It was beautiful, but it was challenging," he said. "Once it's not a kitten, sixty pounds of cat that doesn't do what you want it to do ain't so cool. You can't really, like, brush it off the counter." In their native habitat, caracals hunt antelope. "A friend of mine bought it who lived in downtown D.C. in an apartment, and she had three Siamese cats. By the time it was a year old, it weighed about forty pounds, and it ate her three other cats. Just left, like, half the head. She was just doing what a wildcat's supposed to do."

Because of the risks associated with wildcats, part-wild hybrids are controversial. The Cat Fanciers' Association does not recognize Bengals or any other hybrid breed. In New York State, it's illegal to own a Savannah, unless it's at least five generations removed from a wildcat. "There are, even to this moment, states like Hawaii that do not allow Bengals," Hutcherson said. "There is a Bengal breeder in Ohio who had all her cats confiscated, because Animal Control there decided they were wild animals." So breeders tend to be secretive. "There's this kind of dividing line where we really have to emphasize domestic for policy and politics—versus the actual scientific truth," he said. "It's kind of like, What's being black? People will have these really philosophical and long-drawn-out conversations about what it is to be domestic, what it is to be wild. Can we call it a hybrid and be honest about what's really in the past? And I'm, like, one drop: that's all it takes. It's how society views that one drop that can make it O.K. or not O.K. to be honest about what you are."

Hybrid aficionados are aesthetes, but they are also excited by the suggestion of the primal. "Breeders, we tend to like the more extreme versions," Hutcherson said—the equivalent of a domestic dog bred with a wolf. But he is skeptical of Savannahs, whose first-generation crosses can be the size of a tricycle. "That is fairly troublesome to me," he said. "It doesn't matter how domesticated your cat is. When they play or reach out or jump on you—a ten-pound cat who does that is one thing. A thirty-pound cat that does that, or scratches your daughter when she tries to pick it up, is a totally other thing." It would be fine, he said, if people bred Savannahs to be small. "But there's so much money to be made making them big. People are literally on waiting lists, paying ten, twelve, fifteen thousand dollars—for a cat." He sighed. "I know many servals. They are a dif-

"Margo, I think it's time we talked about us."

ferent character than leopard cats," like the ones that his Bengals descend from. "Leopard cats are shy; servals are much more confident. They are intimidators. They play rough."

Martin Stucki, the proprietor of A1 Savannahs, in Ponca City, Oklahoma, is prone to bluster, like a cat who makes his hair stand on end to exaggerate his size. "People either love me or hate me," he said, and, if it's the latter, "it's jealousy. Me, I don't know jealousy. If you are running the No. 1 cattery in the world, you're doing something right." There's little agreement about which cattery is the world's best, but Stucki, a Swiss-born former musician, has an undeniably impressive operation. He keeps seven helpers at work, bleaching the indoor nursery, where he has dozens of kittens in paper-lined wire cages, and checking on the hundred and twenty servals and Savannahs that he keeps in two enormous converted horse barns. For years, every cat he bred had its DNA mapped and recorded at Texas A. & M. University. On the day I visited, his wife, Kathrin, was delivering a cat to a client in Shanghai.

A1 is surely the most upscale business in Ponca City; Stucki advertises in *Town & Country*, and a Savannah can cost nine thousand dollars for a breedable male, or stud, and as much as thirty-five thousand for a female. But he resists talking about money. "A lot of the people say, 'Oh! Nine thousand dollars for a cat?' That's not the point!" He added, "We have people who save for four years to buy one of our cats. Regular, hardworking, blue-collar people who say, 'This is what I want! I want something exquisite—I don't care if I don't buy any new clothes this month.'" There is something powerful, he said, about "the desire to have something wild in your house."

Stucki breeds Savannahs exclusively. "I had Asian leopard cats, I had caracals; I sold all of that, because I'm a firm believer that, if you do something, you specialize and you be the best," he said. He pointed to an accordion on the kitchen table. "If I play music, I only play the accordion— I apologize, but I'm good at it. I know people, they play accordion, piano, and violin, but when it comes to the accordion? I say, Hey—I know what I'm doing."

Stucki is very careful with his cats. A1 is the only cattery I visited that required a waiver to

"The kid's good."

protect the proprietor if I was injured by an animal. Not that Stucki worries much about such things. He has two young children, and, in videos on YouTube, they roll around the kitchen floor with a Savannah named Magic, who was once listed in *Guinness World Records* as the world's tallest pet cat. Therein lies one of the paradoxes of the hybrid-cat world: people who love these cats tend to boast in equal measure about their wildness and their tameness.

In Benicia, California, Nicholas Oberzire, the owner of the Styled in the Wild cattery, introduced me to his prize cat: Big Kahuna, a muscular orange creature the size of a cocker spaniel, who resides in a tempered-glass cage attached to Oberzire's house. Wire cages present a problem for studs. "They get their hands through, and they chew each other up fighting," Oberzire explained. "There's definitely still wild left in 'em. They can rip you to ribbons."

Oberzire, an aeronautical-and-fuel-science engineer by profession, works with a relatively new breed called a toyger—a Bengal-domestic cross designed to look like a tiny tiger. He pointed out an iridescent quality in Big Kahuna's coat, known to enthusiasts as "glitter," and told me that it was the result of his wild blood. (Hutcherson insists that all the glitter in such hybrids can be traced to a feral cat named Millwood Tory, whom Jean Mill found sleeping in a rhinoceros pen at the New Delhi zoo.) Oberzire said that he takes Big Kahuna out to restaurants and to wine tastings, where he entertains the other patrons by roaring like a jungle cat. "He goes to the dog parks, but I keep him on a leash," Oberzire said. "If a dog thinks he's going to attack him, it'll be the last thing that dog ever does."

Oberzire has an eight-year-old son, who sleeps in a bunk bed next to a wall of caged cats. I asked Oberzire if he ever worried about his child getting hurt, but he was confident that his cats were perfectly trained. "No means no; gentle means gentle!" he said. "The claws retract on command."

"You want to see something that'll blow your mind?" he asked, and brought another toyger into a bathroom. He turned on the tap, and the cat leaped up on the sink to sip from the spigot. As I waited in silence for the trick, Oberzire turned to me expectantly and said, "I bet you've never seen a cat do that!"

Actually, I've seen both of my cats do that: cats like to drink running water, even if they don't have a wild hair on their body. The expectation that cats can be made to change their nature, like wayward teens in a Scared Straight course, is a new development in feline-human relations. Humans bred dogs to be loyal and companionate; cats domesticated themselves. Biologists call them "commensal domesticates," meaning that they can live with humans, and yet, unlike most other domesticated species, they can revert at any time to feral status. What you glean from the general feline vibe is evolutionary truth: cats can take us or leave us.

Recent DNA studies suggest that cats entered the human sphere during the Neolithic period, at the dawn of agriculture, when *Felis silvestris lybica*, the Arabian and African subspecies of wildcat, developed a high tolerance for living among people. (In 2004, researchers in Cyprus found a cat skeleton carefully buried with a human in a ninety-five-hundred-year-old grave.) As grain storage became common and mice became a problem, cats wandered into settlements in the Fertile Crescent. And when the technology of agriculture was transferred to other cultures cats went with it: the genetic fingerprint of all domestic cats can be traced back to the delicate wildcats that decided to improve the human experience with their presence about twelve thousand years ago. It was an anomaly; in 1903, the naturalist H. C. Brooke described the European wildcat, which is genetically almost indistinguishable from *F. lybica,* as "probably the least amenable of all living creatures." But the adaptation was evolutionarily profitable; it provided a distinct survival advantage for those of the species who aligned themselves with humans. "Basically, some of them didn't eat the children," Stephen O'Brien, of the Theodosius Dobzhansky Center for Genome Bioinformatics, at St. Petersburg State University, said. "Eventually, they were invited into the living room."

The mutation that encourages domesticity has never been found, but scientists on the Feline Genome Project—including O'Brien and a consortium of geneticists at U.C. Davis and the University of Pennsylvania—are looking for a "tameness gene." The idea is borrowed from a Russian scientist named Dmitri Belyaev, who, in the late forties, became fascinated by the way dogs evolved to have coats different from wolves'. He had a theory that morphology was connected to temperament, and, as the director of the Institute of Cytology and Genetics at the Russian Academy of Sciences, he initiated a fifty-year study of silver foxes. The foxes were given limited contact with their caretakers, and were scored on their friendliness. (One crucial measure was how often they bit the researchers.) Only the least fearful and least aggressive were bred. After thirty-five generations, Belyaev found, the tame foxes had a much higher than normal percentage of floppy ears and short or curly tails, and had lost the musky fox smell of their wild brethren.

The tameness gene, it seems, brought with it a more doglike aspect. As the animals came to act less wild, they came to look that way, too.

But what hybrid-cat breeders are after is the most exotic look with the tamest possible temperament. In the end, the animals they produce are as far from wild as can be. At Styled in the Wild, Oberzire showed me a cat named Tiki Wild, who was lying in the sink next to several syringes and a bottle of oxytocin—the hormone that stimulates contractions during labor—suckling two day-old kittens. Oberzire lifted one of the thumb-size creatures away from her, and she didn't protest. "This is the time when you see what you have," he said. "You see the stripes? You see the white belly?" He gave the resigned Tiki Wild back her kitten.

Most breeders seem to love their cats, but there's another impulse at work, too. It's a tinkerer's sensibility—the thing that H. G. Wells had in mind when his villain Dr. Moreau talked about his obsession with "the plasticity of living forms." Pointing to Tiki Wild, Oberzire said, "We've gone through four miscarriages on this cat. The first was just blood. The second, two dead kittens were inside her. We took her to the emergency room, they charged me three thousand dollars for giving her two shots of oxytocin, and they told me she needed a C-section." When he balked at the price, the vet suggested putting her down. "Well, that's my favorite little girl! I said, 'I'll come and pick her up. Don't worry about it: I have more drugs than you guys, I have more equipment than you guys have, and obviously more knowledge than you guys have.' So I brought her home and I flushed her. I used a Massengill—your douche." I was confused. "Human," he explained. "I put a full tube of lube inside of her, and I let her sit for a day so she could get some more energy, because she was just about dead. The next day, I gave her about four times the amount of oxytocin."

"I am an artist!" Judy Sugden declared one evening in her kitchen, in Covina, California, as she prepared supper for a couple of hundred cats. "And I have designed and built a cat." Sugden, an architect by training, is the "grande dame of the toygers." Since the mid-eighties, she has spent most of her time trying to concoct a cat with the temperament of a lap-dog and the appearance of a tiger; it will be "small, but it looks like it could take down a gazelle."

Sugden, a graceful sixty-six-year-old with gray hair twisted into a bun on the side of her head, was wearing a leopard-spotted blouse, with sleeves rolled up to reveal forearms crosshatched with scratch marks. She was in something of a frenzy. "I'm just running in all directions," she

said. She ground cooked chicken in a food processor, and mixed it in a giant bowl with spirulina, algae, diatomaceous earth, canned cat food, and multivitamin pills that she crushed with a pair of pliers, then put the grayish mass in the microwave. "They like it mouse temperature," she explained.

She was flying to Cambodia the next morning, to go bird-watching with her husband (the "perennial president of our Audubon Society"), and before she left she wanted to get as many cats as possible out of her yard. Just before Christmas, Animal Control had come to warn her that Los Angeles County law permits only five cats per property, and that she was rather radically in violation. While she was away, she feared, the authorities could raid her property and make off with her life's work. "Animal Control could walk in at any moment and take anything they want," she said. "So I'm sending things out that I just don't want to lose." A dozen breeders around the world were coordinating with her. Some cats would be crated and put on planes to Europe; others would be picked up by breeders driving down from the San Francisco Bay Area.

Sugden carried the mouse-temperature mixture through a grove of palm and eucalyptus trees and began distributing it to her pride, cages of mewing felines lounging in synthetic trees or scampering around. She spoke to them in a high-pitched voice as she went. "Aren't you just the silliest boy who ever there was?" she asked a shiny green-eyed cat. The thought of having him catnapped was alarming. "That would be devastating!" she said. "God. If he got altered and sent out as a pet?" I asked her who he was. "This one is—really soft, thick coat. That's what we like to have." I asked if he had a name. "Uh, no." She laughed. "But he has a chip in him," a way to track him down if he got loose.

Breeders like Sugden engage in unnatural selection, encouraging attributes with no evolutionary advantage. "A domestic has big eyes, wide apart, and a little tiny nose," Sugden said. (No good.) A big cat, like a tiger or a leopard, "has small eyes, close together, and a V-shaped nose." (Ideal, but how to get it? You can't mate a tiger with a tabby.) Sugden's dream cat "has a bunch of genes that are not in any small cat in the world, so I have to build those traits—spot by spot, hair by hair, squinch by squinch of the nose!" She has travelled all over the world looking for cats with traits that could contribute to the breed standard she invented. Anthony Hutcherson, who is a friend of hers, described one of her typical quests: "She was this lone white woman in India and Kashmir looking for cats, paying kids who were coming back with all kinds of creatures."

In the yard, two cats were mating, emitting a shrill, sour sound. "The female screams because the male has spikes on his penis," Sugden said, scooping slop into their cage. The penis of an unneutered cat has barbs all over it, like the treads you drive over when you return a rental car. These spikes abrade the female cat's vagina, triggering ovulation. (As Carl Van Vechten put it in *The Tiger in the House*, feline "love habits, inspired by the hardiest desires, are often supremely cruel.") The spiked cat penis is why it's nearly impossible to artificially inseminate cats; it is why certain tiger populations are persistently endangered, despite human attempts at intervention; and it is why a cat breeder simply can't get by with five cats.

Sugden places the blame for the five-cat rule on the Humane Society and on People for the Ethical Treatment of Animals, which she thinks have undue influence on local government. "They're all together—especially here in Los Angeles, where all the movie stars are PETA," she

June 24, 1974

The

NEW YORKER

Price 50 cents

said. "They believe that all animal ownership is slavery!"

In fact, PETA does not take a purely abolitionist position toward pet ownership. But there is a page on its Web site titled "There's No Such Thing as a 'Responsible Breeder.'" The argument is that "producing animals for sale is a greedy and callous business in a world in which there is a critical and chronic shortage of good homes for dogs, cats, and other animals, and the only 'responsible breeders' are those who . . . get out of the business altogether."

PETA's concern isn't just that the desire for fancy cats distracts attention from homeless cats. "Inbreeding causes painful and life-threatening genetic defects in 'purebred' dogs and cats," the Web site says. Traits that are charming to humans can be unpleasant for the animals endowed with them. More than 80 percent of bulldog litters have to be delivered by cesarean section, because the puppies, bred to have extra-large heads, get stuck in their mothers' birth canals. Cavalier King Charles spaniels are prone to a condition called syringomyelia, the result of their skulls' being too small for their brains.

The essential problem is that genetic changes don't happen in isolation; every perfectly placed spot or stripe carries with it the possibility of another mutation. Inside Sugden's house, she showed me a group of cats she called "faans." They were cross-eyed, cow-hocked, and splayfooted, and, though you couldn't tell from looking, many of them had hydrocephalus, a condition in which "there's nothing in the middle of the brain except liquid." But faans also have a trait that Sugden considers crucial for a perfected toyger: small, rounded ears, very different from a typical domestic cat's pointy triangles.

Sugden has no human children. "I have lousy genetics, so I got myself spayed," she told me. In fact, she is of excellent stock. She is Jean Mill's daughter, and she came up with the idea for the toyger when she noticed some of her mother's flawed Bengals—stripes, rather than spots. Sugden registered the toyger in 1993 with the International Cat Association, a worldwide group with five thousand members, which is the arbiter of the highly artificial standards for perfection in pedigreed cats. Building an

"I mean, God, Philip, what if he doesn't really <u>like</u> Tabby Treat but is only eating it so we'll feel less guilty?"

acceptable cat isn't easy; TICA's breed standards are as exacting as the manual for an intercontinental bomber. At cat shows, all Abyssinians, for instance, must have gently shaped muzzles, with "no evidence of snippiness, foxy appearance, or whisker pinch." Polydactyls—extra toes—are broadly forbidden. A recent breed called a Pixiebob is allowed to have them, but TICA maintains a strict limit of seven toes per paw. Like beauty-pageant contestants, show cats are expected to be pleasantly behaved and of high moral character; they are automatically disqualified for "showing evidence of intent to deceive."

By the time Sugden proposed the toyger as an official breed, the Bengal had become the most popular purebred in the world. "TICA would have laughed at me and turned me away, except that my mother had just done a project that made them a hell of a lot of money," she said. "They've all told me, 'We never thought you could do it.'" But toygers now regularly win championship titles—beating Siamese or Abyssinians or other more established breeds—and Sugden's best cats sell for five thousand dollars. She has deputized several dozen breeders to strive for the ultimate toyger. But they don't always pursue her vision, either because they succeed at developing a single trait, and then, to her dismay, become satisfied with the result, or because they are out-and-out renegades. Sugden recently had a falling out with a fellow-breeder over the ideal dimensions of a toyger's nose and legs. "She says bad things about me," Sugden said. "And she knows nothing! Her cats are ugly."

As Sugden finished her dinner rounds, Jean Mill, a white-haired woman in blue sweatpants, came by to bid her farewell before her travels. "She's having troubles that I never had," Mill said. "I had a wildcat to use, so I had the genetics right there; she can't breed from a tiger so it's much harder. And the government's cracking down on everything!"

But the greatest problem for breeders is their own obsession. Sugden admitted that what started as a quest had become "my addiction," and she told me that she has gone "dead broke" pursuing it. Her breeding enterprise costs her more than a hundred thousand dollars a year, and she has expended all the savings she amassed as an architect. When I visited Anthony Hutcherson, he told me that he, too, had given up a lot to have something wild in his life. "I was in a relationship that ended," he said. "If all your free time is taken up with litter boxes, cat shows, and cat people, it can be challenging. My partner wasn't into cats at all." And, no matter how much he devotes himself to animals, he knows that he'll never be completely satisfied. "What I really, really want is a cat that looks like an ocelot," he said. "But if I were able to get one cat who had 'it' my next question would be, How can I get two?"

In Sugden's kitchen, several of her "best cats" were frolicking on the floor. They were stunning: the light played on their glittery, fire-orange coats. One had flashing golden eyes; another's were glowing green. A sassy toyger jumped up on a table and stretched out a paw to slap at Sugden's face. "Gentle, gentle—you be very good boy," she said, in her high-pitched cat voice. "You don't get to play if you're going to be rough." The cat looked her in the eyes and kept on batting.

|2013|

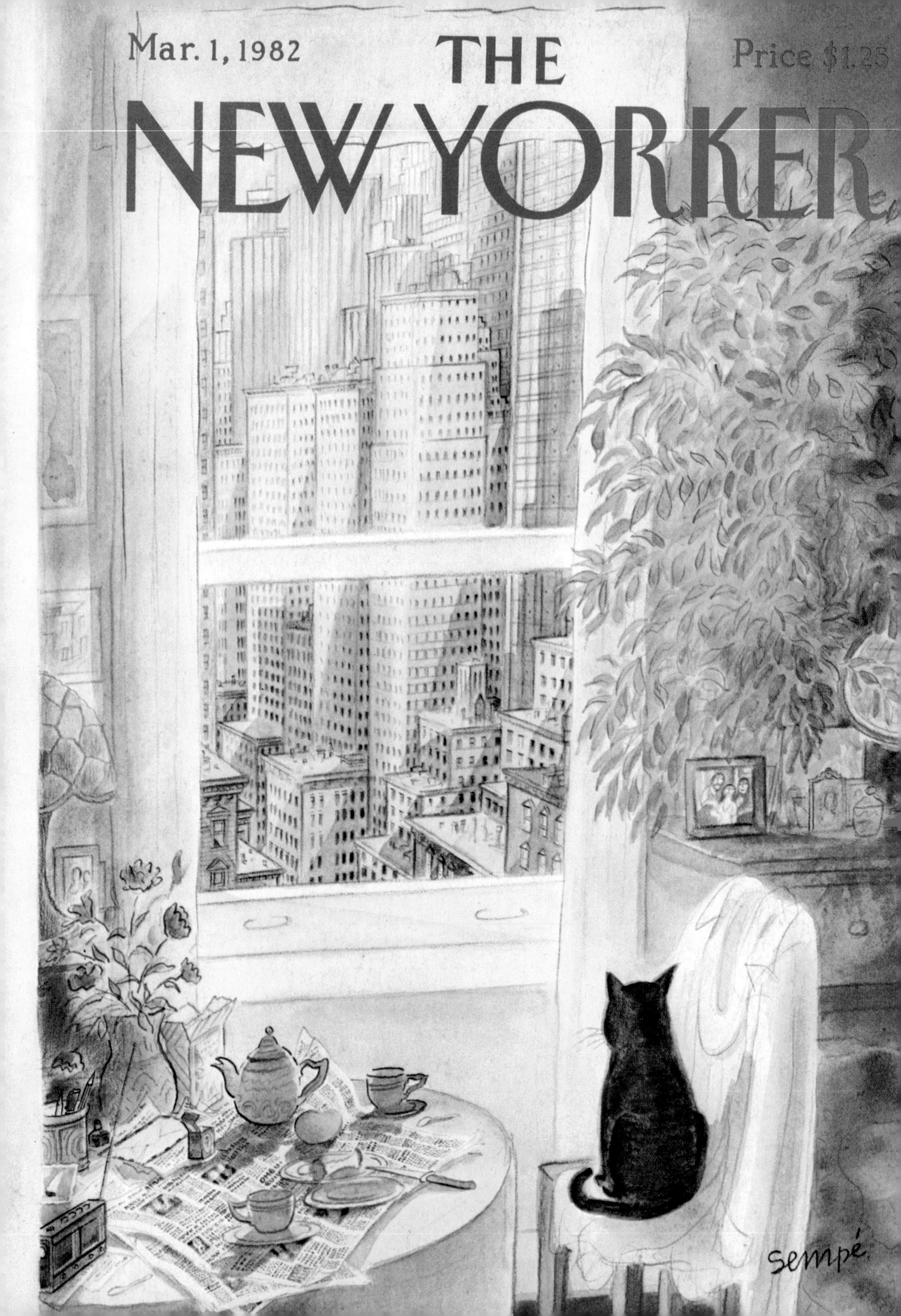
Mar. 1, 1982
THE NEW YORKER
Price $1.25
Sempé

CURIOUS CATS

This cat   At Chopin's apartment: George Sand,
met ———————   Delacroix, Heine, Meyerbeer,
                   Mickawicz

This cat loved music (?)

He met or knew —

     Beethoven in youth.

Schubert	Mendelssohn	} friends
Berlioz	Schumann	
Paganini	Meyerbeer	
Rossini	Chopin	—— friends
Bellini	George Sand — ~~Dudevant~~ ?
Delacroix	Heine
Ingres	Wagner
	Young Brahms.

Eloped to Switzerland with Mme. d'Agoult
                   2 illegit daughters.
                     1 "Son

The famous Ingres portrait — youngest

Loved Dante & Goethe's Faust.

Balzac's Béatrix derived d'Agoult & Liszt.

EDWARD THE CONQUEROR

Fiction

ROALD DAHL

Louisa, holding a dishcloth in her hand, stepped out the kitchen door at the back of the house into the cool October sunshine.

"Edward!" she called. "*Ed-ward!* Lunch is ready!"

She paused a moment, listening; then she strolled out onto the lawn and continued across it—a little shadow attending her—skirting the rose bed and touching the sundial lightly with one finger as she went by. She moved rather gracefully for a woman who was small and plump, with a lilt in her walk and a gentle swinging of the shoulders and the arms. She passed under the mulberry tree onto the brick path, then went all the way along the path until she came to the place where she could look down into the dip at the end of this large garden.

"*Edward!* Lunch!"

She could see him now, about eighty yards away, down in the dip on the edge of the wood—the tallish, narrow figure in khaki slacks and dark-green sweater, working beside a big bonfire with a fork in his hands, pitching brambles onto the top of the fire. It was blazing fiercely, with orange flames and clouds of milky smoke, and the smoke was drifting back over the garden with a wonderful scent of autumn and burning leaves.

Louisa went down the slope toward her husband. Had she wanted, she could easily have called again and made herself heard, but there was something about a first-class bonfire that impelled her toward it, right up close so she could feel the heat and listen to it burn.

"Lunch," she said, approaching.

"Oh, hello. All right—yes. I'm coming."

"*What* a good fire."

"I've decided to clear this place right out," her husband said. "I'm sick and tired of all these brambles." His long face was wet with perspiration. There were small beads of it clinging all over his mustache like dew, and two little rivers were running down his throat onto the turtle-neck of the sweater.

"You better be careful you don't overdo it, Edward."

"Louisa, I do wish you'd stop treating me as though I were eighty. A bit of exercise never did anyone any harm."

"Yes, dear, I know. Oh Edward! Look! Look!"

The man turned and looked at Louisa, who was pointing now to the far side of the bonfire.

"Look, Edward! The cat!"

Sitting on the ground, so close to the fire that the flames sometimes seemed actually to be touching it, was a large cat of a most unusual color. It stayed quite still, with its head on one side and its nose in the air, watching the man and woman with a cool yellow eye.

"It'll get burnt!" Louisa cried, and she dropped the dishcloth and darted swiftly in and grabbed it with both hands, whisking it away and putting it on the grass well clear of the flames.

"You crazy cat," she said, dusting off her hands. "What's the matter with you?"

"Cats know what they're doing," the husband said. "You'll never find a cat doing something it doesn't want. Not cats."

"Whose is it? You ever seen it before?"

"No, I never have. Damn peculiar color."

The cat had seated itself on the grass and was regarding them with a superior, sidewise look. There was a veiled, inward expression about the eyes, something curiously omniscient and pensive, and around the nose a most delicate air of contempt, as though the sight of these two middle-aged persons—the one small, plump, and rosy, the other lean and extremely sweaty—were a matter of some surprise but very little importance. For a cat, it certainly had an unusual color—a pure silvery gray with no blue in it at all—and the hair was very long and silky.

Louisa bent down and stroked its head. "You must go home," she said. "Be a good cat now and go on home to where you belong."

The man and wife started to stroll back up the hill toward the house. The cat got up and followed, at a distance first, but edging closer and closer as they went along. Soon it was alongside them, then it was ahead, leading the way across the lawn to the house, and walking as though it

"Culturally, I'm a cat."

owned the whole place, holding its tail straight up in the air, like a mast.

"Go home," the man said. "Go on home. We don't want you."

But when they reached the house, it came in with them, and Louisa gave it some milk in the kitchen. During lunch, it hopped up onto the spare chair between them and sat through the meal with its head just above the level of the table, watching the proceedings with those dark-yellow eyes, which kept moving slowly from the woman to the man and back again.

"I don't like this cat," Edward said.

"Oh, I think it's a beautiful cat. I do hope it stays a little while."

"Now, listen to me, Louisa. The creature can't possibly stay here. It belongs to someone else. It's lost. And if it's still trying to hang around this afternoon, you'd better take it to the police. They'll see it gets home."

After lunch, Edward returned to his gardening. Louisa, as usual, went to the piano. She was a competent pianist and a genuine music lover, and almost every afternoon she spent an hour or so playing for herself. The cat was now lying on the sofa, and she paused to stroke it as she went by. It opened its eyes, looked at her a moment, then closed them again and went back to sleep.

"You're an awfully nice cat," she said. "And such a beautiful color. I wish I could keep you." Then her fingers, moving over the fur on the cat's head, came into contact with a small lump, a little growth just above the right eye.

"Poor cat," she said. "You've got bumps on your beautiful face. You must be getting old."

She went over and sat down on the long piano bench, but she didn't immediately start to play. One of her special little pleasures was to make every day a kind of concert day, with a carefully arranged program, which she worked out in detail before she began. She never liked to break her enjoyment by having to stop while she wondered what to play next. All she wanted was a brief pause after each piece while the audience, as it were, clapped enthusiastically and called for more. It was so much nicer to imagine an audience, and now and again while she was playing—on the lucky days, that is—the room would begin to swim and fade and darken, and she would see nothing but row upon row of seats and a sea of white faces upturned toward her, listening with a rapt and adoring concentration.

Sometimes she played from memory, sometimes from music. Today she would play from memory; that was the way she felt. And what should the program be? She sat before the piano with her small hands clasped on her lap, a plump, rosy little person with a round and still quite pretty face, her hair done up in a neat bun at the back of her head. By looking slightly to the right, she could see the cat curled up asleep on the sofa, and its silvery-gray coat was beautiful against the purple of the cushion. How about some Bach to begin with? Or, better still, Vivaldi. The Bach adaptation for organ of the D-Minor Concerto Grosso. Yes—that first. Then perhaps a little Schumann. "Carnaval"? That would be fun. And after that—well, a touch of Liszt for a change. One of the "Petrarch Sonnets." The second one—that was the loveliest—the E Major. Then another Schumann, another of his gay ones—"Kinderscenen." And lastly, for the encore, a Brahms waltz, or maybe two of them, if she felt like it.

Vivaldi, Schumann, Liszt, Schumann, Brahms. A very nice program, one that she could play easily without the music. She moved herself a little closer to the piano and paused a moment while someone in the audience—already she could feel that this was one of the lucky days—while someone in the audience had his last cough; then, with the slow grace that accompanied nearly all her movements, she lifted her hands to the keyboard and began to play.

She wasn't, at that particular moment, watching the cat at all—as a matter of fact she had forgotten its presence—but as the first deep notes of the Vivaldi sounded softly in the room, she became aware, out of the corner of one eye, of a sudden flurry, a flash of movement on the sofa to her right. She stopped playing at once. "What is it?" she said, turning to the cat. "What's the matter?"

The animal, who a few seconds before had been sleeping peacefully, was now sitting bolt upright on the sofa, very tense, the whole body aquiver, ears up and eyes wide open, staring at the piano.

"Did I frighten you?" she asked gently. "Perhaps you've never heard music before."

No, she told herself. I don't think that's what it is. On second thought, it seemed to her that the cat's attitude was not one of fear. There was no shrinking or backing away. If anything, there was a leaning forward, a kind of eagerness about the creature, and the face— well, there was rather an odd expression on the face, something of a mixture between surprise and shock. Of course, the face of a cat is a small and fairly expressionless thing, but if you watch carefully the eyes and ears working together, and particularly that little area of mobile skin below the ears and slightly to one side, you can occasionally see the reflection of very powerful emotions. Louisa was watching the face closely now, and because she was curious to see what would happen a second time, she reached out her hands to the keyboard and began again to play the Vivaldi.

This time the cat was ready for it, and all that happened to begin with was a small extra tensing

THE PAW OF A CAT

The first trickle
of water down
a dry ditch stretches
like the paw
of a cat, slightly
tucked at the front,
unambitious
about auguring
wet. It may sink
later but it hasn't
yet.

—Kay Ryan | 2009 |

of the body. But as the music swelled and quickened into that first exciting rhythm of the introduction to the fugue, a strange look that amounted almost to ecstasy began to settle upon the creature's face. The ears, which up to then had been pricked up straight, were gradually drawn back, the eyelids drooped, the head went over to one side, and at that moment Louisa could have sworn that the animal was actually *appreciating* the work.

What she saw (or thought she saw) was something she had noticed many times on the faces of people listening very closely to a piece of music. When the sound takes complete hold of them and drowns them in itself, a peculiar, intensely ecstatic look comes over them that you can recognize as easily as a smile. So far as Louisa could see, the cat was now wearing almost exactly this kind of look.

Louisa finished the fugue, then played the siciliana, and all the way through she kept watching the cat on the sofa. The final proof for her that the animal was listening came at the end, when the music stopped. It blinked, stirred itself a little, stretched a leg, settled into a more comfortable position, took a quick glance round the room, then looked expectantly in her direction. It was precisely the way a concertgoer reacts when the music momentarily releases him in the pause between two movements of a symphony. The behavior was so thoroughly human it gave her a queer, agitated feeling in the chest.

"You like that?" she asked. "You like Vivaldi?"

The moment she'd spoken, she felt ridiculous, but not—and this to her was a trifle sinister—not quite so ridiculous as she knew she should have felt.

Well, there was nothing for it now except to go straight ahead with the next number on the program, which was "Carnaval." As soon as she began to play, the cat again stiffened and sat up straighter; then, as it became slowly and blissfully saturated with the sound, it relapsed into that queer, melting mood of ecstasy that seemed to have something to do with drowning and with dreaming. It was really an extravagant sight— quite a comical one, too—to see this silvery cat sitting up on the sofa and being carried away like this. And what made it more screwy than ever, Louisa thought, was the fact that this music, which the animal seemed to be enjoying so much, was manifestly too *difficult*, too *classical*, to be appreciated by the majority of humans in the world.

Maybe, she thought, the creature's not really enjoying it at all. Maybe it's a sort of hypnotic reaction, like with snakes. After all, if you can charm a snake with music, then why not a cat? Except that millions of cats hear the stuff every day of their lives, on radio and gramophone and piano and, as far as she knew, there'd never yet been a case of one behaving like this. This one was acting as though it were following every single note. It was certainly a fantastic thing.

But was it not also a wonderful thing? Indeed it was. In fact, unless she was much mistaken, it was a kind of miracle, one of those animal miracles that happen about once every hundred years.

"I could see you *loved* that one," she said when the piece was over. "Although I'm sorry I didn't play it any too well today. Which did you like best—the Vivaldi or the Schumann?"

The cat made no reply, so Louisa, fearing she might lose the attention of her listener, went straight into the next part of the program— Liszt's second "Petrarch Sonnet."

And now an extraordinary thing happened. She hadn't played more than three or four bars when the animal's whiskers began perceptibly to twitch. Slowly it drew itself up to an extra height, laid its head on one side, then on the other, and stared into space with a kind of frowning, concentrated look that seemed to say, "What's this? Don't tell me. I know it so well, but just for the moment I don't seem to be able to place it." Louisa was fascinated, and, with her little mouth half open and half smiling, she continued to play, waiting to see what on earth was going to happen next.

NON-CAPTIVE AUDIENCE

A lady who favors classical music—and whose veracity we can vouch for—has written to tell us that her cat has long snoozed on her radio, from time to time, listening to Bach and Beethoven with apparent contentment. Last Sunday, however, he discovered that turning a dial changes the station. Restless during a string-quartet selection, he paced about for a while on the radio, then jumped down to the tabletop on which the radio sits and started turning the knob. He tried a number of programs, giving each one a minute or two, and, finally settling on a disc-jockey show, jumped back onto the radio and stretched out, purring.

| 1950 |

The cat stood up, walked to one end of the sofa, sat down again, listened some more; then all at once it bounded to the floor and leaped up onto the piano bench beside her. There it sat, listening intently to the lovely sonnet, not dreamily this time, but very erect, the large yellow eyes fixed upon Louisa's fingers.

"Well!" she said as she struck the last chord. "So you came up to sit beside me, did you? You like this better than the sofa? All right, I'll let you stay, but you must keep still and not jump about." She put out a hand and stroked the cat softly along the back, from head to tail. "That was Liszt," she went on. "Mind you, he can sometimes be quite horribly vulgar, but in things like this he's really charming."

She was beginning to enjoy this odd animal pantomime, so she went straight on into the next item on the program, Schumann's "Kinderscenen."

She hadn't been playing for more than a minute or two when she realized that the cat had again moved, and was now back in its old place on the sofa. She'd been watching her hands at the time, and presumably that was why she hadn't even noticed its going; all the same, it must've been an extremely swift and silent move. The cat was still staring at her, still apparently attending closely to the music, and yet it seemed to Louisa that there was not now the same rapturous enthusiasm there'd been during the previous piece, the Liszt. In addition, the act of leaving the stool and returning to the sofa appeared in itself to be a mild but positive gesture of disappointment.

"What's the matter?" she asked when it was over. "What's wrong with Schumann? What's so marvellous about Liszt?" The cat looked straight back at her with those yellow eyes that had small jet-black bars lying vertically in their centers.

This, she told herself, is really beginning to get interesting—a trifle spooky, too, when she came to think of it. But one look at the cat sitting there on the sofa, so bright and attentive, so obviously waiting for more music, quickly reassured her.

"All right," she said. "I'll tell you what I'm going to do. I'm going to alter my program specially for you. You seem to like Liszt so much I'll give you another."

She hesitated, searching her memory for a good Liszt; then softly she began to play one of the twelve little pieces from "Der Weihnachtsbaum." She was now watching the cat very closely, and the first thing she noticed was that the whiskers again began to twitch. It jumped down to the carpet, stood still a moment, inclining its head, quivering with excitement, and then, with a slow, silky stride, it walked around the piano, hopped up on the bench and sat down beside her.

They were in the middle of all this when Edward came in from the garden.

"Edward!" Louisa cried, jumping up. "Oh, Edward, darling! Listen to this! Listen what's happened!"

"What is it now?" he said. "I'd like some tea." He had one of those narrow, sharp-nosed, faintly magenta faces, and the sweat was making it shine as though it were a long wet grape.

"It's the cat!" Louisa cried, pointing to it sitting quietly on the piano bench. "Just *wait* till you hear what's happened!"

"I thought I told you to take it to the police."

"But, Edward, *listen* to me. This is *terribly* exciting. This is a *musical* cat."

"Oh, yes?"

"This cat can appreciate music, and it can understand it, too."

"Now, stop this nonsense, Louisa, and let's for God's sake have some tea. I'm hot and tired from cutting brambles and building bonfires." He sat down in an armchair, took a cigarette from a box beside him, and lit it with an immense patent lighter that stood near the box.

"What you don't understand," Louisa said, "is that something extremely exciting has been happening here in our own house while you were out, something that may even be . . . well . . . almost momentous."

"I'm quite sure of that."

"Edward, *please*!"

Louisa was standing by the piano, her little pink face pinker than ever, a scarlet rose high up on each cheek. "If you want to know," she said, "I'll tell you what I think."

"I'm listening, dear."

"I think it might be possible that we are at this moment sitting in the presence of—" She stopped, as though suddenly sensing the absurdity of the thought.

"Yes?"

"You may think it silly, Edward, but it's honestly what I think."

"In the presence of who, for heaven's sake?"

"Of Franz Liszt himself!"

Her husband took a long, slow pull at his cigarette and blew the smoke up at the ceiling. He had the tight-skinned, concave cheeks of a man who has worn a full set of dentures for many years, and every time he sucked at a cigarette, the cheeks went in even more and the bones of his face stood out like a skeleton's. "I don't get you," he said.

"Edward, listen to me. From what I've seen this afternoon with my own eyes, it really looks as though this might actually be some sort of a reincarnation."

"I have a couple of other projects I'm excited about."

"You mean this lousy cat?"

"Don't talk like that, dear, please."

"You're not ill, are you, Louisa?"

"I'm perfectly all right, thank you very much. I'm a bit confused—I don't mind admitting it—but who wouldn't be after what's just happened? Edward, I swear to you—"

"What *did* happen, if I may ask?"

Louisa told him, and all the while she was speaking, her husband lay sprawled in the chair with his legs stretched out in front of him, sucking at his cigarette and blowing the smoke up at the ceiling. There was a thin, cynical smile on his mouth.

"I don't see anything very unusual about that," he said when it was over. "All it is—it's a trick cat. It's been taught tricks, that's all."

"Don't be so silly, Edward. Every time I play Liszt, he gets all excited and comes running over to sit on the stool beside me. But only for Liszt, and nobody can teach a cat the difference between Liszt and Schumann. You don't even know it yourself. But this one can do it every single time. Quite obscure Liszt, too."

"Velcro!"

"Twice," the husband said. "He's only done it twice."

"Twice is enough."

"Let's see him do it again. Come on."

"No," Louisa said. "Definitely not. Because if this *is* Liszt, as I believe it is, or anyway the soul of Liszt or whatever it is that comes back, then it's certainly not right or even very kind to put him through a lot of silly, undignified tests."

"My dear woman! This is a *cat*—a rather stupid gray cat that nearly got its coat singed by the bonfire this morning in the garden. And anyway, what do you know about reincarnation?"

"If his soul is there, that's enough for me," Louisa said firmly. "That's all that counts."

"Come on, then. Let's see him perform. Let's see him tell the difference between his own stuff and someone else's."

"No, Edward. I've told you before, I refuse to put him through any more silly circus tests. He's had quite enough of that for one day. But

I'll tell you what I *will* do. I'll play him a little more of his own music."

"A fat lot that'll prove."

"You watch. And one thing is certain—as soon as he recognizes it, he'll refuse to budge off that bench where he's sitting now."

Louisa went to the music shelf, took down a book of Liszt, thumbed through it quickly, and chose another of his finer compositions—the B-Minor Sonata. She had meant to play only the first part of the work, but once she got started and saw how the cat was sitting there literally quivering with pleasure and watching her hands with that rapturous, concentrated look, she didn't have the heart to stop. She played it right the way through. When it was finished, she glanced up at her husband and smiled. "There you are," she said. "You can't tell me he wasn't absolutely *loving* it."

"He just likes the noise, that's all."

"He was *loving* it. Weren't you, darling?" she said, lifting the cat in her arms. "Oh, my goodness, if only he could talk. Just think of it, dear—he met Beethoven in his youth! He knew Schubert and Mendelssohn and Schumann and Berlioz and Grieg and Delacroix and Ingres and Heine and Balzac. And let me see . . . My heavens, he was Wagner's father-in-law! I'm holding Wagner's father-in-law in my arms!"

"Louisa!" her husband said sharply, sitting up straight. "Pull yourself together." There was a new edge to his voice now, and he spoke louder.

Louisa glanced up quickly. "Edward, I do believe you're jealous!"

"Oh, sure, sure I'm jealous—of a lousy gray cat!"

"Then don't be so grumpy and cynical about it all. If you're going to behave like this, the best thing you can do is to go back to your gardening and leave the two of us together in peace. That will be best for all of us, won't it, darling?" she said, addressing the cat, stroking its head. "And later on this evening we shall have some more music together, you and I, some more of your own work. Oh, yes," she said, kissing the creature several times on the neck, "and we might have a little Chopin, too. You needn't tell me—I happen to know you adore Chopin. You used to be great friends with him, didn't you, darling? As a matter of fact—if I remember rightly—it was in Chopin's apartment that you met the great love of your life, Mme. Something-or-Other. Had three illegitimate children by her, too, didn't you? Yes, you did, you naughty thing, and don't go trying to deny it. I read all about you not so long ago in a book by Mr. Sitwell. So you shall have some Chopin," she said, kissing the cat again, "and that'll probably bring back all sorts of lovely memories to you, won't it?"

"Louisa, stop this at once!"

"Oh, don't be so stuffy, Edward."

"You're behaving like a perfect idiot, woman. And anyway, you forget we're going out this evening, to Bill and Betty's for canasta."

"Oh, but I couldn't *possibly* go out now. There's no question of that."

Edward got up slowly from his chair, then bent down and stubbed his cigarette hard into the ashtray. "Tell me something," he said quietly. "You don't really believe this—this twaddle you're talking, do you?"

"But of *course* I do. I don't think there's any question about it now. And, what's more, I consider that it puts a tremendous responsibility upon us, Edward—upon both of us. You as well."

"You know what I think," he said. "I think you ought to see a doctor. And damn quick, too."

With that, he turned and stalked out of the room, through the French windows, back into the garden.

Louisa watched him striding across the lawn toward his bonfire and his brambles, and she waited until he was out of sight before she turned and ran to the front door, still carrying the cat.

Soon she was in the car, driving to town.

She parked in front of the library, locked the cat in the car, hurried up the steps into the building, and headed straight for the reference room. There she began searching the cards for books on two subjects—"Reincarnation" and "Liszt."

Under "Reincarnation" she found something called *Recurring Earth-Lives—How and Why,* by a man called F. Milton Willis, published in 1921. Under "Liszt" she found two biographical volumes. She took out all three books, returned to the car, and drove home.

Back in the house, she placed the cat on the sofa, sat herself down beside it with her three books, and prepared to do some serious reading. She would begin, she decided, with Mr. F. Milton Willis's work. The volume was thin and a trifle soiled, but it had a good heavy feel to it and the author's name had a nice authoritative ring.

The doctrine of reincarnation, she read, states that spiritual souls pass from higher to higher forms of animals. "A man can, for instance, no more be reborn as an animal than an adult can re-become a child."

She read this again. But how did he know? How could he be so sure? He couldn't. No one could possibly be certain about a thing like that. At the same time, the statement took a good deal of the wind out of her sails.

"Around the center of consciousness of each

of us, there are, besides the dense outer body, four other bodies, invisible to the eye of flesh, but perfectly visible to people whose faculties of perception of superphysical things have undergone the requisite development. . . ."

She didn't understand that one at all, but she read on, and soon she came to an interesting passage that told how long a soul usually stayed away from the earth before returning in someone else's body. The time varied according to type, and Mr. Willis gave the following breakdown:

Drunkards and the unemployable	40/50	years
Unskilled laborers	60/100	"
Skilled workers	100/200	"
The bourgeoisie	200/300	"
The upper-middle classes	500	"
The highest class		
of gentleman farmers	600/1000	"
Those in the Path of Initiation	1500/2000	"

Quickly she referred to one of the other books, to find out how long Liszt had been dead. It said he died in Bayreuth in 1886. That was sixty-seven years ago. Therefore, according to Mr. Willis, he'd have to have been an unskilled laborer to come back so soon. That didn't seem to fit at all. On the other hand, she didn't think much of the author's methods of grading. According to him, "the highest class of gentleman farmers" was just about the most superior being on the earth. Red jackets and stirrup cups and the bloody, sadistic murder of the fox. No, she thought, that isn't right. It was a pleasure to find herself beginning to doubt Mr. Willis.

Later in the book, she came upon a list of some of the more famous reincarnations. Epictetus, she was told, returned to earth as Ralph Waldo Emerson. Cicero came back as Gladstone, Alfred the Great as Queen Victoria, William the Conqueror as Lord Kitchener. Ashoka Vardhana,

King of India in 272 B.C., came back as Colonel Henry Steel Olcott, an esteemed American lawyer. Pythagoras returned as Master Koot Hoomi, the gentleman who founded the Theosophical Society with Mme. Blavatsky and Colonel H. S. Olcott (the esteemed American lawyer, alias Ashoka Vardhana, King of India). It didn't say who Mme. Blavatsky had been. But "Theodore Roosevelt," it said, "has for numbers of incarnations played great parts as a leader of men. . . . From him descended the royal line of ancient Chaldea, he having been, about 30,000 B.C., appointed Governor of Chaldea by the Ego we know as Caesar who was then ruler of Persia. . . . Roosevelt and Caesar have been together time after time as military and administrative leaders; at one time, many thousands of years ago, they were husband and wife. . . ."

That was enough for Louisa. Mr. F. Milton Willis was clearly nothing but a guesser. She was not impressed by his dogmatic assertions. The fellow was probably on the right track, but his pronouncements were extravagant, especially the first one of all, about animals. Soon she hoped to be able to confound the whole Theosophical Society with her proof that man could indeed reappear as a lower animal. Also that he did not have to be an unskilled laborer to come back within a hundred years.

She now turned to one of the Liszt biographies, and she was glancing through it casually when her husband came in again from the garden.

"What are you doing now?" he asked.

"Oh—just checking up a little here and there. Listen, my dear, did you know that Theodore Roosevelt once was Caesar's wife?"

"Louisa," he said, "look—why don't we stop this nonsense? I don't like to see you making a fool of yourself like this. Just give me that goddam cat and I'll take it to the police station myself."

Louisa didn't seem to hear him. She was staring openmouthed at a picture of Liszt in the book that lay on her lap. "My God!" she cried. "Edward, look!"

"What?"

"Look! The warts on his face! I forgot all about them! He had these great warts on his face and it was a famous thing. Even his students used to cultivate little tufts of hair on their own faces in the same spots, just to be like him."

"What's that got to do with it?"

"Nothing. I mean not the students. But the warts have."

"Oh, Christ," the man said. "Oh, Christ God Almighty."

"The cat has them, too! Look, I'll show you."

She took the animal onto her lap and began examining its face. "There! There's one! And there's another! Wait a minute! I do believe they're in the same places! Where's that picture?"

It was a famous portrait of the musician in his old age, showing the fine, powerful face framed in a mass of long gray hair that covered his ears and came halfway down his neck. On the face itself, each large wart had been faithfully reproduced, and there were five of them in all.

"Now, in the picture there's *one* above the right eyebrow." She looked above the right eyebrow of the cat. "Yes! It's there! In exactly the same place! And another on the left, at the top of the nose. That one's there, too! And one just below it on the cheek. And two fairly close together under the chin on the right side. Edward! Edward! Come and look! They're exactly the same."

"It doesn't prove a thing."

She looked up at her husband, who was standing in the center of the room in his green sweater and khaki slacks, still perspiring freely. "You're scared, aren't you, Edward? Scared of losing your precious dignity and having people

think you might be making a fool of yourself just for once."

"I refuse to get hysterical about it, that's all."

Louisa turned back to the book and began reading some more. "This is interesting," she said. "It says here that Liszt loved all of Chopin's works except one—the Scherzo in B Flat Minor. Apparently he hated that. He called it the 'Governess Scherzo,' and said that it ought to be reserved solely for people in that profession."

"So what?"

"Edward, listen. As you insist on being so horrid about all this, I'll tell you what I'm going to do. I'm going to play this Scherzo right now and you can stay here and see what happens."

"And then maybe you will deign to get us some supper."

Louisa got up and took from the shelf a large green volume containing all of Chopin's works. "Here it is. Oh, yes. I remember it. It *is* rather awful. Now, listen—or, rather, watch. Watch to see what he does."

She placed the music on the piano and sat down. Her husband remained standing. He had his hands in his pockets and a cigarette in his mouth, and in spite of himself he was watching the cat, which was now dozing on the sofa. When Louisa began to play, the first effect was as dra-

PROTECTED

Cat-owning couple on a motor tour took their pet to his first hotel. Before going out to dinner, without the cat, they told the day maid they were afraid the animal might escape if the night maid popped in. "Don't worry," said the maid, and when they got back, there was a "Do Not Disturb" card hanging from the outside handle of their door.

| 1951 |

matic as ever. The animal jumped up as though it had been stung, and it stood motionless for at least a minute, the ears pricked up, the whole body quivering. Then it became restless and began to walk back and forth, back and forth, the length of the sofa. Finally, it hopped down onto the floor, and with its nose and tail held high in the air, it marched slowly, majestically, from the room.

"There!" Louisa cried, jumping up and running after it. "That does it! That really proves it!" She came back carrying the cat, which she put down again on the sofa. Her whole face was shining with excitement now, her fists were clenched white, and the little bun on top of her head was loosening and going over to one side. "What about it, Edward? What d'you think?" She was sort of laughing every time she spoke.

"I must say it was quite amusing."

"*Amusing!* My dear Edward, it's the most wonderful thing that's ever happened! Oh, goodness me!" she cried, picking up the cat again and hugging it to her bosom. "Isn't it marvellous to think we've got Franz Liszt staying in the house?"

"Now, Louisa. Don't let's get hysterical."

"I can't help it, I simply can't. And to *imagine* that he's actually going to live with us for always!"

"I beg your pardon?"

"Oh, Edward! I can hardly talk from excitement. And d'you know what I'm going to do next? Every musician in the whole world is going to want to meet him, that's a fact, and ask him about the people he knew—about Beethoven and Chopin and Schubert—"

"He can't talk," her husband said.

"Well—all right. But they're going to want to meet him anyway, just to see him and touch him, and to play their own music to him, modern music he's never heard before."

"He wasn't that great. Now, if it had been Bach or Beethoven . . ."

"Don't interrupt, Edward, please. So what I'm going to do is notify all the important living composers everywhere. It's my duty. I'll tell them Liszt is here, and invite them to visit him. And you know what? They'll come flying in from every corner of the earth!"

"To see a gray cat?"

"Darling, it's the same thing. It's *him*. No one cares what he *looks* like. Oh, Edward, it'll be the most exciting thing there ever was!"

"They'll think you're mad."

"You wait and see." She was holding the cat in her arms and petting it tenderly but looking across at her husband, who now walked over to the French windows and stood there staring out into the garden. The evening was beginning, and the lawn was turning slowly from green to black, and in the distance he could just see the smoke from his bonfire rising straight up in a white column.

"No," he said, without turning round, "I'm not having it. Not in this house. It'll make us both look perfect fools."

"Edward, what do you mean?"

"Just what I say. I absolutely refuse to have you stirring up a lot of publicity about a foolish thing like this. You happen to have found a trick cat. O.K.—that's fine. Keep it, if it pleases you. I don't mind. But I don't wish you to go any further than that. Do you understand me, Louisa?"

"Further than what?"

"I don't want to hear any more of this crazy talk. You're acting like a lunatic."

Louisa put the cat slowly down on the sofa. Then slowly she raised herself to her full small height and took one pace forward. "*Damn* you, Edward!" she shouted, stamping her foot. "For the first time in our lives something really exciting comes along and you're scared to death of having anything to do with it because someone may laugh at you! That's right, isn't it? You can't deny it, can you?"

"Louisa," her husband said. "That's quite enough of that. Pull yourself together now and stop this at once." He walked over and took a cigarette from the box on the table, then lit it with the enormous patent lighter. His wife stood watching him, and now the tears were beginning to trickle out of the inside corners of her eyes, making two little shiny rivers where they ran through the powder on her cheeks.

"We've been having too many of these scenes just lately, Louisa," he was saying. "No, no, don't interrupt. Listen to me. I make full allowance for the fact that this may be an awkward time of life for you, and that—"

"Oh, my God! You idiot! You pompous idiot! Can't you see that this is different, this is—this is something *miraculous*? Can't you see *that*?"

At that point, he came across the room and took her firmly by the shoulders. He had the freshly lit cigarette between his lips, and she could see faint contours on his skin where the heavy perspiration had dried in patches. "Listen," he said. "I'm hungry. I've given up my golf, and I've been working all day in the garden, and I'm tired and hungry and I want some supper. So do you. Off you go, now, to the kitchen and get us both something good to eat."

Louisa stepped back and put both hands to her mouth. "My heavens!" she cried. "I forgot all about it. He must be absolutely famished. Except for some milk, I haven't given him a thing to eat since he arrived."

"Who?"

"Why, *him*, of course. I must go at once and cook something really special. I wish I knew what his favorite dishes used to be. What do you think he would like best, Edward?"

"*Goddam* it, Louisa!"

A CAT / A FUTURE

A cat can draw
the blinds
behind her eyes
whenever she
decides. Nothing
alters in the stare
itself but she's
not there. Likewise
a future can occlude:
still sitting there,
doing nothing rude.

—Kay Ryan | 1995 |

"Now, Edward, please. I'm going to handle this *my* way just for once. You stay here," she said, bending down and touching the cat gently with her fingers. "I won't be long."

Louisa went into the kitchen and stood for a moment, wondering what special dish she might prepare. How about a soufflé? A nice cheese soufflé? Yes, that would be rather special. Of course, Edward didn't much care for them, but that couldn't be helped.

She was only a fair cook, and she couldn't be sure of always having a soufflé come out well, but she took extra trouble this time, and waited a long while to make certain the oven had heated fully to the correct temperature. While the soufflé was baking and she was searching around for something to go with it, it occurred to her that Liszt had probably never in his life tasted either avocado pears or grapefruit, so she decided to give him both of them at once in a salad. It would be fun to watch his reaction. It really would.

When it was all ready, she put it on a tray

and carried it into the living room. At the exact moment she entered, she saw her husband coming in through the French windows from the garden.

"Here's his supper," she said, putting it on the table and turning toward the sofa. "Where is he?"

Her husband closed the garden door behind him and walked across the room to get himself a cigarette.

"Edward, where is he?"

"Who?"

"You know who."

"Ah, yes. Yes, that's right. Well—I'll tell you." He was bending forward to light the cigarette, and his hands were cupped around the enormous patent lighter. He glanced up and saw Louisa looking at him—at his shoes and the bottoms of his khaki slacks, which were damp from walking in long grass.

"I just went out to see how the bonfire was going," he said.

Her eyes travelled slowly upward and rested on his hands.

"It's still burning fine," he went on. "I think it'll keep going all night."

But the way she was staring made him uncomfortable.

"What is it?" he said, lowering the lighter. Then he looked down and noticed for the first time the long thin scratch that ran diagonally clear across the back of one hand, from the knuckle to the wrist.

"*Edward!*"

"Yes," he said, "I know. These brambles are terrible. They tear you to pieces. Now, just a minute, Louisa. What's the matter?"

"*Edward!*"

"Oh, for God's sake, woman, sit down and keep calm. There's nothing to get worked up about. Louisa! Louisa, *sit down!*"

| 1953 |

"Makes you wonder, doesn't it?"

QUESTIONS ABOUT LANGUAGE—CATS

VICKI HEARNE

There used to be, and probably still is, activity in the area called comparative psychology which consists of various attempts to work out ways of studying and quantifying memory and intelligence across different species. There was sometimes a certain amount of difficulty in coming up with experimental designs that gave clear results. (In one case that I remember something of, various animals were shown where food was hidden and then brought back minutes, hours, or days later and watched to see how well they did in finding the food.) I used to hear older experimenters advising younger ones about working with cats. It seems that under certain circumstances if you give cats a problem to solve or a task to perform in order to find food they work it out pretty quickly. But, as I heard, "the trouble is that as soon as they figure out that the researcher or technician *wants* them to push the lever they stop doing it; some of them will *starve* to death rather than do it."

That result fascinated me—I would have dropped everything in order to find out what the cats were trying to do or say to the researchers. After all, when human beings behave that way we come up with a pretty fancy catalogue of virtues in order to account for it. But, of course, I was stupidly supposing that the point of these efforts was to understand animals, and it wasn't at all. The point was simply to Do Science, or so I began to suspect when I heard one venerable professor tell a young researcher, "Don't use cats. They'll screw up your data."

What is it about cats? Among gentler and more tentative philosophers than the investigators I have described, cats are considered unobtrusively ubiquitous, and the philosophers are by and large grateful for this. At least, I hear the sound of gratitude in Montaigne when he says that while our way of talking is to say that one plays with one's cat there is no reason we shouldn't suppose that it is the other way about— that one's cat is playing with one. Montaigne's delicate alertness to such possibilities of grammatical reversal is sadly missing from most modern speculations about language and consciousness, but our cats are still here, which means that the most agreeable of philosophical expressions, the grateful one, is still possible.

The cats who were prepared to starve to death in the laboratories were, no doubt about it, frustrated animals. The refusal of food is a signal made to the cosmos itself when one despairs of signalling to one's chums that something deep in nature is being denied. A mare on the point of foaling will not eat or drink if there is insufficient congruence between her sense of the event she anticipates and the attitudes of the creatures and landscape around her. Children refuse food when

they are overloaded with various phoninesses disguised as love. And when you take a house cat and put it in a situation in which there is only one choice, that of responding in a linear way to human expectations, the cat won't eat if eating entails the performance of a kind of "pleasing" that is a violation of the cat's nature, a distortion of the cat's duties on the planet.

This means not that cats are perverse but, rather, that the pleasures and expectations of human beings are profoundly important to cats. In fact, it suggests that, contrary to popular wisdom, getting it right about pleasing us is in some ways far more to the point of cat nature than it is to the point of dog nature. Dogs are by and large more like human beings in that they are merely amused and relieved when their imitations and approximations of obedience are accepted by us; and their resemblance to us in that way may be one of the reasons it is easier to achieve general agreement on the interpretation of a given doggy action. But cats take the task of pleasing us far more seriously. Science has shown us this. Of course, science has also shown us that merely having some lunkheaded expectation and presenting it to the cat doesn't satisfy the cat. The cat's job includes making us aware of the invented nature of our expectation, and cats can't do this when the bulldozer effect takes over our expectations, as it can in science and in our erotic relationships.

I should interrupt myself and explain what I mean by my simpleminded assault on science in general and behaviorism in particular. I don't

---

Every now and then we come upon a moment of rare, if not intolerable, domestic felicity. We met one the other afternoon when we went to call on a friend and found his three-year-old daughter curled up in a chair, with a book and a languishing Angora cat.

"Please hush," she said to us. "I am reading to Pussy."

We withdrew respectfully, stopping only long enough to discover the name of the book, which she was holding upside down. It was *The Turn of the Screw*, by Mr. Henry James.

| 1942 |

mean that there is much point in merely discarding—for now, at least—such notions as conditioned response and operant behavior. They are far too useful, philosophically and morally. For one thing, thinking about interactions between stimuli and behaviors without reference to internal events can make it turn out that most things are not our fault, thus relieving us of the "bad conscience" that Nietzsche so despised. But there are certain confusions that get into the discussions in practice, usually in the guise of genuine difficulties. The result tends to be that the behaviorist overtly denies the interpretative significance of internal events while covertly making appeal to them when the going gets philosophically rough. The opposite happens, too, of course. Some animal trainers declare themselves the enemies of academic psychology without acknowledging the extent to which things like the stimulus-response model have clarified their thinking and practice. All this is well and good, but it still doesn't turn out that behaviorism in its pure form has come up with a better response to cats' refusals than "Don't use cats. They'll screw up your data."

I am not an especially good observer of cats, so the cat who first caught my attention was one who comes when he is called and who attends to his interests straightforwardly. At least, Koshka comes when *I* call him, and he is tolerably responsive when my female cat, Cynthia, hollers at him. He is also somewhat clumsy, which is why it is possible for me to work out fairly easily what he is up to.

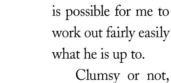

Clumsy or not, he is like all cats in his relationship to straight lines. If he is on the windowsill in the living room and

I put down a bowl of food on the floor in the kitchen, he selects a route to the bowl that takes him over the sofa and the bookcase and he makes it look like a natural route, somewhat in the way a field-trial dog will make his leaps over yawning gullies look natural; it is profoundly important to Koshka that he avoid the stupidities of straight lines. It is because he is clumsy that I was able to see this; the genius of cats is in the way we don't, by and large, think about such things, because cats play so sweetly with our expectations, all the while charming us out of false skepticisms. And they are, as I have said, very serious about this. When they fail at charming us, they move so swiftly to the next meditation that we are hardly aware there has been an attempt, much less a failure.

The philosophical condition that makes the cat's indirections meaningful is one in which we understand that something needs to be restored—that straight lines, the lines of speech and intention, are already lost to us, so that our first impulse toward directness will be irrevocably contaminated. Dogs manifest their sensitivity to that contamination in various ways—most plainly in their refusals to perform complete retrieves without the restorations and consolations of formal training—and cats have their own evasions of postlapsarian invocations. One traditional way of understanding Eden has been to say that it was prelinguistic, and there is something right about that in a world in which "linguistic" means "after Babel." But there is something wrong about it if "prelinguistic" is understood to mean "prior to language," for Adam and Eve and God and all of creation could sing to and call one another. Let us say that Paradise was not so much prior to language—though it was certainly prior to our language—as it was prior to epistemology, prior to doubt about the sources and resources of meaningful resonances.

In such a case, it is important to understand the circumstances in which cats *will* travel in straight lines and under the direction of a human. There are people who work cats for movies. The animal trainer Bill Koehler has had cats whom he could control in the exacting situations in which the cat's movements must be coordinated with directors, cameramen, actors, and scripts. These cats are by and large travelling in straight lines, in response to signals (or "discriminatory cues") and for food rewards. Such cats are spoken of admiringly, with such comments as "Open his cage in the morning and out he comes, jumps on my shoulder, ready to do a job of work" or "The buzzer sounds and that cat makes a beeline, right now." That is to say that the cats are doing in working situations exactly what the researchers I used to listen to failed to get them to do. The trainers are on to something that could be expressed by saying that training is partly a discipline of a kind of negative capability, which they express in various ways. For example, one day we were watching a woman who was a fine handler work her Basenji on retrieving exercises—and Basenjis are notoriously hard to work with. (I once found myself saying that a masochist is a person who is training his or her second Basenji.) Someone in the group of spectators said, "I like what she does with that dog. Doesn't send out any brain waves." Here "brain waves" was a way of referring to a kind of psychic imperialism.

By contrast, in the labs where the cats wouldn't eat I used to see the researcher or the technician or the work-study student walk into the lab, ready to go to work, trying with some degree of sincerity and expertness to be *objective*. This may sound like a corollary of not sending out brain waves, but in fact it was the first mistake I observed. To be objective is to try to approach the condition of being No One in Particular with a View from Nowhere, and cats know better than that. They are uneasy around such people, because people who don't know better tend to ride roughshod over the cat's own knowledge that a cat is Someone in Particular.

Of course, if the caretaker was an undergraduate he would usually still be moved to talk to the cat, to find the grounds of relationship, but in the laboratory situation the impulse would be truncated, the rhythms of attentiveness and response would be offbeat—and the rhythm and harmony of our attention are everything to a cat. Objectivity depends on models of the world and of language which require precisely the flat-footed and contaminated sort of straight line that cats are dedicated to undermining for the sake of clarity and richness of discourse. It has nothing to do with the emptying of self—or, really, ego—which moves poets to come up with expressions like "negative capability." "Scientific objectivity" is, as most people practice it, precisely what the trainers call "brain waves."

I once went to visit Washoe, the first chimpanzee to be taught the American Sign Language. At that time, she was being kept temporarily at Gentle Jungle, a wild-animal training facility that used to rent animals out to movies and television. There were roughly three categories of people going in and out of the main compound. There was the group that included trainers, handlers, and caretakers, there were Hollywood types of one sort and another, and there were academics, who were there mostly because of the presence of the signing chimpanzee. I realized that without consciously thinking about it I was able to identify accurately and from some distance away which group anyone who came in belonged to. I wasn't doing this with clues of clothing, either; almost everyone was in the same sort of jeans, sneakers, and T-shirt. The handlers, I noticed, walked in with a soft, acute, three-hundred-and-sixty-degree awareness; they were receptively establishing mute acknowledgments of and relationships with all of the dozens of pumas, wolves, chimps, spider monkeys, and Galápagos tortoises. Their ways of moving *fit* into the spaces shaped by the animals' awareness. The Hollywood types moved with vast indifference to where they were, and might as well have been on an interior set with flats painted with pictures of tortoises, or on the stage of a Las Vegas night club. They were psychically intrusive, and I remembered the animal trainer Dick Koehler's saying that you could count on your thumbs the number of actors, directors, and so on who could actually respond meaningfully to what an animal was doing. The academics didn't strut quite that way, but they were nonetheless psychically intrusive—they failed to radiate the intelligence the handlers did. Their very hip joints articulated the importance of their

theories. They had too many questions, too many hidden assumptions about their roles as observers. I am talking about nice, smart people, but good handlers don't "observe" animals in this way, from within diagrams of the objective perfor-

mance, and with that stare which makes almost all animals a bit uneasy, and especially cats.

Cats do not observe *us* in this way—but they do observe us, almost continuously, as I learned from a poem of John L'Heureux's, "The Thing About Cats," which closes with a question:

> A cat is not a conscience; I'm not
> Saying that.
> What I'm saying is
>
> why are they looking?

It took me some ten years after being struck by this question to realize that it was the question I had been looking for, or a real question and a real noticing of the fact that our cats are looking at us. This is evidence of my own participation in the culture's ailurophobia.

I just now looked up from my typewriter at one of my own cats, Patrick, snoozing on top of the stereo. Something—perhaps the longish pause in the sounds of typing—alerted him to the change in my mental posture, and he opened an eye, smoothed a whisker, then leaped down and strolled out of the room with a muffled meow. I felt this to be simultaneously an instance of gracious acknowledgment of the moment of contact with me and as gracious a refusal to interrupt me. (I should say that I am quite stern with my cats about their desire to be in between my eyes and whatever piece of paper I am engaged with.)

One could read this small episode in various ways, as mere coincidence or as evidence of my sentimentality about Patrick, but it now occurs to me that the success of language itself may depend a great deal of the time on serendipity, just as it may turn out that the variations of "meow" which our powers can detect are always by accident the right thing to say. Patrick just reentered the room, crossed in front of me with a graceful arch and another unobtrusive comment, and settled in a new observation post—in his basket. This felt like the right thing for him to do during another longish pause, during which I had muttered aloud, wondering where he had got to. It is not, in any event, a *mistake* on his part—to invoke the philosopher J. L. Austin's wonderful distinction about what remarks and actions of his will fit smoothly into my activities. (In "A Plea for Excuses," Austin talks about two instances of shooting a donkey, in one case by accident and in the other case by mistake.)

But Patrick used to make mistakes. This is not easy to remember, and, indeed, he so quickly became adept at judging when it was appropriate for him to cuddle, or request a favor, and at what distance from me he should be under various circumstances, that I might be forgiven for invoking the notion of an unconsciously "programmed" set of behaviors to account for it. We need a new vocabulary term to identify such errors—a nasty word like "mechanomorphism," for example—or some other way of referring to our thoughtless and superstitious habit of attributing mechanical traits to organisms, as though nature dutifully imitated our inventions. Donald R. Griffin has pointed out in his book *Animal Thinking:*

> If . . . an animal thinks about its needs and desires, and about the probable results of alternative actions, fewer and more general instructions are sufficient. Animals with relatively small brains may thus have greater need for simple conscious thinking than those endowed with a kilogram or more of gray matter. Perhaps only we and the whales can afford the luxury of storing detailed behavioral instructions. . . .

But I am in danger here of straying from my investigation. I think that the differences be-

tween the case of dogs and the case of cats, and the different superstitious errors we are led into in the different cases, suggest that what we have made mistakes about is the nature of certain virtues—especially the willingness to please. Consider, for example, that there isn't in our relationships with dogs a phenomenon similar enough to ailurophobia for us to have a popular name for it. People just say that they are afraid of dogs, and the fear of dogs is fairly easy to demolish if the right dog and the right handler are about. The fear of dogs usually has a basis that is at least approximately rational, and this is one reason that someone who is no longer afraid  of Lassie may find his or her fear reappearing with different dogs or in different circumstances, as in the case of a few friends of mine who are no longer at all nervous about my dogs but are still jumpy when a strange dog goes by on the streets.

Ailurophobia is not like this; it is far more resistant to desensitization techniques (which often consist of social introductions) and is perhaps more obviously inexplicable. After all, cats are not used much to guard persons or property and are more or less unresponsive to attack training, whereas there are plenty of dogs in the world who are real man-stoppers, and also quite a few dogs who aren't but brag that they are when you happen by their yards or their cars. I am, for that matter, sometimes afraid of dogs; that is to say, I respect a dog's assertion of a claim to property, and in the case of certain dogs I respect their authority when they say, "Do this, not that."

But the thing about cats is, first of all, that

they are looking at us, and perhaps the thing about ailurophobes is that they don't want to be looked at like that. We are all ailurophobes to the extent that we have bought the culture's "wisdom" about the aloofness and emotional independence of cats, which, as the philosopher Stanley Cavell taught me to understand, is logically very like virtually any other expression of skeptical terror about the independent existence of other minds—such as jealousy and the reassurances it demands, or sexism, or racism. So perhaps the aloofness story is one we tell ourselves in order not to know that we are being looked at. But why should we not want to be looked at?

I find that for me to point out that we have various reasons for wanting to hide doesn't help, if only because that phenomenon has been too often discussed under the heading of pathology, and I am thinking of something that is part of health. And talk in which we say that some people have a fear of intimacy, or that Americans have this fear, or academics have that fear, is similarly unhelpful, as is talk in which we suppose that genuine intimacy, as opposed to its false forms, is "threatening." I don't mean that such ways of talking are wrong—only that what I am interested in is some of the false ideas we have about the nature of intimacy. There is the idea, for example, that intimacy consists in reporting on inner states or feelings. This is at best an odd thing for anyone to think, in light of the fact that when people are actually spending most or all of their conversational time reporting on their feelings they are usually boring, and in extreme cases are as likely to end up locked away somewhere as people who seem to lose entirely the ability to report on their frame of mind when that is appropriate.

There is something that is not *that* that is intimacy. Babies, as Cavell has provocatively reminded us, learn to talk when you talk to them about something—puppies, say, or pumpkins—and not when they are shut up in boxes, and I want to say somehow that intimacy is thinking. It is thinking about *something*—something other than just the parties engaged in the conversation. If you are my friend, I may from time to time need or want to request your response to some happiness or some grief of mine, and in the logic of any friendship love will entail that we agree to do this for each other. But we won't, as C. S. Lewis observes, want to talk about it once the occasion has passed; to do so is displeasing unless our interest becomes philosophical. To dwell on grief and distress or on happiness—or, at least, to dwell in a housebound way on them—is to dwell in some busy ranch of isolation that is not intimacy and is not thinking. To dwell upon it or in it would be what Lewis, speaking from a precisely British metaphysics of talk, calls "embarrassing," and what I, speaking from the animal trainer's sense of things, want to call distraction, as when we say, "It's no use trying to talk to her now. She is distracted out of her wits."

I am thinking of the capacity for intimacy as a virtue, the virtue of friendship—Philia, the emblem of which is two figures holding hands and gazing at some third object. This is unlike Eros, that love whose emblem is two figures gazing at each other. Eros may be—in fact, had probably better be—figured eventually as the intimacy of friendship. A marriage, for example, may be founded on a rich and continuous conversation about the nature of marriage and love, but it cannot, as the women's magazines keep warning, be founded on continuous *declarations* of love. A friend of mine once said crossly, after a particularly trying evening at a couple's house, that she couldn't imagine herself in a marriage, because she didn't feel like spending all of her time praising someone—she preferred thought and conversation. I didn't know enough then to say, "But what that couple was doing tonight—that is not a bad marriage, that isn't marriage."

Some dogs make continuous declarations of love, or seem to, and this can enable some people to survive psychic wildernesses of one sort or another, but it is only training—work—that creates a shared grammar of objects of contemplation outside the dog and the master, and it is there that the best conversations start and, with them, the bonds of that deeper love which consists in thinking. Cats do not declare their love much; they enact it, by their myriad invocations of our pleasure, and they show their understanding of what they are doing—that is, they show the structure of their understanding—in part through their willingness to give up the last moment's enactment for this moment, as though they knew that love, being what refreshes thought, must itself always be discarding us for our refreshment. You may very well get stuck in yesterday's declarations with your spouse or your child, and they may not know how to prevent this in you or in themselves, but your cat will not permit this. The declarations of five minutes ago—that particular arching of the back, that appealing gesture with the paw—may have been true then but now are not, and the cat never allows them to become the bedraggled hermit in our tropes of gesture who, in the words of Wallace Stevens, "comes and goes and comes and goes all day."

One may say, with John Hollander, that our cats are infinitely interpretable texts, but the "text" is something *between* us and our cats; it is the object the cat makes out of our positions relative to each other. We regard it from our viewpoint, they from theirs, which introduces a variation on the theme, as cats seldom want to stand side by side with us holding hands unless they are scared or are in certain crises, as our cat Blue was recently, when kitting for the first time. She didn't want my husband to leave the room, and even reported to him on her frame of mind and feelings. But she was asking for this from him, I suspect, because she knows that he respects her too much to get stuck in some sticky mode of rescue, and can be relied on to go back to the conversation. He doesn't, even while holding hands, send out brain waves. Some people are better at talking with cats than other people are; they have larger capacities for the dreamy yet acute sorts of discourse that most cats seem to favor.

Koshka, the cat I spoke of earlier who was clumsy enough to reveal himself to my blunt perceptions, is somewhat jealous—or, at least, he shows his jealousy more obviously than other cats I have known. He has had to deal, over the years, with a variety of cats, kittens, dogs, and other claimants on the hearth, who disturb the progress of his Poem of Koshka. Nowadays, he betrays only the slightest tendency to sulk and grump, having learned that sulky cats don't please me. But in his youth this was not so. Once, I brought in two fuzzy harlequin-marked kittens and sat playing with them on the couch. Koshka leaped wildly into the middle of this arrangement and then away, and then back again, screaming hoarsely that it wasn't *right*. I batted him in the nose and told him to mind his manners, but Koshka said shrilly that they weren't minding *their* manners, were they? Other,

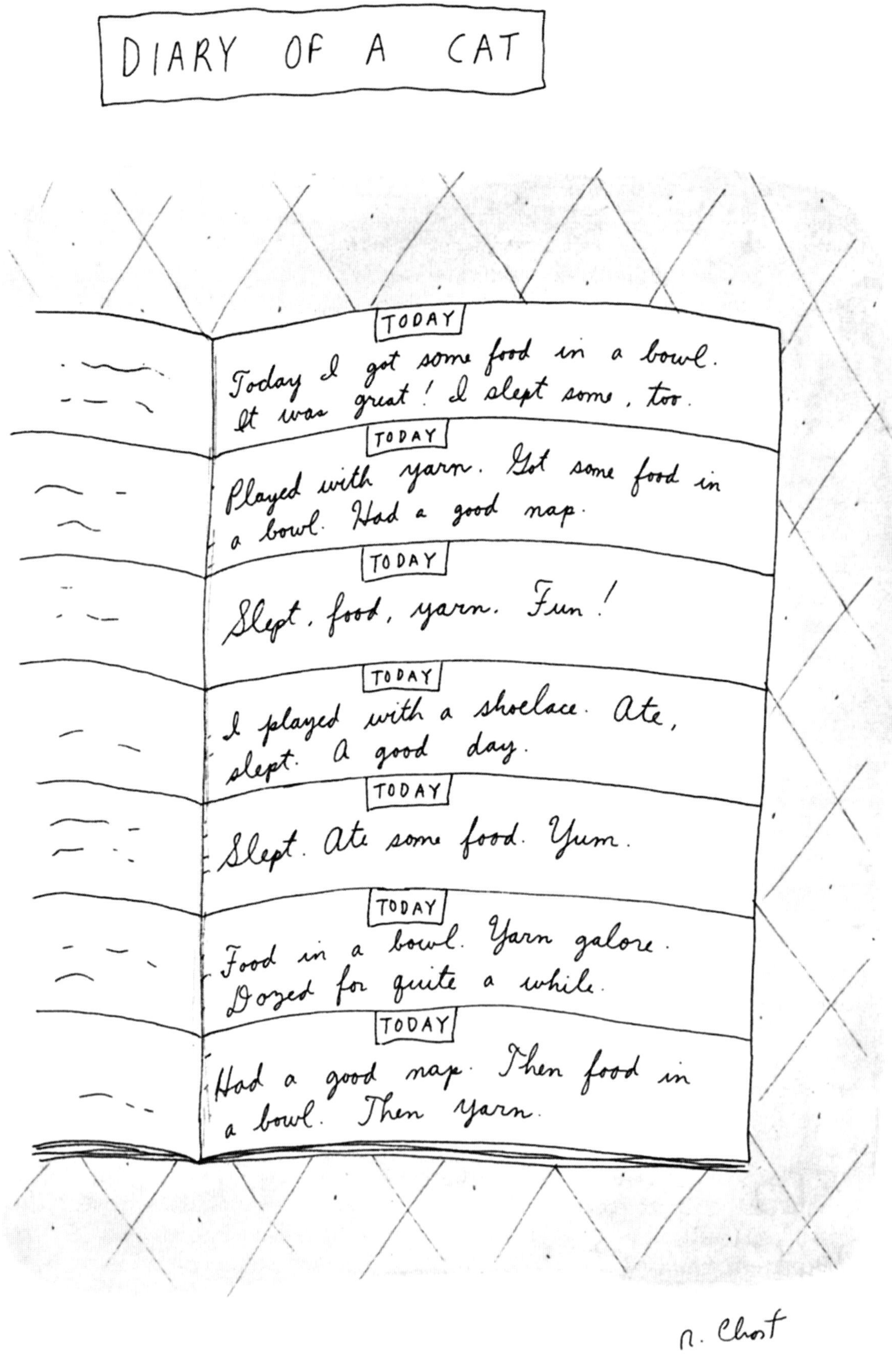

DIARY OF A CAT

TODAY

Today I got some food in a bowl. It was great! I slept some, too.

TODAY

Played with yarn. Got some food in a bowl. Had a good nap.

TODAY

Slept, food, yarn. Fun!

TODAY

I played with a shoelace. Ate, slept. A good day.

TODAY

Slept. Ate some food. Yum.

TODAY

Food in a bowl. Yarn galore. Dozed for quite a while.

TODAY

Had a good nap. Then food in a bowl. Then yarn.

R. Chast

more graceful cats would at this point have taken to washing their paws, perhaps, or have developed a sudden interest in a squirrel outside the window while they worked things out. Koshka retreated to the end of the couch and looked depressed and forlorn, alternately meowing and purring at me in a loud, unseemly way. Then he decided to be a good sport and come up and make friends, but found when he tried to get up that his emotional fit had caused him to get his claws stuck in the couch (a frequent mishap for him), and he had to spend a minute or two working them loose. Once he got loose, he headed for me in a straightforward—a doglike—manner, then seemed to remember himself and went back where he had been, lay down again, got up, and zigzagged his way around the room, stopping to sniff some flowers in a vase, a pile of magazines by the fireplace, until he finally managed to be hunting an invisible fly that was buzzing near me and the kittens. Leaping for the fly, he suddenly "noticed" the kittens and began playing with them, pausing to rub against me, purring this time in a dignified fashion. This is not a remarkable cat story, of course.

What had happened to so rapidly transform his clumsily expressed irritation into graciousness was, I think, precisely that typically feline interest in and focus on my pleasure, which is to say, on my interests—the unstated theme that most of a cat's behavior in relation to his or her friends is variations on. (This isn't from our point of view an infinitely adjustable pleasing, of course; try keeping cats and parakeets together, for example.) Koshka revealed that theme in his from time to time doggy behavior, but most cats don't reveal it so directly; that is why it can seem to us that there is no theme, no focus, to a cat's activities. Cats stalk the web of our imaginations as carefully as they stalk prey, and, by and large, elude our grosser interpretations with skill and care, not because they

wish to remain unknown to us but because they cannot bear to be *falsely* known, known only by the deceptive glare of a single proposition. Perhaps nervousness about being in such a way falsely known is the healthy source of some of our ill health, our various impulses to hide, to make mysteries of ourselves, and is also the healthy source of ailurophobia. Because cats are more adept than we are at evading monolithic propositions of character, they are also less likely to go insane in the way we do, or dogs and horses do, when "pinned to a proposition."

When our friends get it wrong about us, we tend to go about saying urgently to anyone we can collar that People Don't Understand Us—no one understands scholars, or poets, or animal trainers, or diabetics. And then we go on to try to say what is in fact the case; but one monolithic and totalizing proposition is no better than another, has no more power to penetrate pluralities of perception and misperception. This, of course, is another error that cats avoid. When we aim a misinterpretation at them, they slip sidewise so adeptly that it usually seems as if they just happened accidentally to move at the very moment we took aim and fired—as if it were always by accident rather than by mistake that we miss. (Except, it appears, when behaviorists get going in laboratories.) To put it another way, cats have a much more efficient "stroke economy" than we do. Here I am using the term "stroke" to mean any stimulus from outside the organism or, at least, from outside the brain that initiates internal activities. Strokes, that is, start everything else. Strokes like "That's a catchy little tune there" don't have the significance that *Porgy and Bess* does, but strokes are necessary, if not sufficient, to those psychic and physical motions that give us *Porgy and Bess*. "Stroke" means *any* acknowledgment of a creature's existence, including negative and painful ones. These don't have the

"Well, he was on the endangered list, and I thought I could save him."

have, then it is my nature you have acknowledged, something that is, by and large, immortal as long as I am.

"Be" strokes are the only kind that cats are normally interested in, which is why work with them can't go the way work with dogs and horses can. Emotional M&M's are either ignored or resisted if circumstances make it impossible to perform the preferred feline metaphysics. Hence the grammars of approval and disapproval that so madden humans are refused utterly by cats, who appear to be born with something like an intuitive understanding that approval is almost inevitably the flip side of disapproval—in contrast to some (though not all) dogs, who are like us in that they usually have to spend time learning the hard way, if they do learn, why it is that bribery and flattery are so dangerous.

The cat's refusal to be approved of or disapproved of may make it appear that, after all, stimulus-response psychology has explanatory force in their case. Especially if people go on to say that in order to get a cat to perform as Bill Koehler's cats do the "reinforcements" used must be impersonal—the handler's self-esteem must not get into them. Such a way of talking makes tropes of mechanomorphism look philosophically promising. But the advice about the importance of impersonality itself points to fundamental differences between, say, my cat Gumbie and my Jeep Cherokee. My Jeep also

generational power that positive acknowledgments have, but they will keep an organism alive even if unhappy. This is one way of understanding why monkeys will embrace wire mothers, and people will stay in relationships that consist largely or wholly of exchanges that leave the participants feeling lousy. Most social animals seem to be capable of becoming addicted to whatever sort of stroke comes handy. Beyond which, some people seem able to become addicted to "do" strokes rather than "be" strokes—usually in the form of praise for a particular accomplishment rather than for a general way of being. The trouble with "do" strokes is that you can never get enough of them, and their stimulating effect doesn't last very long; hence the dusty trophy cases full of stale strokes that some people clutter up their conversations with. "Be" strokes, by contrast, can last practically forever and don't require further validation from anyone, including, usually, the creature who gave you the stroke in the first place. So that while I may feel set up for anywhere from a minute to several weeks if you tell me that a finished performance is splendid, the thrill will come to an end, whereas if you manage to acknowledge accurately the kind of mind I "refuses" to run if there is sugar in the gas tank, and so is "finicky." But what the Jeep does that we can call "refusing" is plainly figurative, as is a parking meter's behavior when we "feed" it. Neither the Jeep nor the meter cares whether or not I care, does not refuse to be "fed" if I make approval noises at it. This sort of difference is so obvious that I am driven to suppose there must be a very powerful superstition preventing some thinkers from seeing it—thinkers who like to say that a cat cannot be said to be "really" playing with a ball, because a cat does not seem to know our grammar of what "playing with" and "ball" are. This sort of more or less positivist position requires a fundamental assumption that "meaning" is a homogeneous, quantifiable thing, and that the universe is dualistic in that there are only two states of meaning in it—significant and insignificant—and, further, that "significant" means only "significant to me." Such a view demands that we acknowledge that the proposition "Cats are more significant to Vicki than grasshoppers are" is a remark about Vicki, not about cats and grasshoppers in and of themselves, as though Vicki had infinite interpretative powers. Such positivism of meaning often looks like an injunction against the pathetic fallacy, but seems to me to be quite the opposite, and also to be, as some writers have claimed that it is, a view that does not answer to the theoretical demand for parsimony. If, for example, Gumbie hides when guests she doesn't like come to visit, and stalks about after they leave, suspiciously checking on the evidences of their visit, then my sense of the guests and of Gumbie is revised a bit, especially since Gumbie usually behaves this way when guests attempt uncalled-for familiarity with her; from that it follows that Gumbie, if I respect her, is revising the meanings of my world. Of course, I may also say "Oh, Gumbie, don't be such a snob!" and insist on my earlier, friendlier interpretation of the guests and decide that Gumbie is behaving badly. This will still be a function of Gumbie's interpretative powers, including her power to interpret me, without regard for any theories about Gumbie I may start with. Gumbie may also, while disporting herself in the back yard, so draw my attention to grasshoppers that I become interested in them, and maybe take up entomology. If the sentence "Cats are more significant to Vicki than grasshoppers are" is one for which the judgments "true" and "false" are relevant, then it is as much about cats and grasshoppers as it is about Vicki.

"The meaning of life is cats."

KITTEN IN A GRAVEYARD

You pick your way among the dead
With padded and fastidious tread,
Your tail so high, your fur so sleek.
You are the strong and I the weak
Who fear this quiet spot of serried
Tombs where everything is buried
Except the evergreen and stone
For you to whet your claws upon.
I ask to live, if only that
I may be here to stroke you, cat.

—Selma Robinson | 1932 |

Compare it with "Xqrwz are more significant to Vicki than bxryqwixxws are." This is not, in the language I speak, anything for which the judgment "true" or "false" is relevant; it is not about anything.

With Gumbie, the only way to manage to believe that any significance she has is the product of my theories about her is to kill her; allow her to live and she will with every turn, every thoughtful purr and liquidity of comment in her throat, remind me that her relationship to the world is mediated through mine only insofar as that mediation is congruent with the revolving "I am" that is Gumbie. The objections to my saying this are curiously various. Some philosophers would want, of course, to cry out against my attribution to Gumbie of a concept of self, but others would want to say that the cat's unresponsiveness to emotional bribery is "just" a function of the fact that house cats, like tigers, are loners—not social animals, not dependent on the structure and organization of any sort of group. I don't know where this notion comes from in light of the fact that virtually every popular book on owning cats recommends that you have more than one, so that they will keep each other company when you are not at home.

Cats are more likely than horses and dogs in domestic situations (hanging around the house) to force the dimmest of us—temporarily, at least—to abandon our epistemological heavy-handedness. When a cat is made out in a TV cat-food commercial to be performing some sort of minuet by means of photographic manipulations, the very ease with which we can so interpret his image is itself a reminder that it is an interpretation built on sand, and not a full figuration. We do not forget that that cat—the cat himself—remains outside our interpretations. Cats are always saying to us in one way and another, "I am the Cat who walks by himself, and all places are alike to me," as the cat in Kipling's *Just So Stories* does. When a cat looks at us, there is always in the looking the reminder that a cat can look at me or at a king and in both cases equally from the chosen poise of *that* particular angle of grace and speculation.

But, of course, here is the point I am laboring over: Cats are saying that *to us*. They take infinite trouble so that we should continue to be aware of their way of looking. Consider the cat in Kipling. In that story, the first creature to be domesticated was Wild Man, who was "dreadfully wild," we are told. "He didn't even begin to be tame till he met the Woman, and she told him that she did not like living in his wild ways." The next animal was, of course, Wild Dog, who was easily drawn into the amiability of the cave by the Woman when she made "the First Singing Magic in the world." The dog came when called and became, by way of a song, First Friend. Wild Horse was cooperative, too, being charmed and tamed by the Second Singing Magic in the world. And so with Wild Cow. Even the little Bat is a guest rather than an intruder in the cave, and calls the Woman, "O my Hostess and wife of my Host."

But the Cat refused the tale the humans wanted to tell of him, and, indeed, insisted on a revision of the Woman's story about *herself*, with the result that it was the Woman who was charmed, and said, "I knew I was wise, but I did not know I was beautiful. So I will make a bargain with you. If ever I say one word in your praise you may come into the Cave." The Cat agreed to this and negotiated further, for a warm spot by the fire should there be two words in his praise, and the privilege of drinking milk should there be three. As is usual in such stories, the Woman did say three words in his praise, but, of course, not in the way she meant—the world of such tales is a magically logocentric world, in which, as in legal situations, saying "That isn't what I meant" doesn't get us out of it. The Cat, first by tickling and charming Baby, then by purring and so lulling Baby asleep, and finally by catching a mouse, moved the Woman to utter the three words of praise. Kipling goes on to tell of the return of the Man and the Dog at the end of the day, and of their threats to throw things and use teeth should the Cat fail to continue to be kind to Baby and to catch mice. Kipling falters here, I think, for he has it turn out that the threats are effective against the Cat, and I have never seen anyone succeed in making a cat go forward and do something—rather than run away—in response to threats. (In fact, threats aren't really very good motivators for any species that I know of. But that is a somewhat separate issue, which has to do with the reasons cruelty doesn't work very well.) What matters here is that up until the end, when Kipling sentimentally allows the Dog and the Man to succeed with the sort of macho display behavior that cats generally despise, he has the important part right—the Cat's revisionary impulses.

I don't blame Kipling, of course, for his failure to sustain his cat story properly. It is impossi-ble for anyone to stay ahead of a cat. My cat Blue, for example, is becoming a politician these days and has organized the other cats, who are upset with me because I spend too much time talking on the telephone and making airline reservations instead of paying proper attention to creature comforts. Yesterday, a friend called me. When Blue failed to get my attention away from the

Shanahan

telephone, she simply "accidentally" walked on the button that hangs the phone up on her way from the bookcase to her water dish. By the time I worked out what she had been up to, she had given herself a bath, dealt with the mice, and instructed my pit bull further on how to keep the male cats in line.

It is pleasing to watch kittens practicing these revisionary impulses—stalking a shadow with sidewise hops, and so on, or playing with parts of their own bodies and those of Mama and their littermates with that odd regard for the intended nature of the tail, paw, or ear which makes us tend to say that the kitten chasing his tail doesn't know that it is his tail. What the kitten is born to know is that it is his or her own Tale, the tale of the cat's limitlessly metamorphosing stances toward us and the rest of the world.

I feel again the hot breath of someone wanting to give me a lecture from the opening series in Life Sciences 121a: The Interpretation of Behavior, and tell me that the behaviors I am talking about are explainable as the result of predatory mechanisms in the cat. There is, as usual, an implied "merely" in this, as if in the first place something as difficult and as important as hunting weren't a likely basis for play and tale, and as such also a source of figures of thought in the development of friendships. Believing such a notion consistently would entail denying that any utterance can be a poem, because all or some of its grammar and diction can be shown to have sources in survival modes necessitated by, say, droughts during the Pleistocene.

There are differences between the friendships of humans with cats and those with other human beings. The cat's insistence on being himself brings pleasure, whereas such an insistence in human-to-human loves is too often done clumsily and painfully and may result in

the static of Quarrel rather than in the Heart of philosophy. But I have been for too long trying to indicate in prose what is more properly celebrated in verse—those turns and graces by means of which not only those who are Beloved Others but philosophy itself consoles us for the very fact of Otherness which drives us to philosophy. Some Eastern thinkers speak of "the gap" and then say no more about it. Dogs, people, and horses are all likely to try foolishly to close the gap, to deny what Stanley Cavell has called our "differences from one another—the one everything the other is not," and to deny "human separation, which can be accepted, and granted, or not. Like the separation from God." Cats live in a kind of ever-changing song or story in and of the gap. Here is "Kitty and Bug," by John Hollander:

```
           I        a
        cat     who
        coated in a
        dense shadow
        which I cast
        along myself
         absorb the
          light you
         gaze at me
         with can yet
         look at a king
        and not be seen
        to be seeing any
      more than himself
       a motionless seer
       sovereign of gray
      mirrored invisibly
    in the seeing glass
   of air Whatever I am
  seeing is part of me
  As you see me now my
  vision is wrapped in
  two green hypotheses
   darkness blossoming
    in two unseen eyes
      which pretend to be
       intent on a spot of        bug
        upon
         the
         rug
       Who
       can
        see
          how
           eye
           can
        know
```

TOOTH AND CLAW

Fiction

T. CORAGHESSAN BOYLE

The weather had absolutely nothing to do with it—though the rain had been falling off and on throughout the day and the way the gutters were dripping made me feel as if despair were the mildest term in the dictionary—because I would have gone down to Daggett's that afternoon even if the sun were shining and all the fronds of the palm trees were gilded with light. The problem was work. Or, more specifically, the lack of it. The boss had called at 6:30 A.M. to tell me not to come in, because the guy I'd been replacing had recovered sufficiently from his wrenched back to feel up to working, and, no, he wasn't firing me, because they'd be on to a new job next week and he could use all the hands he could get. "So take a couple days off and enjoy yourself," he'd rumbled into the phone in his low, hoarse, uneven voice, which always seemed on the verge of morphing into something else altogether—squawks and bleats or maybe just static. "You're young, right? Go out and get yourself some tail. Get drunk. Go to the library. Help old ladies across the street. You know what I mean?"

It had been a long day: breakfast out of a cardboard box while cartoon images flickered and faded and reconstituted themselves on the TV screen, and then some desultory reading, starting with the newspaper and a couple of *National Geographics* I'd picked up at a yard sale; lunch at the deli, where I had ham-and-cheese in a tortilla wrap and exchanged exactly eleven words with the girl behind the counter ("No. 7, please, no mayo." "Have a nice day." "You, too"), and a walk to the beach that left my sneakers sodden. And, after all that, it was

265

still only three o'clock in the afternoon and I had to force myself to stay away from the bar till five, five at least.

I wasn't stupid. And I had no intention of becoming a drunk like all the hard-assed old men in the shopping-mall-blighted town I grew up in, silent men with hate in their eyes and complaint eating away at their insides—like my own dead father, for that matter—but I was new here, or relatively new (nine weeks now and counting), and Daggett's was the only place I felt comfortable. And why? Precisely because it was filled with old men drinking themselves into oblivion. It made me think of home. Or feel at home, anyway.

The irony wasn't lost on me. The whole reason I'd moved out to the Coast to live, first with my Aunt Kim and her husband, Waverley, and then in my own one-bedroom apartment with kitchenette and a three-by-six-foot balcony with a partially obscured view of the Pacific, half a mile off, was so that I could inject a little excitement into my life and mingle with all the college students in the bars that lined State Street cheek to jowl, but here I was hanging out in an old-man's bar that smelled of death and vomit and felt as closed in as a submarine, when just outside the door were all the exotic, sunstruck glories of California. Where it never rained. Except in winter. And it was winter now.

I nodded self-consciously at the six or seven regulars lined up at the bar, then ordered a Jack-and-Coke, the only drink besides beer that I liked the taste of, and I didn't really like the taste of beer. There were sports on the three TVs hanging from the ceiling—this was a sports bar—but the volume was down and the speakers were blaring the same tired hits of the sixties that I could have heard back home. Ad nauseam. When the bartender—*he* was young, at least, as were the waitresses—set down my drink, I made a comment about the weather, "Nice day for sunbathing, isn't it?," and the two regulars nearest me glanced up with something like interest in their eyes. "Or maybe bird-watching," I added, feeling encouraged, and they swung their heads back to the familiar triangulation of their splayed elbows and cocktail glasses and that was the end of that.

It must have been seven or so, the rain still coming down and people briefly enlivened by the novelty of it as they came and went in spasms of umbrella furling and unfurling, when a guy about my age—or, no, he must have been thirty, or close to it—came in and took the seat beside me.

He was wearing a baseball cap, a jean jacket, and a T-shirt that said "Obligatory Death," which I took to be the name of a band, though I'd never heard of them. His hair was blond, cut short around the ears, and he had a soul beard that was like a pale stripe painted under his lip by an unsteady hand. We exchanged the standard greeting—*What's up?*—and then he flagged down the bartender and ordered a draft beer, a shot of tomato juice, and two raw eggs.

"Raw eggs?" the bartender echoed, as if he hadn't heard right.

"Yeah. Two raw eggs, in the shell."

The bartender—his name was Chris, or maybe it was Matt—gave a smile and scratched the back of his head. "We can do them over easy or sunny-side up or poached even, but *raw*, I don't know. I mean, nobody's ever requested raw before—"

"Ask the chef, why don't you?"

The bartender shrugged. "Sure," he said, "no problem." He started off in the direction of the kitchen, then pulled up short. "You want toast with that, home fries, or what?"

"Just the eggs."

Everybody was watching now, any little drama worth the price of admission, especially on a night like this, but the bartender—Chris, his name was definitely Chris—just went down to the other end of the bar and communicated the order to the waitress, who made a notation in her pad and disappeared into the kitchen. A moment went by, and then the man turned to me and said in a voice loud enough for everybody to hear, "Jesus, this music sucks. Are we caught in a time warp here, or what?"

The old men—the regulars—glanced up from their drinks and gave him a look, but they were gray-haired and slack in the belly and they knew their limits.

"Yeah," I heard myself say, "it really sucks," and before I knew it I was talking passionately about the bands that meant the most to me even as the new guy poured tomato juice in his beer and sipped the foam off the top, while the music rumbled defiantly on and people with wet shoes and dripping umbrellas crowded in behind us. The eggs, brown-shelled and naked in the middle of a standard dinner plate, were delivered by Daria, a waitress I'd had my eye on, though I hadn't yet worked up the nerve to say more than hello and goodbye to her. "Your order, sir," she said, easing the plate down on the bar. "You need anything with that? Ketchup? Tabasco?"

"No," he said, "that's fine," and everyone was waiting for him to crack the eggs over his beer, but he didn't even look at them. He was looking at Daria, holding her with his eyes. "So, what's your name?" he asked, grinning.

She told him, and she was grinning, too.

"Nice to meet you," he said, taking her hand. "I'm Ludwig."

"Ludwig," she repeated, pronouncing it with a "V," as he had, though as far as I could tell—from his clothes and accent, which was pure Southern California—he wasn't German. Or if he was he sure had his English down.

"Are you German?" Daria was flirting with him, and the realization of it began to harden me against him in the most rudimentary way.

"No," he said. "I'm from Hermosa Beach, born and raised. It's the name, right?"

"I had this German teacher last year? His name was Ludwig, that's all."

"You're in college?"

She told him she was, which was news to me. Working her way through. Majoring in business. She wanted to own her own restaurant someday.

"It was my mother's idea," he said, as if he'd been mulling it over. "She was listening to the 'Eroica' Symphony the night I was born." He shrugged. "It's been my curse ever since."

"I don't know," she said. "I think it's kind of cute. You don't get many Ludwigs, you know?"

"Yeah, tell me about it," he said, sipping his beer.

She lingered, though there were other things she could have been doing. "So, what about the eggs?" she said. "You going to need utensils, or—"

"Or what? Am I going to suck them out of the shell?"

"Yeah," she said, "something like that."

He reached out a hand cluttered with silver to embrace the eggs and gently roll them back and forth across the gleaming expanse of the plate. "No, I'm just going to fondle them," he said, and got the expected response: she laughed. "But does anybody still play dice around here?" he called down the bar as the eyes of the regulars slid in our direction and then away again.

In those days—and this was ten years ago or more—the game of Horse was popular in certain California bars, as were smoking, unprotected sex, and various other adult pleasures that may or may not have been hazardous to your health. There were five dice, shaken in a cup, and you slammed that cup down on the bar, trying for the highest cumulative score, which was thirty. Anything could be bet on, from the next round of drinks to ponying up for the jukebox.

The rain hissed at the door and it opened briefly to admit a stamping, umbrellaless couple. Ludwig's question hung unanswered on the air. "No? How about you, Daria?"

"I can't—I'm working."

He turned to me. I had no work in the morning or the next morning, either—maybe no work at all. My apartment wasn't what I'd thought it would be, not without somebody to share it with, and I'd already vowed to myself that I'd rather sleep on the streets than go back to my aunt's, because going back there would represent the worst kind of defeat. *Take good care of my baby, Kim*, my mother had said when she dropped me off. *He's the only one I've got.*

"Sure," I said. "I guess. What're we playing for—for drinks, right?" I began fumbling in my pockets, awkward—I was drunk, I could feel it. "Because I don't have, well, maybe ten bucks—"

"No," he said, "no," already rising from his seat, "you just wait here, just one minute, you'll see," and then he was out the door and into the grip of the rain.

Daria hadn't moved. She was dressed in the standard outfit for Daggett's employees—shorts, white ankle socks, and a T-shirt with the name of the establishment blazoned across the chest, her legs pale and silken in the flickering light of the fake fireplace in the corner. She gave me a sympathetic look, and I shrugged to show her that I was ready for anything, a real man of the world.

There was a noise at the door—a scraping and shifting—and we all looked up to see Ludwig struggling with something there against the backdrop of the rain. His hat had been knocked askew and water dripped from his nose and chin. It took a moment, one shoulder pinning the door open, and then he lifted a cage—a substantial cage, two and a half feet high and maybe four feet long—through the doorway and set it down against the wall. No one moved. No one said a word. There was something in the cage, the apprehension of it as sharp and sudden as the smell it brought with it, something wild and alien and very definitely out of the ordinary on what to this point had been a painfully ordinary night.

Ludwig wiped the moisture from his face with a swipe of his sleeve, straightened out his hat, and came back to the bar, looking jaunty and refreshed. "All right," he said, "don't be shy—go have a look. It won't bite. Or it will, it definitely will, just don't get your fingers near it, that's all."

I saw coiled limbs, claws, yellow eyes. Whatever it was, the thing hadn't moved, not even to blink. I was going to ask what it was when Daria, still at my side, said, "It's a cat, some kind of wildcat, right? A what—a lynx or something?"

"You can't have that thing in here," one of the regulars said, but already he was getting up out of

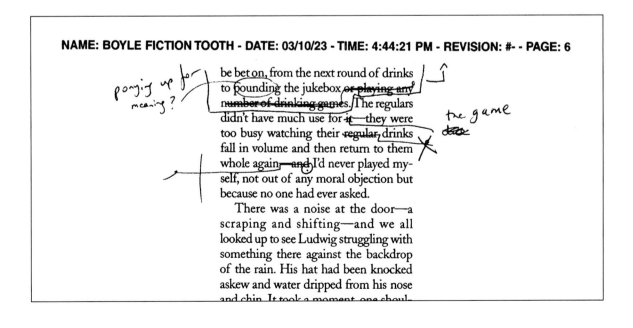

his seat to have a look at it—everyone was getting up now, shoving back chairs and rising from the tables, crowding around.

"It's a serval," Ludwig was saying. "From Africa. Thirty-five pounds of muscle and quicker than a snake."

And where had he got it? He'd won it, in a bar in Arizona, on a roll of the dice.

How long had he had it? Two years.

What was its name? Cat. Just Cat. And, yes, it was a male, and, no, he didn't want to get rid of it but he was moving overseas on a new job and there was just no way he could take it with him, so he felt that it was apropos—that was the word he used, "apropos"—to give it up in the way he'd got it.

He turned to me. "What was your name again?"

"Junior," I said. "James, Jr., Turner, I mean. James Turner, Jr. But everybody calls me Junior." I wanted to add, "Because of my father, so people

wouldn't confuse us," but I left it at that, because it got even more complicated considering that my father was six months dead and I could be anybody I wanted.

"O.K., Junior, here's the deal," Ludwig said. "Your ten bucks against the cat, one roll. What do you say?"

I wanted to say that I had no place for the thing, that I didn't want a cat of any kind or even a guinea pig or a fish in a bowl and that the ten dollars was meaningless, but everyone was watching me and I couldn't back out without feeling the shame rise to my face—and there was Daria to consider, because she was watching me, too. "Yeah," I said. "Yeah, O.K., sure."

Sixty seconds later, I was still solvent and richer by one cat and one cage. I'd got lucky—or unlucky, depending on how you want to look at it—and rolled three fives and two fours; Ludwig rolled a combined eleven. He finished his beer in a gulp, took my hand to seal the deal, and then

"Well, you don't look like an experimental psychologist to me."

started toward the door. "But what do I feed it?" I called. "I mean, what does it eat?"

"Eggs," he said. "It loves eggs. And meat. Raw. No kibble, forget kibble. This is the real deal, this animal, and you need to treat it right." He was at the door, looking down at the thing with what might have been wistfulness or satisfaction, I couldn't tell which, then he reached down behind the cage to unfasten something there—a gleam of black leather—and toss it to me: it was a glove, or a gauntlet, actually, as long as my arm. "You'll want to wear this when you feed him," he said, and then he was gone.

For a long moment, I stared at the door, trying to work out what had happened, and then I looked at the regulars—at the expressions on their faces—and at the other customers, locals or maybe even tourists, who'd come in for a beer or a burger or the catch of the day and had all this strangeness thrust on them, and finally at the cage. Daria was bent beside it, cooing to the animal inside, Ludwig's eggs cradled in one hand. She was short and compact, conventionally pretty, with the round eyes and symmetrical features of an anime heroine, her running shoes no bigger than a child's, her blond hair pulled back in a ponytail, and I'd noticed all that before, over the course of weeks of study, but now it came to me with the force of revelation. She was beautiful, a beautiful girl propped on one knee, while her shorts rode up in back and her T-shirt bunched beneath her breasts, offering this cat—my cat—the smallest comfort, as if it were a kitten she'd found abandoned on the street.

"Jesus, what are you going to do with the thing?" Chris had come out from behind the bar and he was standing beside me now, looking awed.

I told him that I didn't know. That I hadn't

planned on owning a wildcat, hadn't even known they existed—servals, that is—until five minutes ago.

"You live around here?"

"Bayview Apartments."

"They accept pets?"

I'd never really given it much thought, but they did, they must have—the guy next door to me had a pair of yapping little dogs with bows in their hair, and the woman down the hall had a Doberman that was forever scrabbling its nails on the linoleum when she came in and out with it, which she seemed to do about a hundred times a day. But this was something different. This was something that might push at the parameters of the standard lease. "Yeah," I said, "I think so."

There was a single slot where the door of the cage fastened that was big enough to receive an egg without crushing its shell, and Daria, still cooing, rolled first one egg, then the other, through the aperture. For a moment, nothing happened. Then the cat, hunched against the mesh, shifted position ever so slightly and took the first egg in its mouth—two teeth like hypodermics, a crunch, and then the soft frictive scrape of its tongue.

Daria rose and came to me with a look of wonder. "Don't do a thing till I get off, O.K.?" she said, and in her fervor she took hold of my arm. "I get off at nine, so you wait, O.K.?"

"Yeah," I said. "Sure."

"We can put him in the back of the storage room for now, and then, well, I guess we can use my pickup."

I didn't have the leisure to reflect on how complex things had become all of a sudden, and even if I had I don't think I would have behaved any differently. I just nodded at her, stared into her plenary eyes and nodded.

"He's going to be all right," she said, and

added, "He will," as if I'd been disagreeing with her. "I've got to get back to work, but you wait, O.K.? You wait right here." Chris was watching. The manager was watching. The regulars had all craned their necks and half the dinner customers, too. Daria patted down her apron, smoothed back her hair. "What did you say your name was again?"

So I had a cat. And a girl. We put the thing in the back of her red Toyota pickup, threw a tarp over it to keep the rain off, and drove to Vons, where I watched Daria march up and down the aisles seeking out kitty litter and the biggest cat pan they had (we settled for a dishpan, hard blue plastic that looked all but indestructible), and then it was on to the meat counter. "I've only got ten bucks," I said.

She gave me a withering look. "This animal's got to eat," she informed me, and she reached back to slip the band from her ponytail so that her hair fell glistening across her shoulders, a storm of hair, fluid and loose, the ends trailing down her back like liquid in motion. She tossed her head impatiently. "You do have a credit card, don't you?"

Ten minutes later, I was directing her back to my building, where she parked next to the Mustang I'd inherited when my father died, and then we went up the outside stairs and along the walkway to my apartment, on the second floor. "I'm sorry," I said, swinging open the door and hitting the light switch, "but I'm afraid I'm not much of a housekeeper." I was going to add that I hadn't expected company, either, or I would have straightened up, but Daria just strode right in, cleared a spot on the counter, and set down the groceries. I watched her shoulders as she reached into the depths of one bag after another and extracted the forty-odd dollars' worth of chicken

parts and rib-eye steak (marked down for quick sale) that we'd selected in the meat department.

"O.K.," she said, turning to me as soon as she'd made space in the refrigerator for it all, "now where are we going to put the cat, because I don't think we should leave it out there in the truck any longer than we have to, do you? Cats don't like the rain, I know that—I have two of them. Or one's a kitten, really." She was on the other side of the kitchen counter, a clutter of crusted dishes and glasses sprouting colonies of mold between us. "You have a bedroom, right?"

I did. But if I was embarrassed by the state of the kitchen and living room—this was my first venture at living alone, and the need for order hadn't really seemed paramount to me—then the thought of the bedroom, with its funk of dirty clothes and unwashed sheets, the reeking work-boots and the duffelbag out of which I'd been living, gave me pause. Here was this beautiful apparition in my kitchen, the only person besides my aunt who'd ever stepped through the door of my apartment, and now she was about to discover the sad, lonely disorder at the heart of my life. "Yeah," I said. "That door there, to the left of the bathroom." But she was already in the room, pushing things aside, a frown of concentration pressed between her eyes.

"You're going to have to clear this out," she said. "The bed, everything. All your clothes."

I was standing in the doorway, watching her. "What do you mean, 'clear it out'?"

She lifted her face. "You don't think that animal can stay caged up like that, do you? There's hardly room for it to turn around. And that's just cruel." She drilled me with that look again, then put her hands on her hips. "I'll help you," she said. "It shouldn't take ten minutes."

Then it was up the stairs with the cat, the two of us fighting the awkwardness of the cage.

We kept the tarp knotted tightly in place, both to keep the rain off the cat and to disguise it from any of my neighbors who might happen by, and, though we shifted the angle of the thing coming up the stairs, the animal didn't make a sound. We had a little trouble getting the cage through the doorway—the cat seemed to concentrate its weight as if in silent protest—but we managed, and then we maneuvered it into the bedroom and set it down in the middle of the rug. Daria had already arranged the litter box in the corner, atop several sheets of newspaper, and she'd taken my biggest stewpot, filled it with water, and placed it just inside the door, where I could get to it easily. "O.K.," she said, glancing up at me with a satisfied look, "it's time for the unveiling," and she bent to unfasten the tarp.

The overhead light glared, the tarp slid from the cage and puddled on the floor, and there was the cat, pressed to the mesh in a compression of limbs, its yellow eyes seizing on us. "Nice kitty," Daria cooed. "Does he want out of that awful cage? Hmm? Does he? And meat—does he want meat?"

So far, I'd gone along with everything in a kind of daze, but this was problematic. Who knew what the thing would do, what its habits were, its needs? "How are we going to—" I began, and left the rest unspoken. The light stung my eyes, and the alcohol whispered in my blood. "You remember what that guy said about feeding him, right?" In the back of my head, there was the smallest glimmer of a further complication: once he was out of the cage, how would we—how would I—ever get him back into it?

For the first time, Daria looked doubtful. "We'll have to be quick," she said.

And so we were. Daria stood at the bedroom door, ready to slam it shut, while I leaned forward, my heart pounding, and slipped the bolt on

Sign in front of a home in Van Nuys, California:

FOR SALE
SIAMESE CATS
BEAUTIFUL AND INTELLIGENT
THE CADILLAC OF CATS

| 1951 |

the cage. I was nimble in those days—twenty-three years old and with excellent reflexes despite the four or five Jack-and-Cokes I'd downed in the course of the evening—and I sprang for the door the instant the bolt was released. Exhilaration burned in me. It burned in the cat, too, because at the first click of the bolt it came to life as if it had been hot-wired. A screech tore through the room, the cage flew open, and the thing was an airborne blur slamming against the cheap plywood panel of the bedroom door, even as Daria and I fought to force it shut.

In the morning (she'd slept on the couch, curled up in the fetal position, faintly snoring; I was stretched out on the mattress we'd removed from the bedroom and tucked against the wall under the TV), I was faced with a number of problems. I'd awakened before her, jolted out of a dreamless sleep by a flash of awareness, and for a long while I just lay there watching her. I could have gone on watching her all morning, thrilled by her presence, her hair, the repose of her face, if it weren't for the cat. It hadn't made a sound, and it didn't stink, not yet, but its existence was communicated to me nonetheless—it was there, and I could feel it. I would have to feed it, and after the previous night's episode, that was going to require some thought and preparation, and I would have to offer Daria something, too, if only to hold her here a little longer. Eggs, I could scramble some

THE NEW YORKER

eggs, but there was no bread for toast, no milk, no sugar for the coffee. And she would want to freshen up in the bathroom—women always freshened up in the morning, I was pretty sure of that. I thought of the neatly folded little matching towels in the guest bathroom at my aunt's and contrasted that image with the corrugated rag wadded up on the floor somewhere in my own bathroom. Maybe I should go out for bagels or muffins or something, I thought—and a new towel. But did they sell towels at 7-Eleven? I didn't have a clue.

We'd stayed up late, sharing the last of the hot cocoa out of the foil packet and talking in a specific way about the cat that had brought us to that moment on the greasy couch in my semi-darkened living room and then more generally about our own lives and thoughts and hopes and ambitions. I'd heard about her mother, her two sisters, the courses she was taking at the university. Heard about Daggett's, the regulars, the tips—or lack of them. And her restaurant fantasy. It was amazingly detailed, right down to the number of tables she was planning on, the dinnerware, the cutlery, and the paintings on the walls, as well as the décor and the clientele—"Late twenties, early thirties, career people, no kids"—and a dozen or more of the dishes she would specialize in. My ambitions were more modest. I'd told her how I'd finished community college without any particular aim or interest, and how I was working setting tile for a friend of my aunt and uncle; beyond that, I was hoping to maybe travel up the coast and see Oregon. I'd heard a lot about Oregon, I told her. Very clean. Very natural up there. Had she ever been to Oregon? No, but she'd like to go. I remembered telling her that she ought to open her restaurant up there, someplace by the water, where people could look out and take in the view. "Yeah," she'd said,

"that'd be cool," and then she'd yawned and dropped her head to the pillow.

I was just getting up to see what I could do about the towel in the bathroom, thinking vaguely of splashing some aftershave on it to fight down any offensive odors it might have picked up, when her eyes flashed open. She didn't say my name or wonder where she was or ask for breakfast or where the bathroom was. She just said, "We have to feed that cat."

"Don't you want coffee or anything—breakfast? I can make breakfast."

She threw back the blanket and I saw that her legs were bare. She was wearing the Daggett's T-shirt over a pair of shiny black panties; her running shoes, socks, and shorts were balled up on the rug beneath her. "Sure," she said. "Coffee sounds nice." And she pushed her fingers through her hair on both sides of her head and then let it all fall forward to obscure her face. She sat there a moment before leaning forward to dig a hair clip out of her purse, arch her back, and pull the hair tight in a ponytail. "But I am worried about the cat, in new surroundings and all. The poor thing—we should have fed him last night."

Perhaps so. And I certainly didn't want to contradict her—I wanted to be amicable and charming, wanted to ingratiate myself in any way I could—but we'd both been so terrified of the animal's power in that moment when we'd released it from the cage that neither of us had felt up to the challenge of attempting to feed it. Attempting to feed it would have meant opening that door again, and that was going to take some thought and commitment. "Yeah," I said. "We should have. And we will, we will, but coffee, coffee first—you want a cup? I can make you a cup?"

So we drank coffee and ate the strawberry Pop-Tarts I found in the cupboard above the sink and made small talk as if we'd awakened together a hundred mornings running, and it was so tranquil and so domestic and so right I never wanted it to end. We were talking about work and about what time she had to be in that afternoon, when her brow furrowed and her eyes sharpened and she said, "I wish I could see it. When we feed it, I mean. Couldn't you, like, cut a peephole in the door or something?"

I was glad for the distraction, damage deposit notwithstanding. And the idea appealed to me: now we could see what the thing—my pet—was up to, and if we could see it then it wouldn't seem so unapproachable and mysterious. I'd have to get to know it eventually, have to name it and tame it, maybe even walk it on a leash. I had a brief vision of myself sauntering down the sidewalk, this id with claws at my side, turning heads and cowing the weight lifters with their Dobermans and Rottweilers, and then I fished my power drill out from under the sink and cut a neat hole, half an inch in diameter, in the bedroom door. As soon as it was finished, Daria put her eye to it.

"Well?"

"The poor thing. He's pacing back and forth like an animal in a zoo."

OH, GOSH! YOGA IN TWENTY MINUTES.

She moved to the side and took my arm as I pressed my eye to the hole. The cat flowed like molten ore from one corner of the room to the other, its yellow eyes fixed on the door, the dun, faintly spotted skin stretched like spandex over its seething muscles. I saw that the kitty litter had been upended and the hard blue plastic pan reduced to chewed-over pellets, and wondered about that, about where the thing would do its business if not in the pan. "It turned over the kitty pan," I said.

She was still holding my arm. "I know."

"It chewed it to shreds."

"Metal. We'll have to get a metal one, like a trough or something."

I took my eye from the peephole and turned to her. "But how am I going to change it—don't you have to change it?"

Her eyes were shining. "Oh, it'll settle down. It's just a big kitty, that's all"—and then for the cat, in a syrupy coo—"Isn't that right, kittums?" Next, she went to the refrigerator and extracted one of the steaks, a good pound and a half of meat. "Put on the glove," she said, "and I'll hold on to the doorknob while you feed him."

"What about the blood—won't the blood get on the carpet?" The gauntlet smelled of saddle soap and it was gouged and pitted down the length of it; it fit me as if it had been custom-made.

"I'll press the blood out with a paper towel—here, look," she said, dabbing at the meat in the bottom of the sink and then lifting it on the end of a fork. I took the fork from her and together we went to the bedroom door.

I don't know if the cat smelled the blood or if it heard us at the door, but the instant I turned the knob it was there. I counted three, then jerked the door back just enough to get my arm and the dangle of meat into the room even as the cat exploded against the doorframe and the meat vanished. We pushed the door to—Daria's face was flushed and she seemed to be giggling or gasping for air—and then we took turns watching the thing drag the steak back and forth across the rug as if it still needed killing. By the time the cat was done, there was blood everywhere, even on the ceiling.

After Daria left for work, I didn't know what to do with myself. The cat was ominously silent and when I pressed my eye to the peephole I saw that it had dragged its cage into the far corner and was slumped behind it, apparently asleep. I flicked on the TV and sat through the usual idiocy, which was briefly enlivened by a nature show on the Serengeti that gave a cursory glimpse of a cat like mine—"The serval lives in rocky kopjes, where it keeps a wary eye on its enemies, the lion and the hyena, feeding principally on small prey, rabbits, birds, even snakes and lizards," the narrator informed me in a hushed voice—and then I went to the sandwich shop and ordered the No. 7 special, no mayo, and took it down to the beach. It was a clear day, all the haze and particulate matter washed out of the air by the previous day's deluge, and I sat there with the sun on my face and watched the waves ride in on top of one another while I ate and considered the altered condition of my life. Daria's face had got serious as she stood at the door, her T-shirt rumpled, her hair pulled back so tightly from her scalp I could make out each individual strand. "Take care of our cat now, O.K.?" she said. "I'll be back as soon as I get off." I shrugged in a helpless, submissive way, the pain of her leaving as acute as anything I'd ever felt. "Sure," I said, and then she reached for my shoulders and pulled me to her for a kiss—on the lips. "You're sweet," she said.

So I was sweet. No one had ever called me sweet before, not since childhood, anyway, and I have to admit the designation thrilled me, bloomed inside me like the promise of things to come. I began to see her as a prime mover in my life, her naked legs stretched out on the couch, the hair falling across her shoulders at the kitchen table, her lips locked on mine. But as I sat there eating my ham-and-cheese wrap a conflicting thought came to me: there had to be someone in her life already, a girl that beautiful, working in a bar, and I was deluding myself to think I had a chance with her. She had to have a boyfriend—she could even be engaged, for all I knew. I tried to focus on the previous night, on her hands and fingers—had she been wearing a ring? And, if she had, then where was the fiancé, the boyfriend, whoever he was? I hated him already, and I didn't even know if he existed.

The upshot of all this was that I found myself in the cool subterranean glow of Daggett's at three-thirty in the afternoon, nursing a Jack-and-Coke like one of the regulars while Daria, the ring finger of her left hand as unencumbered as mine, cleared up after the lunch crowd and set the tables for the dinner rush. Chris came on at five, and he called me by my name and refreshed my drink before he even glanced at the regulars, and for the next hour or so, during the lulls, we conversed about any number of things, beginning with the most obvious—the cat—but veering into sports, music, books, and films, and I found myself expanding into a new place altogether. At one point, Daria stopped by to ask if the cat was settling in—Was he still pacing around neurotically or what?—and I could tell her with some assurance that he was asleep.

"He's probably nocturnal," I said, "or something like that." And then, with Chris looking on, I couldn't help adding, "You're still coming over, right? After work? To help me feed him, I mean."

She looked to Chris, then let her gaze wander out over the room. "Oh, yeah," she said, "yeah," and there was a catch of hesitation in her voice. "I'll be there."

I let that hang a moment, but I was insecure and the alcohol was having its effect and I couldn't leave it alone. "We can drive over together," I said, "because I didn't bring my car."

She was looking tired by the end of her shift, the bounce gone out of her step, her hair a shade duller under the drab lights, and even as I switched to coffee I noticed Chris slipping her a shot of something down at the end of the bar. I'd had a sandwich around six, and then, so as not to seem overanxious, I'd taken a walk, which brought me into another bar down the street, where I had a Jack-and-Coke and didn't say a word to anyone, and then I'd returned at eight to drink coffee and hold her to her promise.

We didn't say much on the way over to my place. It was only a five-minute drive, and there was a song on that we both liked. Plus, it seemed to me that when you were comfortable with someone you could respect the silences. I'd gone to the cash machine earlier and in a hopeful mood stocked up on breakfast things—eggs, English muffins, a quart each of no-fat and 2-percent milk, an expensive Chinese tea that came in individual foil packets—and I'd picked up two bottles of a local Chardonnay that was supposed to be really superior, or at least that was what the guy in the liquor department had told me, as well as a bag of corn chips and a jar of salsa. There were two new bathroom towels hanging on the rack beside the medicine cabinet, and I'd given the whole place a good vacuuming and left the dishes to soak in a sink of scalding water and the last few molecules of dish soap left in the plastic container I'd brought with me from my aunt's. The final touch was a pair of clean sheets and a light blanket folded suggestively over the arm of the couch.

Daria didn't seem to notice—she went straight to the bedroom door and affixed her eye to the peephole. "I can't see anything," she said, leaning into the door, the muscles of her calves flexing as she went up on her toes. "It's too bad we didn't think of a night-light or something."

I was watching her out of the corner of my eye—admiring her, amazed all over again at her presence—while working the corkscrew in the bottle. I asked her if she'd like a glass of wine. "Chardonnay," I said. "It's a local one, really superior."

"I'd love a glass," she said, turning away from the door and crossing the room to me. I didn't have wineglasses, so we made do with the milky-looking water glasses my aunt had dug out of a box in her basement. "I wonder if you could maybe slip your arm in the door and turn on the light in there," she said. "I'm worried about him. And, plus, we've got to feed him again, right?"

"Sure," I said, "yeah, no problem," but I was in no hurry. I refilled our glasses and broke out the chips and salsa, which she seemed happy enough to see. For a long while, we stood at the kitchen counter, dipping chips and savoring the wine, and then she went to the refrigerator, extracted a slab of meat, and began patting it down with paper towels. I took her cue, donned the gauntlet, braced myself, and jerked the bedroom door open just enough to get my hand in and flick on the light. The cat, which of course had sterling night vision, nearly tore the glove from my arm, and yet the suddenness of the light seemed to confuse it just long enough for me to salvage the situation. The door slammed on a puzzled yowl.

Daria immediately put her eye to the peephole. "Oh my God," she murmured.

"What's he doing?"

"Pacing. But here, you have a look."

The carpeting—every last strip of it—had been torn out of the floor, leaving an expanse of dirty plywood studded with nails, and there seemed to be a hole in the plasterboard just to the left of the window. A substantial hole. Even through the closed door I could smell the reek of cat piss or spray or whatever it was. "There goes my deposit," I said.

She was right there beside me, her hand on my shoulder. "He'll settle down," she assured me, "once he gets used to the place. All cats are like that—they have to establish their territory is all."

"You don't think he can get inside the walls, do you?"

"No," she said, "no way. He's too big."

The only thing I could think to do, especially after an entire day of drinking, was to pour more wine, which I did. Then we repeated the ritual of the morning's feeding—the steak on the fork, the

blur of the cat, the savage thump at the door—and took turns watching it eat. After a while, bored with the spectacle—or perhaps "sated" is a better word—we found ourselves on the couch and there was a movie on TV and we finished the wine and the chips and we never stopped talking, a comment on this movie leading to a discussion of movies in general, a reflection on the wine dredging up our mutual experiences of wine tastings and the horrors of Cribari red and Boone's Farm and all the rest. It was midnight before we knew it and she was yawning and stretching.

"I've really got to get home," she said, but she didn't move. "I'm wiped. Just wiped."

"You're welcome to stay over," I said, "I mean, if you don't want to drive, after the wine and all—"

A moment drifted by, neither of us speaking,

and then she made a sort of humming noise—"Mmm"—and held out her arms to me even as she sank down into the couch.

I was up before her in the morning, careful not to wake her as I eased myself from the mattress where we'd wound up sleeping because the couch was too narrow for the two of us. My head ached—I wasn't used to so much alcohol—and the effigy of the cat lurked somewhere behind that ache, but I felt buoyant and optimistic. Daria was asleep on the mattress, the cat was hunkered down in his room, and all was right with the world. I brewed coffee, toasted muffins, and fried eggs, and when she woke I was there to feed her. "What do you say to breakfast in bed?" I murmured, easing down beside her with a plate of eggs over easy and a mug of coffee.

I was so intent on watching her eat that I barely touched my own food. After a while, I got up and turned on the radio and there was that song again, the one we'd heard coming home the night before, and we both listened to it all the way through without saying a word. When the d.j. came on with his gasping juvenile voice and lame jokes, she got up and went to the bathroom, passing right by the bedroom door without a thought for the cat. She was in the bathroom a long while, running water, flushing, showering, and I felt lost without her. I wanted to tell her that I loved her, wanted to extend a whole list of invitations to her: she could move in with me, stay here indefinitely, bring her cats with her, no problem, and we could both look after the big cat together, see to its needs, tame it, and

"Never, ever, think outside the box."

make it happy in its new home—no more cages, and meat, plenty of meat. I was scrubbing the frying pan when she emerged, her hair wrapped in one of the new towels. She was wearing makeup and she was dressed in her Daggett's outfit. "Hey," I said.

She didn't answer. She was bent over the couch now, stuffing things into her purse.

"You look terrific," I said.

There was a sound from the bedroom then, a low moan that might have been the expiring gasp of the cat's prey, and I wondered if it had found something in there, a rat, a stray bird attracted to the window, an escaped hamster or lizard. "Listen, Junior," she said, ignoring the moaning, which grew higher and more attenuated now, "you're a nice guy, you really are."

I was behind the Formica counter. My hands were in the dishwater. Something pounded in my head, and I knew what was coming, heard it in her voice, saw it in the way she ducked her head and averted her eyes.

"I can't— I have to tell you something, O.K.? Because you're sweet, you are, and I want to be honest with you."

She raised her face to me all of a sudden, let her eyes stab at mine and then dodge away again. "I have a boyfriend. He's away at school. And I don't know why . . . I mean, I just don't want to give you the wrong impression. It was nice. It was."

The moaning cut off abruptly on a rising note. I didn't know what to say—I was new at this, new and useless. Suddenly I was desperate, looking for anything, any stratagem, the magic words that would make it all right again. "The cat," I said. "What about the cat?"

Her voice was soft. "He'll be all right. Just feed him. Be nice to him." She was at the door,

the purse slung over one shoulder. "Patience," she said, "that's all it takes. A little patience."

"Wait," I said. "Wait."

"I've got to go."

"Will I see you later?"

"No," she said. "No, I don't think so."

As soon as her pickup pulled out of the lot, I called my boss. He answered on the first ring, raising his voice to be heard over the ambient noise. I could hear the tile saw going in the background, the irregular banging of a hammer, the radio tuned to some jittery right-wing propagandist. "I want to come in," I said.

"Who is this?"

"Junior."

"Monday, Monday at the earliest."

I told him I was going crazy cooped up in my apartment, but he didn't seem to hear me. "What is it?" he said. "Money? Because I'll advance you on next week if you really need it, though it'll mean a trip to the bank I wasn't planning on. Which is a pain in the ass. But I'll do it. Just say the word."

"No, it's not the money, it's just—"

He cut me off. "Don't you ever listen to anything I say? Didn't I tell you to go out and get yourself laid? That's what you're supposed to be doing at your age. It's what I'd be doing."

"Can't I just, I don't know, help out?"

"Monday," he said.

I was angry suddenly and I slammed the phone down. My eyes went to the hole cut in the bedroom door and then to the breakfast plates, egg yolk congealing there in bright-yellow stripes, the muffin, Daria's muffin, untouched but for a single neat bite cut out of the round. It was Friday. I hated my life. How could I have been so stupid?

There was no sound from the bedroom, and as I laced my sneakers I fought down the urge to go to the peephole and see what the cat had accomplished in the night—I just didn't want to think about it. Whether it had vanished like a bad dream or chewed through the wall and devoured the neighbor's yapping little dogs or broken loose and smuggled itself onto a boat back to Africa, it was all the same to me. The only thing I did know was that there was no way I was going to attempt to feed that thing on my own, not without Daria there. It could starve, for all I cared, starve and rot.

Eventually, I fished a jean jacket out of a pile of clothes on the floor and went down to the beach. The day was overcast and a cold wind out of the east scoured the sand. I must have walked for hours and then, for lack of anything better to do, I went to a movie, after which I had a sandwich at a new place downtown where college students were rumored to hang out. There were no students there as far as I could see, just old men who looked exactly like the regulars at Daggett's, except that they had their square-shouldered old wives with them and their squalling unhappy children. By four I'd hit my first bar, and by six I was drunk.

I tried to stay away from Daggett's—*Give her a day or two*, I told myself. *Don't nag, don't be a burden*—but at quarter of nine I found myself at the bar, ordering a Jack-and-Coke from Chris. Chris gave me a look, and everything had changed since yesterday. "You sure?" he said.

I asked him what he meant.

"You look like you've had enough, buddy."

I craned my neck to look for Daria, but all I saw were the regulars, hunched over their drinks. "Just pour," I said.

The music was there like a persistent annoyance, dead music, ancient, appreciated by no one, not even the regulars. It droned on. Chris set down my drink and I lifted it to my lips. "Where's Daria?" I asked.

"She got off early. Said she was tired. Slow night, you know?"

I felt a stab of disappointment, jealousy, hate. "You have a number for her?"

Chris gave me a wary look, as if he knew something I didn't. "You mean she didn't give you her number?"

"No," I said. "We never—well, she was at my house . . ."

"We can't give out personal information."

"To me? I said she was at my house. Last night. I need to talk to her, and it's urgent—about the cat. She's really into the cat, you know?"

"Sorry."

I threw it back at him. "You're sorry? Well, fuck you—I'm sorry, too."

"You know what, buddy—"

"Junior, the name's Junior."

He leaned into the bar, both arms propped before him, and in a very soft voice he said, "I think you'd better leave now."

It had begun to rain again, a soft patter in the leaves that grew steadier and harder as I walked home. Cars went by on the boulevard with the sound of paper tearing, and they dragged whole worlds behind them. The street lights were dim. There was nobody out. When I came up the hill to my apartment, I saw the Mustang standing there under the carport, and though I'd always been averse to drinking and driving—a lesson I'd learned from my father's hapless example—I got behind the wheel and drove up to the job site with a crystalline clarity that would have scared me in any other state of mind. There was an aluminum ladder there, and I focussed on that—the picture of it lying against the building—until I arrived and hauled it out of the mud and tied it to the roof of the car, without a thought for the paint job or anything else.

When I got back, I fumbled in the rain with my overzealous knots until I got the ladder free and then I hauled it around back of the apartment building. I was drunk, yes, but cautious, too—if anyone had seen me, in the dark, propping a ladder against the wall of an apartment building, even my own apartment building, things could have got difficult in a hurry. I couldn't very well claim to be painting, could I? Not at night. Not in the rain. Luckily, though, no one was around. I made my way up the ladder, and when I got to the level of the bedroom the odor hit me, a rank fecal wind sifting out of the dark slit of the window. The cat. The cat was in there, watching me. I was sure of it. I must have waited in the rain for fifteen minutes or more before I got up the nerve to fling the window open, and then I ducked my head and crouched reflexively against the wall. Nothing happened. After a moment, I made my way down the ladder.

I didn't want to go into the apartment, didn't want to think about it, didn't know if a cat that size could climb down the rungs of a ladder or leap twenty feet into the air or unfurl its hidden wings and fly. I stood and watched the dense black hole of the window for a long while and then I went back to the car and sat listening to the radio in the dark until I fell asleep.

In the morning—there were no heraldic rays of sunshine, nothing like that, just more rain—I let myself into the apartment and crept across the room as stealthily as if I'd come to burgle it. When I reached the bedroom door, I put my eye to the peephole and saw a mound of carpet propped up against an empty cage—a den, a makeshift den—and only then did I begin to feel something for the cat, for its bewilderment, its fear and distrust of an alien environment: this was no rocky kopje, this was my bedroom on the second floor of a run-down apartment building in a seaside town a whole continent and a fathomless ocean away from its home. Nothing moved inside. Surely it must have gone by now, one great leap and then the bounding limbs, grass beneath its feet, solid earth. It was gone. Sure it was. I steeled myself, pulled open the door, and slipped inside. And then—and I don't know why—I pulled the door shut behind me.

| 2003 |

WET THURSDAY

A stiff wind off the channel
Linking the chimney's mutterings
With rain; the shaken trees,
Mile after mile, greening the sand.
Turn to the fire as the afternoon
Turns gray. Then, suddenly,
The locked door opens without sound,
Thunder shaking the sky, to usher in
A monstrous cat that seems
Far older than the oldest carp
In the waters under the earth,
Moving like a shadow over the floor
To warm its frozen paws
Before the fire. He turns,
Smiling into the woodbox,
And says, "*Felis libyca domestica*
They call me, kept by man for catching
Rats and mice. Of Eastern or
Egyptian origin. Now to be
Your spiteful and envenomed shadow. Here
Will I live out my nine and evil lives
Before your very interesting fire.
And the days, months, years, are endless."

Wind pounds along the coast.
The trees bend double to the sand.
The cat sleeps like an old campaigner
During this season of the long rains.

—WELDON KEES | 1948 |

BLUEBELL REGAINED

BRENDAN GILL

If, in the past, we've seemed partial to reports of the various kinds of misadventures that befall the human inhabitants of this city (what happens to a man who finds himself locked in an office building late at night, what happens to a couple marooned on a desert island in the East River), it isn't because we lack interest in the misadventures of the animal inhabitants. On the contrary, our curiosity about them mounts with every passing year, in proportion to our bewilderment at their managing to survive here at all. Surely, we've reasoned, if a city built by human beings for their own occupancy is so often a hazardous place for them to live in, it must be a hundred times more hazardous for dogs, cats, and other pets, who had no voice in designing the city and only dumbly consent to reside in it out of devotion to their masters. Yet how little we learn of the adventures, some with happy endings, others with sad, that the poor creatures go through! Had they the knack of speech, how instructive their reminiscences might be!

The above is by way of introducing what is, considering that it came from human beings, a fairly full account of an adventure that recently befell a cat named Bluebell. A three-year-old white cat who lives in Scarsdale but whose adventure took place on the upper East Side, Bluebell belongs to a girl named Jean, who is four years her senior and received her as a gift from the family butcher. Bluebell loves the cozy security of cars and often takes cat naps in them. Late the other afternoon, having spotted a secure-looking Oldsmobile outside a neighbor's house, she entered it through an open window and curled up on the back seat for a snooze. The car was owned by the neighbor's mother, who lives in New York but nearly always spends the day in Scarsdale. Her visit concluded, the lady got into the car and drove back to town, unaware of Bluebell on the back seat. She left the car in front of her apartment building, on East Seventy-ninth Street, between Lexington and Third. A garage attendant picked up the car that evening, and another attendant brought it around the next morning, in time for the day's run to

Scarsdale. As the lady got into the car, she noticed Bluebell on the back seat, awake this time and hungry. Assuming that Bluebell lived in the vicinity and had hopped into the car a few moments before, the lady shooshed her out onto the sidewalk. Bluebell, who had never thought of New York as a nice place to visit, much less live in, reluctantly gave in to being shooshed.

Meanwhile, Jean was desolate. She had first missed Bluebell about seven the previous evening, when the cat failed to show up for her evening meal. After a hasty search of the neighborhood, Jean had gone home, had drawn a picture of Bluebell, to show to strangers, and, accompanied by her mother, had undertaken a second, and more thorough, search. No Bluebell. The next afternoon, Bluebell still having failed to show up, Jean drew a better likeness of her and, with her mother, made a third desperate search. Again no Bluebell. Early the morning after that, the lady in New York telephoned; she had just heard from her daughter that the little girl next door had lost a white cat, and was it possible that . . . ? Jean and her mother thought it was. Armed with the two dishes from which Bluebell was accustomed to eat and drink, they drove straight to Seventy-ninth Street. All they had to go on was that a certain cat had been shooshed out of a certain car on a certain block at a certain hour the day before. Gallantly, they set off along Seventy-ninth Street, Jean showing her drawing of Bluebell to apartment-house doormen, delivery boys, and the like, and her mother rattling Bluebell's two dishes—a sound that had always brought her racing. They came on a doorman across the street who remembered seeing the white cat shooshed out of the car. To the best of his recollection, the cat had headed east, so Jean and her mother headed east, too. In the very next block, they met a doorman who had made friends the day before with a cat that looked like Jean's drawing of Bluebell. He had given the cat a saucer of milk at lunchtime and, when he went off duty at four, had handed her over to a friend of his who ran a fruit-and-vegetable store on the corner of Eighty-first Street and York Avenue and who loved cats.

Jean and her mother hurried to the fruit store. The proprietor said yes, he'd been given the cat by his friend the doorman—a nice cat, just like Jean's picture—and had passed her along to a lady customer. He didn't know the lady's name, but he was pretty sure of where she lived. He marched Jean and her mother up and down Eighty-first Street between First Avenue and York Avenue, a block that consists mostly of old brownstone cold-water flats. At an upper window of one of the brownstones, he recognized the face of a lady who, he told Jean, was a friend of the lady he had given the cat to. He shouted up to the lady to ask her where her friend lived, and the lady pointed to the house next door. Entering the house next door, Jean and her mother learned that a new cat was in residence on the fourth floor. Up they dashed to the fourth floor, knocked on a door, and, when the door was opened, beheld, in a cardboard box by a kerosene stove, the cynosure of five entranced children, Bluebell. "She's just eaten a mouse!" the chil-dren cried. Bluebell, who, as far as Jean and her mother knew, had never eaten anything less dainty than chopped kidneys in her life, was looking extremely pleased with herself. Jean's mother explained the situation to the mother of the five children and gave the children as much change as she could find in her purse to help assuage the pain of their loss. Then Jean bent down and gathered up Bluebell. From the moment she and her mother started looking for a lost cat in the midst of the biggest city on earth until the moment they found her, exactly fifty-eight minutes had elapsed.

| 1954 |

KIKIMORA

Fiction

JEAN RHYS

The bell rang. When Elsa opened the door, a small, fair, plump young man advanced, bowed, and said, "Baron Mumtael."

"Oh yes, please come in," said Elsa. She was aware that her smile was shy, her manner lacking in poise, for she had found his quick downward and upward glance intimidating. She led the way and asked him to sit down.

"What a very elegant dinner suit you are wearing," said Baron Mumtael mockingly.

"Yes, isn't it? . . . Oh, I don't think it is really," said Elsa distractedly. "I hate myself in suits," she went on, plunging deep into the scorn of his pale blue eyes.

"The large armchair is of course your husband's and the smaller one yours," said the Baron, quirking his mouth upward. "What a typical interior! Where shall I sit?"

"Sit wherever you like," said Elsa. "The interior is all yours. Choose your favorite bit." But his cold glance quelled her, and she added, twittering, "Will you . . . Do have a drink."

Bottles of whiskey, vermouth, and soda water stood on a red lacquered tray. "I'll have vermouth," said Baron Mumtael firmly. "No soda, thank you. And you?"

"A whiskey I think," Elsa said, annoyed that her hands had begun to shake with nervousness.

"How nice is ice on a hot afternoon in London. Are you . . . Have you lived in America?"

"No. Oh, no." She gulped her whiskey-and-soda quickly.

"Charming," said Baron Mumtael, watching her maliciously. "Charming. I'm so glad you're not an American. I think some American women are a menace, don't you? The spoilt female is invariably a menace."

"And what about the spoilt male?"

"Oh the spoilt male can be charming. No spoiling, no charm."

"That's what I always say," said Elsa eagerly. "No spoiling, no charm."

"No," said Baron Mumtael. "None. None at all. Will your husband be long, do you think?"

"I think not. I think here he is."

After Stephen came in, the tension lessened. Baron Mumtael stopped fidgeting and settled down to a serious discussion of the politics of his native land, his love of England, and his joy at having at last become a naturalized Englishman.

Elsa went out of the room to put the finishing touches to the meal. It was good, she thought. He would have to appreciate it. And indeed, the first time he addressed her, after they sat down, he said, "What delicious food. I congratulate you."

"It all came from various shops in Soho," Elsa lied.

"Really delicious. And that picture fascinates me. What is it supposed to be?"

"Paradise."

A naked man was riding into a dark-blue sea. There was a sky to match, palm trees, a whale in one corner, and a butterfly in the other. "Don't you like it?" she asked.

"Well," said Baron Mumtael, "I think it's colorful. It was painted by a woman, I feel sure."

"No, it was painted by a man," said Elsa. "He said he put in the whale and the butterfly because everything has its place in Paradise."

"Really," said Baron Mumtael. "I shouldn't have thought so. One can only hope not. Please tell me which shop in Soho supplied the guinea fowl and really delicious sautéed potatoes."

"I've forgotten," said Elsa vaguely. "Somewhere around Wardour Street or Greek Street. I'm so bad at remembering where places are. Of course you have to fry the potatoes up with on-

"The fact that you cats were considered sacred in ancient Egypt cuts no ice with me."

ions and then you get something like *pommes lyonnaises*."

But Baron Mumtael had already turned away and was continuing his conversation with Stephen about the next war. He gave it three months. (It was 1938 and he wasn't far wrong.)

The black cat, Kikimora, who had been sitting quietly in the corner of the room, sprang onto his lap. The Baron looked surprised, stroked the animal cautiously, then sprang up and said, "My God! She's scratched me, quite badly." And indeed there was blood on the finger he was holding up.

"I can't think what's come over him," Elsa said. "I've never known him do such a thing before. He's so staid as a rule. You naughty, bad cat." She snatched him up and flung him outside the door. "I'm so very sorry."

"Elsa spoils that cat," Stephen said.

"I think," said Baron Mumtael, "that something ought to be done about my finger. You can't be too careful about the scratches of a she-cat. If you'd be so kind as to let me have some disinfectant?"

"He's not a she-cat, he's a he-cat," said Elsa.

"Really," said Baron Mumtael. "Can you let me have some disinfectant? That is, if you have any," he added.

"I've got Lysol and peroxide of hydrogen," said Elsa belligerently, repeated whiskeys having given her courage. "Which will you have?"

"My *dear* Elsa . . ." said Stephen.

She left them and locked herself in the bathroom. When she came back, Baron Mumtael was still holding his finger up, talking politics.

"I haven't forgotten the cotton wool," she said.

At last the finger was disinfected and a spotless white handkerchief wrapped round it. "One can't be too careful with a she-cat," Baron Mumtael kept repeating. And Elsa, breathing deeply,

would always answer, "He's not a she-cat, he's a he-cat."

"Goodbye," said Baron Mumtael as he left. "I shall never forget your charming evening's entertainment. Or your so very elegant dinner suit. It's been quite an experience. All so typical."

As soon as he was out of the door Elsa said, "What a horrible man!"

"I didn't think so," Stephen said. "I thought he was rather a nice chap. It's a relief to meet somebody who doesn't abuse the English."

"Abuse the English?" said Elsa. "He'd never abuse the English. It must be comforting to be able to take out naturalization papers when you find your spiritual home."

"You hardly shone," Stephen said.

"Of course I shone. He brought out all my sparkle. He was so nice, wasn't he?"

"I didn't notice that he wasn't nice," said Stephen.

"No. You wouldn't," Elsa muttered.

She went into the kitchen, caught up the cat and began to kiss it. "My darling cat. My darling black velvet cat with the sharp claws. My angel, my little gamecock. . . ."

Kikimora purred and even licked a tear off her face with his rough tongue. But when he struggled and she put him down he yawned elaborately and walked away.

Elsa went to the bedroom, took off the suit she had been wearing, and with the help of a pair of scissors began to tear it up. Stephen heard the rending noise and called out, "What on earth are you doing?"

"I'm destroying my feminine charm," Elsa said. "I thought I'd make a nice quick clean job of it."

| 1976 |

OLD WOMAN

Fiction

IVY LITVINOV

To most people the Miss Gullivers seemed the same age. One of them was known to be older than the other, but which only the insurance man knew. They weren't so very old—not seventy or eighty or anything like that. Sixty something, you know, going on for seventy. Old ladies. And they weren't so very much alike, really. One had light-blue eyes and prominent teeth and the other wore spectacles and had a mole on her chin, but people bestowed Miss Jessica's teeth on Miss Madge or Miss Madge's mole on Miss Jessica in the most callous manner and still could not remember which was which. Nobody ever looked at them longer than it took to register: "The Miss Gullivers," or if either of them was met separately: "I saw one of the Miss Gullivers in the post office this morning." Even a distant relative who lived in Huddersfield did not know one from the other, and when, on one of her infrequent visits to London, she knocked at the door of her cousins' house was liable to say indiscriminately, whichever opened to her knock, "You get more and more like Jessica every day."

It had not always been like this with the Miss Gullivers. They had been Jessie and Maddie to their father and mother, and nobody ever forgot that Jessie was the elder. All through their childhood Jessie was the clever one and Maddie the good one, the sunny-natured. When they went on errands and later to day school, it was always Jessie who chose the side streets to be taken and Maddie who had to follow, with rage in her heart, and when it was Maddie who asked, "May we paint?" or "May we play with plasticine?" the choice was always Jessie's. It was Jessie who chose the books at the library, and Maddie had to read

Little Women and *Eric or Little by Little* when what she really would have liked was *Black Beauty*.

There was even an air of ambiguity about the Miss Gullivers' cat, for though ten years old, Nelson had the spurious youthfulness that dependence on others and constant petting sometimes give to the aged. And why should a rich tab of matronly appearance be called Nelson and yet be invariably referred to as "she"? Nelson had come into the world on Trafalgar Day in a set of five kittens, all reported by the milkman to be boys and distributed among friends and acquaintances on that understanding. When, almost simultaneously, they produced five kittens apiece, there was consternation in five London households. Nelson had two families in little over a year and the Miss Gullivers felt they could not face a lifetime of finding homes for kittens every few months. But the prospect of periodical massacres of the innocents appalled their cat-compassionate hearts, and the milkman, called in for consultation, advised them to send Nelson to the vet. After much heartburning this was done, half a crown extra being paid for an anesthetic, and Nelson came back insured against kittens. Till then she had been as playful as a kitten herself, but she soon fell into staid dozing ways, scarcely looking up when a ping-pong ball was bounced under her nose and turning disdainfully from her clockwork mouse. And yet her mistresses had their work cut out to keep her away from the goldfish bowl, and she would sit for hours on the windowsill gazing at the sparrows flitting in the branches of the old sycamore tree in the yard, untucking her folded paws now and again and fidgeting uneasily. A curved breast feather poised on the carpet, a speck of slowly wavering fluff in the air aroused sleeping reflexes, and Miss Jessica and Miss Madge would cling to one another when their idol leaped from her statuesque repose to lunge at the fluff in midair, or pounce stiff-legged on the rocking feather. But her predatory instincts were moribund; she never again brought a dead bird or a quivering mass of frog to lay at the feet of her mistresses.

Nelson soon lost the delicious greed her slaves had ministered to with such joyous ardor. She never seemed to have an appetite, and the infrequent visitor who happened in while Nelson was being coaxed to eat was admitted by Miss Jessica (or was it Miss Madge?) with a finger held to her parted lips, while Miss Madge (if it was not Miss Jessica) might be discovered with her knitting held rigid on her knees. Looking round, the visitor saw nothing but a cat lapping cream

"Dolly—Gregory Strong, author of 'A World History of Cats.' Need I say more?"

from the far side of a saucer on the floor. Only when it turned away, languidly licking its chops, and sprang powerfully up to the top of the sofa, did Miss Jessica (or perhaps Miss Madge) move a chair for the visitor, explaining with a deprecatory smile that the least thing put Nelson off her feed.

The fourth member of this not so jocund company was Silver, the minnow. The leaden-stepping hours paid out in seconds by the grandfather clock in the drawing room ground the wrinkles ever deeper into the Miss Gullivers' faces and even seemed to weigh upon Nelson's more resilient frame. But what has the heavy plummet's pace to do with a two-inch minnow darting a million million times from its tiny thicket of waterweeds, plunging back again just when it seemed it must stub its blunt nose against the side of the bowl? Silver's eye remained firmly protuberant, no crow's-feet marred the surface of its shining armor, its taut contours were immune to the flabbiness of age. Visitors sometimes expressed surprise that the Miss Gullivers did not keep a budgerigar. A bird would be no less suited than a fish to coexistence with a cat, and would surely be a more rewarding pet. But Silver had been "sent" to them, left by an unknown hand in a jam jar on the back doorstep, and they had not had the heart to send him back. Besides, where was there to send him? So they brought the jar in and set it on the scullery floor. Nelson was on the spot immediately, though, just before, they had searched the house for her in vain. Fascinated, they watched her dip her paw into the jar, with-

Overheard on the fringe of Gramercy Park, smartly costumed mother to teen-age daughter: "You must understand, dear, that we're not the sort of people who give clever names to cats."

| 1963 |

draw it sharply, and shake off a few chill drops. She licked perfunctorily at the pads under her claws, never removing her arch, ferocious gaze from the tiny silver boomerang in the jar. The second time the paw went deeper into the water and came out loaded, but the moment the harsh air entered the minnow's gill chambers it shot upward and dropped like a stone back into the jar. Nelson made another tentative dab at the surface of the water, but a tiny jet splashing up and falling in a drop on her nose seemed to discourage her. Annoyed and puzzled (Miss Jessica and Miss Madge knew and could interpret all Nelson's expressions), she drew her paw toward her for a short, sharp lick, set it down daintily, and minced out of the scullery. Miss Jessica made the revolting suggestion that the minnow should be boiled for Nelson's tea, but Miss Madge knew she didn't mean it. She had said it just to tease her sister. Miss Madge understood this from the way Miss Jessica picked up the jar and shooed Nelson (who had come back again and was looking on with blazing eyes) into the back yard.

Silver was housed in a fishbowl that Miss Madge recovered from a hatbox in the attic. The sisters remembered this bowl with unexpressed remorse. It had been the prison of three goldfish, the consolation of their bedridden mother's last years. All three had died soon after her funeral, because neither of the sisters (younger then and so heartless) could see why *she* should be the one to feed them.

Miss Madge sat long on the floor of the attic, gazing with brimming eyes into the glass bowl between her hands. Through its side she could see the shiny black wall of the hatbox, narrower at the bottom, spreading gracefully upward, like a lily, or like an inverted top hat. It had indeed once contained a top hat, and the pad of green plush used to smooth its glossy sides still lay in tissue paper at the bottom. The hat had been their father's, the very symbol of his dignity, only taken out for weddings and funerals, or for periodical inspection. The box stood under the marital bed long after Father's death, but when Mother died Miss Jessica had taken it and sent the topper to a jumble sale. Guy Fawkes Day was the only day in the year that one of the Miss Gullivers went out shopping alone, the other staying at home with Nelson, the windows shut and the curtains drawn—the popping rockets and raucous cries played havoc with Nelson's nerves and they did not like to leave her alone in the house. On Guy Fawkes Day Miss Madge was sure she had seen Father's top hat balanced over a ghastly white face borne past her on trundling wheels. Later in the day she had come upon an abandoned go-cart at the corner of the public house. In it was a sagging figure with a top hat jammed over its face. That night she had dreamed confused jack-in-the-box dreams, of Punch, of Judy, of the dog Toby, and a limp figure flung down down into blackness. And now she sat on the attic floor with the bowl on her knees, and remembered how her father had always loved her the best, how she and Jessie had giggled and kissed and quarrelled, but Jessie always had her own way about everything. . . . And how life was passing and nothing had ever really happened to either of them.

Silver was in greater danger of being overcherished than neglected. Miss Madge attended to him more closely than his primitive needs required, ever fancying he looked hungry or his water needed changing. Miss Jessica insisted on training the light from an electric bulb over the bowl for two hours every day, having read that fish required ultraviolet rays. Miss Madge was afraid the glare would give Silver a headache and bought a blue bulb of immense power. The poetry of life was never quite dead for Miss Madge: to stand and stare gave her a satisfaction of which she was almost ashamed. (She was one of the few women who could watch a baby at play without longing to pick it up.) Once, she had come back from early-morning church to find that the wild iris in a bottle on the windowsill had freed itself from its sheaf; if she had not gone to church she might have witnessed the final click as the delicately sprung petals were released. The thought almost made her hate the vicar. She would release a fly from the toils of golden syrup and watch for an hour its herculean efforts to scrape the cloying film to the edge of its wings in tiny beads, which fell one at a time onto the table. And she never wearied of watching the water sift through the filaments of Silver's subtly articulated tail.

Silver was the only fish in the house, but otherwise his hold on identity was slight. His sex was bestowed on him firmly from the very beginning, but there was nobody to vouch for it. He might just as well have been a girl-fish. And then one day a small boy came to the back door with another minnow, in a Crosse & Blackwell jar. He explained that it was he who had left Silver on the back doorstep, and now he had brought another to keep him company. The Miss Gullivers were positively excited at this idea and the transfer from jam jar to fishbowl was expeditiously made under the keenly interested eyes of Nelson before you could say knife. Miss Jessica gave the little boy majestic permission to come the next day and see how the minnows were getting on. She even gave him a biscuit and watched him out of sight.

Back in the drawing room she found Miss Madge and Nelson in a state of agitation. The new minnow was floating belly up in the fishbowl and Silver was swimming serenely to and fro in the middle depths. Victorious Silver! He would

"I've done it again."

ment Silver entered the charmed circle of ambiguity. Was he, or was he not, really Silver? The Miss Gullivers put all doubts resolutely from them, but in their hearts they were never *quite* sure.

Silver brought fresh complications into the lives of the Miss Gullivers, each of whom lived in perpetual anxiety lest the other should have left the drawing-room door open. And even when one of them was in the room, even when they were both there, they had to keep a sharp lookout in case Nelson jumped on the windowsill. Nelson's very presence there was enough to set Silver darting frenetically to the bottom of the bowl, and once they had only just been in time to pull the terrible hooked paw out of the water.

Each morning the Miss Gullivers set out for a row of shops parallel to Jocelyn Terrace, where they lived, to do the shopping for themselves and their pensioners. It made no difference whether they turned down Budd Street, Lupin Street, or Caitlin Place, since their house was in the middle of the Terrace. Miss Jessie did not mind which of the three side streets they took so long as it was not the one preferred by her sister. If Miss Madge took a tentative step toward Budd Street, Miss Jessie marched resolutely on to Lupin Street. At the subtlest indication that Miss Madge intended to stop at the traffic light, Miss Jessica would turn and cross the road the other way, and Miss Madge, tense with frustration, would follow. After Miss Madge had come back from a whole month in hospital, she did think Miss Jessie would allow her an invalid's privilege. But no,

not tolerate a rival in his realm. The Miss Gullivers were sorry for the poor stranger, of course, but gave him to Nelson to play with. And they were sorry to have to tell the little boy the new minnow was dead. They allowed him to come into the drawing room again, whereupon he staunchly declared that the minnow swimming triumphantly out of the weeds was the new minnow—he knew every spot on its body. According to this horrid boy, it was Silver who had been routed, killed by the newcomer and played with and subsequently eaten by Nelson. Nothing could convince the Miss Gullivers of this; they, too, knew every spot on their minnow's body. Miss Madge even knew his different expressions and could see when he was tired or out of spirits by the changing rhythms of his fins. From that mo-

Miss Jessica waited as usual for her sister almost to turn the corner into Caitlin Place and then stalked on to Lupin Street, sure of being followed. Then let her! thought Miss Madge, and trudged stubbornly along the pavement of Caitlin Place. From this day they had gone to the shops along different streets, and there was a new problem: to anticipate each other's choice, never to be trapped into the semblance of surrender. Usually they met unsmiling outside the pet shop or the butcher's, but sometimes they stopped in their tracks, simultaneously visited by the harrowing apprehension that they had forgotten to shut the drawing-room door. They would have been saved this agony if one of them had stayed at home, or they could have gone shopping on alternate days, but their jealous ardor made this impossible.

To indifferent eyes, the passage of the years left no traces of change in the sisters, and none but indifferent eyes ever rested on Miss Jessie or Miss Madge now. Increasing deafness, failing eyesight, asthmatic breathing, absentmindedness almost amounting to amnesia are taken for granted in the old. The tremor of the hand, the tic that sets the head a-bobbing were noted by few, and even when noted were undifferentiated. Was it Miss Jessie whose left hand shook and Miss Madge whose head kept nodding, or was the one whose hand shook Miss Madge and . . . And— Oh, shut up, can't you?, people said before these speculations were completed.

Miss Madge was the first to go (that month in hospital). She had no illness, was not a day in bed, but one afternoon when they were seated in silence with their needlework beside the fire and Miss Jessica had begun to wonder if it wasn't time to put the kettle on, Miss Madge let her work drop on her knees and said very faintly, "Jessie."

And that was all. Nelson began jumping onto Miss Madge's knee and down again, mewing, and almost the first thing Miss Jessica had had to do was to carry her out of the room. Resting her withered cheek on the warm, domed head, she thought, No one will ever call me Jessie again. The absurd—almost blasphemous in the circumstances—question arose in her mind: What would Nelson call me if she could speak?

Miss Jessica wept when she saw Miss Madge looking so calm and beautiful laid out amidst spring flowers on her bed. But when the thought visited her: Who will cry when I am dead?, she sobbed.

And one morning Nelson was found stretched on her side on the drawing-room hearth, the tip of her tongue showing between clenched teeth. Miss Jessica had a slight stroke the next day. Through all this death and devastation, Silver mounted his watery treadmill as if defying time and death to catch him up.

Miss Jessica's stroke left her much as usual but for a kind of landslide from her left eyebrow to the point of her chin. The cousin came up from Huddersfield, solicitors were consulted, and the house and most of the furniture were sold. Only the grandfather clock turned out to be of any value, and it was snapped up as a period piece by a prowling American the moment it made its appearance in a Fulham shopwindow. A seaside cottage was found for Miss Jessica and furnished with the comfortable armchair, the bed, and the drawing-room carpet, and other unsold pieces. Mrs. Yorke next door promised to keep an eye on Miss Jessica, and soon a new Nelson came into her life. He had turned up on Miss Jessica's doorstep one morning, in sad plight after a night of storm during which a ship went down with all hands in full sight of the cliffs. The romantic view was taken that the cat had been sent to console her in her loneliness. Nobody knew what Miss Jessica herself thought about it, but she gave the name of Nelson to the stranger—a half-grown tom, black, with an ample shirtfront and one white paw. It was too strenuous for such an old lady to be always keeping an active cat away from the fishbowl, and Silver had to be given to two little boys who were staying with their parents at Mrs. Yorke's next door. A cat was more company than a minnow, after all, and Miss Jessica had never been so devoted to Silver as had Miss Madge. When the visitors returned to town they left Silver behind, and their landlady's husband took the bowl down to the edge of the sea and tipped him into an outgoing wave, where he died immediately.

Miss Jessica was no longer known by her Christian name, or by any name at all. The fisher people called her "the old 'oman next to Mrs. Yorke's" and the boy from the village shop left her groceries with Mrs. Yorke's order, saying, "The eggs and the golden syrup is for the old 'oman." Miss Jessica lived quietly through the winter, and Nelson grew into a fine, purring cat. When summer came round again, seaside visitors stroked the black pussy seated so proudly under its own rooftree, and a small girl whose father and mother brought her to live at Mrs. Yorke's for the summer took to sitting on Miss Jessica's porch step to fondle Nelson and chat with the old lady. People saw Miss Jessica's lips moving and little Pattie looking into her face, nodding gravely and stammering out shrill, half-inarticulate phrases, and wondered what the two could be talking about. Pattie's father, who had exhibited in the Royal Academy ten years before, did a picture of the porch with Pattie seated at the old woman's feet—only you couldn't see their faces properly and Nelson wasn't there at all. They forgot to send Pattie in to say goodbye when they went

back to town in the autumn, and by next summer Miss Jessica was dead and her cottage taken by a family from London.

"A pity," said Pattie's mother. "It would have just suited us. We ought to have gone round and said goodbye to the poor old thing." Pattie's father was sorry, too; he had hoped to go on with his picture and send it to the Royal Academy. But Pattie burst into tears. "Why did she die?" she asked, looking up wildly. "I didn't want her to be died."

| 1973 |

ELECTRICAL STORM

Dawn an unsympathetic yellow.
Cra-aack!—dry and light.
The house was really struck.
Crack! A tinny sound, like a dropped tumbler.
Tobias jumped in the window, got in bed—
silent, his eyes bleached white, his fur on end.
Personal and spiteful as a neighbor's child,
thunder began to bang and bump the roof.
One pink flash;
then hail, the biggest size of artificial pearls.
Dead-white, wax-white, cold—
diplomats' wives' favors
from an old moon party—
they lay in melting windrows
on the red ground until after sunrise.
We got up to find the wiring fused,
no lights, a smell of saltpetre,
and the telephone dead.

The cat stayed in the warm sheets.
The Lent trees had shed all their petals:
wet, stuck, purple, among the dead-eye pearls.

—ELIZABETH BISHOP | 1960 |

May 11, 1968

THE NEW YORKER

Price 35 cents

W. Steig

from GETTING THROUGH TO THE OTHERS

EMILY HAHN

In a collection of papers written by various experts in the field of what Professor Thomas A. Sebeok, of Indiana University, has called "zoosemiotics"—in other words, animal communication—each writer tries valiantly to define what he means by the term, and, if no two of them actually agree on a definition, at least they provide a most stimulating lot of theories. As Professor Sebeok himself tells us, "speech is the principal, but by no means the only, mechanism whereby communities are knit into social organizations via a systematic flow of messages exchanged over interpersonal communication channels." There are other mechanisms, he points out: such "sensory modalities" as auditory and visual signals, touch, smell, taste, even temperature signals. Gulls communicate with each other by means of postures and movements as well as calls. The male American alligator roars to attract the female, but she is also attracted by the fountain of water sent up by the roars, and by a musky smell from the glands in his mouth. The more I have read about the subject, the less I have felt I knew. In search of really practical ideas about animal communication, I have turned to zoos and the people who work in them.

At the Arizona-Sonora Desert Museum, in Tucson, which houses creatures indigenous to the region, I asked my questions of Charles L. Hanson, curator of birds and mammals. "There are lots of things we don't understand about animal signals," he admitted. We were sitting in a pleasant office surrounded by low-lying shrubs and here and there a tree. A pair of small ferrets were making free with the place, running about, wrestling with each other, and sometimes taking mock refuge in the

298

bookcases. They emitted shrill, tiny squeaks, like rusty machinery, as they boxed and scampered. Facing Dr. Hanson across another desk sat the zoo's curator of education, Doris Ready. Every so often, she had to stop listening to the conversation to answer a telephoned inquiry about school visits or publications. "Why animals react as they sometimes do to strangers is a puzzle," said Hanson. "I know there are criticisms of observations made in a zoo, on the ground that the situation is so artificial that such observations have no validity. I don't think that's true. Even in an artificial situation, the animals still reflect intelligence levels, communication levels, and behavioral patterns that are characteristic and valid, and these should be given serious consideration, because, after all, they simply cannot be made in the wild. It's the only opportunity we have to document. I think most people are beginning more to accept such knowledge. When we see the relation between bobcat and human being here, for instance, there's no reason to suppose that it differs radically from communication between bobcat and bobcat in the wild. Certainly we shouldn't just ignore it, though the interpretation, of course, is always open to question. I must admit that here at the museum we are emotionally involved with our animals, and such involvement precludes objectivity. Even so, the observations themselves are valid. Interpretations by other people are quite all right as long as one doesn't throw out the material."

We talked for a while about relationships between animals in captivity—between animal and animal as well as between animal and man. Doris Ready told me that she had raised at her home a kit fox, one of the little animals that live in the western deserts. The fox, a female, has lived in the house ever since she was very small, and has made one or two strange friendships in the process, the most familiar one being with the Ready cat.

"An ordinary house cat?" I asked.

"Yes, just a cat. When the fox was only a few weeks old and the cat was about a year and a half, they met for the first time. I wasn't at all sure of the cat's reaction, so I held on to him while the fox investigated, and then I held the fox so the cat could relax, and after a while it seemed safe to let them both go. For a while—I forget how long, exactly—nothing happened, but one day when they were both out in the yard, all of a sudden the fox began doing her thing behind a bush—dodging and posturing, ears laid back, making a kind of giggling sound. Then the cat jumped into the air and started playing like a kitten, chasing the fox, and that was just what the fox wanted. They played around like that all over the place. Sometimes they chased each other in the house, fox after cat. Then the fox finally began the grooming thing, starting to nibble, nibble, nibble on the cat, and the cat didn't care for it at all. He kept backing away."

Hanson explained to me, "Kit foxes' teeth are admirably constructed for grooming. The muzzle is quite long, and at the tip are the small front teeth they use in the exercise. They love to groom each other."

Mrs. Ready took up her story. "Well, the fox kept doing it, and then one day—I don't remember just when it was—the cat started grooming the fox back. Nowadays when the cat doesn't feel like it he just walks off. Other times, they groom each other for as much as ten or fifteen minutes. Sometimes you have a wet fox and a wet cat. They take turns: after the fox has groomed for a while, she seems to feel it's her turn, and she stands there sort of leaning toward the cat with her eyes half closed."

"The only time the cat objects is when the fox starts grooming his ears," Hanson said. "But she can't be stopped. It's an important part of the kit fox's social behavior. I told Michael Fox about it. You know who he is, don't you? The man who studies canine-and-cat behavior. Well, I told him about this unusual intergeneric social behavior, and he was interested. It didn't really surprise him, though. He said a kit fox is so extroverted and so social that if you deprived it all other animal association it would even groom an elephant."

"We had another weird combination of friendships," Mrs. Ready said ruminatively. "We had a black vulture that we raised from an egg. When it was about half grown, I tried to introduce it to the cat, and the cat split. It wasn't seen again for the rest of the day. But the fox took to the vulture right away, and they would chase each other back and forth, back and forth. The fox always initiated the play, and I'm not sure if the vulture really enjoyed it. It's hard to tell. A vulture doesn't have quite as expressive a face as a fox has."

"A kit fox can relate to absolutely anything," declared Hanson. "For that reason, one subspecies, the San Joaquin Valley kit fox, is an endangered animal. It thinks the whole world is its friend."

"Except one animal," said Doris Ready. "I once brought home a skunk and put it on the floor, and the fox walked right by as if it weren't there. All the animals ignored that skunk."

"Sure," said Hanson. "The skunk wears a flash pattern, black and white, that says 'Avoid,' and all other animals do avoid it—except the domestic dog. I guess that sort of caution has been bred out of dogs—which is inconvenient sometimes. Maybe you could cross kit foxes with cocker spaniels and come up with dogs that would avoid skunks. You haven't seen Mike Fox's project yet—the crosses he's made between coyotes and beagles. They've produced some strange animals: some pups look like beagles and act like coyotes, and some look like coyotes and act like beagles. Some are beagles with ears that stand up, others are coyotes with drooping ears. He certainly got some bizarre-looking animals. Of course, he isn't breeding them for looks but to study the genetics of behavior, behavioral anomalies, hy-

brid characteristics. Do you know that the coyote has been bred in captivity and is sometimes sold in pet shops? It happens, especially around here, which is too bad, as only an exceptional adult coyote can be handled by man. Among these crosses of Michael Fox's, some are quite beagle-like in their relationships with man, but others develop coyote characteristics as they get older."

Doris Ready brought the subject back to her kit fox, saying that, although it was indeed ordinarily very affectionate, it had different reactions to different people, and was well aware of the identity of various callers at the house. "She likes the human beings she's known since she was a little bitty baby, but with new people it's as if she makes up her mind on sight. She takes an instant dislike to some, who don't seem to relate very well to animals. Sometimes she nips their ankles. But my mother, who, as a matter of fact, isn't usually very good with animals, is a great favorite with her. You wonder what it is—how it is that animals happen to like certain people, don't you?"

"It's an interesting thing," Hanson agreed. "What clues do the higher animals use to relate to a human being? As you say, Doris, it isn't necessarily the person's attitude. I'm convinced of that. It can't be a matter of smell, either. It used to be thought that animals might be turned off by the adrenalin pumping in a frightened or worried human being, because it produced an olfactory clue that the animal might pick up and would interpret as a sign of anger or fear, but you sometimes see an animal take a great liking to somebody through a glass door or a window. One thing we know—the animal makes a decision very quickly. You can watch it happening. Doris can see it with her kit fox, and I can with a bobcat I keep as a pet. I can tell immediately what the bobcat thinks of a person—whether he thinks, You're O.K., I can relate to you, or You're somebody I really don't like, and if you come in here I'll show you how much I don't like you. It's absolutely incredible, and I don't know how it happens."

I told them about an experience of that sort which I had one day at the Whipsnade zoo, in England, when I was walking there with my husband. Whipsnade has large outdoor paddocks to accommodate the hoofed animals, and as we were walking past one of these, which was full of various placid grazing beasts, we saw one animal running toward us. It was a gnu, and its eyes were fixed on my husband, Charles. It ran straight into the fence, as if it were trying to attack him. It recoiled from the collision, but a moment later it was trying again with all its might to get at Charles. It followed us all the way along, inside the fence, until it could go no farther, showing every sign of enmity. "What do you suppose it was all about?" I asked now. "To my certain knowledge, Charles has never hurt a gnu in his life, and he hardly ever goes to zoos. Perhaps something about him reminded the animal of an old enemy. What do you think?"

"No telling," said Hanson. "Take cats. Their etiquette is very interesting. If you want to get along with a cat, you have to know several basic things. Most people when they see a cat—that is, if they like cats—want to pet it and cuddle it. They may say something, too, like 'Hi there!' Now, that isn't the way. You want to look at the animal just for a minute, and after your eyes meet, you must turn your eyes away, to show the cat that you aren't being aggressive—because the aggressive posture of the cat is the locked-eye gaze and various other attitudes, depending on the subspecies, that mean, 'I am threatening you.' Cats will transfer this reaction to human beings, and when the stranger says 'Hi!' a cat will, according to its nature, back away or make a threatening gesture or merely ignore him. There are certain rigid rules of cat etiquette which you don't violate if you are really going to get acquainted with it. With some cats in captivity, this response is, in time, eroded away, and they become accepting, but some others never give it up."

I asked if he thought it was true that cats always know when they meet people who can't bear them.

Hanson said he didn't think so. He had taken such people in to see his bobcat, he said, and nothing happened, though on one occasion the bobcat sensed from the visitor's recoil how he felt, and gave him a little push. "It was a testing thing," he said. "He was trying to sense what the man would do. Distressing for the man, of course, but not important. The cat didn't bite or attack, or anything—just pushed, just tested. In other cases, he simply ignored the people. Yet I've seen times when people weren't quite sure they wanted to meet a bobcat, and he was charming. One would like to know just what is communicated. Often, I know I'm communicating with him but I don't know what I'm saying or how I'm saying it. There's no rule I can come up with." He paused, puffing at his pipe, and thought.

| 1978 |

GUARDIANS

In my sick daughter's room
The household animals gather.
Our black tom poses lordly on
The sun-warmed windowsill.
A spaniel sleeps by her slippers,
Keeping one weather eye open.
For once, they agree to differ:
Nary a sound, or spit of bother.
Aloof and hieratic as guardians,
They seem wiser than this poor animal
Her father, tiptoeing in and out,
Ferrying water bottle, elixirs, fruit,
His unaccustomed stockinged stealth
Tuned anxiously to a child's breath.

—JOHN MONTAGUE | 1995 |

CAT THERAPIST

LOIS METZGER

"Cat therapy," says Carole Wilbourn, "consists of making owners aware of the strong needs and feelings of their cats and then changing the cats' environment to accommodate those needs." In eighteen years in the business, Carole has seen ten thousand cats, with a success rate, according to one veterinarian, of 75 percent. Carole lives in the West Village with a black cat, Ziggy Stardust, and a Siamese, Sunny Blue. Before leaving for a therapy session, Carole always tells her cats, calmly and matter-of-factly, "I'll be gone for about an hour and I'll see you later." Carole does not think that her cats understand the words. "But they pick up feelings of love and security," she says, "and know I'm not leaving forever."

People find out about Carole from reading one of her books (*Cats Prefer It This Way, The Inner Cat, Cat Talk, Cats on the Couch*), or by being referred to her by New York veterinarians, or by seeing her listing in the Yellow Pages under "Cats," or by running across one of her weekend consultations at Paw'N Claw, a Greenwich Village pet-supply store; she visits a person's home, sees the person's cat, and charges from thirty-five to eighty dollars an hour. In recent years, she says, more and more veterinarians have begun to recognize that cats undergo real stress brought on by fear, jealousy, anger, and loss. "Emotional problems can cause medical problems. That's why you have to treat the *total* cat."

Carole is exactly five feet tall, with short, bouncy brown hair and round hazel eyes. Not long ago, we accompanied her on a couple of lower-Manhattan house calls.

BYRON: A beautiful, big nine-year-old tabby with dark-brown and black patches and a white chest, Byron lives in a small one-bedroom apartment in the West Village with three other cats—his brother, Jamie; his mother, Tuna; and his father, Little Guy—and with two people, Joyce and Billy. Byron's problem is Little Guy— he is terrified of his father. "The parent cats are only nine months older than their children," Joyce explained. "And Byron is actually bigger and stronger than Little Guy. A couple of times a year, when we're not home, they really fight. We know because of the fur on the floor—mostly Little Guy's. Afterward, Little Guy is fine, even pleased, but Byron, our sweetest cat, is devastated."

Little Guy is a part-Siamese black cat with intense green eyes. "Little Guy stands close to Byron and stares, giving him a piercing look," Joyce says. "Byron starts to cringe and hiss."

"It's hard to get mad at Little Guy," Billy said. "He's such a clown—a riot with people."

Both Billy and Joyce are magazine editors and freelance writers, and Joyce does volunteer work at the Bronx Zoo. "We've been together four years, and got married a few months ago," Joyce said. "Since then, Byron's been worse, spending almost all his time by himself, hiding from the other cats."

"Cats are fierce creatures of habit," Carole said. "Even a subtle change, like new slipcovers on the sofa, can seem to them very dramatic. Wedding preparations can be traumatic."

Carole was sitting with Joyce and Billy in their living room, surrounded by all the cats except Byron. Joyce, a pretty woman with curly brown hair, was wearing a gray sweatshirt that had a pattern of black pawprints running from hip to shoulder.

"It's so rare to have a whole family of cats," Carole said. "Especially the father, who's usually a stray tom nobody knows."

"I got Little Guy for Tuna thinking he was another female," Joyce said. "But he wasn't, and before I could blink an eye Tuna was pregnant. She gave birth at three in the morning, after waiting for me to get home from a date. First came Jamie, then Byron, who has a big head and was a breech birth. Tuna was in labor for two hours, and I had to help her."

Carole's jaw fell. "So often I tell people that problems stem from kitten-hood, and they look at me funny," she said. "It's wonderful that you were actually there and could tell us about it."

With the help of some dry food, Joyce coaxed Byron out from a hiding spot behind the refrigerator. Carole gave him a toy. "I'm not giving toys to the other cats, so that Byron will feel special," she said. But Little Guy threw Byron a devilish stare, and Byron stayed away from his new toy.

"In the middle of the night, Byron comes downstairs and meows and meows," Joyce said. "It's as if he had an imaginary friend."

Carole went off to one side of the room and made some notes, and then returned. "Imagine a person sitting beside you squirming and cracking his knuckles and humming off-key, for hours on end," she said. "That's what it's like for Little Guy to be near Byron, who's been anxious since birth. Little Guy moves too close to Byron because he's hypersensitive to anxiety and wants Byron to relax. It's one reason cats jump in the laps of people who don't like cats. Unfortunately, Little Guy's method is about as useful as slapping a hysterical person. But if Byron loosens up, Little Guy won't bother him. Tranquillizers can help.

So will popcorn, since that's Byron's favorite treat. Refer to him as Little Guy's son—it's a pleasant connection, and Byron will pick up good feelings. Byron seems sweet and passive, but even across a room I can feel his immense energy. Get that big cat in him out."

The next day, Joyce called Carole to say that Byron had had a wonderful day—no hissing and no hiding.

"He knew he was getting help," Carole said to us. "I was so moved. Poor Byron."

NED: Ned, a ten-year-old black-and-white cat, lives in a large, cozy country-house kind of loft in Tribeca with two English bulldogs, Porky and Beans, and with Alan, an attorney now studying for a doctorate in psychology at the New School, and Sondra, a Pan Am flight attendant, registered nurse, speech therapist, actress, and karate black belt. During the house call, Alan was studying in a room off the living room, and Porky and Beans were sleeping in a gated playpen area. "I grew up on a farm in Wisconsin," Sondra said. "I have bulldogs because they remind me of the pigs."

Sondra had called Carole because Ned had been lonely and depressed since the death last summer of their other cat, Buster, and she wanted to know if Ned needed a new cat. Sondra told her story: "During one of those hot, hot weeks last August, Alan and I went out of town, after taking Porky and Beans to a farm in Connecticut and asking our neighbor to feed the cats. One day, he realized that one of the cats hadn't come around to eat. He found Ned sitting next to the body of Buster. No one knows just what happened to Buster—it may have been the heat. I went through all of Elisa-

beth Kübler-Ross's stages of grief. I sat in the spot where Buster used to sleep, and spoke to him."

Sondra, who has thick dark hair and wears it pulled back in a braid, was now sitting on an L-shaped brown tweed sofa. "I got Ned at the A.S.P.C.A.," she went on. "He was crying at the time, and he kept on crying for four years—even though I got Buster three months after I got him, and they became best friends. They loved each other."

Ned came into the living room a bit diffidently. He jumped into Sondra's lap and hid his head under her arm.

Carole talked for a while about a children's party in St. Vincent's Hospital, and then she crouched on the floor beside Ned. "That was people chatter," she said to him. "I talked people chatter so the attention would be off you and you could feel like a cat. Now you're relaxed, and I'm relaxed, and Sondra's relaxed."

Carole gave Ned some catnip and a toy, which he liked, and asked him, "Ned, what do you want? A cat? A kitten? Want to be left alone? Tell me, Ned."

Then she went off to write her notes.

When she came back, she said, "Ned has always been a sensitive soul. Now he's suffering from separation anxiety and an abandonment complex, because you were both away when Buster died. Wait a little longer. Don't get another cat yet. Look on this as Ned's nurture time. He needs to become the cat he wants to be. Ned, this is your nurture time."

Ned looked at her and blinked.

| 1984 |

CAT 'N' MOUSE

Fiction

STEVEN MILLHAUSER

The cat is chasing the mouse through the kitchen: between the blue chair legs, over the tabletop with its red-and-white checkered tablecloth that is already sliding in great waves, past the sugar bowl falling to the left and the cream jug falling to the right, over the blue chair back, down the chair legs, across the waxed and butter-yellow floor. The cat and the mouse lean backward and try to stop on the slippery wax, which shows their flawless reflections. Sparks shoot from their heels, but it's much too late: the big door looms. The mouse crashes through, leaving a mouse-shaped hole. The cat crashes through, replacing the mouse-shaped hole with a larger, cat-shaped hole. In the living room, they race over the back of the couch, across the piano keys (delicate mouse tune, crash of cat chords), along the blue rug. The fleeing mouse snatches a glance over his shoulder, and when he looks forward again he sees the floor lamp coming closer and closer. Impossible to stop—at the last moment, he splits in half and rejoins himself on the other side. Behind him the rushing cat fails to split in half and crashes into the lamp: his head and body push the brass pole into the shape of a trombone. For a moment, the cat hangs sideways there, his stiff legs shaking like the clapper of a bell. Then he pulls free and rushes after the mouse, who turns and darts into a mousehole in the baseboard. The cat crashes into the wall and folds up like an accordion. Slowly, he unfolds, emitting accordion music. He lies on the floor with his chin on his upraised paw, one eyebrow lifted high in disgust, the claws of his other forepaw tapping the floorboards. A small piece of plaster drops on his head. He raises an outraged eye.

305

A framed painting falls heavily on his head, which plunges out of sight between his shoulders. The painting shows a green tree with bright-red apples. The cat's head struggles to rise, then pops up with the sound of a yanked cork, lifting the picture. Apples fall from the tree and land with a thump on the grass. The cat shudders, winces. A final apple falls. Slowly it rolls toward the frame, drops over the edge, and lands on the cat's head. In the cat's eyes, cash registers ring up "No Sale."

The mouse, dressed in a bathrobe and slippers, is sitting in his plump armchair, reading a book. He is tall and slim. His feet rest on a hassock, and a pair of spectacles rest on the end of his long, whiskered nose. Yellow light from a table lamp pours onto the book and dimly illuminates the cozy brown room. On the wall hang a tilted sampler bearing the words "Home Sweet Home," an oval photograph of the mouse's mother with her gray hair in a bun, and a reproduction of Seurat's *Sunday Afternoon* in which all the figures are mice. Near the armchair is a bookcase filled with books, with several titles visible: *Martin Cheddarwit*, Gouda's *Faust*, *The Memoirs of Anthony Edam*, *A History of the Medicheese*, the sonnets of Shakespaw. As the mouse reads his book, he reaches without looking toward a dish on the table. The dish is empty: his fingers tap about inside it. The mouse rises and goes over to the cupboard, which is empty except for a tin box with the word "Cheese" on it. He opens the box and turns it upside down. Into his palm drops a single toothpick. He gives it a melancholy look. Shak-

ing his head, he returns to his chair and takes up his book. In a bubble above his head a picture appears: He is seated at a long table covered with a white tablecloth. He is holding a fork upright in one fist and a knife upright in the other. A mouse butler dressed in tails sets before him a piece of cheese the size of a wedding cake.

From the mousehole emerges a red telescope. The lens looks to the left, then to the right. A hand issues from the end of the telescope and beckons the mouse forward. The mouse steps from the mousehole, collapses the telescope, and thrusts it into his bathrobe pocket. In the moonlit room, he tiptoes carefully, lifting his legs very high, over to the base of the armchair. He dives under the chair and peeks out through the fringe. He emerges from beneath the armchair, slinks over to the couch, and dives under. He peeks out through the fringe. He emerges from beneath the couch and approaches the slightly open kitchen door. He stands flat against the doorjamb, facing the living room, his eyes darting left and right. One leg tiptoes delicately around the jamb. His stretched body snaps after it like a rubber band. In the kitchen, he creeps to a moonlit chair, stands pressed against a chair leg, begins to climb. His nose rises over the tabletop: he sees a cream pitcher, a gleaming knife, a looming pepper mill. On a breadboard sits a wedge of cheese. The mouse, hunching his shoulders, tiptoes up to the cheese. From a pocket of his robe he removes a white handkerchief that he ties around his neck. He bends over the cheese, half closing his eyes, as if he were sniffing a flower. With a crashing sound, the cat springs onto the table. As he chases the mouse, the tablecloth bunches in waves, the sugar bowl topples, and waterfalls of sugar spill to the floor. An olive from a fallen cocktail glass rolls across the table, knocking into a cup, a salt-

THE CAT SITUATION

Somebody is always at us for something, and last week it was a lady wanting to rent a stuffed cat. She wrote that she was willing to pay three dollars, possibly four if it was a very dreadful cat. The stuffed-cat situation in town is pretty much as follows—we know because we have just finished calling up the taxidermists. Murgatroyd Brothers, 509 East 144th Street, have a black-and-white one they will rent for ten dollars a week provided you give them a fifteen-dollar deposit. Fred Sauter, 42 Bleecker Street, has a gray-and-white one he would let go for three dollars a week, or you could buy it, and he would dye it black, for twenty dollars. Or you could supply the cat and he would mount it for twenty. M. J. Hofmann, of 989 Gates Avenue, Brooklyn, has two gray-and-white numbers: one Persian lying down and an alley sitting up. He also offers a black kitten lying down. He would rent any of these for six dollars a week or sell them for thirteen dollars apiece—which he assured us was a very special price.

That's the situation.

| 1933 |

shaker, a trivet: the objects light up and cause bells to ring, as in a pinball machine. On the floor, a brigade of ants is gathering the sugar: one ant catches the falling grains in a bucket, which he dumps into the bucket of a second ant, who dumps the sugar into the bucket of a third ant, all the way across the room, until the last ant dumps it into a waiting truck. The cat chases the mouse over the blue chair back, down the chair legs, across the waxed floor. Both lean backward and try to stop as the big door comes closer and closer.

The mouse is sitting in his armchair with his chin in his hand, looking off into the distance with a melancholy expression. He is thoughtful

May 12, 1973   Price 50 cents

THE
NEW YORKER

by temperament, and he is distressed at the necessity of interrupting his meditations for the daily search for food. The search is wearying and absurd in itself, but is made unbearable by the presence of the brutish cat. The mouse's disdain for the cat is precise and abundant: he loathes the soft, heavy paws with their hidden hooks, the glinting teeth, the hot, fish-stinking breath. At the same time, he confesses to himself a secret admiration for the cat's coarse energy and simplicity. It appears that the cat has no other aim in life than to catch the mouse. Although the faculty of astonishment is not highly developed in the mouse, he is constantly astonished by the cat's unremitting enmity. This makes the cat dangerous, despite his stupidity, for the mouse recognizes that he himself has long periods when the cat fades entirely from his mind. Moreover, despite the fundamental simplicity of the cat's nature, it remains true that the cat is cunning: he plots tirelessly against the mouse, and his ludicrous wiles require in the mouse an alert attention that he would prefer not to give. The mouse is aware of the temptation of indifference; he must continually exert himself to be wary. He feels that he is exhausting his nerves and harming his spirit by attending to the cat; at the same time, he realizes that his attention is at best imperfect, and that the cat is thinking uninterruptedly, with boundless energy, of him. If only the mouse could stay in his hole, he would be happy, but he cannot stay in his hole, be-

cause of the need to find cheese. It is not a situation calculated to produce the peace of mind conducive to contemplation.

The cat is standing in front of the mousehole with a hammer in one hand and a saw in the other. Beside him rests a pile of yellow boards and a big bag of nails. He begins furiously hammering and sawing, moving across the room in a cloud of dust that conceals him. Suddenly, the dust clears and the cat beholds his work: a long, twisting pathway that begins at the mousehole and passes under the couch, over the back of the armchair, across the piano, through the kitchen door, and onto the kitchen table. On the tablecloth, at the end of the pathway, is a large mousetrap on which sits a lump of cheese. The cat tiptoes over to the refrigerator, vanishes behind it, and slyly thrusts out his head: his eyes dart left and right. There is the sound of a bicycle bell: *ring ring*. A moment later, the mouse appears, pedalling fiercely. He speeds from the end of the pathway onto the table. As he screeches to a stop, the round

"Projectile hairballing."

wheels stretch out of shape and then become round again. The mouse is wearing riding goggles, a riding cap, and gloves. He leans his bicycle against the sugar bowl, steps over to the mousetrap, and looks at it with interest. He steps onto the mousetrap, sits down on the brass bar, and puts on a white bib. From a pocket of his leather jacket he removes a knife and fork. He eats the cheese swiftly. After his meal, he replaces the knife and fork in his pocket and begins to play on the mousetrap. He swings on a high bar, hangs upside down by his legs, walks the parallel bars, performs gymnastic stunts. Then he climbs onto his bicycle and disappears along the pathway, ringing his bell. The cat emerges from behind the refrigerator and springs onto the table beside the mousetrap. He frowns down at the trap. From the top of his head he plucks a single hair: it comes loose with the sound of a snapping violin string. Slowly, he lowers the hair toward the mousetrap. The hair touches the spring. The mousetrap remains motionless. He presses the spring with a spoon. The mousetrap remains motionless. He bangs the spring

with a sledgehammer. The mousetrap remains motionless. He looks at the trap with rage. Cautiously, he reaches out a single toe. The mousetrap springs shut with the sound of a slammed iron door. The cat hops about the table holding his trapped foot as the toe swells to the size of a light bulb, bright red.

The cat enters on the left, disguised as a mouse. He is wearing a blond wig, a nose mask, and a tight black dress slit to the thigh. He has high and very round breasts, a tiny waist, and round, rolling hips. His lips are bright red, and his black lashes are so tightly curled that when he blinks his eyes the lashes roll out and snap back like window shades. He walks slowly and seductively, resting one hand on a hip and one hand on his blond hair. The mouse is standing in the mousehole, leaning against one side with his hands in his pockets. His eyes protrude from their sockets in the shape of telescopes. In the lens of each telescope is a thumping heart. Slowly, as if mesmerized, the mouse sleepwalks into the room. The cat places a needle on a record, and rumba music begins to play. The cat dances with his hands clasped behind his neck, thrusting out each hip, fluttering his long lashes, turning to face the other way: in the tight black dress, his twitching backside is shaped like the ace of spades. The mouse faces the cat and begins to dance. They stride back and forth across the room, wriggling and kicking in step. As they dance, the

cat's wig comes loose, revealing one cat ear. The cat dances over to a bearskin rug and lies down on his side. He closes his long-lashed eyes and purses his red, red lips. The mouse steps up to the cat. He reaches into his pocket, removes a cigar, and places it between the big red lips. The cat's eyes open. They look down at the cigar, look up, and look down again. The cat removes the cigar and stares at it. The cigar explodes. When the smoke clears, the cat's face is black. He gives a strained, very white smile. Many small lines appear in his teeth. The teeth crack into little pieces and fall out.

The cat is lying on his back in his basket in the kitchen. His hands are clasped behind his head, his left knee is raised, and his right ankle rests sideways on the raised knee. He is filled with rage at the thought of the mouse, who he knows despises him. He would like to tear the mouse to pieces, to roast him over a fire, to plunge him into a pan of burning butter. He understands that his rage is not the rage of hunger and he wonders whether the mouse himself is responsible for evoking this savagery, which burns in his chest like indigestion. He despises the mouse's physical delicacy, his weak arms as thin as the teeth of combs, his frail, crushable skull, his fondness for books and solitude. At the same time, he is irritably aware that he admires the mouse's elegance, his air of culture and languor, his easy self-assurance. Why is he always reading? In a sense, the mouse intimidates the cat: in his presence, the cat feels clumsy and foolish. He thinks obsessively about the mouse and suspects with rage that the mouse frequently does not think about him at all, there in his brown room. If the mouse was less indifferent, would he burn with such hatred? Might they learn to live peace-

fully together in the same house? Would he be released from this pain of outrage in his heart?

The mouse is standing at his workbench, curling the eyelashes of a mechanical cat. Her long black hair is as shiny as licorice; her lips look like licked candy. She is wearing a tight red dress, black fishnet stockings, and red high heels. The mouse stands the mechanical cat on her feet, unzips the back of her dress, and winds a big key. He zips up the dress and aims her toward the mousehole. In the living room, the mechanical cat struts slowly back and forth; her pointy breasts stick out like party hats. The cat's head rises over the back of the armchair. In his eyes appear hearts pierced by arrows. He slithers over the chair and slides along the floor like honey. When he reaches the strutting cat, he glides to an upright position and stands mooning at her. His heart is thumping so hard that it pushes out the skin of his chest with each beat. The cat reaches into a pocket and removes a straw boater, which he places on his head at a rakish angle. He fastens at his throat a large polka-dot bow tie. He becomes aware of a ticking sound. He removes from his pocket a round yellow watch, places it against his ear, frowns, and returns it to his pocket. He bends close to the face of the cat and sees in each of her eyes a shiny round black bomb with a burning fuse. The cat turns to the audience and then back to the dangerous eyes. The mechanical cat blows up. When the smoke clears, the cat's skin hangs in tatters about him, revealing his raw pink flesh and a pair of polka-dot boxer shorts.

Outside the mousehole, the cat is winding up a mouse that exactly resembles the real mouse. The mechanical mouse is wearing

"People are O.K., but I prefer little pieces of string."

dous breath and blows out the fuse with such force that for a moment the cake is slanted. Now the cat grins, licks his teeth, and opens his jaws. He hears a sound. The cake is ticking loudly: *tock tock, tock tock.* Puzzled, the cat holds it up to one ear. He listens closely. A terrible knowledge dawns in his eyes.

The cat rides into the living room in a bright-yellow crane. From the boom hangs a shiny black wrecking ball. He drives up to the mousehole and stops. He pushes and pulls a pair of levers, which cause the wrecking ball to be inserted into a gigantic rubber band attached to a gigantic slingshot. The rubber band stretches back and back. Suddenly, it releases the shiny black ball, which smashes into the wall. The entire house collapses, leaving only a tall red chimney standing amid the ruins. On top of the chimney is a stork's nest, in which a stork sits with a fishing pole. He is wearing a blue baseball cap. Below, in the rubble, a stirring is visible. The cat rises unsteadily, leaning on a crutch. His head is covered with a white bandage that conceals an eye; one leg is in a cast and one arm in a sling. With the tip of his crutch, he moves away a pile of rubble and exposes a fragment of baseboard. In the baseboard we see the unharmed mousehole. Inside the mousehole, the mouse sits in his chair, reading a book.

a bathrobe and slippers, stands with hands in pockets, and has a pair of eyeglasses perched at the end of its nose. The cat lifts open the top of the mouse's head, which is attached in the manner of a hinged lid. He inserts a sizzling red stick of dynamite and closes the lid. He sets the mouse in front of the hole and watches as it vanishes through the arched opening. Inside, the mouse is sitting in his chair, reading a book. He does not raise his eyes to the visitor, who glides over with its hands in its pockets. Still reading, the mouse reaches out and lifts open the head of his double. He removes the sizzling dynamite, thrusts it into a cake, and inserts the cake into the mouse's head. He turns the mechanical mouse around and continues reading as it walks out through the arch. The cat is squatting beside the hole with his eyes shut and his fingers pressed in his ears. He opens his eyes and sees the mouse. His eyebrows rise. He snatches up the mouse, opens its head, and lifts out a thickly frosted cake that says "Happy Birthday." In the center of the cake is a sizzling red stick of dynamite. The cat's hair leaps up. He takes a tremen-

The mouse understands that the clownishly inept cat has the freedom to fail over and over again, during the long course of an inglorious lifetime, while he himself is denied the liberty of a single mistake. It is highly unlikely, of course, that he will ever be guilty of an error, since he is much cleverer than the cat and immediately sees through every one of his risible stratagems. Still, might not the very knowledge of his superiority lead to a relaxation of vigilance that will prove fatal, in the end? After all, he is not invulnerable; he is invulnerable only insofar as he is vigilant. The mouse is bored, deeply bored, by the ease with which he outwits the cat; there are times when he longs for a more worthy enemy, someone more like himself. He understands that his boredom is a dangerous weakness against which he must perpetually be on his guard. Sometimes he thinks, If only I could stop watching over myself, if only I could let myself go! The thought alarms him and causes him to look over his shoulder at the

mousehole, across which the shadow of the cat has already fallen.

The cat enters from the left, carrying a sack over one shoulder. He sets the sack down beside the mousehole. He unties a rope from the neck of the sack, plunges both hands in, and carefully lifts out a gray cloud. He places the cloud in the air above the mousehole. Rain begins to fall from the cloud, splashing down in great drops. The cat reaches into the sack and removes some old clothes. He swiftly disguises himself as a peddler and rings the mouse's bell. The mouse appears in the arched doorway, leaning against the side with his arms folded across his stomach and his ankles crossed as he stares out at the rain. The cat removes from the sack an array of mouse-size umbrellas, which he opens in turn: red, yellow, green, blue. The mouse shakes his head. The cat removes from the sack a yellow slicker, a pair of hip boots, a fishing rod and tackle box. The mouse shakes his head. The cat removes a red rubber sea horse, a compressed-air tank, a diving bell, a rowboat, a yacht. The mouse shakes his head, steps into his house, and slams the door. He opens the door, hangs a sign on the knob, and slams the door again. The sign reads "Not Home." The rain falls harder. The cat steps out from under the

NORELDO, THE MENTAL MARVEL, READS THE MIND OF HIS CAT, NED.

cloud, which rises above his head and begins to follow him about the room. The storm grows worse: he is pelted with hailstones the size of golf balls. In the cloud appear many golfers, driving golf balls into the room. Forked lightning flashes; thunder roars. The cat rushes around the room trying to escape the cloud and dives under the couch. His tail sticks out. Lightning strikes the tail, which crackles like an electric wire. The couch rises for an instant, exposing the luminous, electrified cat rigid with shock; inside the cat's body, with its rim of spiked fur, his blue-white skeleton is visible. Now snow begins to fall from the cloud, and whistling winds begin to blow. Snow lies in drifts on the rug, rises swiftly up the sides of the armchair, sweeps up to the mantelpiece, where the clock looks down in terror and covers its eyes with its hands. The cat struggles slowly through the blizzard but is soon encased in snow. Icicles hang from his chin. He stands motionless, shaped like a cat struggling forward with bent head. The door of the mouse-hole opens and the mouse emerges, wearing earmuffs, scarf, and gloves. The sun is shining. He begins shovelling a path. When he comes to the snow-cat, he climbs to the top of his shovel and sticks a carrot in the center of the snowy face. Then he climbs down, steps back, and begins throwing snowballs. The cat's head falls off.

The cat is pacing angrily in the kitchen, his hands behind his back and his eyebrows drawn down in a V. In a bubble above his head a wish appears: He is operating a circular saw that moves slowly, with high whining sounds, along a yellow board. At the end of the board is the mouse, lying on his back, tied down with ropes. The image vanishes and is replaced by another: The cat, wearing an engineer's hat, is driving a great train along a track. The mouse is stretched across the middle of the track, his wrists fastened to one rail and his ankles to the other. Sweat bursts in big drops from the mouse's face as the image vanishes and is replaced by another: The cat is turning a winch that slowly lowers an anvil toward the mouse, who is tied to a little chair. The mouse looks up in

S. GROSS

"Eddie, you are one hell of a mouse!"

terror. Suddenly, the cat lets go of the crank and the anvil rushes down with a whistling sound as the winch spins wildly. At the last moment, the mouse tumbles away. The anvil falls through the bubble onto the cat's head.

The cat understands that the mouse will always outwit him, but this tormenting knowledge serves only to inflame his desire to catch the mouse. He will never give up. His life, in relation to the mouse, is one long failure, a monotonous succession of unspeakable humiliations; his unhappiness is relieved only by moments of delusional hope, during which he believes, despite doubts supported by a lifetime of bitter experience, that at last he will succeed. Although he knows that he will never catch the mouse, who will forever escape into his mousehole a half inch ahead of the reaching claw, he also knows that only if he catches the mouse will his wretched life be justified. He will be transformed. Is it therefore his own life that he seeks, when he lies awake plotting against the mouse? Is it, when all is said and done, himself that he is chasing? The cat frowns and scratches his nose.

The cat stands before the mousehole holding in one hand a piece of white chalk. On the blue wall he draws the outline of a large door. The mousehole is at the bottom of the door. He draws the circle of a doorknob and opens the door. He steps into a black room. At the end of the room stands the mouse with a piece of chalk. The mouse draws a white mousehole on the wall and steps through. The cat kneels down and peers into the mousehole. He stands up and draws another door. He opens the door and steps into another black room. At the end of the room stands the mouse, who draws an-

other mousehole and steps through. The cat draws another door, the mouse draws another mousehole. Faster and faster they draw: door, hole, door, hole, door. At the end of the last room, the mouse draws on the wall a white stick of dynamite. He draws a white match, which he takes in his hand and strikes against the wall. He lights the dynamite and hands it to the cat. The cat looks at the white outline of the dynamite. He offers it to the mouse. The mouse shakes his head. The cat points to himself and raises his eyebrows. The mouse nods. The stick of dynamite explodes.

The cat enters on the left, wearing a yellow hard hat and pushing a red wheelbarrow. The wheelbarrow is piled high with boards. In front of the mousehole, the cat puts down the handles of the barrow, pulls a hammer and saw from the pile of boards, and thrusts a fistful of black nails between his teeth. He begins sawing and hammering rapidly, moving from one end of the room to the other as a cloud of dust conceals his work. Suddenly, the dust clears and the cat beholds his creation: he has constructed a tall guillotine, connected to the mousehole by a stairway. The blue-black glistening blade hangs between posts high above the opening for the head. Directly below the opening, on the other side, stands a basket. On the rim of the basket the cat places a wedge of cheese. The cat loops a piece of string onto a lever in the side of the guillotine and fastens the other end of the string to the wedge of cheese. Then he tiptoes away with hunched shoulders and vanishes behind a fire shovel. A moment later, the mouse climbs the stairs onto the platform of the guillotine. He stands with his hands in the pockets of his robe and contemplates the blade, the opening for the head, and

CAT'S PAJAMAS

R. Chast

the piece of cheese. He removes from one pocket a yellow package with a red bow. He leans over the edge of the platform and slips the loop from the lever. He thrusts his head through the head hole, removes the piece of cheese from the rim of the basket, and sets the package in its place. He ties the string to the package, slides his head back through the hole, and fits the loop of the string back over the lever. From his pocket he removes a large pair of scissors, which he lays on the platform. He next removes a length of rope, which he fastens to the lever so that the rope hangs nearly to the floor. On the floor, he stands cross-ankled against the wheel of the barrow, eating his cheese. A moment later, the cat leaps onto the platform. He looks up in surprise at the unfallen blade. He crouches down, peers through the head hole, and sees the yellow package. He frowns. He looks up at the blade. He looks at the yellow package. Gingerly, he reaches a paw through the opening and snatches it back. He frowns at the string. A cunning look comes into his eyes. He notices the pair of scissors, picks them up, and cuts the string. He waits, but nothing happens. Eagerly, he thrusts his head through the opening and reaches for the package. The

mouse, eating his cheese with one hand, lazily tugs at the rope with the other. The blade rushes down with the sound of a roaring train; a forlorn whistle blows. The cat tries to pull his head out of the hole. The blade slices off the top half of his head, which drops into the basket and rolls noisily around like a coin. The cat pulls himself out of the hole and stumbles about until he falls over the edge of the platform into the basket. He seizes the top of his head and puts it on like a hat. It is backward. He straightens it with a half turn. In his hand, he sees with surprise the yellow package with the red bow. Frowning, he unties it. Inside is a bright-red stick of dynamite with a sizzling fuse. The cat looks at the dynamite and turns his head to the audience. He blinks once. The dynamite explodes. When the smoke clears, the cat's face is black. In each eye a ship cracks in half and slowly sinks in the water.

The mouse is sitting in his chair with his feet on the hassock and his open book face down on his lap. A mood of melancholy has invaded him, as if the brown tones of his room had seeped into his brain. He feels stale and out of sorts: he moves within the narrow compass of his mind, utterly devoid of fresh ideas. Is he perhaps too much alone? He thinks of the cat and wonders whether there is some dim and distant possibility of a connection, perhaps a companionship. Is it possible that they might become friends? Perhaps he could teach the cat to appreciate the things of the mind, and learn from the cat to enjoy life's simpler pleasures. Perhaps the cat, too, feels an occasional sting of loneliness. Haven't they much in common, after all? Both are bachelors, indoor sorts, who enjoy the comforts of a cozy domesticity; both are secretive; both take pleasure in plots and schemes. The more the mouse pursues this line of thought, the more it seems to him that the cat is a large, soft mouse. He imagines the cat with mouse ears and gentle mouse paws, wearing a white bib, sitting across from him at the kitchen table, lifting to his mouth a fork at the end of which is a piece of cheese.

The cat enters from the right with a chalkboard eraser in one hand. He goes over to the mousehole, bends down, and erases it. He stands up and erases the wall, revealing the mouse's home. The mouse is sitting in his chair with his feet on the hassock and his open book face down on his lap. The cat bends over and erases the book. The mouse looks up in irritation. The cat erases the mouse's chair. He erases the hassock. He erases the entire room. He tosses the eraser over his shoulder. Now there is nothing left in the world except the cat and the mouse. The cat snatches him up in a fist. The cat's red tongue slides over glistening teeth sharp as ice picks. Here and there, over a tooth, a bright star expands and contracts. The cat opens his jaws wider, closes his eyes, and hesitates. The death of the mouse is desirable in every way, but will life without him really be pleasurable? Will the mouse's absence satisfy him entirely? Is it conceivable that he may miss the mouse, from time to time? Is it possible that he needs the mouse, in some disturbing way?

As the cat hesitates, the mouse reaches into a pocket of his robe and removes a red handkerchief. With swift circular strokes he wipes out the cat's teeth while the cat's eyes watch in surprise. He wipes out the cat's eyes. He wipes out the cat's whiskers. He wipes out the cat's head. Still held in the cat's fist, he wipes out the entire cat, except for the paw holding him. Then, very carefully, he wipes out the paw. He drops lightly down and slaps his palms together. He looks about. He is alone with his red handkerchief in a blank white world. After a pause, he begins to wipe himself out, moving rapidly from head to toe. Now there is nothing left but the red handkerchief. The handkerchief flutters, grows larger, and suddenly splits in half. The halves become red theatre curtains, which begin to close. Across the closing curtains, words write themselves in black script: "The End."

| 2004 |

ACKNOWLEDGMENTS

A good anthology sidles up to you and brushes its sleek flanks against your shins. It *claims* you. But who can lay claim to it? This anthology, certainly, was a collective endeavor, and the collective includes Roger Angell, Jordan Awan, Katia Bachko, Jennifer Backe, Chris Curry, Deanna Donegan, Noah Eaker, Hendrik Hertzberg, Trevor Hoey, Whitney Johnson, Susan Kamil, Mina Kaneko, Anthony Lane, Rachel Lee, Maria Lokke, Bob Mankoff, Pam McCarthy, Chloe McConnell, Caitlin McKenna, Wyatt Mitchell, Françoise Mouly, Lynn Oberlander, Erin Overbey, Beth Pearson, James Pomerantz, David Remnick, Joshua Rothman, Eric Simonoff, and—last only alphabetically!—Susan Turner. Some of these worthies pounced on permissions or swatted away dangling impediments; others groomed for errors, chased down archival images, scratched out page designs, or simply gave inspiration by combing their whiskers and looking wise. Special thanks go to the cat-herding Henry Finder and to Giles Harvey, who clawed through the magazine's copious archives, finding the fun among the fur balls.

CONTRIBUTORS

MARGARET ATWOOD is a poet, novelist, and literary critic. Her books include *The Handmaid's Tale*, which won the Arthur C. Clarke Award; *The Blind Assassin*, which won the Booker Prize; and the MaddAddam trilogy, featuring quasi-humans endowed with the ability to purr.

THOMAS BELLER began contributing to *The New Yorker* in 1991. He is the author of a short-story collection, *Seduction Theory;* a novel, *The Sleep-Over Artist;* and a memoir, *How to Be a Man: Scenes from a Protracted Boyhood.*

SALLY BENSON (1897–1972) was a screenwriter who also contributed many short stories to *The New Yorker,* some of which served as the basis for the film *Meet Me in St. Louis.*

BURKHARD BILGER has been a staff writer at *The New Yorker* since 2001. He is the author of *Noodling for Flatheads*, which was a finalist for the PEN/Martha Albrand Award. His work has been anthologized three times in *Best American Science and Nature Writing*, twice in *Best American Sports Writing*, and once each in *Best Food Writing*, *Best Technology Writing*, and *Best American Science Writing.*

ELIZABETH BISHOP (1911–1979) published her first poem in *The New Yorker* in 1940. She won a Pulitzer Prize in 1956 for *Poems: North & South—A Cold Spring* and was elected to the American Academy of Arts and Letters in 1976.

T. CORAGHESSAN BOYLE has published nine short-story collections and fourteen novels, including *T. C. Boyle Stories II, The Women,* and *When the Killing's Done.*

MAEVE BRENNAN (1917–1993) joined the staff of *The New Yorker* in 1949 and for many years wrote the column "The Long-Winded Lady" for the Talk of the Town. She published two volumes of short stories, *In and Out of Never-Never Land* and *Christmas Eve,* most of which appeared originally in *The New Yorker.*

JOHN BROOKS (1920–1993) joined *The New Yorker* as a staff writer in 1949 and wrote numerous pieces for the magazine about the world of high finance. His books include *Once in Golconda: A True Drama of Wall Street 1920–1938* and *The Takeover Game: The Men, the Moves, and the Wall Street Money Behind Today's Nationwide Merger Wars.*

HENRI COLE is a poet whose books include *Touch, Blackbird and Wolf,* and *Middle Earth,* which was a finalist for the Pulitzer Prize. He teaches at Ohio State University and is the poetry editor of *The New Republic.*

HENRY S. F. COOPER began contributing to *The New Yorker* in 1969. From 1969 to 1987, he wrote a regular column called "Letter from the Space Center." He has written eight books about NASA and space exploration, including *Apollo on the Moon* and *The Evening Star: Venus Observed.*

ROALD DAHL (1916–1990) was a novelist, short-story writer, and poet and one of the world's best-selling children's authors. His books include *James and the Giant Peach, Charlie and the Chocolate Factory, Fantastic Mr. Fox, My Uncle Oswald,* and *Kiss Kiss.*

WOLCOTT GIBBS (1902–1958) joined *The New Yorker* in 1927 as a writer and editor. He became known for the varied Profiles, parodies, and reminiscences he contributed and for his exacting editing of others. In 1940, he became the magazine's drama critic, and in 1950 his play *Season in the Sun* (adapted from his earlier book about Fire Island bohemianism) became a Broadway hit.

BRENDAN GILL (1914–1997) joined *The New Yorker* in 1936 and wrote the long-running "Sky Line" column for the magazine. His numerous books include *Many Masks: A Life of Frank Lloyd Wright* and *Here at the New Yorker,* a memoir of his time at the magazine.

DANA GOODYEAR joined *The New Yorker* in 1999. She is the author of two books of poems, *Honey and Junk* and *The Oracle of Hollywood Boulevard,* and a book about foodie culture, *Anything That Moves.*

ROBERT GRAVES (1895–1985) was born in London and produced more than 120 books in his long life, including the First World War memoir *Goodbye to All That,* the historical novel *I, Claudius,* and *The White Goddess: A Historical Grammar of Poetic Myth.* His poems appeared in *The New Yorker* for a quarter of a century, starting in 1950.

EMILY HAHN (1905–1997) was an American author and journalist whose many books include *Look Who's Talking!,* on animal communication, and *No Hurry to Get Home,* a memoir.

VICKI HEARNE (1946–2001) was a writer and animal trainer. Her books include *Adam's Task: Calling Animals by Name.*

HENDRIK HERTZBERG, a senior editor and staff writer, was a *New Yorker* Talk of the Town reporter from 1969 to 1977. After a fifteen-year hiatus as a White House speechwriter and then editor of *The New Republic,* he returned to *The New Yorker* in 1992. He is the author of *Politics: Observations and Arguments, 1966–2004* and *¡Obamanos!: The Birth of a New Political Era.*

TED HUGHES (1930–1998) was a poet and children's writer whose books include *Crow, Birthday Letters,* and *The Iron Man.* He was the British poet laureate from 1984 until his death.

WELDON KEES (1914–1955) was a poet, novelist, and painter whose books include *The Last Man* and *The Fall of the Magicians.*

JAMAICA KINCAID began contributing to *The New Yorker* in 1974. Her books include *At the Bottom of the River, Annie John, The Autobiography of My Mother,* and *See Now Then.*

E. F. Kinkead (1906–1992) was a staff writer and editor at *The New Yorker* for fifty-eight years. His books include *Wilderness Is All Around Us: Notes of an Urban Naturalist* and *Central Park*.

Katherine T. Kinkead (1910–2001) joined the staff of *The New Yorker* in 1942. She was one of the first women reporters for the magazine.

Anthony Lane joined *The New Yorker* in 1993. In addition to his biweekly film reviews, he contributes book reviews and other works of criticism, for which he has received a National Magazine Award. *Nobody's Perfect*, a collection of his pieces for the magazine, was published in 2003.

Ariel Levy joined *The New Yorker* as a staff writer in 2008. She is the author of *Female Chauvinist Pigs: Women and the Rise of Raunch Culture*.

Ivy Litvinov (1889–1977) was the author of several novels, including *The Measure of Our Youth, Garden Oats*, and *A Pen and Ink Passion*.

Patricia Marx has been contributing to *The New Yorker* since 1989. She is a former writer for *Saturday Night Live* and the author of several books, including the novels *Him Her Him Again the End of Him* and *Starting from Happy* (both of which were finalists for the Thurber Prize) and several children's books, among them *Now Everybody Really Hates Me* and *Meet My Staff*.

William Matthews (1942–1997) was a poet and essayist whose books include *A Happy Childhood* and *Time & Money*, which won the National Book Critics Circle Award.

Peter Matthiessen is a novelist and nature writer. His books include *The Snow Leopard* and *Shadow Country*, both of which won the National Book Award.

Lois Metzger is the author of several young adult novels, most recently *A Trick of the Light*.

Steven Millhauser is the author of many novels and short-story collections, including *Dangerous Laughter, Edwin Mullhouse*, and *Martin Dressler*, which won the Pulitzer Prize.

John Montague is the author of several books of poetry, including *Poisoned Lands* and *Tides*.

Paul Muldoon, *The New Yorker*'s poetry editor, has published numerous books of poetry, including *The Annals of Chile*, which won the T. S. Eliot Prize, and *Moy Sand and Gravel*, which won the Pulitzer Prize.

Haruki Murakami is the author of many novels and short-story collections, including *Kafka on the Shore, Norwegian Wood, The Wind-Up Bird Chronicle*, and *1Q84*. His work has been translated into more than forty languages, and his honors include the Franz Kafka Prize and the Jerusalem Prize.

Susan Orlean began contributing articles and Talk of the Town pieces to *The New Yorker* in 1987 and became a staff writer in 1992. She is the author of *The Orchid Thief, The Bullfighter Checks Her Makeup, My Kind of Place*, and *Rin Tin Tin*.

Amy Ozols is a writer and producer for *Late Night with Jimmy Fallon*.

Robert Pinsky is a poet whose books include *An Explanation of America, Jersey Rain, Gulf Music, The Figured Wheel*, and a new book about poetry, *Singing School*.

J. F. POWERS (1917–1999) was a novelist and short-story writer whose books include *Morte d'Urban* and *Wheat That Springeth Green*.

ALASTAIR REID is a poet and translator whose books include *Outside In: Selected Prose* and *Inside Out: Selected Poetry and Translations*. He has published celebrated translations of Jorge Luis Borges and Pablo Neruda.

JEAN RHYS (1890–1979) was a novelist and short-story writer whose books include *Voyage in the Dark, Wide Sargasso Sea,* and *Good Morning, Midnight*.

SELMA ROBINSON (1899–1977) was a poet and short-story writer who began contributing to *The New Yorker* in 1926.

KAY RYAN has published seven volumes of poetry, including *The Best of It: New and Selected Poems, Elephant Rocks, Say Uncle,* and *The Niagara River*. She was the United States poet laureate from 2008 to 2010.

DAVID SCHICKLER is a screenwriter and author. His books include the novels *Kissing in Manhattan* and *Sweet and Vicious,* and *The Dark Path,* a memoir. He won an O. Henry Award for his story "The Smoker."

SUSAN SHEEHAN has written for *The New Yorker* since 1961. Her books include *Ten Vietnamese* and *Is There No Place on Earth for Me?,* which won the Pulitzer Prize.

TOM SLEIGH is a poet, essayist, and dramatist. His books include *The Chain, Space Walk,* and *Army Cats*.

GEORGE STEINER began writing for *The New Yorker* in 1966 and has contributed more than two hundred reviews to the magazine. His many books include *The Portage to San Cristobal of A.H., In Bluebeard's Castle, After Babel,* and *Real Presences*.

ROBERT SULLIVAN began contributing to *The New Yorker* in 1991. He is the author of several books, including *Rats, The Meadowlands, The Whale Hunt,* and *My American Revolution*.

BERNARD TAPER was a staff writer for *The New Yorker* for thirty-nine years. He is the author of several books, including *Balanchine: A Biography* and *Cellist in Exile: A Portrait of Pablo Casals*.

JAMES THURBER (1894–1961) joined *The New Yorker* in 1927 as an editor and writer; his cartoons began to appear there four years later. His books include two children's classics—*The 13 Clocks* and *The Wonderful O*—and an autobiography, *My Life and Hard Times*.

JOHN UPDIKE (1932–2009) contributed fiction, poetry, essays, and criticism to *The New Yorker* for half a century. He published twenty-three novels, including the Pulitzer Prize–winning *Rabbit Is Rich* and *Rabbit at Rest,* and seventeen books of short stories, eight collections of poetry, five children's books, a memoir, and a play.

SYLVIA TOWNSEND WARNER (1893–1978) was a novelist, short-story writer, and poet. She published thirty books, including *Lolly Willowes* and *Summer Will Show*.

E. B. WHITE (1899–1985) joined the staff of *The New Yorker* in 1927. He wrote the children's classics *Stuart Little, Charlotte's Web,* and *The Trumpet of the Swan*. He received the Presidential Medal of Freedom in 1963 and was awarded an honorary Pulitzer Prize in 1978 for his work as a whole.

WALLACE WHITE began contributing to *The New Yorker* in 1960 and wrote more than 150 pieces for the magazine over the next three decades.

THOMAS WHITESIDE (1918–1997) joined the staff of *The New Yorker* in 1950 and worked at the magazine for forty-one years. He published eleven books, including *The Blockbuster Complex*.

FRANZ WRIGHT is a poet whose books include *F, Going North in Winter, God's Silence,* and *Walking to Martha's Vineyard,* which won the Pulitzer Prize.

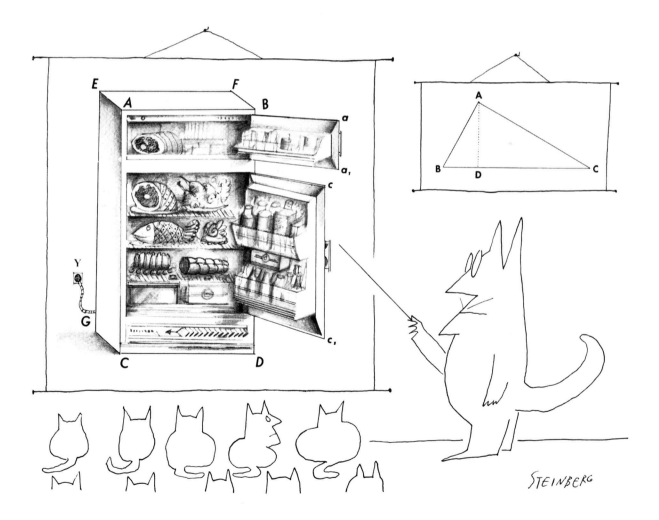

ILLUSTRATION CREDITS

220: Mark Peckmezian
229: André François
232: J. J. Sempé
252: Saul Steinberg
266: Peter Stemmler
269: Galley page of "Tooth and Claw" by T. Coraghessan Boyle.
274: Garrett Price
297: William Steig
308: André François

Cartoons by Charles Addams (69, 121), Harry Bliss (227), George Booth (103, 106, 144–45, 181), Roz Chast (258, 316), Frank Cotham (113, 294), Leo Cullum (viii, 128, 276, 280), Joe Dator (81, 178), Eldon Dedini (134, 248), Liza Donnelly (199), J. C. Duffy (242), Ed Fisher (200), Ed Frascino (260), Alex Gregory (96, 286), Sam Gross (59, 84, 100, 158, 261, 270, 314), William Hamilton (230), J. B. Handelsman (288), Bruce Eric Kaplan (236, 312), Edward Koren (78), Arnie Levin (166, 279, 310), Lee Lorenz (182), Robert Mankoff (12, 99, 122), Henry Martin (151, 185), Paul Noth (224), Donald Reilly (88), Mischa Richter (38), Victoria Roberts (165), Bernard Schoenbaum (72), Danny Shanahan (87, 263), Edward Sorel (172), William Steig (4), Saul Steinberg (vii, 55, 325), Mick Stevens (9, 43, 147, 194, 306), James Stevenson (209), Mike Twohy (xi, 241), Dean Vietor (215), Robert Weber (212, 223, 291), Christopher Weyant (22), Shannon Wheeler (92), Gahan Wilson (313), Jack Ziegler (66, 70, 163, 309)

Spot art by Christoph Abbrederis, Peter Arkle, Tom Bachtell, George Booth, Pierre Clemente, Jules Feiffer, André François, Olaf Hajek, Edward Koren, Pascal Lemaître, Jacques Loustal, Daniel Maja, Mariscal, Ever Meulen, Mr. Bingo, Filip Pagowski, Gary Panter, Philippe Petit-Roulet, Emmanuel Pierre, Quickhoney, Robert Risko, Deborah Ross, Ronald Searle, J. J. Sempé, Otto Soglow, Edward Sorel, William Steig, Saul Steinberg, Anders Wenngren, Gahan Wilson

This book was set in Adobe Caslon. William Caslon released his first typefaces in 1722. His types were based on seventeenth-century Dutch old style designs, which were then used extensively in England. Because of their incredible practicality Caslon's designs met with instant success. Caslon's types became popular throughout Europe and the American colonies; printer Benjamin Franklin hardly used any other typeface. The first printings of the American Declaration of Independence and the Constitution were set in Caslon. For her Caslon revival, designer Carol Twombly studied specimen pages printed by William Caslon between 1734 and 1770. Ideally suited for text, Adobe Caslon is right for magazines, journals, book publishing, and corporate communications.